General editor: Andrew S. Thompson

Founding editor: John M. MacKenzie

When the 'Studies in Imperialism' series was founded by Professor John M. MacKenzie more than thirty years ago, emphasis was laid upon the conviction that 'imperialism as a cultural phenomenon had as significant an effect on the dominant as on the subordinate societies'. With well over a hundred titles now published, this remains the prime concern of the series. Cross-disciplinary work has indeed appeared covering the full spectrum of cultural phenomena, as well as examining aspects of gender and sex, frontiers and law, science and the environment, language and literature, migration and patriotic societies, and much else. Moreover, the series has always wished to present comparative work on European and American imperialism, and particularly welcomes the submission of books in these areas. The fascination with imperialism, in all its aspects, shows no sign of abating, and this series will continue to lead the way in encouraging the widest possible range of studies in the field. 'Studies in Imperialism' is fully organic in its development, always seeking to be at the cutting edge, responding to the latest interests of scholars and the needs of this ever-expanding area of scholarship.

Mistress of everything

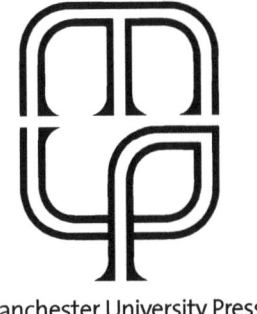

Manchester University Press

SELECTED TITLES AVAILABLE IN THE SERIES

WRITING IMPERIAL HISTORIES
ed. Andrew S. Thompson

EMPIRE OF SCHOLARS
Tamson Pietsch

HISTORY, HERITAGE AND COLONIALISM
Kynan Gentry

COUNTRY HOUSES AND THE BRITISH EMPIRE
Stephanie Barczewski

THE RELIC STATE
Pamila Gupta

WE ARE NO LONGER IN FRANCE
Allison Drew

THE SUPPRESSION OF THE ATLANTIC SLAVE TRADE
ed. Robert Burroughs and Richard Huzzey

HEROIC IMPERIALISTS IN AFRICA
Berny Sèbe

Mistress of everything

QUEEN VICTORIA IN INDIGENOUS WORLDS

Edited by
Sarah Carter and Maria Nugent

MANCHESTER UNIVERSITY PRESS

Copyright © Manchester University Press 2016

While copyright in the volume as a whole is vested in Manchester University Press, copyright in individual chapters belongs to their respective authors, and no chapter may be reproduced wholly or in part without the express permission in writing of both author and publisher.

Published by Manchester University Press
Oxford Road, Manchester M13 9PL
www.manchesteruniversitypress.co.uk

British Library Cataloguing-in-Publication Data
A catalogue record for this book is available from the British Library

ISBN 978 1 7849 9140 1 hardback

First published 2016

ISBN 978 1 5261 3688 6 paperback

First published 2018

The publisher has no responsibility for the persistence or accuracy of URLs for any external or third-party internet websites referred to in this book, and does not guarantee that any content on such websites is, or will remain, accurate or appropriate.

Typeset by Out of House Publishing

CONTENTS

List of maps and figures—vii
List of contributors—ix
Acknowledgements—xii
Maps—xiii

Introduction: Indigenous histories, settler colonies and
Queen Victoria   *Maria Nugent and Sarah Carter*   1

Part I – Monarch, metaphor, memory

1 'We have seen the son of Heaven/We have seen the Son of Our Queen': African encounters with Prince Alfred on his royal tour, 1860   *Hilary Sapire*   25

2 'We rejoice to honour the Queen, for she is a good woman, who cares for the Māori race': Loyalty and protest in Māori politics in nineteenth-century New Zealand   *Michael Belgrave*   54

3 'The faithful children of the Great Mother are starving': Queen Victoria in contact zone dialogues in western Canada   *Sarah Carter*   78

4 The politics of memory and the memory of politics: Australian Aboriginal interpretations of Queen Victoria, 1881–2011   *Maria Nugent*   100

Part II – Royal relations

5 'My vast Empire & all its many peoples': Queen Victoria's imperial family   *Barbara Caine*   125

6 Māori encounters with 'Wikitoria' in 1863 and Albert Victor Pomare, her Māori godchild   *Chanel Clarke*   144

7 Southern African royalty and delegates visit Queen Victoria, 1882–95   *Neil Parsons*   166

Part III – Sovereign subjects?

8 Sovereignty performances, sovereignty testings: The Queen's currency and imperial pedagogies on Australia's south-eastern settler frontiers   *Penelope Edmonds*   187

CONTENTS

9 Bracelets, blankets and badges of distinction: Aboriginal subjects and Queen Victoria's gifts in Canada and Australia   *Amanda Nettelbeck*   210

10 Chiefly women: Queen Victoria, Meri Mangakahia, and the Māori parliament   *Miranda Johnson*   228

Select bibliography—246
Index—249

LIST OF MAPS AND FIGURES

Maps

1. South Africa c. 1860, indicating places mentioned in the text — page xiii
2. North and South Islands of New Zealand indicating locations of places and regions mentioned in the text — xiv
3. Provinces, territories and administrative districts of Canada, 1881–86 — xv
4. The south-eastern Australian states (formerly colonies) indicating locations of places, including Aboriginal settlements, mentioned within the text. Names in brackets refer to earlier nomenclature — xvi

Figures

1.1 'Gaika Chief Sandile and his counsellors'. [F.A.V. York?]. (National Library of South Africa (Cape Town) Special Collections, ALBX.19, Sir George Grey Album circa 1860–1890, INIL 15798) — 34

1.2 'Zulu Kafirs at the foot of the Drakensburg, Natal'. (Photographed by HRH Prince Alfred, 01.09.1860. National Library of South Africa (Cape Town) Special Collections, Album 166, 'Prince Alfred's Visit (1860) Album') — 43

1.3 'Assemblage of warriors of Chief Goza's tribe'. (Killie Campbell Library, University of KwaZulu-Natal, Album C59/001–106) — 45

1.4 'Ngoza ka Ludaba and his men wearing ceremonial dress worn to welcome Prince Alfred in Pietermaritzburg, 1860'. (Killie Campbell Library, University of KwaZulu-Natal, d37-54, Zulu Chiefs Album 3; image described as: 'Chief Ngoza in full war costume, and his indunas') — 47

2.1 Tāwhiao, the Māori king, and Te Morehu Maipapa (also known as Major Wiremu Te Wheoro), in London, 1884. (National Library of Australia, NK2783, Rex Nan Kivell Collection) — 69

2.2 Te Morehu Maipapa (also known as Major Te Wheoro), Ngai Naho Chief and Member of Parliament for Western Māori, 1879–84 (Auckland Libraries, 4-2736, Sir George Grey Special Collections) — 70

2.3 The statue of Queen Victoria at Ohinemutu (Auckland Libraries, 35-R1263, Sir George Grey Special Collections) — 72

3.1 Henry Prince (Mis-koo-kenew/Red Eagle). (Archives of Manitoba, N10501) — 89

LIST OF FIGURES

3.2 ' "Pow-wow" between Marquess of Lorne and Blackfoot people, September 1881', pencil sketch by Sydney P. Hall, from sketchbook entitled 'Canada 1878 North West 1881' (Original in National Archives of Canada, PA-1211–56. This copy courtesy of Glenbow Archives, University of Alberta)   93

4.1 Deputation of Victorian Aborigines at the Governor's levee, 1863 (State Library of Victoria, Melbourne, Australia. Published with permission: Joy Murphy, Senior Wurundjeri Elder)   105

5.1 *The Secret of England's Greatness* (Queen Victoria presenting a Bible in the Audience Chamber at Windsor), Thomas Jones Baker, c. 1863 (© National Portrait Gallery, London)   127

5.2 Sarah Forbes Bonetta (Sarah Davies), Camille Silvy (© National Portrait Gallery, London)   134

6.1 *The New Zealand Chiefs at Wesley's House*, James Smetham, 1863 (University of Otago, Hocken Collections, Uare Taoka o Hakena)   149

6.2 Hare and Hariata Pomare and child Albert Victor Pomare, 1863, London, John Jabez Mayall (Alexander Turnbull Library, Wellington, New Zealand, PA2-1130)   158

6.3 Christening set presented by Queen Victoria to Albert Victor Pomare. (The Bishop of Auckland and Auckland War Memorial Museum, New Zealand)   159

7.1 Queen Victoria statue vandalised in 'defence' of Zuma, Port Elizabeth, South Africa, 5 March 2010. (Gallo Images/Contributor. Licensed: Getty Images)   179

8.1 Coin, 1843, Head of the Queen on obverse. Photographer: Justine Philip, 2010. (Museum Victoria, Melbourne, Australia)   191

8.2 'Gold Girl', from the series *Oz Omnium Rex et Regina*, 2008, artist: Darren Siwes. (© Darren Siwes/Licensed by Viscopy, 2015/Courtesy: Darren Siwes and GAGPROJECTS, Adelaide, South Australia)   202

8.3 'Gold Female', from the series *Oz Omnium Rex et Regina*, 2008, artist: Darren Siwes. (© Darren Siwes/Licensed by Viscopy, 2015/Courtesy: Darren Siwes and GAGPROJECTS, Adelaide, South Australia)   203

9.1 'Treaty medal presented to chiefs and councillors of treaties no. 1–7'. (National Library and Archives of Canada, Ottawa, PA-117764)   214

9.2 'The Queen's Birthday at Brisbane: distribution of blankets to the aboriginals [sic], 1873'. (State Library of Victoria, Melbourne, Australia, AS12/07/73/68. Published with permission: Maxine Briggs, Koori Liaison Officer)   221

10.1 Meri Te Tai Mangakahia. (Auckland War Memorial Museum, New Zealand, Davis Collection, C5101)   237

10.2 *Queen with Moko*, Barry Ross Smith, 2008. (Courtesy: Barry Ross Smith)   243

CONTRIBUTORS

Michael Belgrave is a historian and foundation member of Massey University's Albany campus. He has published widely on treaty and Māori history, including as lead editor of *Waitangi Revisited: Perspectives on the Treaty of Waitangi* (OUP). He is the author of *Historical Frictions: Maori Claims and Reinvented Histories*. He is currently completing a book to be published by Auckland University Press on the aftermath of the New Zealand Wars, focusing on the peace-making which occurred between the Kīngitanga and the Colonial Government over the King Country.

Barbara Caine is Professor of History and Dean of the Faculty of Arts and Social Sciences at the University of Sydney. She has written extensively on nineteenth-century British History and on the relationship between history and biography. Her most recent monographs are *Bombay to Bloomsbury: A Biography of the Strachey Family* (2005) and *Biography and History* (2010).

Sarah Carter is Professor and Henry Marshall Tory Chair at the University of Alberta where she has a joint appointment in the Department of History and Classics, and Faculty of Native Studies. She is the author of multiple articles and books including *The Importance of Being Monogamous: Marriage and Nation-Building in Western Canada* (2008) and *Aboriginal People and Colonizers of Western Canada* (1999). Her most recent co-edited collection (with Patricia McCormack) is *Recollecting: Lives of Aboriginal Women of the Canadian Northwest and Borderlands* (2011).

Chanel Clarke is of Māori descent and has tribal affiliations to Ngāpuhi, Te Rarawa, Ngāti Porou and Waikato-Tainui. She is the Curator Māori at the Auckland Museum and is currently undertaking her PhD at the University of Otago in New Zealand. Her specific collection interests are the social and cultural aspects of dress and textiles in both traditional and contemporary contexts. She has been the recipient of numerous awards and grants including Fulbright New Zealand and the American Association of Museums International Partnerships Programme.

Penelope Edmonds is Australian Research Council Future Fellow and Associate Professor, History and Classics, School of Humanities, University of Tasmania. Her research interests are in colonial and postcolonial histories in the Australian and Pacific region. Her most recent book is *Settler Colonialism and (Re)conciliation: Frontier Violence, Affective Performances, and Imaginative Refoundings* (Cambridge Imperial and Postcolonial Studies series, Palgrave, 2016).

Miranda Johnson is a lecturer in the Department of History at the University of Sydney. She works on Indigenous histories in settler colonial states. Her book, *The Land is Our History: Indigeneity, Law and the Settler State* (Oxford University Press, 2016), examines Indigenous claims-making in the late-twentieth century in Australia, Canada, and New Zealand as a profoundly transformative and paradoxical phenomenon that has left lasting legacies in these countries. Born and raised in New Zealand, Johnson studied and taught in the United States before moving to Australia.

Amanda Nettelbeck is Professor in the School of Humanities at the University of Adelaide. Her publications have centred on the history and memory of the settler colonial frontier and the colonial governance of Indigenous people. She is co-author with Robert Foster of *Out of the Silence: The History and Memory of South Australia's Frontier Wars* (2012), *In the Name of the Law: William Willshire and the Policing of the Australian Frontier* (2007) and *Fatal Collisions: The South Australian Frontier and the Violence of Memory* (2001). A collaborative book with Russell Smandych, Louis Knafla and Robert Foster, *Fragile Settlements: Aboriginal Peoples, Law and Resistance in South-West Australia and Prairie Canada*, will be published by UBC Press in 2016.

Maria Nugent is Fellow in the School of History's Australian Centre for Indigenous History at the Australian National University in Canberra. She is the author of *Botany Bay: Where Histories Meet* (2005) and *Captain Cook was Here* (2009). She contributed to the British Museum's 2015 exhibition, *Indigenous Australia: Enduring Civilisation*. Between 2011 and 2015, she held an Australian Research Council Future Fellowship, and was Visiting Professor of Australian Studies at the University of Tokyo in 2015–16. She publishes on Australian Indigenous and settler-colonial history and memory.

Neil Parsons is a London-based independent scholar, former Professor of History at the University of Botswana. He is the author of many books including *A New History of Southern Africa* (1982), a biography of *Seretse Khama 1921–1980* (1995), *King Khama Emperor Joe and the Great White Queen* (1998), and *Clicko the Wild Dancing Bushman* (2009). He is currently completing an illustrated volume titled *Black and White Bioscope: Silent Cinema in Southern Africa 1895–1923*.

CONTRIBUTORS

Hilary Sapire is Senior Lecturer in the history of the British Empire and Southern Africa in the Department of History, Classics and Archaeology, Birkbeck College, University of London. She has written widely on modern South African history. She is a former editor of the *Journal of Southern African Studies*, and her publications include (with Robert Edgar) *African Apocalypse: The Story of a Twentieth-Century South African Prophet* (Ohio University Press, 1999) and (with Christopher Saunders) *Southern African Liberation Struggles: New Local, Regional and Global Perspectives* (University of Cape Town Press, 2012). She is currently writing a book on the history of royal tours to southern Africa.

ACKNOWLEDGEMENTS

All but one of the chapters in this volume were presented at a symposium 'Queen Victoria in the Colonies: Ideas, Interpretations, Interactions' convened by Maria Nugent at The Australian National University in December 2013. Our thanks to everyone who participated in that event for two days of very stimulating discussion and exchange of ideas. Unfortunately, and for various reasons, not all of the papers presented could be included. Subsequent to the symposium, Hilary Sapire accepted our invitation to contribute a chapter on South Africa, which was less well represented in the symposium programme than the other three settler colonies of New Zealand, Australia and Canada. We are indebted to her for that. We wish to acknowledge the considerable support provided by The Australian National University. In particular, our thanks to the School of History (and in particular the then head, Dr Douglas Craig) and its Australian Centre for Indigenous History (especially Professor Ann McGrath) for encouragement, funds and administrative support provided. Thanks also to the Visiting Fellows scheme in the College of Arts and Social Science at ANU, which supported Sarah Carter's participation in the symposium. Generous funding was also received from external sources, including the Australian Research Council, the Academy for the Social Sciences in Australia, and the Department of History at Monash University. Maria especially thanks Dr Blake Singley for his assistance with organising the symposium and his good humour throughout.

All of the participants responded with alacrity to the prospect of an edited collection, and we have enjoyed working with each of them on it. We were pleased when Manchester University Press accepted our proposal because we knew of its high scholarly standards and review processes, and excellent publication values. We appreciated the helpful and encouraging comments from anonymous reviewers on the proposal and manuscript. Our particular thanks to Emma Brennan for her support and for shepherding us through the publication process. In helping us prepare the manuscript for publication, we owe a debt to Dr Gretchen Albers, Calgary, Alberta, for her outstanding editorial work completed under very tight deadlines, and also to Peter Johnson who created the location maps for us. The final stages were undertaken while Maria Nugent was based at the Center for Pacific and American Studies at the University of Tokyo. Special thanks to Professor Yasuo Endo, Professor Fumiko Nishizaki and Associate Professor Kenryu Hashikawa for their hospitality and support.

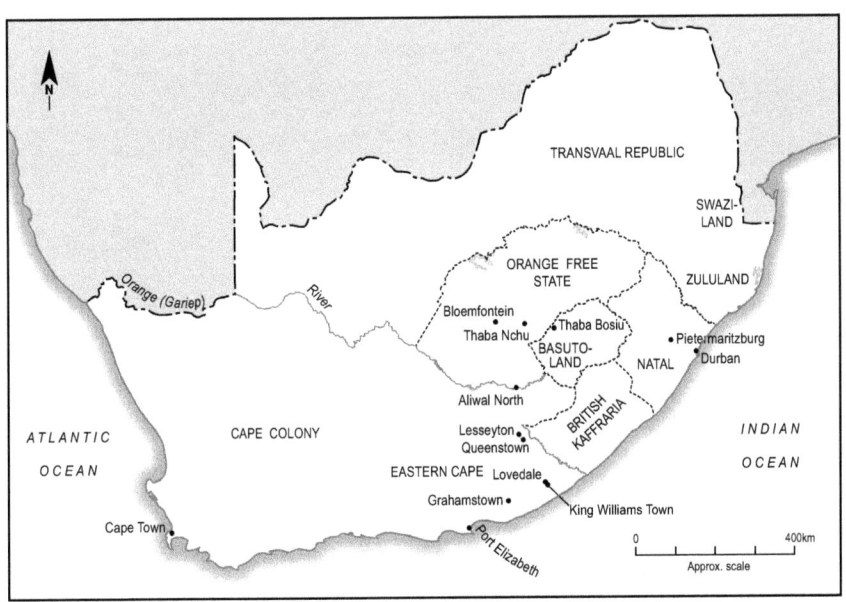

Map 1 South Africa c. 1860, indicating places mentioned in the text.

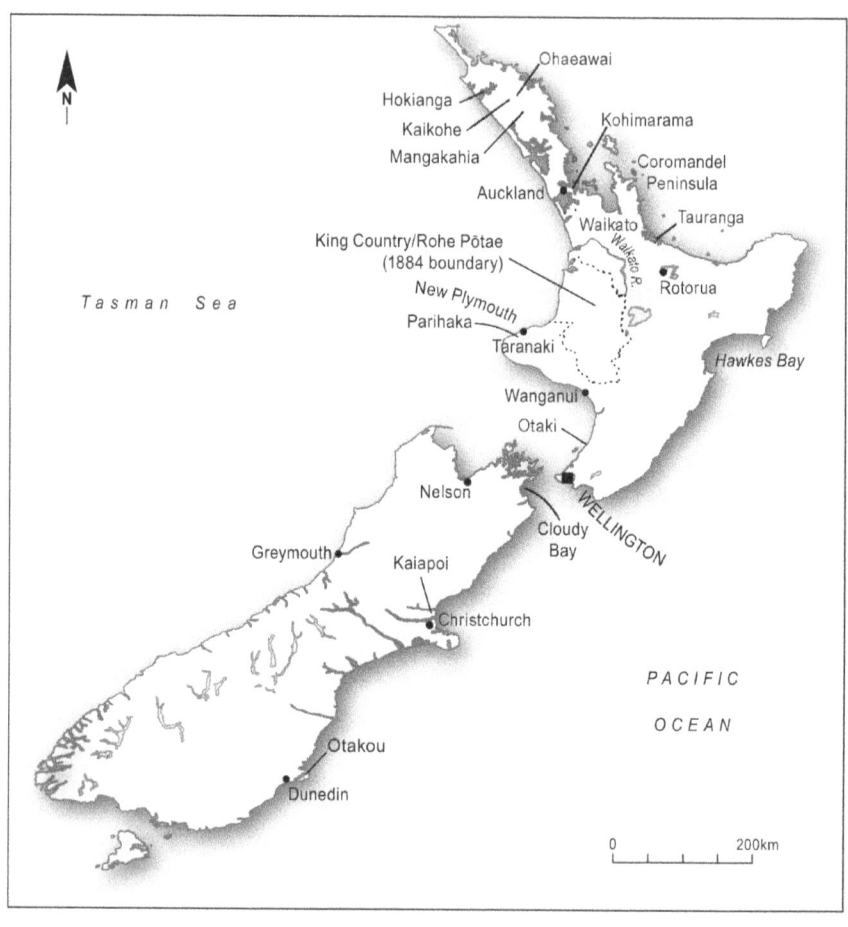

Map 2 North and South Islands of New Zealand, indicating locations of places and regions mentioned in the text.

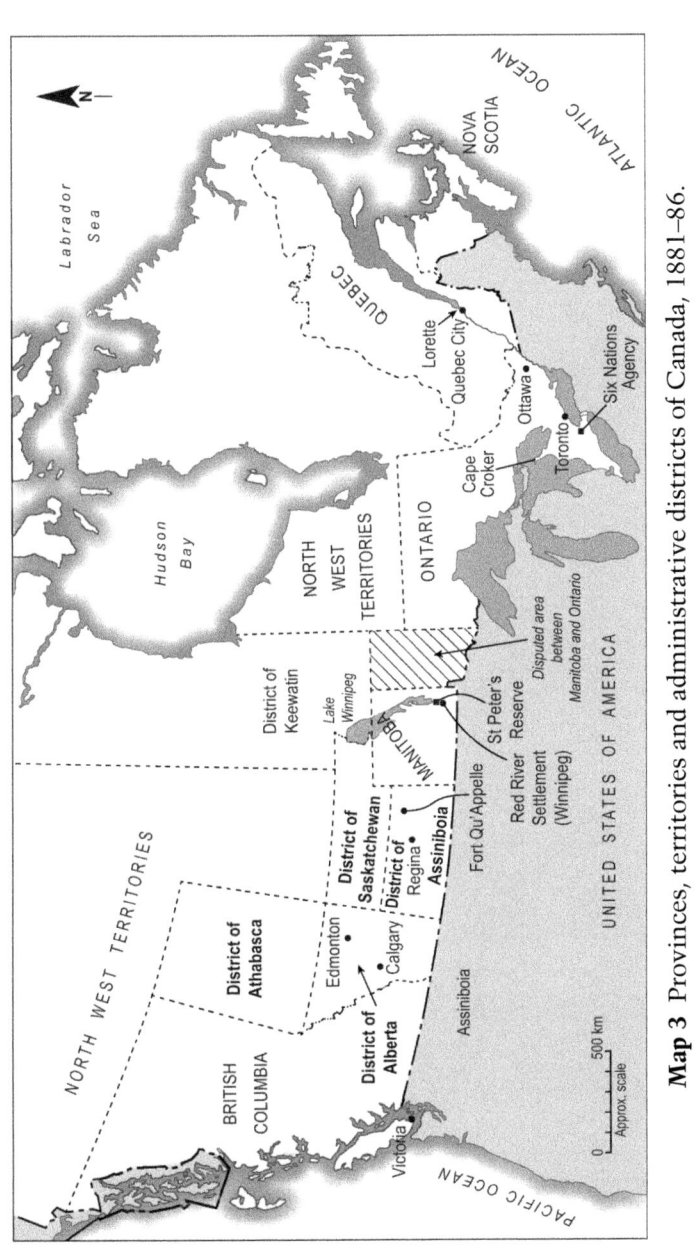

Map 3 Provinces, territories and administrative districts of Canada, 1881–86.

Map 4 The south-eastern Australian states (formerly colonies), indicating locations of places, including Aboriginal settlements, mentioned within the text. Names in brackets refer to earlier nomenclature.

INTRODUCTION

Indigenous histories, settler colonies and Queen Victoria

Maria Nugent and Sarah Carter

When Prince William and the Duchess of Cambridge visited Canada in 2011, journalists would occasionally weave into their reports a reference to Queen Victoria. Describing their visit to northern Canada, one report opened with the tidbit that the Prince met with 'aboriginal groups who still refer affectionately to his ancestor Queen Victoria as "grandmother"'. Mixing myth with history, it went on to assert that the 'area aboriginals signed the British monarchy's first Arctic treaty 112 years ago … with William's great-great-great-grandmother, Queen Victoria'.[1] The journalist, perhaps unknowingly, was contributing to the continuation of a long tradition whereby successive royal visitors to Canada (as in other British colonies) were represented and welcomed in ways that highlighted their descent from Queen Victoria, registering the ways in which she, above all other British monarchs, had come to occupy a privileged place in Indigenous people's histories, traditions, and memories. Moreover, the newspaper report reflected and nourished the persistence of a widely held belief that treaties and other agreements made during British colonisation of Indigenous territories had been made personally with Queen Victoria.[2] Here, as elsewhere in the British world, she was cast as intimately involved with and implicated in promises and agreements made between Indigenous people and Britain (or Britons). One aim of this collection is to plumb the ideas and interpretations, like those that this example evokes, which Indigenous people have formulated and articulated *about* – or, more accurately, *through* – Queen Victoria in response to the colonial encounter.[3] It explores the multivalent ways in which Indigenous people in Australia, New Zealand, Canada, and South Africa engaged – or sought to engage – Queen Victoria in their lives and struggles, including by incorporating her into their intellectual thought, political rhetoric, and narrative traditions. On the flipside, so to speak, the collection also considers the ways in which the Crown's representatives employed the figure of the monarch in their dealings with the peoples that British colonisation displaced, as well as how Queen Victoria viewed her Indigenous 'subjects' (see Caine Chapter 5 especially).

'Queen Victoria' denotes more than merely the name by which the monarch was known. As many of the chapters amply illustrate, Queen Victoria was a name or phrase with many and multiplying meanings and associations, and which could easily be used metaphorically, metonymically, or analogically as well as serving more prosaic uses as a term of address. Within colonial contexts, Queen Victoria referred not only to the person on the throne, but was also used widely as shorthand or synonym for the Crown, for the British government and for the Empire – or some approximation or amalgam of all three. Our title – *Mistress of Everything* – a description used by Plains Cree spokesman Pahsung in 1881 during a visit to Fort Qu-Appelle by Queen Victoria's son-in-law, the Marquis of Lorne (discussed in Carter Chapter 3) registers Queen Victoria's capacious meanings and associations for Indigenous people (as for others). By using the term 'Indigenous' to describe interlocutors or interpretations, for instance, we register our primary interest in the experiences, practices, and perspectives of the peoples displaced and dispossessed, often violently, as a result of British imperial expansion during Queen Victoria's long reign.

We have purposely limited the scope of the collection to the settler colonies of Canada, New Zealand, Australia, and southern Africa. While we are aware that Indigenous and other colonised peoples elsewhere in the British world during the nineteenth century also developed 'traditions' and 'narratives' incorporating the figure of Queen Victoria (India, Fiji, and the British West Indies are obvious examples),[4] our concentration on the settler colonies is for the scope provided for comparative and transnational perspectives. As Annie Coombes outlines in her introduction to *Rethinking Settler Colonialism*, these countries share 'a number of features in terms of their colonial histories', in their relationships to the imperial metropolitan centre, in the composition of their colonial communities, and consequently, in their cultural and political institutions. It is not for nothing, then, that many recent historical studies and collections seeking to respond to the repeated call for an expanded view of British history that takes into account its overseas colonies, or aiming for a rapprochement between settler-national and imperial-Commonwealth historiographies, or pursuing 'transnational' or 'interconnected' approaches to writing imperial-colonial history, choose to cover much the same geographical ground as we do.[5] But while these colonies and the nations they spawned share much in common, their differences are notable as well. Where their distinctiveness springs from, Coombes argues, is 'fundamentally contingent on their relationship to and with the various Indigenous communities they ... encountered' as well as in the histories of their colonising 'dealings' with them.[6] Within these national contexts, then, the nature of relations and interactions between British settlers/colonisers and Indigenous people is a defining feature of their past and their present.

It is in this spirit that we believe a singular focus on Queen Victoria comes into its own. In each of the places we cover are to be found broadly comparable colonial cultures of monarchy with Queen Victoria as a centrepiece, and so the chapters cohere to suggest interconnections and overlaps in the ways in which Indigenous people participated in and engaged with those practices, symbols, and cultures to mobilise Queen Victoria for their own purposes.[7] At the same time, though, detailed and empirically rich analysis and micro-studies of Indigenous interpretations of and interactions with Queen Victoria opens out onto quite distinct histories of Indigenous and settler relations, revealing in the process some of the particularities and pluralities of Indigenous people's struggles for rights, recognition, and redress. And although many examples of Indigenous people's engagements around Queen Victoria have already been discussed in a wide range of scholarship, we note that they have been mainly confined to national or regional historiographies.[8] This volume represents a first attempt to bring such work together into productive dialogue and to apply some comparative and transnational perspectives to it.

Needless to say, Queen Victoria is an especially generous 'site' for the kinds of historical and cultural analysis we pursue here. This is not least because she reigned for such a long time. Her reign was inaugurated in mid-1837 and ended with her death in early 1901. These were, by any measure, six significant decades for Indigenous peoples in Britain's settler colonies. Not only did they witness the continued and increased influx of British settlers, who, as Alan Lester and Fae Dussart put it, 'did the work of violent Indigenous dispossession' even as they were met with 'the resilient and sovereign peoples' who fought against colonial incursion.[9] This was also a period, as Lisa Ford has recently described it, 'when technologies of settler governance intruded on Indigenous life with new intimacy and persistence'.[10]

Victoria's reign coincided with a shift in British imperial policy and practice, and paralleled a series of landmark events in empire-wide and localised histories of British colonisation. The early phase of her reign in late 1830s and early 1840s articulated with processes that Lester and Dussart have recently mapped in their book *Colonization and the Origins of Humanitarian Governance*, in which they show that 'amelioration policies were translated into policies for the protection of Indigenous peoples in southern Africa, the Australian colonies and New Zealand', as well as in Canada, as they acknowledge, although it is not included in their study.[11] Under these general conditions, Queen Victoria emerged as something of a poster child for 'benevolent' or 'humanitarian' colonisation. The British Crown's local representatives in the colonies were inclined to represent her in such terms in their dialogue and dealings with Indigenous people. Yet, as Ann Curthoys argues, 'this strategy had an unintended consequence: over time, Indigenous people began to see the Queen as an alternative source of authority, as someone who could help them in their battle with settler governments and people, especially in their quest for the return of their land'.[12]

In the later decades of Victoria's reign, Indigenous people were often in desperate need of an external ally – an 'alternative source of authority' – particularly as settler autonomy grew apace through the gradual granting of self-government to the settler colonies and as their own political power and autonomy was, as a result, threatened and reduced.[13] As Julie Evans et al. note, the 'shift in power from central to more localised control by European systems of law and government' within the settler colonies from the 1830s onwards had 'serious consequences for indigenous peoples', often prompting 'appeals to the Crown to abide by British justice, forcing the British Government of the day to respond to their concerns independently of the local authorities'.[14] Contests and conflicts between Indigenous peoples and settlers are, as many of our authors note, registered in the astute ways in which Queen Victoria could be mobilised by Indigenous people to challenge British settler claims about justice, fairness, and humane treatment, to hold them to account for their actions, and to push for redress of the situations in which they found themselves as a result of further settler encroachment.[15]

The sheer ubiquity of Queen Victoria's imprint and symbolic and cultural presence in colonial contexts also made 'her' abundantly available for imaginative incorporation into Indigenous people's thought, rhetoric, and politics.[16] Reminders and inscriptions of the British sovereign were seemingly everywhere – whether in the names for places, on the currency and stamps that circulated, as the signatory to documents and deeds, as the occasion for public holidays, in photographs displayed in churches or reproduced in newspapers, and in various other modes too many to mention.[17] In settler colonial contexts, Indigenous people were constantly exposed to Queen Victoria. They might be occasionally paid visits by the monarch's sons, as Hilary Sapire's chapter describes, or more often by colonial governors (one of whom in Canada was her son by marriage), as Sarah Carter discusses. Indigenous people were regular recipients of royal rhetoric, whether delivered to them by visiting princes, resident missionaries, government officials, or ordinary settlers, and they were commonly deemed in need of lessons in imperial loyalty and subjecthood, as Amanda Nettelbeck's chapter in particular shows. As more than a name, Queen Victoria became incorporated into the lexicons and vernaculars that were used for cross-cultural conversations carried out on colonial frontiers, as Penelope Edmonds explores in her chapter.

Taken together, the chapters reveal the range and breadth of meanings that accrued to Queen Victoria during the course of her reign – and afterwards. As a shared figure or symbol, drawn on by British settlers and authorities, imperial institutions, and (Colonial Office) bureaucrats and Indigenous people alike,[18] and not least in their ongoing dialogues with each other, Queen Victoria was embroidered into far-reaching debates and discourses on such crucial matters as rights and responsibilities, community and belonging, citizenship and non-citizenship, race and difference, and authority, sovereignty, and destiny. We have noted the ways Queen Victoria became associated with protection, charity, and benevolence, but as monarch she could just as easily be deployed in exchanges about the recognition of Indigenous people's sovereignty, the nature of imperial and Indigenous authority and power, Indigenous claims to compensation for land and other losses, their own royal status and structures and its relationship to the royal house of Britain, and the bases for their qualifications and claims as 'imperial citizens'.[19]

In some respects this was nothing new. In all of the contexts explored in the volume, Indigenous people grafted Queen Victoria onto pre-existing understandings about, earlier relationships with, and continuing creative uses of, the British monarch (see Belgrave Chapter 2, Parsons Chapter 7, and Carter Chapter 3, especially). But, as a number of scholars and biographers have noted, the young queen also provided something special and novel.[20] As a female monarch who quickly acquired a reputation for charity, concern, and virtue, reference to Queen Victoria could be introduced into colonial/Indigenous discussions to provide a quite specific set of inflections, often gendered: a theme that Miranda Johnson pursues in her chapter on the ways in which some Māori women drew on Queen Victoria as a narrative device in their debates with Māori men regarding matters of authority and autonomy. Likewise, the emphasis on Queen Victoria as a maternal figure, translated commonly into descriptions of her as a 'great mother', is also a recurring theme across a number of the chapters, but one that is refracted through understandings of kinship or authority within particular cultural contexts and traditions that help to reveal the meaningful particularities that lie beneath a common metaphor.

Our approach to studying Indigenous histories and experiences via a sustained focus on Queen Victoria (and, to a lesser extent, vice versa) highlights a number of concepts and themes. Prominent among them is 'loyalty', a theme that continues to engage scholars as they seek to understand the politics of Indigenous people (or individuals) in Britain's settler colonies, especially in the period from the middle of the nineteenth century to the middle of the twentieth when an 'affective' engagement with the monarch, beginning with Queen Victoria, became increasingly noticeable.

Loyalty and devotion to the Queen was promoted and nurtured among all her scattered subjects and colonists, not just the Indigenous people of the Empire. According to imperialists, she generated a 'mystic reverence' amongst all her people.[21] She was the emblem of imperial unity as well as maternal love, 'standing watchful guide over her magnificent realms'.[22] An imperial enthusiast wrote in tribute after her death that Victoria built an empire on love: 'She was a royal conqueror indeed, for she conquered the whole world, but it was by love ... [H]er power was such as no sovereign who ruled by force, or right or ability, ever commanded. Thus out of the seeming weakness of a woman on the throne was perfected the strength of an Empire.'[23] Indigenous people were typically portrayed by imperial apologists as even surpassing British settlers in their allegiance and devotion, implying that they were delighted to accept and live peacefully under the rule of a woman they worshipped.

Historians have at times been confounded and unsettled by Indigenous people's seemingly exaggerated expressions of fealty to the Queen. Interpretations have covered a spectrum from assumptions of gullible naivety to assertions of conscious and knowing strategy. As Heather Goodall observes in relation to Australian Aboriginal people's generally positive interpretations of Queen Victoria, they 'have often been described rather patronisingly as reflections of Aboriginal people's gullability ... [or as] examples of Aboriginal naiveté in feeling gratitude and loyalty to the Queen for her benevolence and charity, while failing to recognise the British Crown as the cause of their dispossession'. Goodall concludes that both of 'these readings severely underestimate the factual knowledge held by Aboriginal people in the period, and the symbolic power of their account'.[24] In a more recent discussion, which some of our authors cite, Andrew Thompson has helpfully argued in relation to South Africa (one of our locations) that to understand the 'loyalist theme ... we must distance ourselves from the narrow but more familiar idea of loyalism that sees it as an overzealous, gratuitous, almost pathological affirmation of imperialism among minorities and fringe groups'.[25] He proposes instead to approach it as a 'broad church in which very different kinds of imperial "faith" could (however uncomfortably) coexist', which were expressed in diverse modes towards different 'objects', whether Britain, Downing Street, or the Crown, and which 'was fuelled by different interests and put to different purposes'.[26]

Similarly, reappraising expressions of loyalty on the part of Indigenous people in Britain's colonies can also contribute to new perspectives on their claim-making and broader politics across the nineteenth century and into the twentieth. The conundrum of loyalty is a theme that Sukanya Banerjee has addressed in her recent study of the claims of South Asian Indians to 'imperial citizenship' in the late Victorian era, in which she argues that expressions of 'imperial loyalty played a mediating role in articulating the claims to rights and an equality of a "we", not least because any rhetoric of citizenship hinges quite dramatically on notions of loyalty'.[27] In this way, she makes an important argument that a politics of imperial citizenship, underwritten often by a discourse of imperial loyalty, belongs to a history of anti-colonial thought, providing a much longer genealogy for it than is often credited.[28]

Chapters in this collection pursue similar questions about how to interpret expressions of affection for the Queen and to situate their meanings within broader political agendas and visions. Through careful analysis, a number of authors show the ways in which 'affective' modes of speaking and of expressing relationships to a distant queen were a medium for hardnosed and clear-eyed political agendas, or for extending the terms of engagement between Indigenous people and settlers, or indeed among Indigenous people themselves (see, for instance, Johnson Chapter 10 and Sapire Chapter 1). Some, like Sarah Carter in her chapter, show that proclamations of loyalty were more often than not accompanied by demands that the monarch and her representatives respect or restore Indigenous rights and protect Indigenous people from rapacious colonisers and settler interests. Others, such as Michael Belgrave, illustrate the ways in which loyalty could be slippery and changeable, at times asserted and at others disavowed or renounced. Whatever the case, our authors are in agreement that Indigenous expressions of loyalty unsettle the self-serving settler myth of unstinting adulation of Indigenous people for the British sovereign.

Not all Indigenous statements about or attitudes towards Queen Victoria were, of course, delivered (shrouded?) in the language of loyalism or characterised by positively inflected feelings of attachment and affection. They could just as easily be expressly and unambiguously critical of the British Crown, especially when it came to negotiations over land and to what were roundly perceived as broken promises and unfulfilled terms of agreements. As various authors show, Queen

Victoria – as the embodiment of the Crown – was often invoked during transactions involving land acquisition and treaty negotiations, and she became in the process closely and personally associated with particular agreements (for examples, see Belgrave Chapter 2, Carter Chapter 3, Edmonds Chapter 8). This also contributed to her incorporation into rich storytelling and other interpretative traditions as well as her longevity as a recursive figure within the politics of memory that always attends Indigenous/settler relationships and that continues to be a feature within the 'post imperial', 'postcolonial' present (see, for instance, Nugent Chapter 4, Parsons Chapter 7, Edmonds Chapter 8, Clarke Chapter 6).

One evocative example will suffice to underline the point. At the Treaty 4 negotiations in 1874 in Canada, prominent Cree chief Kawâhkatos was present – and later recalled an incident. One of the Queen's representatives, he recounted, spread a cloth on the ground and placed bags of money on it, and explained through an interpreter how many bags the Queen had sent. According to Kawâhkatos, a chief replied: 'Tell the Queen's representative to empty the money and fill the bags with dirt. Tell him to take the bags back to England to the Queen. She has paid for that much land.'[29] Anecdotes and remembrances like these come in many versions, and can be found within colonial archives across Canada, New Zealand, Australia, and southern Africa. It is not surprising that Queen Victoria should feature so widely in the records and remembrances of negotiations over land, because land was and is at the very core of histories of settler colonies and of the fraught and unresolved relations between Indigenous people and settlers. What this particular example illustrates well is the ways in which Queen Victoria was so often cast as a mediating figure in these histories, a figure onto which, for instance, competing claims of generosity or fairness and miserliness or underhandedness could be inscribed.

By juxtaposing studies drawn from different settler colonies and interrogating the function or role given to Queen Victoria within Indigenous people's own historical interpretations, what emerges once again is evidence for the distinct histories that have arisen from the nature of settler/Indigenous encounters and relations in each of these places. At the most obvious level, differences occur in relation to whether or not treaties between Indigenous people and the British Crown were made. (No treaties were made in Australia, as Edmonds Chapter 8, Nettelbeck Chapter 9, and Nugent Chapter 4, show.) But the differences are more subtle than this as well. They are indexed, for instance, in the diversity of interpretations and claim-making incorporating Queen Victoria in some regions and the notable uniformity

INTRODUCTION

in other places. In her chapter on South Africa, Hilary Sapire notes, 'The variety of expressions of monarchical devotion ... reflected the different stages and depths of the experience of colonisation and British cultural hegemony'. Contrast this with the single, collective interpretation of the Queen's apparent role in land matters that was shared over a quite large geographical area by Aboriginal people in south-east Australia, as Nugent's chapter makes clear. Other historical differences registered within the collection derive from histories of war and conflict, both between Indigenous people and Britons within the colonies as well as in regard to Indigenous people's participation in imperial wars; levels of parliamentary representation and political rights accorded to Indigenous people or concomitantly the disenfranchisement of Indigenous people and their loss of the rights to self-govern; the relative mobility of Indigenous people (both to Britain or across regions) and contact with international organisations and networks; and literacy, education, and Christian conversion.

As our discussion so far demonstrates, many of the contributors are interested in the discursive 'production' of Queen Victoria by Indigenous people and the 'performance' of relationships to her situated within broader histories of Indigenous–imperial–colonial relations. The focus is on Indigenous people as interlocutors and agents in the various social, cultural, and imaginative processes by which, as Mark McKenna puts it, monarchy is 'performed into being'.[30] An interest in performance and the spaces of performance – whether they occur in the Queen's state rooms (Clarke Chapter 6, Parsons Chapter 7, Caine Chapter 5) or during a royal or vice-regal tour (Sapire Chapter 1, Carter Chapter 3), or are elements within a commemorative event (Edmonds Chapter 8, Nettelbeck Chapter 9, Belgrave Chapter 2), or are the speeches and statements made in other public settings (Nugent Chapter 4, Johnson Chapter 10) – necessarily draws attention to different cultures and practices of diplomacy, oratory, remembrance, and gift-giving. Repeatedly, the discussions reveal what often appears as a 'coincidence of ritual' when Indigenous and settler practices of diplomacy, claim-making, and transactional events meet. But they just as often show the mistranslations and misinterpretations that occur within – constitute even – the contact zones and 'middle grounds'[31] in which Queen Victoria was liberally employed as a mediating device between what were often radically different worldviews, expectations, and power dynamics.

One question that emerges from all of this is how to conceive of 'Indigenous politics' – or indeed politics in general. The volume as a whole does not present any single position on this, and in fact there is some tension, contradictions even, between authors in terms of the ways in which they understand and write about political action and thought. For instance, some are inclined to interpret it in terms of public forms of action and appeal aimed at – and preferably resulting in – improved circumstances and material and measurable outcomes, such as, for instance, the reaffirmation of treaty terms or increased provisions from the Crown.[32] For those authors, Indigenous people's dealings with or uses of Queen Victoria, in whatever mode and in whatever context, are invariably (perhaps inevitably) judged as being of only limited political value or as 'failures' or 'disappointments'. Others, though, adopt a view in which all action is in a sense 'political' and in which politics exists or is constituted in and by doing – or being and becoming. For them, the 'discursive' matters a great deal, as they consider the ways in which words and language – at its most 'performative'[33] – can work to 'wedge' open spaces, as Miranda Johnson describes it in her chapter, for telling or articulating alternative accounts of self and of history.

Finally, the chapters taken together also provide, even if only incidentally, plenty of evidence of the contributions that Indigenous people in the settler colonies made to British imperial culture and especially to cultures of monarchy. This reminds us, as McKenna notes, that 'popular monarchism in the British Empire during the nineteenth and twentieth centuries was created and sustained by "British people" *and* Indigenous subjects in all their diversity, particularly in the dialogue between imperial authorities and colonies' (emphasis added).[34] Our emphasis on Indigenous interpretations of Queen Victoria and the dialogical and 'cross-cultural' production of her meanings and symbolism provides some corrective to scholarship – and, indeed, the vast popular literature as well – which is slanted towards domestic British perspectives, although there is certainly evidence that this is changing, and this collection is part of the shift.[35] When attention was first turned to view the monarchy and Empire from outside the metropole, such as by David Cannadine in his classic text *Ornamentalism*, the perspective offered, as indeed some critics noted, tended to be 'top down' or projected outwards from centre to margin.[36] As Antoinette Burton has noted, '*Ornamentalism* ... offered the view from above: a promontory perspective which privileged monarchy as the fount of social, aesthetic and national values, as well as the source from which all imperial ideals emanated'.[37]

In place of studying projections fanning outwards from the centre, the studies presented in our volume tend to work from the ground up by exploring the ways in which the symbolic vocabularies and vernaculars of monarchy, empire, sovereignty, and the Crown (among other things) were produced – or at the very least, co-produced – by colonised communities and constituencies, and taken up within broader political repertoires and cultures. This reflects a recent reorientation in histories of empire, conceived around metaphors of 'webs' of connection or integrated imperial networks that trace the movements of things, ideas, and people from colony to colony rather than in a straight line from centre to periphery, although in this volume we have not explicitly attempted to map the trans-colonial or empire-wide circulation of ideas about Queen Victoria.[38] We do not, for instance, consider here the influence of Indigenous people's engagements with Queen Victoria in one colonial context on other situations, although we do commend such an approach.[39]

Before moving on to provide summaries of the chapters, it is worth noting that much of the scholarship presented here is only possible because of methodological innovations over the last few decades, particularly in areas of Indigenous history, cultural history, visual and material culture studies, narrative and memory studies, and post-colonial studies. Until reasonably recently, some historians might have been inclined to argue that such kinds of analysis aimed at teasing out the meanings of Indigenous people's words and actions were not possible given the fragmentary nature of the archival record and its often second-hand or densely mediated nature. Although the nature of the archive, and especially the relative dearth of Indigenous-authored texts, remains a challenge for scholarship in this vein – one which our authors acknowledge – a combination of interpretative and methodological approaches can glean from the evidence available the probable meanings of reported speech, fragmentary writings, and records of performances and their communicative contexts, intent, and reception. Indeed, a number of the chapters provide lessons in reading 'against' and 'along' the archival grain, in combining historical, art historical, and ethnographic approaches, and in contextualising both at micro and macro levels telling moments preserved within the historical record, even if only faintly.[40] Although they are all empirically grounded, some contributors use seemingly small and ephemeral incidents in order to pursue larger arguments about, for instance, the workings of cross-cultural exchanges and diplomacy, the articulation and refinement of political visions and claims, and the charged processes by which knowledge and authority were constructed – and challenged – on colonial borderlands.

Interpreting not only what was said (or recorded as said), but also the communicative modes and practices by which they were said and the communicative contexts in which they were transmitted, is a feature of some of the analysis offered. For some authors, there is a necessary focus on orality, including styles of oratory and occasions for oration (Johnson Chapter 10, Carter Chapter 3, Sapire Chapter 1, Nugent Chapter 4). For others, there is attention to the ways in which the presentation of certain objects was designed to convey meanings and to enact things, such as to initiate a relationship of reciprocity or to affirm equivalence in authority and status (Clarke Chapter 6, Belgrave Chapter 2, Nettelbeck Chapter 9). Attention is likewise given to the processes of translation and publication. In some cases, a return to the original archival record to check a source reveals what had been deleted or skewed during publication in the popular press, providing a very different meaning and serving a completely other agenda than the one intended by the speaker. A heavy editorial hand was often evident as well in the derogatory ways in which Indigenous speech and action was represented. To inform their interpretations of past events, other contributors pay attention to the recursive interplay between past and present, either by using contemporary sources, such as recorded oral history, or otherwise considering the ways in which certain past ideas and interpretations travel through time and place, acquiring new meanings and associations in the process (see Nugent Chapter 4 especially).

Just as interpreting Indigenous people's statements and perspectives presents challenges, so does testimony from or attributed to Queen Victoria herself. A few chapters (Caine Chapter 5, Clarke Chapter 6, and Parsons Chapter 7, particularly) draw on Victoria's journals as source material, but as with other chapters, they read this material with an eye to the contexts within which the monarch's own ideas and impressions were shaped and influenced. Barbara Caine's chapter is especially attuned to the monarch's milieu as she considers what to make of Queen Victoria's own intimate, as well as epistolary, relations with Indigenous individuals along with her own friends, acquaintances, and family members living and working in the settler colonies.

The book is structured in three sections, each of which highlights a particular mode of engagement or interpretation, though there are clear interconnections across the sections and across individual chapters as well (as the discussion above demonstrates).

In Part I: 'Monarch, metaphor, memory', we examine a range of interpretations of and ideas about Queen Victoria and the expression of them within and through various modes of cultural production, myth-making and memory-work. The chapters in this section combine to provide detailed discussion of the discursive construction and uses of Queen Victoria by Indigenous people in South Africa (the Cape and Natal in particular), New Zealand, western Canada and south-eastern Australia.

Hilary Sapire's chapter discusses Prince Alfred's royal tour to South Africa in 1860. Royal tours, as Sapire notes, were an innovation of Queen Victoria's reign, and became one of the most powerful 'sites' through which ideas about the monarch took root in the colonies and were occasions for public claim-making by Indigenous people about the responsibilities of Britain and settler governments to them. African encounters with Prince Alfred 'made flesh the mythology of the "Great White Queen" in ways that neither portraits nor celebrations could achieve', she writes. Throughout the chapter, Sapire explores how the symbolism of Queen Victoria was deployed in pursuit of greater 'rights' for black South Africans, including consideration of the uses of the rhetoric of loyalism. Engagements at the height of Victoria's reign had enduring significance, not least because they helped shape future ceremonial rituals, particularly the royal visits of the twentieth century, coronations, and events surrounding the death of British monarchs.

In his chapter, Michael Belgrave provides a broad study of Māori attitudes towards Queen Victoria from 1840. He analyses the many and changing Māori relationships with Queen Victoria and the intense Māori debates that centred on her. Some Māori communities expressed loyalty to the Queen early in her reign. Through her association with the Treaty of Waitangi in 1840, the idea emerged that she would protect Māori rights, and that she was distinct from her colonial government. Others rejected and opposed her, contesting the view that the Queen stood above settler politics. Sceptics of the idea that a distant queen could protect their rights initiated the Māori King Movement. Belgrave demonstrates how Victoria was incorporated into Māori systems of status, that she had 'mana'. By the late 1880s there was widespread Māori support for the Queen, because her name could be mobilised to represent their causes to both colonial and imperial governments. There remained a pattern of 'affection and protest': declarations of loyalty were followed by criticisms of the failure of settler governments to live up to the Queen's righteousness and the provisions of the treaty.

In a chapter that builds on her earlier and much-cited publications on Canadian First Nations and Queen Victoria, Sarah Carter uses St. Peter's Reserve, a settlement in western Canada, to explore a series of 'contact zones' that emerged across the nineteenth century in which ideas about Queen Victoria were produced, challenged, and honed as part of an ongoing discourse between Indigenous people and settler authorities concerning what the Crown had promised, failed to deliver, and still owed. Carter's analysis subtly moves beyond a simple dichotomous view, in which the Queen meant one thing to settlers and something else entirely to First Nations, or in which all First Nations' statements about her were essentially and straightforwardly strategic. The picture she paints is more nuanced than that. She does illustrate, as some other chapters do, that it could be advantageous at times to juxtapose the Queen's supposed morality with the failures of settler governments, but other considerations and impulses were at play as well. Moreover, she shows that settlers were much invested in ideas about Indigenous people as loyal subjects of the Queen, because it served their own myths about Canada's reputation as humane and benign colonisers.

In the following chapter, Maria Nugent takes as her focus a widely shared claim about Queen Victoria as the personal source of reserve lands, which has circulated among Aboriginal people in south-east Australia for three or four generations, seemingly impermeable to any alteration or interpretative innovation. Despite appearances, though, Nugent's discussion recovers a multiplicity of rhetorical purposes that this claim performed, each of which speaks to the changed conditions of Aboriginal people's lives during the second half of the nineteenth century and across the twentieth. She considers the diverse contexts of its public articulation and evocation, underlining her interest in the ways in which this 'epigrammatic history' with Queen Victoria at its heart worked within a broader politics of memory that attended (and attends still) to Indigenous-settler relations in Australia.

The chapters in Part II: 'Royal Relations' focus on personal, even intimate, modes of interaction and relations between various Indigenous people and Queen Victoria – or members of her immediate family, who sometimes served as proxies for her. In these chapters, Queen Victoria features, even if only opaquely, as a real person – in embodied form, as it were – and at home in the imperial centre. We encounter her mainly through her journals and in her audiences with Indigenous visitors.

In her chapter, Barbara Caine explores the nature and scope of Queen Victoria's own interest in and engagement with her Empire beyond Europe. This is, as Caine notes, a surprisingly muted theme in the vast and ever-expanding literature – scholarly and popular – on the lives, loves, and legacies of Victoria. Caine's chapter begins to redress this lacuna. In a discussion that is alert to the very real limits on Queen Victoria's power as a 'constitutional monarch', Caine discusses some of the ways in which she sought to use personal influence in colonial matters that intermittently garnered her attention. She suggests that Queen Victoria operated within the interstices of Empire – in the spaces where her personal connections and networks intersected with the machineries and workings of imperial expansion and governance. One notable way in which the monarch engaged with the colonies was through personal involvement in the lives of children, particularly some who found themselves dislocated as a result of British colonisation. These pseudo-maternal relationships, some much closer than others, were one of the avenues through which Victoria came to know about colonial situations. At the same time, these relationships also

INTRODUCTION

represent, as Caine argues, a means by which Queen Victoria sought to resolve the paradox 'presented by her simultaneous enthusiasm for imperial expansion and her sympathy for some of the victims of that expansion'.

Most of the children or youths who Victoria 'adopted' were, as Caine underlines, deposed royals, but she also occasionally appointed herself 'godmother' to some other young colonial 'subjects', including a Māori baby, whom Chanel Clarke discusses in Chapter 6 of this volume. This is, it must be said, a curious episode within the history of interactions between Indigenous people and Queen Victoria. The expectant mother and her husband were travelling with a Māori group in England in 1863, during which time they met with the Queen. To interpret the series of exchanges that occurred, Clarke applies the methods of cultural history as well as a curator's sensibility to tease out the meanings carried by dress, style, and comportment, the functions and expectations of gift-giving and diplomatic traditions, and the techniques by which visual representations, both photographs and portraits, helped to framed the public story of the meeting between Māori and the monarch. As with other chapters, Clarke carries her discussion through to contemporary times by considering the ways in which the Queen's gift of a christening set to the baby continues to have resonance for descendants.

In a chapter that reprises some of his earlier work, Neil Parsons charts southern African regal delegations to Queen Victoria, drawing on accounts of their reactions to their audiences with the monarch, as well as the Queen's journal entries on these encounters. In each case the Colonial Office assisted to stage these meetings, and arranged visits to sites and institutions intended to showcase the might and superiority of England, but refused to consider the Indigenous viewpoint. These missions also had no impact on colonial governments in southern Africa. After her reign, Parsons shows that attitudes to Victoria were varied and ambiguous among southern Africans depending on the relationship with the Empire. Where Africans were defeated by the British, or abandoned as allies, for example, the Queen was viewed as an 'evil chief', while for others she was recalled as a guarantor of justice and honour.

In the third section of the book, Part III: 'Sovereign Subjects?', our contributors continue to interrogate the ways in which Queen Victoria featured in exchanges and debates in settler colonial contexts about matters such as sovereignty, political autonomy, rights to land, and what it meant to be made into or to become 'imperial subjects'.

Penelope Edmonds uses an exchange involving an object bearing the Queen's image – in this case a coin – as a provocation for considering competing and incomplete claims of British sovereignty over

Indigenous people and their lands in south-east Australia. She considers a series of what she calls 'sovereignty performances' to show the ways in which during the early part of Queen Victoria's reign settler debates over sovereignty and its limits in Australia were in flux. Such casual performances of sovereignty, where newly colonised subjects were tested, are also implicit claims for European sovereignty, she argues, in what were at this time 'anomalous legal zones', to use Lauren Benton's phrase.[41] Edmonds brings her discussion to the present through a consideration of some contemporary artwork that returns to questions of female monarchs and sovereignty within 'republican' and 'postcolonial' visions of Australia.

In the following chapter, and the only explicitly comparative study in the collection, Amanda Nettelbeck also draws on material objects to frame her discussion. She compares the different contexts in which Aboriginal people figured as recipients of the Queen's gifts in commemorative moments that asserted British sovereignty in nineteenth-century Canada and Australia, and that were perceived to affirm Aboriginal people's status as the Queen's subjects. In considering how these gifts were received and how they circulated, the chapter explores some of the different meanings they generated, and the potentially unsettled relationships they implied between the Crown and Indigenous people in Australia and Canada respectively.

Miranda Johnson's chapter takes as its focus the Māori parliament (Kotahitanga) in New Zealand, which existed for a decade between 1892 and 1902. She provides an especially insightful analysis of the historical problem of Māori loyalty to the British monarch and the questions of autonomy that expressions of loyalty raised. Despite the devastation wrought on their people and their lands in the latter decades of the nineteenth century at the hands of white British settlers and imperial troops, in the late nineteenth century loyalty to the Queen and the right to be self-governing were notions in close tension with one another. Attending to diverse expressions of loyalty, Johnson's interest is in the purposes they served in dialogues and debates about Māori men's and Māori women's status and rights in particular. She argues that Māori women were suffering from the imposition of colonial rule in particular ways, notably the loss of recognition of their entitlements to land rights and their lack of representation at the national level. In this context, Queen Victoria became a useful 'narrative device' as some Māori women spelt out in the parliament their claims to autonomy and chiefly status as rightful landholders. Johnson argues 'that by centring the figure of Queen Victoria in their various demands, the Māori protagonists of this story laid claim to their own space *beside* the settler state, and *in* the

British Empire', but she also notes the fundamental paradox whereby they depended on an external authority to authorise their own claims to self-governance.

It is clear from several of the chapters that even in these 'post imperial', 'postcolonial' times Queen Victoria's symbolic resonance is not yet a spent force. Neil Parsons' closing example of the vandalism of a monument to Queen Victoria in Port Elizabeth in South Africa in 2010, Maria Nugent's mention of an Australian Aboriginal activist's reference to Queen Victoria in a speech to the Occupy Movement in London in 2011, Chanel Clarke's description of how a gift from Queen Victoria to a Māori infant is used within contemporary Waitangi Tribunal hearings in New Zealand, and Penelope Edmonds' discussion of Darren Siwes' photographic artworks that play with representations of sovereigns on Australian coins, all point in different ways to the continuing, recursive uses of Queen Victoria within broader conversations about the enduring legacies of British imperialism and colonialism for Indigenous people in settler-colonial nations. Many other examples could be drawn in here, including, for instance, Anishinaabe artist Rebecca Belmore's videoed performance piece, *Victorious*, produced in 2008, in which she clothed a proxy Queen Victoria in newspaper and honey to the strains of 'God Save the Queen' as a comment on imperial power.[42]

While we have touched only lightly on contemporary situations in which the figure of Queen Victoria is invoked, nevertheless one of our hopes for the collection is that it will make a contribution to growing interdisciplinary interest in Indigenous people's creative, performative, and discursive engagements with and reinscriptions of histories of imperial expansion and Indigenous dispossession. And we hope that it might also inspire especial interest in the ways in which the symbolically weighty figure of Queen Victoria continues to be produced, 'performed into being', and deployed and circulated within the fraught politics of history and memory – and of recognition and redress – that are a defining feature of the public life of settler-colonial societies, communities, and nations.

Notes

1 'Prince William and wife Kate meet aborigines in Canada', *The Australian* (AFP) (6 July 2011).
2 See, for instance, J. R. Miller, 'Victoria's "Red Children": The "Great White Mother" and native–newcomer relations in Canada', *Native Studies Review*, 17:1 (2008), 1–23. Following current convention in Australia and Canada, we have capitalised the word "Indigenous" throughout the book, except where an author has indicated a preference to use the lower case form.

3 Tim Rowse, *After Mabo: Interpreting Indigenous Traditions* (Melbourne: Melbourne University Press, 1993), pp. 13–14. For relevant discussions of Indigenous stories and oral histories about Queen Victoria and other members of the British family as a response to imperial expansion and the colonial encounter, see: Keith Thor Carlson, 'Aboriginal diplomacy: The Queen comes to Canada and Coyote goes to London', in J. Marshall Beier (ed.), *Indigenous Diplomacies* (London: Palgrave Macmillan, 2009), pp. 156–70; Keith Thor Carlson, 'The Indians and the Crown: Aboriginal memories of royal promises in Pacific Canada', in Colin M. Coates (ed.), *Majesty in Canada: Essays on the Role of Royalty* (Toronto: Dundern Press, 2006), pp. 68–95; Maria Nugent, '"The queen gave us the land": Aboriginal people, Queen Victoria and historical remembrance', *History Australia*, 9:2 (2012), 182–200; John Sharp, 'Land claims in Namaqualand: The Komaggas Reserve', *Review of African Political Economy*, 21:6 (September 1994), 403–14.
4 See, for instance, Tracey Banivanua Mar, 'Imperial literacy and Indigenous rights: Tracing transoceanic circuits of modern discourse', *Aboriginal History*, 37 (2013), 19. For a brief mention of how Queen Victoria features in contemporary post-colonial politics in Fiji, see John Fraenkel, 'Post-colonial political institutions in the South Pacific Islands: A survey', in David Hegarty and Darrell Tryon (eds), *Politics, Development and Security in Oceania* (Canberra: ANU Press, 2013), p. 38. For some recent work on British royalty in West Indian middle-class culture, see: Anne Spry Rush, *Bonds of Empire: West Indians and Britishness from Victoria to Decolonization* (Oxford: Oxford University Press, 2011). For other relevant recent discussions, see: David Killingray, '"A good West Indian, a Good African, and, in short, a good Britisher": Black and British in a colour-conscious empire, 1760–1950', *The Journal of Imperial and Commonwealth History*, 36:3 (2008), 363–81; Arianne Chernock, 'Queen Victoria and the "Bloody Mary of Madagascar"', *Victorian Studies*, 55:3 (Spring 2013), 425–49.
5 See, for instance, Julie Evans, Patricia Grimshaw, David Philips, and Shurlee Swain, *Equal Subjects, Unequal Rights: Indigenous Peoples in British Settler Colonies, 1830–1910* (Manchester: Manchester University Press, 2003); Alan Lester and Fae Dussart, *Colonization and the Origins of Humanitarian Governance: Protecting Aborigines across the Nineteenth-Century British Empire* (Cambridge: Cambridge University Press, 2014), which tracks the spread of 'protectionism' across Australia, New Zealand, and South Africa (but not Canada); Lisa Ford and Tim Rowse (eds), *Between Indigenous and Settler Governance* (London: Routledge, 2012), which covers the CANZUS states – Canada, Australia, New Zealand, and the United States – but also includes one chapter on South Africa; Annie E. Coombes (ed.), *Rethinking Settler Colonialism: History and Memory in Australia, Canada, Aotearoa New Zealand and South Africa* (Manchester: Manchester University Press, 2006). Coombes cites Donald Denoon, *Settler Colonialism: The Dynamics of Dependent Development in the Southern Hemisphere* (Oxford and New York: Oxford University Press, 1983) as a pioneering example of working across settler colonial contexts. In Australia, recently, there has been some debate about conceptualisations of 'settler colonial studies' and 'settler colonialism' as a dominant explanatory concept. See Tim Rowse, 'Indigenous heterogeneity', *Australian Historical Studies*, 45:3 (2014), 297–310, and Lorenzo Verancini, 'Defending settler colonialism', *Australian Historical Studies*, 45:3 (2014), 311–16.
6 Annie E. Coombes, 'Introduction: Memory and history in settler colonialism', in Coombes (ed.), *Rethinking Settler Colonialism*, pp. 1–4.
7 There is an established scholarship on cultures of monarchy and royalty in colonial contexts during the Victorian era and since. See, for instance, Mark McKenna, 'Monarchy: From reverence to indifference', in D. Schreuder and S. Ward (eds), *Australia's Empire* (Oxford: Oxford University Press, 2008), pp. 261–87; Annette Shiell and Peter Spearitt (eds), *Australians and the Monarchy* (Melbourne: National Centre for Australian Studies, 1993); Philip W. Pike, *The Royal Presence in Australia, 1867–1986* (Adelaide, S.A.: Royalty Publishing, 1986); Peter J. Boyce, *The Queen's Other Realms: The Crown and its Legacy in Australia, Canada and New Zealand*

INTRODUCTION

(Sydney: Federation Press, 2008); Colin M. Coates (ed.), *Majesty in Canada: Essays on the Role of Royalty* (Toronto: Dundern Press, 2006); Ged Martin, 'Queen Victoria and Canada', *American Review of Canadian Studies*, 13:3 (1983), 215–34; Phillip Buckner, 'Casting daylight upon magic: Deconstructing the royal tour of 1901 to Canada', *Journal of Imperial and Commonwealth History*, 31:2 (2003), 158–89; Ian Radforth, *Royal Spectacle: The 1860 Visit of the Prince of Wales to Canada and the United States* (Toronto: University of Toronto Press, 1987); James H. Murphy, *Abject Loyalty: Nationalism and monarchy in Ireland During the Reign of Queen Victoria* (Washington, DC: Catholic University Press of America, 2001); Phillip Buckner, 'The royal tour of 1901 and the construction of an imperial identity in South Africa', *South African Historical Journal*, 41:4 (1991), 324–48; Terence Ranger, 'The invention of tradition in colonial Africa', in Eric Hobsbawm and Terence Rangers (eds), *The Invention of Tradition* (Cambridge: Cambridge University Press, 1983), pp. 211–62. Hilary Sapire, 'African loyalism and its discontents: The royal tour of South Africa, 1947', *The Historical Journal*, 54:1 (March 2011), 215–40.

8 For a selection from this work, see: Sarah Carter, '"Your great mother across the salt sea": Prairie First Nations, the British Monarchy and the vice-regal connection to 1900', *Manitoba History* 48 (Autumn 2004/Winter 2005), 34–48; Henry Wade 'Imagining the Great White Mother and the Great King: Aboriginal tradition and royal representation at the "Great Pow-wow" of 1901', *Journal of the Canadian Historical Association*, 11:1 (2000), 87–108; Ruth B. Phillips, 'Making sense out/ of the visual: Aboriginal presentations and representations in nineteenth-century Canada', *Art History*, 27:4 (September 2004), 593–615; Ian Radforth, 'Performance, politics, and representation: Aboriginal people and the 1860 royal tour of Canada', *Canadian Historical Review*, 84:1 (March 2003), 1–32; Cecilia Haig-Brown, 'The "Friends" of Nahnebahwequa', in C. Haig-Brown and David A. Nock (eds), *With Good Intentions: Euro-Canadian and Aboriginal Relations in Colonial Canada* (Vancouver: UBC Press, 2005), pp. 132–57; John Lonsdale, 'Ornamental constitutionalism in Africa: Kenyatta and the two queens', *Journal of Imperial and Commonwealth History*, 34:1 (March 2006), 87–103; Roger Levine, 'Prince Alfred in King William's Town, South Africa: 13 August 1860', *Rethinking History: The Journal of Theory and Practice*, 14:1 (2010), 137–44; Neil Parsons, *King Khama, Emperor Joe, and the Great White Queen: Victorian Britain through African Eyes* (Chicago, IL: University of Chicago Press, 1998); Sharp, 'Land claims in Namaqualand'; Jessie Mitchell, '"It will enlarge the ideas of the natives": Indigenous Australians and the tour of Prince Alfred, Duke of Edinburgh', *Aboriginal History*, 34 (2010), 197–216; Ian Henderson, 'Planetary lives: Edward Warrulan, Edward John Eyre and Queen Victoria', *English Studies in Africa*, 57:1 (2014), 66–80; Nugent, 'The queen gave us the land'.

9 Lester and Dussart, *Colonization and the Origins of Humanitarian Governance*, p. 14.
10 Lisa Ford, 'Locating Indigenous self-determination in the margins of settler sovereignty', in L. Ford and T. Rowse (eds), *Between Indigenous and Settler Governance* (London: Routledge, 2012), p. 1.
11 Lester and Dussart, *Colonization and the Origins of Humanitarian Governance*, p. 4.
12 Ann Curthoys, 'Indigenous subjects', in Schreuder and Ward (eds), *Australia's Empire*, p. 94.
13 For discussion of the implications of self-government for Indigenous people and politics in the Australian colonies, see: Ann Curthoys, 'Taking liberty: Towards a new political historiography of settler self-government and Indigenous activism', in Kate Fullagar (ed.), *The Atlantic World in the Antipodes: Effects and Transformations since the Eighteenth Century* (Newcastle upon Tyne: Cambridge Scholars Press, 2012), pp. 237–54.
14 Evans *et al.*, *Equal subjects, unequal rights*, p. 8.
15 Mark McKenna, 'Transplanted to savage shores: Indigenous Australians and British birthright in the mid-nineteenth-century Australian colonies', *Journal of Colonialism and Colonial History*, 13:1 (Spring 2012), npgs.
16 David Cannadine, *Ornamentalism: How the British Saw Their Empire* (London: Allen Lane, 2001); McKenna, 'Monarchy', p. 263.

17 John Plunkett, *Queen Victoria: First Media Monarch* (Oxford: Oxford University Press, 2003).
18 For a comparison of Australian Indigenous interpretations of another imperial figure, Captain James Cook, see: Deborah Bird Rose, 'The saga of Captain Cook: Remembrance and morality', in Bain Attwood and Fiona Magowan (eds), *Telling Stories: Indigenous History and Memory in Australia and New Zealand* (Sydney: Allen and Unwin, 2001), pp. 61–79; Chris Healy, 'We know your mob now: histories and their cultures', *Meanjin*, 49:3 (1990), 512–23; Maria Nugent, *Captain Cook Was Here* (Melbourne: Cambridge University Press, 2009).
19 Sukanya Banerjee, *Becoming Imperial Citizens: Indians in the Late-Victorian Empire* (Durham, NC: Duke University Press, 2010); see also Daniel Gorman, *Imperial Citizenship: Empire and the Question of Belonging* (Manchester: Manchester University Press, 2006).
20 See, especially, Dorothy Thompson, *Queen Victoria: Gender and Power* (London: Virago, 2008).
21 Duncan Bell, 'The idea of a patriot queen? The monarchy, the constitution and the iconographic order of Greater Britain, 1860–1900', *The Journal of Imperial and Commonwealth History*, 34:1 (March 2006), 8.
22 *Ibid.*, p. 6.
23 'Victoria as Empire Builder', *The Review of Reviews* (March 1901), p. 259. This is an excerpt from an article by C. de Thierry in the March *United Service Magazine*. C. de Thierry was the 'pen name' of New Zealand journalist Jessie Weston who lived in London.
24 Heather Goodall, *Invasion to Embassy: Land in Aboriginal Politics in New South Wales, 1770–1972* (Sydney: Allen and Unwin, 1996), p. 102. For a recent argument against interpreting these new identifications as only 'strategic' rather than as a 'deeply felt reformation of self', see: Tim Rowse, 'The identity of Indigenous political thought', in Ford and Rowse (eds), *Between Indigenous and Settler Governance*, pp. 95–107.
25 Andrew Thompson, 'The languages of loyalism in Southern Africa, c. 1870–1939', *English Historical Review*, 118:477 (June 2003), 619. For other relevant scholarship on the politics of loyalism, see: Vivian Bickford-Smith, 'African nationalist or British loyalist? The complicated case of Tiyo Soga', *History Workshop Journal*, 71:1 (2011), 75–97; Hilary Sapire, 'African loyalism and its discontents: The royal tour of South Africa, 1974', *The Historical Journal*, 54:1 (March 2011), 215–40; Hilary Sapire, 'Ambiguities of loyalism: The Prince of Wales in India and Africa, 1921–2 and 1925', *History Workshop Journal*, 73 (2012), 37–65.
26 Thompson, 'The languages of loyalism', pp. 619–20.
27 Banerjee, *Becoming Imperial Citizens*, p. 26.
28 See also, Marilyn Lake and Henry Reynolds, *Drawing the Global Colour Line: White Men's Countries and the Question of Racial Equality* (Melbourne: Melbourne University Press, 2008).
29 Quoted in Neal McLeod, *Cree Narrative Memory From Treaties to Contemporary Times* (Saskatoon: Purich Publishing Ltd., 2007), p. 93.
30 McKenna, 'Monarchy', p. 261. For another recent discussion of Indigenous interlocutors engaged with imperial policy and practice, see: Zoe Laidlaw, 'Indigenous interlocutors: Networks of imperial protest and humanitarianism in the mid-nineteenth century', in Jane Carey and Jane Lydon (eds), *Indigenous networks: Mobility, Connections and Exchange* (London: Routledge, 2014), pp. 114–39. See also, Elizabeth Elbourne, 'Indigenous peoples and imperial networks in the early nineteenth century: The politics of knowledge', in Phillip Buckner and R. Douglas Francis (eds), *Rediscovering the British World* (Calgary: University of Calgary Press, 2005), pp. 59–85.
31 The term 'middle ground' for these cross-cultural contact zones is taken from: Richard White, *The Middle Ground: Indians, Empires, and Republics in The Great Lakes Region, 1650–1815* (Cambridge: Cambridge University Press, 1991 [2011]).

INTRODUCTION

32 For an insightful discussion of this in the Australian context during the late Victorian era and up to the end of the First World War, see: Jessica Horton, 'Rewriting political history: Letters from Aboriginal people in Victoria, 1886–1919', *History Australia*, 9:2 (2012), 166–75.
33 J. L. Austin, *How to do Things with Words* (Oxford: Clarendon Press, 1975).
34 McKenna, 'Monarchy', p. 265.
35 See also: Anne Spry Rush, *Bonds of Empire: West Indians and Britishness from Victoria to Decolonization* (Oxford: Oxford University Press, 2011).
36 Cannadine, *Ornamentalism*. For critiques in this vein, see: Tony Ballantyne (ed.), 'From orientalism to ornamentalism: Empire and difference in history', Special issue of *Journal of Colonialism and Colonial History*, 3:1 (2002), with articles by Geoff Eley, Mrinalini Sinha, Peter H. Hoffenberg, Peter H. Hansen, Antoinette Burton, Madhavi Kale, Jane Samson, and Jean Marie Allman. See also: Ian Christopher Fletcher's review of *Ornamentalism: How the British Saw Their Empire* by David Cannadine in *Victorian Studies*, 45:3 (Spring 2003), 532–4; Paul Smith, 'Refuge for the Aristocracy', *London Review of Books*, 23:12 (12 June 2001), pp. 30–1.
37 Antoinette Burton, 'Déjà vu all over again', in Ballantyne (ed.), 'From orientalism to ornamentalism'.
38 See, for instance, Tony Ballantyne and Antoinette Burton (eds), *Moving Subjects: Mobility, Intimacy and Gender in an Age of Global Empire* (Durham, NC: Duke University Press, 2009); Alan Lester, 'British settler discourse and the circuits of empire', *History Workshop Journal*, 54:1 (2002), 27–50.
39 See, for example, John Sharp and Emile Boonzaier, who note similarities between claims that Queen Victoria had granted reserves in Namaqualand with those found in parts of Canada: John Sharp and Emile Boonzaier, 'Ethnic identity as performance: Lessons from Namaqualand', *Journal of South African Studies*, 20:3 (Sept. 1994), 411. Political scientist Ravi de Costa uses histories of Indigenous people in Australia, Canada, and New Zealand petitioning the British monarch and other authorities to trace the emergence of 'indigeneity' as a global identity. Ravi de Costa, 'Identity, authority, and the moral worlds of Indigenous petitions', *Comparative Studies in Society and History*, 48:3 (2006), 669–98.
40 Ann Laura Stoler, *Along the Archival Grain: Epistemic Anxieties and Colonial Common Sense* (Princeton, NJ: Princeton University Press, 2009).
41 Lauren Benton, *A Search for Sovereignty: Law and Geography in European Empires, 1400–1900* (Cambridge: Cambridge University Press, 2009), p. 30.
42 http://extract.gruntarchives.org/rebecca-belmore-victorious.html#lightbox, accessed 27 February 2015.

PART ONE

Monarch, metaphor, memory

CHAPTER ONE

'We have seen the son of Heaven/We have seen the Son of Our Queen': African encounters with Prince Alfred on his royal tour, 1860

Hilary Sapire

At the indaba (ceremonial meeting) at Eshowe, Zululand, in honour of the visiting royal family, King George VI, Queen Elizabeth, and the Princesses Elizabeth and Margaret, on 19 March 1947, Chief Albert Luthuli of the Groutville Reserve, the future African National Congress (ANC) President and Nobel Peace Prize winner, rose to deliver the address of welcome on behalf of the 'Zulu nation'. Hailing the King in the idiom of isiZulu praise poetry, he proclaimed, 'Just as when the lion roars, all nature is hushed, as when Your Majesty speaks to us we will listen to Your Majesty in silent awe'. He then saluted the King as a descendant of the Queen Victoria 'as is our custom, by praising the deeds of Your Royal House':

> We recall with veneration the illustrious reign of Victoria the Great White Queen, who embodied in her person the regal attributes of power and justice, of mercy and peace. We remember with gratitude, how, when her armies had conquered our warriors in battle, she graciously sent for our king, and when he arrived in her august presence, she spoke to him, not words of wrath and vengeance, but the words of a Mother to her erring son, and then sent him back to us again. We shall ever, with affection and reverence, honour her name.[1]

'Our king' to whom Luthuli referred was the vanquished Cetshwayo ka Mpande, who after the British invasion of Zululand in 1879 had been exiled to Cape Town where he was kept in civil custody until permitted to return to his divided kingdom in January 1883. Luthuli was not alone in invoking the Great White Queen during the Southern African royal tour of 1947; from the Ciskei to Bechuanaland 'native representatives' eulogised her and spoke with reverence of her qualities of mercy and the special meaning she held for their political communities. In his address to King George VI at the indaba in Umtata in the Transkei where loyalists had long stressed the benevolence of the Queen, Chief Jeremiah Moshesh described the 'memories of Queen Victoria' as 'the treasures of our old men'.[2]

There is much to be remarked upon in these vignettes of the 1947 indabas with their ornamentalist pageantry and reaffirmations of faith in the monarchical connection in an era when such attachments might seem obsolete. Luthuli's well-worked loyalism and the language of deference in his paean to the King, for example, contrasts strikingly with the frank opposition to white supremacy that increasingly characterised the wartime ANC and that would become even more apparent after 1948 with the accession to power of Afrikaner nationalists. As a number of writers have argued, however, such espousals of loyalism and monarchist fidelity from African *amarespectables* (Christianised, educated elites) and traditionalist chiefs from the late nineteenth to the mid-twentieth centuries should not be read literally as the naive internalisation of the imperial creed by craven 'Black Englishmen'. It was rather a variant of imperial 'faith' that expressed itself in an amalgam of strategies, attitudes, and values, in which the British Crown figured as a source of protection and succour against the wrongs of settlers, colonial states, and the 'betrayals' of British governments. Despite the repeated failures of monarchy and British governments to fulfil African expectations, the proclamation of loyalty to Crown and Empire as a riposte to colonial despotisms and racism endured well into the twentieth century and was not incompatible with the enunciation of nationalist pride and consciousness. Indigenous Africans of the region, like many black subjects across the Empire, imputed to and projected upon the British monarchy their own subjective meanings. As Anne Spry Rush has put it, writing about Jamaica and Britain, this loyalism embodied the idea that the sovereign, if he or she knew, would make things right.[3]

In turn, the idea of the British monarch as a potential redeemer was rooted in the Victorian age, and it is with its early development in South Africa that this chapter is concerned. Queen Victoria as liberator, the font of freedoms and rights for all the Empire's subjects, became a resonant trope in African political discourses and social imaginary until the mid-twentieth century. Liberator of the slaves, embodiment of colour-blind justice, guardian of equality before the law, a source of rights who stood above and beyond the machinations of settler politicians, she was a potent symbol for Africans who sought greater political freedoms and the standard against which subsequent administrations were held. For many, her gender and maternal devotion represented an advantage in a sovereign. Expressing the desire to have 'a woman rule us again' and comparing the reign of George V unfavourably with that of Queen Victoria, an amaXhosa informant told an anthropologist in the 1930s that 'it is only grandmothers who have sense'.[4]

While the image of Victoria became redolent with nostalgia for a period in which nobler values were seen to have prevailed, its very malleability is reflected in the fact that the idea of the Queen's maternal love could be radically inverted. In a poem published in the journal *Isigidimi* in the late nineteenth century when the vaunted freedoms of the liberal Cape came under attack, she appears as predatory and deceitful:

> Awake, rock rabbits of the Mountains of the Night
> She darts out her tongue to the very skies
> That rabbit-snake with female breasts
> who suckled and fostered the trusty Fingoes
> Thereafter to eat them alive.[5]

A similar metaphor was deployed by the Prince Msini, adviser to King Sobhuza of Swaziland in the mid-1920s, in the face of failures to obtain official guarantees of protection from South African territorial ambitions. 'The milk that we suckled at the time of our grandmother, Queen Victoria, has now turned bitter like aloe', he lamented.[6] Reminiscing about his youthful lessons at the feet of grizzled elderly chiefs about his people's history, Nelson Mandela wrote in similar vein of Chief Joyi railing against the white man who had told the amaThembu that 'their true chief was the great white queen across the ocean and that they were her subjects. But the white queen brought nothing but misery and perfidy to black people: if she was a chief, she was an evil chief.'[7] Benefactor or 'evil chief', adored or satirised, Queen Victoria loomed large as a symbol of freedoms promised – and denied – in elite and popular African thought.

Whilst many studies have focused on the role of the non-racial franchise, the operation of colonial courts and the paternalism of officials and missionaries in sustaining the notion of the Queen's benevolence, more recently, scholars have drawn attention to the ways in which this idea was purveyed in material culture, ceremonial form, performance, and visual media. In non-literate cultures, visual spectacle and performance were particularly effective in conveying the ideology of Victoria the Good and her place at the apex of the colonial social order. In turn, the growth of mass print and visual culture assisted in reinventing and humanising the monarchy in both British national life and that of its overseas empire in novel ways.[8] Reproductions of Queen Victoria's image adorned the walls of missions and houses of modernising African Christians in Southern Africa especially after the Jubilees of 1887 and 1897.

The aural and visual impact of the fanfare of royal birthdays, jubilees, and coronations with their bonfires, illuminations, triumphal arches and parades were effective, as were the celebrations of the ending of slavery in Cape Town, in underlining the ideological association of Victorian rule in the Cape with freedom.[9] This chapter focuses on another Victorian invention, the royal tour, made possible by the revolutions in technology that shrank the world and enabled royal figures to meet with their remotest subjects. Royal tours more than any other form of imperial propaganda confirmed the reality of the imperial monarch's existence. It was during the 1860 visit of the Queen's son Prince Alfred to South Africa that many Africans first met a royal personage face to face on their home ground in encounters that made flesh the mythology of the 'Great White Queen'. These were the obverse of the progresses (documented in Neil Parsons' chapter in this volume) whereby delegations of indigenous African leaders travelled to the imperial metropolis in the last decades of the nineteenth century to plead with the Queen and her government to intercede with the colonial authorities in the final phases of the conquest and subordination of southern African societies.

Although there were precedents for colonial ceremonial through which officials sought to legitimise their authority and dramatise the power of the British Empire, a new repertoire of royal ceremonial that symbolised the central role of the British monarchy was first aired in 1860. Fashioned from British, colonial, and indigenous ceremonial and courtly practices, gatherings such as indabas or pitsos at which the royal visitor or government official delivered admonitory homilies to assembled chiefs and followers, exchanged gifts and formal addresses, and witnessed performances of obeisance and displays of 'native' spectacle, were first improvised during this inaugural Southern Hemisphere royal tour. During Prince Alfred's visit, as in subsequent royal visits, African leaders took advantage of their momentary prominence in public national life to press territorial or political claims and assert their cultural pride and identity. Through their self-presentation, dress, dignified occupation of ceremonial space accorded them, their petitioning and letter-writing, they countered the many troubling stereotypes and exotic representations of Africans that appeared in the copious press and publicity ephemera, and sometimes subverted the very purposes of such encounters. Whether appealing to the Queen – through the Prince – bypassing local officialdom, asserting their demands, making manifest their loyalty, or sharing in the festivities in the crowds of flag- and lantern-festooned streets, various sections of the Queen's southern African subjects made the visit meaningful to themselves and thereby contributed to the development of imperial culture and the mythology of 'The Great White Queen'. The variety of expressions of monarchical devotion, in turn, reflected the different stages and depths of colonisation and British cultural hegemony by the middle of the century. In the Cape Colony, where colonial power and influence were most pronounced, celebrations of the Prince's presence were especially elaborate and prolific, and provoked complex responses from indigenous African and 'coloured' communities. For Christian improvers from amaMfengu communities of Port Elizabeth and Grahamstown to mission station Khoekhoe, amaMfengu, and amaXhosa in the frontier regions, the Prince's visit confirmed their loyalist faith, while the scripted enactment of obeisance required of the defeated amaNgqika Paramount Chief Sandile (ca. 1820-78) made that encounter an ambiguous and unsettling one. No attempt was made to introduce the Prince to the amaGcaleka King, Sarhili, who remained unreconciled to British rule. By contrast, the indigenous semi-independent leaders Moshoeshoe of the BaSotho and Moroka of the Barolong in Transorangia, who retained only a measure of autonomy in a fluid situation prior to the final phases of colonial conquest, used the opportunity of meeting with the Prince to reassert claims for protection under the British flag. The Zulu kingdom to the north of the colony of Natal, on the other hand, ruled by 'the great survivor', Mpande ka Senzangakhona, who successfully maintained amaZulu sovereignty and independence, was, like Gcalekaland, excluded from the Prince's itinerary. But there were already early signs of the internal and external threats that Mpande's kingdom would face in the following decade. Indeed, when Mpande's son Cetshwayo, the recognised heir to the amaZulu throne at the time of Alfred's visit, met visiting British royalty in 1882, it was as a beaten chief, colonial subject, and supplicant. The tour thus also marks a transitional moment before the completion of the processes of the dispossession of still independent peoples, and a lull in the 'hundred years' war between settlers and the amaXhosa of the Eastern Cape. It marked a pause too before a mercantile world gave way to an industrial and more rigid racial order for whose inhabitants Queen Victoria's reign stood as a more generous age when the cultural assimilation of Africans, especially at the Cape, was positively encouraged. This chapter attempts to capture that moment; it focuses on the ways in which British royal protocol and new ceremonial rituals were first developed as tools of colonial governance reflecting a gradual shift of power from military governors to local officials and ultimately, responsible governments based on a qualified franchise. It also explores the experience and subjective responses of individual Africans who met with the Queen's second son in 1860.

Prince Alfred's visit to South Africa was the brainchild of the Governor of the Cape Colony and High Commissioner, Sir George Grey. His proposal that one of the Queen's sons should visit to inaugurate the new breakwater in Table Bay was seized upon with alacrity in Britain. It came at a time when Empire royal tours were seen as a means of lifting the monarchy above everyday politics, uniting its diverse peoples around the Crown and rewarding colonies for their loyalty.[10] Although the Queen did not travel beyond Britain, she dispatched her sons and grandsons as emissaries of the Crown in grand transoceanic progresses. Prince Alfred's tour took place in the same year that his brother, the Prince of Wales, visited Canada. Then, in 1867, Prince Alfred toured Australia, visiting New Zealand in 1868, and later India in 1869. Meanwhile the Prince of Wales travelled to Egypt and to India in 1875. After Victoria's death in 1901, her grandson toured Australia and in 1903, her third son, Arthur, represented the Crown at the imperial coronation ceremony in India. By the end of her reign, largely as a result of these world-spanning tours the Queen was indisputably the 'great white empress'.[11]

The vision of Sir George Grey, the controversial Governor, was stamped on a tour that provided him with the opportunity to visually display the advances in 'civilisation' achieved in the colony under his watch as well as to redeem himself in the eyes of former critics in the Colonial Office who had thwarted his plans to reverse Britain's withdrawal from the interior and blocked his expansionist and federal schemes. The inauguration of the breakwater in Table Bay, a museum and new library in Cape Town, together with visits to educational institutions he had supported, underlined his role in promoting the colony's cultural and intellectual life and developing its communication networks. The royal tour of the frontier regions threaded through and thereby visually drew together those territories that his federal plans would have knitted together more palpably.[12] The juxtaposition of the feats of civility and progress against the 'barbarism' of heathen tribes reinforced a triumphal narrative of progress that was the leitmotif of the memorial volume of the tour, whilst evidence of neat mission stations and hard-working Christian African apprentices demonstrated the fruits of Grey's civilising mission.[13] But this tour, like all royal tours, was broad enough for different groups to project upon it their own desires and agendas. Natal publicists highlighted possibilities for investment and immigration in their young colony, whilst progressives and liberals emphasised the political maturity and progress attained by the Cape Colony and Natal with the recent conferrals of representative government. A key message projected in the press coverage was of the unity of diverse peoples around the Crown, a notion that flattered this young colonial society but strained credulity given the recent histories of conflict amongst Boer, British, and African.

One of the aims of the tour was to deploy the idiom of monarchy in the service of colonial governance of indigenous societies. The historian Richard Price suggests that Sir George Grey 'invented' the royal tour, replacing the humiliating rites of authority that a previous Governor, Sir Harry Smith, had imposed in his 'Great Meetings' with amaXhosa chiefs with more inclusive rituals incorporating the symbols of the British royal family.[14] In Prince Alfred's visit, Grey espied a means of conveying the notion of the personal rule of a monarch who could have given no greater proof of her great interest than of 'sending her son, who she so dearly loved to this distant country'.[15] With his gift for self-advertisement, and reversing the familial metaphor through which imperial subjecthood was constructed, Grey also presented himself during the tour as acting *in loco parentis* for the monarch herself.[16] He shared with both his predecessor Sir Harry Smith and Natal's influential Secretary for Native Affairs, Sir Theophilus Shepstone, an appreciation of the value of ceremony as a means of legitimising colonial authority.[17] Indeed, the tour's great meetings with Africans orchestrated by Grey and Shepstone anticipated the Victorian durbars in India in which indigenous monarchical symbolism was used to endorse imperial hierarchy, although the ornamentalist theatrics in both subcontinents were crucially also responses to the mid-century's crises of colonial rule: the Indian Revolt in one and the amaXhosa Cattle Killing episode in the other.

Manipulating the monarchical idiom – indigenous and British – could entail the representation of colonial officials as legatees of indigenous rulers, be they Mughal emperors or African chiefs. In South Africa, whilst Governor Sir Harry Smith had claimed that chiefs regarded him with 'heart and voice' as their Inkosi Inkulu, Shepstone would assume the mantle of the King Shaka ka Senzangakhona himself. It was nonetheless always made clear in day-to-day colonial rule as it was in ceremonial theatre that indigenous chiefs were firmly subordinated to colonial authority and junior in status to the supreme imperial monarch. At the time of the Prince's visit, the amaXhosa chiefs' power had been eviscerated; those not imprisoned on Robben Island were functionaries of the colonial state. Similarly, although Shepstone famously sought to conserve and work with chiefly influence and culture in an early experiment in indirect rule, the chiefs to whom the Prince was introduced in Natal were state appointees or iziphakanyiswa – those who had been 'raised up' by the government. In turn,

Africans' imaginative and affective engagement with these constructions of authority reflects adjustments made to indigenous conceptions of honour and political legitimacy in a rapidly changing configuration of power and authority.

The period immediately preceding the tour had been one of great turbulence with warfare on both the eastern frontier and in the northern regions beyond the Orange River where immigrant Boer, Briton, and Griqua jostled with African communities for land, sovereignty, and influence. The process had begun with earlier expansion of Dutch settlement into the territories of Khoe pastoralists and amaXhosa farmers prior to the formal British occupation of the Cape in 1815. Intensified colonisation of the Eastern Cape by English settlers from the 1820s onwards exacerbated tensions in this region, and by the time of the tour the 'hundred years' war had not reached its denouement. The amaXhosa were recovering from the devastation of the Cattle Killing of 1856, their society traumatised in its wake and the region of British Kaffraria opened to white settlement. Originating as a response to cattle disease, it had been transformed into a millenarian movement in which the slaughter of cattle was seen as a means to resurrect warrior ancestors, cleanse the land, and drive the British into the sea. In the process, 400,000 cattle were killed by followers of the amaNgqika Paramount Chief Sandile, and their grain stocks destroyed. By 1858, around 30,000 starving amaXhosa had migrated to the colony for work, and the region known as Kaffraria was denuded of militant leadership; amaNgqika chiefly authority was fatally undermined, and chiefs became dependents of the colonial state.[18] To the north where Boers and mixed-race Griqua had trekked with their sheep, cattle, and slaves, warfare and conflict punctuated the decades preceding the tour. In the early 1850s, the British abandoned the regions to the north of the Orange River. In granting independence to the Orange Free State and Transvaal Republic in the early 1850s, the British divested themselves of responsibility for policing and regulating these regions, and of the treaty systems and alliances with indigenous and Griqua leaders that had provided the latter with a semblance of protection from the encroachments and ambitions of their neighbours, especially land-hungry Boer farmers. Although there had been no frontier war in Natal, the thousands of African refugees who migrated to the colony, established under the British in 1842, had experienced internecine violence and war with the amaZulu, and sought respite from years of lawlessness. It is against this background of instability in the region that African responses to the Prince's progress can be understood.

In 'the land of Sandile's Ancestors'

After a rapturous reception in Cape Town, the month-long progress by wagon and horseback through the Eastern Cape, Orange Free State, and Natal began. From Port Elizabeth through to Durban, a crammed programme of levees, dinners, hunting expeditions, meetings with settlers, displays of 'barbaric pomp', and visits to mission stations was laid on for the Prince, culminating in the return to Cape Town on the frigate HMS *Euryalus* in the company of the defeated amaNgqika chief Sandile. However superficial his encounters with Africans, from his Khoe escorts and the amaqhira (diviners) who greeted him in Port Elizabeth to the elegant figure of the Presbyterian minister, Tiyo Soga, a considerable component of the Prince's itinerary comprised encounters with indigenous peoples, their leaders, missionaries, and 'native officials'. What the Prince made of these meetings is unclear, but purportedly, it was his hope that his visit would have a galvanising effect on

> the many tribes which he has met with and those which will hear of him, into a more united family, raise the character of Christian institutions and establish a feeling towards England through the person of the Queen which nothing short of Her own presence could instil into a savage mind.[19]

Sir George Grey went to some lengths to bring the amaNgqika chief, Sandile, and the Prince together.[20] Having been imprisoned during the War of the Axe in 1846–47, deposed in 1850 prior to the War of Mlanjeni, and faced with catastrophic losses following the Cattle Killing, Sandile seemed amenable to playing the part of cowed chief. This assigned role was graphically illustrated in an illumination in Grahamstown featuring a 'full length portrait of the Kafir Chief Sandilla, in his kaross, holding forth a branch, emblematic of peace, and trampling an assegai under his foot'.[21] With an entourage of his councillors and 600 followers, the flesh and blood Sandile met with the Prince at the town of Stutterheim. Here, a councillor, Jyala addressed the Prince, expressing the people's joy at his presence and the comfort they took from their sovereign's love and regard. In one of two carefully scripted speeches delivered on Sandile's behalf, the amaNgqika declared their submission:

> We are now no longer a people, we have destroyed ourselves by war. When we have committed our last act of final suicide and national destruction we were restored to life by the representation of our sovereign, for this we beg of your Royal Highness to hear our thanks. We are now supported by her bounty and Sandille [sic] lives. He has made himself nothing. We his people are nothing. His emblems of royalty have been lost in war – and had he yet his warrior's plumes – and how may

they be placed at the foot of your Royal Highness as the tribute due to the son of our Queen. (See also Figure 1.1)²²

While escorting the Prince from Stutterheim to Queenstown, Sandile's party was invited to accompany the visitors to Cape Town on HMS *Euryalus*, the object of which was to inspire confidence in Grey and in the goodwill of the English. The city sights were intended to impress Sandile with the power of Britain 'so that he may learn something for the future good and peace of his people'. Conscious of the fate of other chiefs on Robben Island, it was only on the condition that Charles Brownlee, the amaNgqika commissioner, and Tiyo Soga accompany him that Sandile agreed to the scheme.²³ Whilst the royal party continued with their tour, Sandile's entourage visited a tailor in King Williams Town before proceeding to the frigate in Port Elizabeth. On board, Sandile and his men were 'lionized'; they had their own cabins, were 'waited upon by two negroes', and provided with an excellent repast by the captain on their first day.²⁴ In Cape Town, Sandile was treated as a visiting royal, visiting the best homes, including that of the LMS Missionary, Reverend W. Thompson, who spoke to him of the Bible and how 'it had made the once-savage Britain a great power'.

Figure 1.1 AmaNgqika Chief Sandile and his councillors.

Accepting the gifts of a 'gay purse', handkerchiefs, and Indian chain, Sandile claimed it was the happiest evening he had spent in Cape Town.[25] He attended the ceremony to inaugurate the new breakwater, visited the Zonnebloem Academy for 'kafir chieflings' where he left his daughter to be educated, went to a circus and 'fancy fair', and witnessed the naval pageantry staged for the Prince's departure. It was in Cape Town that Sandile presented the second speech of obeisance, which one historian suggests was probably composed by the Governor:

> Our present position and circumstances brought about by our mad resistance to the authority and the power of the English people has been a great warning to the other tribes in South Africa, and it is now our determination that our loyal and faithful service to your Royal Mother shall be an example for the invitation of these tribes.[26]

It is difficult to see what Sandile gained from this royal visit. He probably was heartened by the attentions shown him; his arrival at Zonnebloem College, for example, evidently provoked greater excitement amongst its African pupils than did the visit of the Prince.[27] But the historian Mostert describes him as returning to his home as a despised and dethroned chief who was reduced to begging 'in the most abject terms' for three pence from a small boy visiting his kraal in 1869.[28] Yet, when the amaGcaleka King Sarhili became involved in what would be the final frontier war eight years later, Sandile rallied to the cause, basing himself in the Isidinge forests near Stutterheim where he had first met the Prince. Refusing to surrender, Sandile was fatally wounded and died in May 1878. Although he had enacted a humiliating performance of submission during the Prince's tour in 1860, he remained consistent in his resistance to colonial occupation and is remembered in isiXhosa oral tradition with a respect and honour denied him by his colonial overlords.

Some of our knowledge of Sandile's encounter with British royalty comes from the observations of Tiyo Soga, the Presbyterian minister, writer, and composer of hymns who had accompanied Sandile to Cape Town. The son of a councillor of both Chief Sandile and his father Chief Ngqika, he had his feet in both his father's world and that of the missions, churches, and schools. He was educated at his mother's behest in the mission station at Chumie, thereafter at Lovedale, and for his university education in Scotland, where he was ordained as a minister. Returning to the colony in 1857 with his Scottish wife, he set about establishing his mission at Mgwali with Sandile's blessing. Whilst scholars debate about Soga's 'true' identity – British loyalist or African nationalist – it is uncontested that his attitude towards the Crown and Queen was deeply reverential. Moreover, as Vivian Bickford-Smith suggests, his monarchical devotion and admiration of most things British did not preclude the love of his own people that can be taken as a form of nationalism.[29] His dedication to the monarchy was marked; when in Scotland, he had walked from Glasgow and Dumbarton to catch a glimpse of the Queen and would mark her birthday in his journal. He expressed the desire 'to have all the natives brought in God's providence, under the influence of the English Government, to smother all causes of irritation and heartburning, and to approve themselves the faithful subjects of the best friend of all men, Queen Victoria'![30] On the death of her husband, Prince Albert, Prince Consort, he wrote that 'if any spectacle is calculated to call forth the finest sensibilities of our being, as dutiful subjects, it is that of contemplating Her Majesty in the present sorrowful position as a desolate, bereaved widow'.[31] For Soga, as for many black loyalists, the Queen and Britain represented benevolent forces, and though not unaware of the violence perpetrated by British soldiers and the racial prejudices of white settlers, he placed his hopes in the progress that British rule, science, and Christian culture promised for his countrymen. Indeed, he saw the Cattle Killing as an opportunity for long-term changes and 'future salvation'.[32]

It is thus unsurprising that he viewed the Prince's presence in the colony as of some moment and that he took pride in being associated with the tour and the 'excitement and enthusiasm' he witnessed in the mission stations in his area.[33] He was deeply affected by people's reactions to the 'noble gift' of a bound Bible that he was given by the Prince.[34] It is from Soga's pen that we have the most detailed descriptions from an African of the Prince and his party:

> And what shall I say in admiration of the noble qualities of the second son of our beloved Queen? My loyalty now knows no bounds! I speak as a man and a minister. I never saw a young man who had more admirable qualities for making a future great man. Modesty – unassuming modesty – is the crowning ornament of them all. Sandile and his councillors are full of his praises, and no wonder.[35]

Not only did the Prince's visit confirm Soga's devotion to the Queen but he believed that it had succeeded in reconciling his countrymen to the rule of Sir George Grey, who had been widely blamed for inciting the Cattle Killing as a means of dispossessing the amaXhosa. According to Soga, Sandile's safe return from Cape Town had quashed local rumours that he would never return and had restored trust in the Governor: 'The Kafirs will now more than ever place confidence in his word, and appreciate his desire of doing good to them and their children'.[36]

Soga was not behind in using the visit as an opportunity to request support from the Governor for the establishment of a second mission. According to one scholar, it was on the voyage that Soga's 'transfrontier' credentials came into their own as he mediated between Grey and Sandile, securing title for the Mgwali station and financial support for his mission.[37] Soga thus came away from his meeting with British royalty with enlarged prospects for his mission and career. He lived for only a decade after the tour, so he did not witness the last futile struggle of the amaXhosa against British rule, the erosion of the rights and freedoms of the liberal Cape embodied by the Queen, or the growth of a new kind of modern politics amongst the amaXhosa in which his youngest son, A. K. Soga, one of the founder members of the ANC, would play a signal part. But he must have deeply impressed his admiration for the Great White Queen on his children, for A. K. Soga would go on to advocate the establishment of a memorial fund in tribute to 'Queen Victoria the Good' early in the new century.

Soga's expressions of joy and hope at the Prince's visit in 1860 were echoed in the crowds of Christianised amaMfengu, Tamboekies, and amaNgqika, who thronged to see him in Port Elizabeth, King Williams Town, Grahamstown, and Queenstown, and at the mission stations of Healdtown, Lovedale, St Marks and St Johns, and Lesseyton. As the royal party entered the towns, they were greeted by banners bearing the message "Bota Inkosi" (Welcome Prince), evergreen arches, and the commotion of noisy parades. The Tamboekies sang out, "We have seen the son of Heaven/We have seen the Son of Our Queen"'.[38] The association between Christian faith and love for the Queen was made explicit in King Williams Town: 'We have been taught by the Word of God to love our Queen'. In their addresses, headmen and other representatives thanked the Queen for sending her son to them and for returning their 'wise' Governor, Sir George Grey (after his recall to London).[39] At St Marks Mission, a speaker proclaimed Grey as the 'saviour' who had redeemed them from death after they had 'blindly followed the words of the false prophet, Umhlakaza'.[40] The Tamboekies' address in Queenstown is illustrative of the genre:

> Prince Alfred, Son of our Beloved Queen! – We greatly rejoice at beholding thee. We never thought our eyes would behold a Prince of the Royal House, and even now it seems like a dream.[41]

No prior intimation had been given to the Prince of this tribute, and he was thus unprepared for a speech in response. Whilst the historian should be wary of reading literally into the elevated language of loyal addresses, petitions, and memorials (which, like indigenous oral praise poetry and oratory often contained an element of criticism of holders of power), the spontaneity of the gesture and quasi-religious tone suggest that these were not simply 'strategic' offerings. Similar observations might be made of two accounts of mission schoolboys of the Prince's visit to King Williams Town. Written undoubtedly to please teachers, and published to amuse whites – because of their naive expression – or to demonstrate the success of missionaries' civilising policies, they nonetheless offer a rare African view of the spectacle:

> At King Williams Town I arrived in the evening and saw great fires, and the echoes of guns and of cannons, and things of fire running in the wind. I saw beautiful pieces of cloth upon many houses and things built up with evergreens. Upon them were put writings – it was written on them saying 'Welcome Prince Alfred'. I saw upon another thing that was built with evergreens there was the likeness of the crown of Victoria, and the likeness of a shipman holding the crown, and on another side a likeness of a soldier holding even the crown of the Queen. I saw also many candles and in all places, and where there was town I saw a great many people the place was filled where the son of the Queen was. At leaving too, *I saw him, that famous person; how small he was*.[42]

'Children of our mother's love?': Moshoeshoe, Moroka, and the Prince

From the Eastern Cape, the Prince's party travelled towards the Orange Free State, and it was en route to the capital Bloemfontein that a meeting was staged with Moshoeshoe (ca. 1786–1870), paramount chief (Morena o Moholo) of the Southern Sotho and founder of the BaSotho kingdom.[43] Renowned as an adaptor and innovator, Moshoeshoe's pre-eminence and power rested on his ability to win the loyalty of followers and acquire new ones during the violent upheavals known as the Difaqane on the highveld in the early 1820s. From his mountain base, Thaba Bosiu, from which he raided his neighbours, Moshoeshoe built up a sizeable federal state under his authority. Cementing fealty through the mafisa (cattle-loaning) system and his reputation for wisdom and magnanimity, he was also deft in his diplomatic dealings. He recognised the value of missionaries and the literacy they conferred upon his state in the region's changing relations of power, earning the epithet monna oa litaba (the man who knows how to handle public affairs). Soon after the intrusion of Boer farmers into the fertile Caledon River valley, Governor Lord Napier signed an agreement that established the western boundary of Moshoeshoe's territory and recognised his sovereignty between Orange and Caledon and some territory to the north of the Caledon, though Moshoeshoe consistently maintained that his land was where his people lived. He welcomed the establishment five years later, in 1848, of the Orange River Sovereignty by Sir Harry Smith as a protection against Boer expansionism, but responded with force on two occasions when the British attempted to compel BaSotho compliance with the agreed boundaries. When a British punitive expedition attacked his capital in 1853, he was conciliatory, requesting that he no longer be 'considered an enemy of the Queen'.[44] Though he criticised the British denial of arms to the BaSotho, Moshoeshoe recognised that it was the Boers who posed the greater threat. The establishment of the independent Orange Free State in 1854 and the withdrawal of British power from the region thus came as a disappointment though he reassured his followers that one day 'Queen Victoria will come back among us. On that day I shall rejoice as I rejoice at the rising of the sun'.[45] Within two years, in response to further Boer encroachment, Moshoeshoe's cavalry found themselves fighting and defeating the Orange Free State in battle. Yet another boundary was set up in an agreement brokered by Sir George Grey at the town of Aliwal North. It was in this unsettled situation that the Prince's visit was announced. For Moshoeshoe, this was an opportunity to go over the head of Sir George Grey and appeal directly to the British Queen to guarantee his nation's territorial integrity and autonomy.

The Prince's arrival in Aliwal North where his meeting with Moshoeshoe took place was preceded by the arrival of 600 men from the Wittenbergen Native Reserve in 'full native costume with assegais and shields' with their superintendent, J. Austen, and by Moshoeshe's cavalcade of 300 armed and mounted followers bearing flags with messages in Sesotho such as 'Molimo o boluke Mofumagli' (God Save the Queen) and 'Bona ngbana Victoria' (See the children of Victoria). According to a press report,

> When Moshesh arrived a loud volley was fired in the air, and for a moment everything was obscured in a cloud of dust and smoke. When it cleared off, the old chief was seen uncovered before the Queen's son, who took off his hat, bowed gracefully and stretched out his hand. Upon this Moshesh, giving his hat to his son, quickly pushed forward and seized the offered hand, as Sir George introduced him amid loud cheers and firing which the Prince and the Governor, now as all along the road before, vainly tried to prevent.[46]

While Moshoeshoe appears to have caused as much, if not more, excitement than the Prince, demonstrating an eye for spectacle equal to that of the Governor, one of his biographers has stated that the septuagenarian was more deferential towards the young Prince than he had been to any other white figure of authority and that this reflected his shrewd understanding of political power. He recognised that only the British had the potential to protect his kingdom and his people.[47]

In a private meeting, he expressed his wish 'that the relations which existed between him and the British Government in the time of Sir Harry Smith and other Governors might be restored'. Steering the conversation into safer currents, Sir George Grey advised Moshoeshoe to write to the Queen directly with his request.[48] The meeting was concluded with the exchange of gifts: leopard skins and two karosses from Moshoeshoe and on the latter's request, signed photographic portraits. Moshoeshoe and his councillors in return sat for the tour's photographer, Mr Yorke. Moshoeshoe needed no prompting to write to the Queen. He presented two letters addressed to her. In the first, he declared himself equal as an ally, and in the second, he stated, 'My prayer to-day is that I may be restored to the same position among the Queen's servants that I first held. ... Let whatever fault I may have committed be today forgiven'.[49] He would later make explicit his terms for a 'protectorate':

> I will be under the Queen as her subject and my people will be her subjects also, but under me ... the Queen rules my people only through me ... I should wish that such laws be submitted to the council of the Basutos, and when they are accepted by my Council, I will send to the Queen and inform her that they have become law.[50]

It took some time before Moshoeshoe's policy of seeking protection from Britain bore fruit. In 1866, his son Tsekelo (who had conducted the three-part rendering of 'God Save the Queen' in welcome of the Prince) led a delegation to London, but was refused an audience with the Queen. Two years later, Moshoeshoe received the anticipated letter telling him that the Queen had been 'graciously pleased to receive him and his people as 'subjects of the British Throne'. In his letter to the High Commissioner, Moshoeshoe replied: 'I am glad that my people should have been allowed to rest and to lie under the large folds of the flag of England before I am not more'.[51] Basutoland was then annexed to the Cape Colony to serve as a reservoir of labour, food, and ponies for the new diamond mines of Griqualand West. But colonial administration was abortive, culminating in rebellion and war in 1879. It was only in 1891 that peace was restored, and the imperial protectorate desired by Moshoeshoe was finally imposed on the country.

Moshoeshoe was the most significant of the quasi-independent African leaders to meet with the Prince, but Chief Moroka (ca. 1795–1880) of the Barolong also grasped the opportunity of a brief audience with the Prince to proclaim his loyalty to the Queen. Moroka's polity had its origins in the Sotho-Tswana political community established to the north of the Vaal river in the late eighteenth century by Seleka, a descendant of the warrior chief Tau. In the early 1830s, Moroka led a party of Barolong and other refugees together with three Wesleyan missionaries from the turmoil of the Difaqane in search of a suitable place in which to settle. With Moshoeshoe's permission, they established a settlement at Thaba Nchu in what would become the southern Orange Free State. Although they came under Moshoeshoe's sovereignty, relations were fraught with tension and misunderstandings. Moroka, also a canny power broker, formed alliances with Boer trekkers and fought against Moshoeshoe as he did against Mzilikazi's invading amaNdebele armies During the period of the Orange River Sovereignty from 1848, he entered a tenuous alliance with the British resident, but when the British withdrew in 1854, Thaba Nchu became politically independent and recognised as such by the republican Orange Free State.[52] Nonetheless, Moroka and the Wesleyan missionaries were alarmed by the withdrawal of British protection. At the behest of the missionary Ludendorf, Moroka wrote to the Special Commissioner Sir George Clerk accusing the Queen and her government of favouring the Boers over his own people. 'Are then the Boers alone children of our mother's love? … has our mother only one breast?', he asked.[53] Moroka understood well the need to cultivate British support and influence. He wrote to Sir George Grey in 1860, the year of the tour, welcoming him back after his temporary recall, and asked him to thank the Queen 'for being an eye to the blind, in sending a God-fearing man as Governor and High Commissioner to this benighted land'.[54] Following Grey's advice he sent his sons to schools in Grahamstown, Cape Town, and Lovedale. This decision, like his subsequent encouragement of an Anglican mission to settle at Thaba Nchu, reflected his desire to sustain political links with Britain given increasingly strained relations with the Free State and the BaSotho.

The tour provided Moroka with the chance to demonstrate his loyalty to the Crown by responding to the request to 'beat up the game' in the surrounds of Bloemfontein for a great hunting expedition for the Prince's entourage. In the days before the royal party's arrival, a thousand mounted and armed men under the direction of Moroka and his stepson Chief Tshipinare rounded up and enclosed 20,000 to 30,000 game. The hunting event, immortalised in a painting by Thomas Baines, was remembered long after the tour's end. Some 6,000 head of game including wildebeest, bonteboks, springboks, hartebeest, and quagga were slaughtered, and several Barolong were injured or trampled to death in the melee. 'Most of the sportsmen looked more like butchers than sportsmen', wrote one observer of the carnage.[55]

Moroka was granted a brief meeting with the Prince in Bloemfontein after the hunt, as was the Griqua captain, Adam Kok III, who likewise was threatened by settler land hunger. The details of their discussions with the Prince were not related in Major Cowell's report to Prince Albert; these matters, he suggested, would be properly addressed in correspondence with the Governor. But Chief Moroka pointedly alluded to the royal tour in his subsequent correspondence. In a letter to Grey, he referred to Barolong loyalty, and revisited the theme of their abandonment by Her Majesty's government and deprivation of the flag's protective cover. He thanked the Queen for sending the Prince among them and hoped that as 'His Royal Highness enters the Museum and his eye fall on the trophies of the hunt near Bloemfontein, he will kindly remember the red Barolong Tribe which surrounded him'.[56] He also asked of Grey that the Prince 'take my children now at the Cape, to England, and make good men of them'. The Prince could not comply with this request, but when Sir George Grey was recalled to England in the following year, he was accompanied by Samuel Lehulere, Moroka's third and surviving son, who attended school in Canterbury and would later identify himself 'not as a Barolong nor a tribesman but as a citizen of the British Empire'.[57]

Moroka's polity, however, would not come under British protection. After the wars between Moshoeshoe and the Free State in 1865 in which Moroka sided with the Boers, the Free State president formally recognised the independence of the Rolong people within the republic's borders, and increasingly, Thaba Nchu's people were drawn into a burgeoning new economy centred on the diamond town Kimberley. After Moroka's death in 1880, a bitter succession dispute between his stepson Tshipinare whose claim was recognised by the Free State and his son Samuel Lehulere resulted in Thaba Nchu's annexation by the Orange Free State in July 1884 and the dispossession of thousands of Barolong who sought sanctuary in Basutoland under Moshoeshoe's successor, Letsie. Repeated attempts by Samuel Lehulere to solicit British aid against the Orange Free State and gain recognition as a 'deposed prince' came to naught. Thus, while the Prince's meeting with Moshoeshoe in 1860 would be incorporated into a foundation story of Basutoland featuring the benevolent Queen and Moshoeshoe, Moroka's encounter with the Prince bore no political fruit.[58] The Rolong polity was incorporated into the Orange Free State; Moroka's favoured stepson and chosen heir, Tshipinare, who had helped him gather in the game for the Prince in 1860, was assassinated by Lehulere and his supporters, the latter banished permanently from his ancestral home.[59]

Gathering of native clans: the Prince in Natal

When the Prince's entourage crossed the Drakensberg and entered the colony of Natal, they were hailed by loyal African crowds performing impromptu 'war dances' and by Zikhali ka Matiwane of the Ngwane, a prominent refugee from violent political struggles in Zululand who had successfully reconstituted his following on the slopes of the Drakensberg as one of Secretary for Native Affairs, Theophilus Shepstone's chiefs (Figure 1.2). Natal's sparse white population, scattered in small settlements and the two main towns, was vastly outnumbered by the African population living under their chiefs on the 12 per cent of the land 'reserved' for their occupation. African administration was dominated by Shepstone, renowned for his role in developing indirect rule and segregation and his flair for ceremonial display. In a colony where settlers were a minority, where Africans had never been conquered, and where fears of an amaZulu invasion were never far from the surface, Shepstone saw the need to recognise African rights to some of the land as well as to rule through intermediaries who undertook the day to day work of communication and coercion in the colony. Rewarding and recognising loyal chiefs, he divided leaders and ensured his position of authority as Somtsewu ka Sonzica (father of whiteness), cultivating a style of personal rule based on his understanding of African chiefly court tradition. He presented himself as an intermediary between the oral isiZulu and colonial worlds, exploiting his 'great white chief' persona; after the tour, he went to Zululand to recognise Cetshwayo's claim to the Zulu throne, and in an improvised coronation ceremony in 1873, he assumed the very mantle of Shaka, the founder of the Zulu kingdom.[60]

Figure 1.2 Inkosi Zikhale ka Matiwane Ngwane and his men welcome Prince Alfred, 1860.

Ruling through subordinate chiefs was necessary in subduing refractory chiefdoms, and Shepstone accordingly rewarded loyal chiefs with positions of influence that rivalled those of hereditary chiefs. This was the route to power of his induna (councillor), Ngoza ka Luduba, the appointed chief of the Qamu ('the government' tribe), who would play a starring role in the African ceremony of welcome to the Prince. Ngoza probably came to the colony with Mpande (ca. 1798–1872) in the mid-1840s, having served in the Zulu army during Dingane's reign. While working in a Pietermaritzburg kitchen, he came to the attention of Shepstone for assisting in putting down a recalcitrant chief and was thereafter 'raised up' as a government chief presiding over large numbers in the Mngeni valley near Pietermaritzburg.[61]

Shepstone had a strong hand in organising the African pageantry in Pietermaritzburg where the crowning celebration of African loyalism took place in a massive indaba of an estimated crowd of 4,000. Prominent in the ceremony, he also choreographed the delivery of loyal speeches and directed the acclaimed Zulu 'war dance' performed in the Prince's honour (Figure 1.3).[62] Well in advance, chiefs had been invited to perform this 'ceremonial dance of homage' before the son of the Queen though they were instructed to leave their assegais behind and to excise elements of the dance in the interests of brevity. The colony was scoured for the feathers and oxtail brushes for their regalia, causing costs to soar overnight.[63] Dwelling in sensationalist terms on waves of writhing bodies, deafening sounds and fearsome sights, colonial press reports of the 'war dance' were lurid:

> They advance, they retreat, they leap aloft in the air, they kneel and crouch to the ground, placing their shields before them. They become frantic, brandishing their spear-sticks, and kicking with knee and foot against their shields. They see their enemy, and yell at him like a pack of demoniac hounds ... Now they retreat, holding their shields behind them, and hissing like a host of wriggling serpents between their teeth. Awful fellows![64]

Shepstone doubtless had a hand in drafting the loyal addresses: Zikhali had declared that the Prince's presence was proof that 'the Great Queen beyond the water ... does care for us, for she has sent her heart to us'.[65] In similar vein, in a speech agreed upon by the chiefs, Shepstone declaimed, 'Long may the Queen reign ... may she know that she has black subjects as well as white, who shall fight for her'.[66]

While artifice characterised all the meetings with Africans throughout the tour, this was especially marked in Pietermaritzburg, for rather than presenting a legitimate hereditary ruler to the Prince, Ngoza was an appointed chief, a cotton farmer whose characteristic dress was breeches and pilot coat. The ruler of the Zulu kingdom,

Figure 1.3 'Assemblage of warriors of Chief Goza's tribe' (original title), 1860.

Mpande presided over his domains to the north, his power untouchable by his white neighbours. Nonetheless, like all 'invented traditions', the Zulu 'war dance' was rooted in culture and history; massed dance performances demonstrating the power of kings had been performed since the founding of the Zulu kingdom, but the form and function had changed under the conditions of colonialism. The intimidating effect of dances in which troupes performed in regiments, in imitation of the structure of the Zulu army, had led to settler attempts to ban some dances and restrict large African gatherings. In 1857, a bill was promulgated to secure 'the better protection and peace' of the colony by prohibiting any 'coloured person' from 'assembling together at any tribal meeting, public meeting, dances of the first fruits, or war dances'.[67] It was Shepstone, once again flouting the views of the labour and land-hungry settlers, who opposed this law. While agreeing to restrictions on African access to arms proposed in the bill, he reasoned that practices emphasising the power of the Zulu king should be permitted, but adapted to project British authority: '(A)nnual gatherings of tribes … might be made useful to the Government' as occasions at which government representatives might remind those assembled of their 'duty to the Government, to whites and each other, promulgate any new regulation or laws, remind them of old ones, and check any objectionable proceedings which occasionally find place in their ceremonies'.[68] This early incarnation of indabas as arenas for the simultaneous enunciation of 'monarchical paternalism', 'traditional' culture and the staging of 'native spectacle' would reach its fullest expression in the interwar years of the next century.[69]

We do not know what Ngoza and his followers made of their encounter with the British Prince. It can be assumed that some of the reported euphoria was genuine even if it derived as much from the pleasures of performing a dance with deep cultural resonances as it did from the sightings of an English prince. It is also undeniable that the Shepstonian indirect rule that was visually dramatised in the ceremonies was valued by many chiefs and commoners as a guarantee of order and security. Ngoza's personal standing, moreover, had been confirmed by his prominence and his presentation to the Prince of a gift of a battle axe. In recognition of his growing renown, Ngoza and his people were subsequently requested to sit for the photographer Thomas Bowman in the fabulous apparel they had worn for the 'war dance' (see Figure 1.4). The photograph in turn was widely circulated in the colony and beyond as a representation of amaZulu traditional culture, militarism, and independent authority – in contrast to the oral record's depiction of Ngoza as a 'dog' of Shepstone.[70]

The authorities were also satisfied that the Prince's physical presence had made a signal impression on Africans. One writer thought it noteworthy that a powerful earthquake soon after the visit prompted much deliberation about its meaning. 'The visit of a child of the great Queen, and a trembling of the farm ground, happening within a few days of each other', he wrote, 'must of necessity have some connection, and so in the Kafir mind His Royal Highness Prince Alfred was responsible for the earthquake'.[71] If African cupidity had been confirmed, the message about the danger they nonetheless presented to the colony had reached its target. The Prince's tutor Major Cowell came away with an understanding that whilst savagery had indeed been subdued in the colony, Africans posed an ongoing threat to colonial control and required the continued firm hand of white authority.

> [They] appear to have a great respect for the white man and regard for the English, but I should be sorry to see them armed, and I am inclined to think that they may give us some trouble yet if we are not very careful. They do not appear such powerful men as the Kaffirs of Kaffraria nor do I think that they would prove nearly so formidable to us, as our later enemies have been, but their number must render them subjects of suspicion.[72]

Figure 1.4 Ngoza ka Ludaba and his men wearing ceremonial dress worn to welcome Prince Alfred in Pietermaritzburg, 1860.

Conclusion

The tour was pronounced by the colonial press a success, a vindication of the governorship of Sir George Grey, marking a decisive shift from earlier policies of vacillation. Major Cowell declared that it had demonstrated to the African population 'the greatness of the country with which they have yet come into contact'[73] and made 'the natives aware of the existence of the Queen':

> [T]hey say that they questioned her existence, and that they considered her name as meaning the Government, much the same way as the Sepoy considered 'Company Bahadoor' a Myth, tho' with far less reason. They now believe in her as a living being and their Queen.[74]

Such claims were not entirely without foundation. Just as the delegations of 'dusky potentates' who visited the Queen in the 1880s and 1890s were impressed by her physical presence, so were many Africans moved by the sight of the teenage Prince and the idea of his mother sending him to her 'children' far away. Yet, these encounters were profoundly ambivalent events that highlighted the narrowness of options available to indigenous societies in a period when settler power was in the ascendant. While Moshoeshoe and Moroka used the ceremonial space provided by the tour to their own advantage, Sandile's subordination was emphasised. However, the latter would not comply with a subsequent request to meet another touring Englishman – the novelist Anthony Trollope – in 1877. Whether it was because he was preparing to join King Sarhili in the final frontier war or because, as Trollope supposed, he was too drunk, Sandile kept well away from this encounter. But the imiDushane chief, Siwani, who did attend the 'street levee', conveyed frank disillusionment in the failed promises of the colonial authorities and dissatisfaction at the lack of respect accorded to chiefs. In response to Trollope's comment on the advantages of civilisation that the Xhosa now enjoyed – 'trousers, for instance', Siwani replied:

> We were told we must come in and see you, and therefore put on our trousers. Very uncomfortable they are, and we wish that you and the trousers and the magistrates, but above all the prisons, would go away and out of the country altogether.[75]

If the royal tour did not reconcile all amaXhosa chiefs to British authority and the Crown, the event can be seen as a pivotal moment in the development of a regional loyalist tradition in which the British Crown was powerfully symbolic.[76] This was particularly so for many amaMfengu for whom an explicit association with the British monarchy had begun after their 'emancipation' from the amaXhosa when representatives of 17,000 Mfengu refugees had gathered under a milkwood tree in the Peddie district and sworn an oath to obey the King, accept Christianity, and educate their children. They were rewarded with further confiscated amaXhosa lands in return for their assistance to the colonial forces in subsequent frontier wars. In turn, they secured the lion's share of positions as clerks, teachers, and traders in the colony, confirming the amaMfengu self-ascription as modernisers and the carriers of a universal Christian civilisation.[77] A repertoire of rituals, such as sending memorials to Queen Victoria – the 'true' paramount chief – and the establishment in the early twentieth century of 14 May as a day of thanksgiving for the 'Emancipation of the Fingos', emerged as a means of underlining amaMfengu distinctiveness. The royal visit was reciprocated when the renowned amaMfengu leader, Veldtman Bikitsha, visited the Queen in 1892 and presented her with a shield and assegai as 'a sign that we have never feared a white man and have never lifted our hand against any of your people ... [and] a sign of all the kindness for which we are indebted to you.'[78] But, as William Beinart and Colin Bundy point out, there was no rigid dichotomy between amaMfengu and amaXhosa: it was precisely because the expectations of *all* loyalists of the region were shattered that it was from their combined ranks that some of the most bitter twentieth-century rebels arose.[79]

Although Africans in this part of the country were estranged from and angered by successive twentieth-century South African administrations, royal visits and royal occasions continued to evoke nostalgia, even if avowals of loyalty often contained an undertone of discontent. During the royal visit of 1947, Professor D. D. T. Jabavu, former leader of the All African Convention, wrote that the tour reminded him of the 1897 jubilee celebrations when Queen Victoria 'cabled to the African people in King Williams Town to … wish all her subject people a happy celebration'. 1947 was a transfiguring moment, when people temporarily forgot their 'social sullenness and political depression'.[80]

The 1860 tour evoked varied responses. But it can be understood as an event that shaped, and was shaped by, a creative engagement with the idea of a benevolent Queen across the waters, and as a crucial moment in which a tradition of 'black loyalism', with all its ambiguities, was born. It was the first of a succession of royal progresses and processionals through which British colonial authority was projected and during which that loyalism was celebrated and contested. This tradition ended decisively exactly 100 years later with Sir Harold Macmillan's 'Wind of Change' tour of Africa during which Britain's 'exit strategy' from the continent was announced. Instead of the outpouring of black loyalism that characterised Prince Alfred's tour, Macmillan's visit was occluded by the dramatic Sharpeville uprising and massacre, and followed within eighteen months by South Africa's withdrawal from the Commonwealth.[81] In turn, African nationalists, driven underground and into exile by the government, turned towards the United Nations and the international anti-apartheid movements as new global allies in their struggles for freedom and democracy.

Acknowledgements

I acknowledge my thanks to Her Majesty Queen Elizabeth II for her gracious permission to quote from the Royal Archives (RA) Windsor. Comments from Saul Dubow, Albert Grundlingh, Cindy McCreery and Maria Nugent, and discussions with Neil Parsons who generously shared his research, were invaluable in drafting this chapter. I thank Dr Gustav Heindrich for research assistance. Research for the larger project was supported by the Leverhulme Trust.

Notes

1 National Archives, Pretoria (NA), Native Affairs Department (NAD), or BAO 7619 112/378, vol. 1, 'To His Most Excellent Majesty George the Sixth by the Grace of God of Great Britain, Ireland and the British Dominions Beyond the Seas, King, Defender of the Faith, Emperor of India', 19 March 1947.
2 *Imvo Zabantsundu* (15 March 1947).
3 Anne Spry Rush, 'Imperial identity in colonial minds: Harold Moody and the League of Coloured Peoples, 1931–1950', *Twentieth Century British History*, 13:4 (2002), 356–83.
4 Monica Wilson, *Reaction to Conquest: Effects of Contact with Europeans on the Pondo of South Africa* (London: Oxford University Press, 1961), pp. 140–9.
5 Cited in S. Brock, 'James Stuart and Lovedale: A Reappraisal of Missionary Attitudes and African Response in the Eastern Cape, South Africa, 1870–1905' (PhD thesis, University of Edinburgh, 1974), fn 9, pp. 222–3, cited in N. Hogan, 'The posthumous vindication of Zachariah Gqishela: Reflections on the politics of dependence at the Cape in the nineteenth century', in S. Marks and A. Atmore (eds), *Economy and Society in Pre-industrial South Africa* (London: Longman, 1980), p. 277. 'Trusty Fingoes' (amaMfengu) were refugees from the mfecane and displaced amaXhosa commoners of the Eastern Cape who became clients of the amaGcaleka Xhosa and subsequently formed alliances with the British in several wars against the amaXhosa, receiving land grants and protection in reward.
6 Hilda Kuper, *Sobhuza II: Ngwenyama and King of Swaziland* (London: Duckworth, 1978), p. 93.
7 Nelson Mandela, with Richard Stengel, *Long Walk to Freedom: The Autobiography of Nelson Mandela* (London: Little, Brown and Co., 1994), p. 22. Criticisms of Queen Victoria and her descendants' perfidy were also often buried within apparently laudatory speeches and petitions.
8 John Plunkett, *Queen Victoria: First Media Monarch* (Oxford: Oxford University Press, 2003); J. M. Mackenzie, 'The global gaze', in J. M. Mackenzie (ed.), *The Victorian Vision: Inventing New Britain* (London: V and A Publications, 2001), pp. 241–63.
9 Vivian Bickford-Smith, 'Meanings of freedom: Social position and identity among ex-slaves and their descendants in Cape Town, 1875–1910', in Nigel Worden and Clifton Crais (eds), *Breaking the Chains: Slavery and Its Legacy in the Nineteenth-Century Cape Colony* (Johannesburg: Witwatersrand University Press, 1994), p. 310.
10 Theo Aronson, *Royal Ambassadors: British Royalties in Southern Africa, 1860–1947* (Cape Town: David Phillip, 1975), Ch. 1; Charles V. Reed, *Royal Tourists, Colonial Subjects and the Making of a British World, 1860–1911* (Manchester: Manchester University Press, 2016); Richard Price, *Making Empire: Colonial Encounters and the Creation of Imperial Rule in Nineteenth-Century Africa* (Cambridge: Cambridge University Press, 2008), pp. 345–51; R. S. Levine, 'Prince Alfred in King William's Town, South Africa: 13 August, 1860', *Rethinking History*, 14:1 (2010), 137–44; J. Guy, '"A paralysis of perspective": Image and text in the creation of an African chief', *South African Historical Journal*, 47:1 (2002), 51–74; Saul Dubow, *A Commonwealth of Knowledge: Science, Sensibility and White South Africa, 1820–2000* (Oxford: Oxford University Press, 2006), pp. 67–70.
11 Plunkett, *Queen Victoria*, p. 241.
12 Aronson, *Royal Ambassadors*.
13 *Progress of H.R.H. Prince Alfred Ernest Albert, Through the Cape Colony, British Kaffraria, the Orange Free State and Port Natal in the Year 1860* (Cape Town: Saul Solomon, 1861).
14 Price, *Making Empire*, p. 346.
15 *Progress of H.R.H. Prince Alfred*, p. 67.
16 Dubow, *A Commonwealth of Knowledge*, p. 70.

17 Shepstone may have observed Smith's activities while working as a translator in government service in the Eastern Cape. R. A. Moyer, 'A History of the Mfengu of the Eastern Cape 1815–1865' (PhD thesis, University of London, 1976), p. 180, fn 1.
18 As a consequence, ran the tour's commemorative volume, 'the political power of the Kafirs is hopelessly broken ... and British law has for ever superseded the crude though not uninteresting laws and usages of the self-outwitted and defeated savage'. *Progress of H.R.H. Prince Alfred*, p. iv.
19 Royal Archives (RA), VIC/ADDA20/69, Major Cowell to Prince Albert, 5 September 1860.
20 J. B. Peires, *The House of Phalo: A History of the Xhosa People in the Days of Their Independence* (Johannesburg: Ravan Press, 1981).
21 *Progress of H.R.H. Prince Alfred*, pp. 39–40.
22 NA (Cape Town), GH 8/48, Letters from Native Chiefs Residents Eastern Cape Frontier, 1856–1860, 15 August 1860, pp. 750–54.
23 Letter dated 3 December 1860 (from The Letter Book, 7 April–11 March 1862), in Donovan Williams (ed.), *The Journal and Selected Writings of the Reverend Tiyo Soga* (Cape Town: A. A. Balkema, 1983), p. 43.
24 J. A. Chalmers, *Tiyo Soga: A Page of South African Mission Work* (Edinburgh: Andrew Elliot, 1878), p. 210.
25 *Juvenile Missionary Magazine*, January 1861.
26 NA, GH 8/48, Letters from Native Chiefs Residents Eastern Cape Frontier, 1856–1860, pp. 744–6, 'The words of farewell salutation from Sandille and his councillors to the young great Chief "Alfred"', 18 September 1860; Price, *Making Empire*, p. 348.
27 J. Hodgson, 'A History of Zonnebloem College 1858 to 1870: A Study of Church and Society' (MA dissertation, University of Cape Town, 1975), pp. 290–1.
28 Noel Mostert, *Frontiers: The Epic of South Africa's Creation and the Tragedy of the Xhosa People* (London: Pimlico, 1992), pp. 1234–9.
29 Vivian Bickford-Smith, 'African Nationalist or British Loyalist? The complicated case of Tiyo Soga', *History Workshop Journal*, 71:1 (2011), 74–97.
30 Chalmers, *Tiyo Soga*, p. 214; Bickford-Smith, 'African Nationalist', p. 87.
31 Chalmers, *Tiyo Soga*, p. 259.
32 Bickford-Smith, 'African Nationalist', p. 86.
33 T. Soga to Dr Somerville, 1 March 1861, in Williams (ed.), *The Journal and Selected Writings of the Reverend Tiyo Soga*, p. 43; Tolly Bradford, *Prophetic Identities: Indigenous Missionaries and British Colonial Frontiers* (Vancouver: UBC, 2012), Ch. 2.
34 Chalmers, *Tiyo Soga*, p. 214.
35 *Ibid.*, pp. 307–8.
36 *Ibid.*, p. 219.
37 Donovan Williams, *Umfundisi: A Biography of Tiyo Soga, 1820–1871* (Lovedale, South Africa: Lovedale Press, 1978), p. 33.
38 RA, VIC/ADDA20/69, Major Cowell to Prince Albert, 18 August 1860.
39 W. Lee Rees and L. Rees, *The Life and Times of Sir George Grey, K.C.B* (Auckland: H. Brett, 1892), p. 257.
40 Rees and Rees, *Life and Times*, p. 261.
41 *Grahamstown Journal* (4 and 11 September 1860).
42 *Cape Chronicle* (14 September 1860).
43 Peter Sanders, *Moshoeshoe: Chief of the Sotho* (London: Heinemann, 1975); Leonard Thompson, *Survival in Two Worlds: Moshoeshoe of Lesotho, 1786–1870* (London: Oxford University Press, 1975).
44 Peter Sanders, *The Last of the Queen's Men: A Lesotho Experience* (Johannesburg: Witwatersrand University Press and Morija, Lesotho: Morija Museum and Archives, 2000), p. 125.
45 Sanders, *Moshoeshoe*, pp. 101 and 241; Sanders, *The Last of the Queen's Men*, pp. 128–9.

46 *Advertiser and Mail* (5 September 1860).
47 Thompson, *Survival in Two Worlds*, p. 268.
48 RA, VIC/ADDA20/69, Major Cowell to Prince Albert, 18 August 1860.
49 Letter from Chief Moshoeshoe to His Royal Highness Prince Alfred, 18 August 1860, in George McCall Theal (ed.), *Basutoland Records: Copies of Official Documents of Various Kinds, Accounts of Travellers*, vol. II (Cape Town: Government Printers, 1883), pp. 568–9.
50 Sanders, *Moshoeshoe*, pp. 249 and 254–5.
51 Peter Sanders, *'Throwing Down White Man': Cape Rule and Misrule in Colonial Lesotho, 1871–1884* (Morija, Lesotho: Morija Museum and Archives, 2010), p. 11.
52 Colin Murray, *Black Mountain: Land, Class and Power in the Eastern Orange Free State, 1880s–1980s* (Edinburgh: Edinburgh University Press, 1992), Ch. 2; S. M. Molema, *Chief Moroka: His Life, His Times, His Country and His People* (Cape Town: Methodist Publishing House, 1951).
53 Cited in J. and J. Comaroff, *Of Revelation and Revolution: Christianity, Colonialism, and Consciousness in South Africa*, vol. 1 (Chicago, IL and London: University of Chicago Press, 1991), pp. 280–1.
54 National Library of South Africa, Special Collections, MSB 223, 5 File 8 Moroka to Sir George Grey, cited in K. Schoeman, 'From the collections of the S.A. Library: Sir George Grey and the African chiefs', *Quarterly Bulletin of the South African Library*, 48:1 (1993), 10–14.
55 Major General Bissett, *Sport and War or Recollections of Fighting and Hunting in South Africa from the Years 1834 to 1869 With a Narrative of His Royal Highness the Duke of Edinburgh's Visit to the Cape* (London: John Murray, 1875), p. 196.
56 Chief Moroka to Sir George Grey, 4 September 1860, in Theal (ed.), *Basutoland Records*, pp. 572–3.
57 Paul S. Landau, *Popular Politics in the History of South Africa, 1400–1948* (Cambridge: Cambridge University Press, 2010), p. 149.
58 Before the Royal Family arrived in Basutoland in 1947, an advance guard of Africans gathered to salute the royal party at the site of Moshoeshoe's meeting with the Prince. *Imvo Zabantsundu* (13 March 1947).
59 Landau, *Popular Politics*, pp. 162–70.
60 Jeff Guy, *The View Across the River: Harriet Colenso and the Zulu Struggle against Imperialism* (Cape Town: David Phillip, 2001), p. 38.
61 Guy, 'A Paralysis of Perspective', p. 54; John Lambert, *Betrayed Trust: Africans and the State in Colonial Natal* (Pietermaritzburg: University of Natal Press, 1995), p. 26.
62 *Natal Courier* (5 September 1860).
63 National Library of South Africa, Special Collections, MSB 223, 8 (18), Gathering Native Clans: Dr Mann (no. 39), *Gathering of Native Clans at Pietermaritzburg*.
64 *Progress of H.R.H. Prince Alfred Ernest Albert*, p. 97.
65 *The Visit of His Royal Highness Prince Alfred to the Colony of Natal* (London: Jarold and Sons, 1860), p. 9.
66 Mann, 'The Gathering'.
67 House of Commons Parliamentary Records, Correspondence between Governor of Natal and Colonial Office with respect to Sum reserved from General Revenues of Colony for Disposal of Crown; Correspondence on Growth of Cotton by Natives, 1860 Session. Also cited in T. Firenzi, 'The changing functions of traditional dance in Zulu society: 1830–Present', *International Journal of African Historical Studies*, 45:3 (2010), 403–25, on p. 410, fn 26–7.
68 *Ibid*.
69 T. Ranger, 'Making Northern Rhodesia imperial: Variations on a royal theme', *African Affairs*, 79:316 (1980), 349–73.
70 Guy, 'A Paralysis of Perspective'.
71 Mann, 'The Gathering'.
72 Major Cowell to Prince Albert, 4 September 1860.
73 Extract from *The Cape Argus*, 'Progress', p. 158.
74 RA, VIC/ADDA 20/69, Major Cowell to Prince Albert, 15 August 1860.

75 Anthony Trollope, *South Africa: A Reprint of the 1878 Edition with an Introduction and Notes by J. H. Davidson* (Cape Town: Balkema, 1973), p. 161.
76 During the Royal Visit of 1947, *Imvo Zanbantsundu* published an article (1 February 1947) about the 1860 visit to the region, noting that many of the arches had been made by Africans, and addresses of welcome had been given by 'Christian chiefs'. 'Years have passed, and now, King George, great grandson of Queen Victoria is coming to visit the land of Sandile's ancestors'.
77 Anonymous, 'Ethnicity and pseudo-ethnicity in the Ciskei', in Leroy Vail (ed.), *The Creation of Tribalism in Southern Africa* (Berkeley and Los Angeles: UCLA Press, 1991), p. 398.
78 R. Moyer, 'History of the Mfengu', pp. 246–52; André Odendaal, *The Founders: The Origins of the ANC and the Struggle for Democracy in South Africa* (Auckland Park: Jacana, 2012), pp. 154–5.
79 William Beinart and Colin Bundy, *Hidden Struggles in Rural South Africa: Politics and Popular Movements in the Transkei and Eastern Cape, 1890–1930* (Johannesburg: Ravan Press, 1987), p. 10.
80 *South African Outlook* (1 April 1947).
81 Saul Dubow, 'Macmillan, Verwoerd and the "Wind of Change" speech', *Historical Journal*, 54:4 (2011), 1087–114.

CHAPTER TWO

'We rejoice to honour the Queen, for she is a good woman, who cares for the Māori race': Loyalty and protest in Māori politics in nineteenth-century New Zealand

Michael Belgrave

Queen Victoria was married on 10 February 1840. Four days earlier, on the other side of the world, she had unknowingly been given a wedding present. Around forty Māori rangātira (chiefs) had signed a treaty with her representative, Captain William Hobson, agreeing that he form a government in New Zealand in her name. Eventually over 500 rangātira, from up and down the country, placed their marks or their signatures to copies of the Treaty of Waitangi.[1] In the text, Queen Victoria promised to protect the rights of chiefs, their authority, and their property, and those of their tribes, in anticipation of a dramatic influx of British settlers. She also agreed to protect them as her own subjects. By early 1840, ships of colonists were already on their way: the first had even arrived before the treaty was signed. Lieutenant Governor Hobson, strongly supported by English missionaries, argued that only by becoming subjects of Her Majesty could Māori be preserved from the consequences of the rapid influx of European settlers. By the time of Victoria's death, in January 1901, Māori had been swamped by 750,000 Europeans – two-thirds of them New Zealand born – while the Māori population reached its nadir at around 40,000 from an estimated 100,000 in 1840. Although represented in the New Zealand Parliament, Māori have been regarded as constitutionally and politically on the margins of a British world at the height of its self-confidence.[2] The sixty glorious years for Victoria were sixty years of turbulence and dispossession for her Māori subjects. Following her death, Māori circumstances improved, land loss slowed, and the population began to increase.

In exploring Māori relationships with Queen Victoria, and there were many, the level of Māori marginalisation and Māori responses to such a period of dramatic change can be reassessed. Victoria personified empire, and Māori responses to being included in the British Empire were linked to their many relationships to the Queen. Although threatened with complete displacement by the sheer force of nineteenth-century colonisation, at the end of Victoria's reign Māori were firmly part of the Empire. Their marginalisation and their resilience can be explained through their relationships – personal, symbolic, and constitutional – with the distant Queen, a woman whose authority had proved inescapable. Through the transformation of Māori life occurring over the period of her reign, Queen Victoria would remain an ambiguous and ambivalent figure. For many Māori, she would become a guarantor of rights denied. Some Māori tribes maintained an intense political loyalty to the Queen from 1840 and pledged their military support to suppress the supposed rebellion of others. Others saw no inconsistency between fighting imperial troops and maintaining loyalty to a Māori king while accepting an overarching authority of the Queen. A number, however, rejected the Queen every bit as much as they rejected the missionaries, the Governor, and constitutional control by a settler parliament. Some Māori went to London to visit the Queen. Initially the expeditions were personal and political reminders that Māori were Victoria's subjects, but from the early 1880s, they had the added and leading objective to embarrass the colonial government. They were staged to remind Great Britain and the Queen of her promises in 1840 and expose the extent to which these promises, in Māori eyes, had been discarded by her settler parliament. The Queen was a passive participant in almost every debate about how to resist, how to contain, and how to benefit from an increasingly powerful European world. An assertion of loyalty in the name of the Queen, depending on who made it and when, could be as much a plea for constitutional autonomy from settlers and their parliament as were more determined rejections of her authority. What was important was her presence.

British intervention in New Zealand came at the end of the extended humanitarian debate on the impact of colonisation on Aborigines, reflected in the report to the House of Commons Select Committee on Aborigines, otherwise known as the Buxton Report, after its chair Thomas Fowell Buxton. This 'high point of humanitarian influence'[3] has been the subject of increasing interest by historians of the 'new imperial history', and its significance in the establishment of the New Zealand colony has long made it a topic of interest for New Zealand historians.[4] The committee heard evidence from both those promoting the colonisation of New Zealand and those opposing it, pitting the political economy of Edward Gibbon Wakefield against the evangelical humanitarianism of the New Zealand missions of the Church Missionary Society (CMS) and the Wesleyans.[5] The missionary societies demanded that Māori be left alone, free to become Christianised and 'civilised' while maintaining their sovereign independence. Anything else, they argued, would threaten their very existence. Buxton agreed, but Wakefield went anyway, forcing the CMS and the newly formed Aborigines Protection Society to encourage Crown intervention to contain the excesses of colonisation.[6] The language of the Treaty of Waitangi reflected this humanitarian moment, acknowledging the coexistence of settlers and Māori, but prioritising Māori rights to protection over the rights of settlers.

Although never again as influential as they were in the 1830s, these humanitarian networks continued to promote Aboriginal causes in the decades following.[7] Māori became part of these networks, some corresponding with the Aborigines Protection Society.[8] Without these networks and the assistance of people like Frederick Chesson, the society's secretary, Māori missions to London in the 1880s would have been impossible. While British supporters of Aboriginal rights understood something of the complexity of different Indigenous communities, Māori visitors were cast into a more generalised role as Aborigines as they fitted into personal associations with well-placed British sympathisers. These relationships were defined by British political debates and European representations of the Indigenous. Māori, like other Indigenous people, responded by tailoring their submissions and their behaviour to suit the role of supplicant subject.[9] The challenge is how to make sense of Māori relationships with Queen Victoria in a way that recognises Māori as culturally distinct people, driven by their own varied responses to empire, while at the same time acknowledging the experiences shared with others from Canada, the other Australasian colonies, and Africa. If, as Andrew Thompson has argued, this delicate balance of difference and affinity applies to settler colonists, it is even more essential for Indigenous peoples, whether Zulu loyalists or Māori.[10] The task is not simply a matter of identifying what was distinctly Māori and what was not, but of also exploring how relationships with Queen Victoria, as Ravi de Costa argues in his work on petitioning the monarch,[11] allowed Māori to become Indigenous as well as Māori, becoming aware both of a common sense of membership in empire and alienation from it.

Queen Victoria had so many different roles in New Zealand – constitutional, symbolic, political, and personal – that it is difficult to reconcile all of them. Constitutionally, she was head of state, guarantor of Māori rights under the Treaty of Waitangi, but also the head of a settler state, intent on marginalising and even replacing Māori on the land. The Queen was a symbol of majesty while at the same time she was friendly and personable to those Māori who did get to meet her. She was the object of petitions and memorials, some of loyalty and others of protest, but all assertions of Māori identity. Performances of loyalty, celebrations of anniversaries, and royal visits allowed Māori to claim inclusion in the new colonial society. Her monarchy provided a model for a Māori King Movement that sometimes saw itself as alongside the Queen and at other times rejected her. Relationships with the Queen also played out in tribal politics as loyalists and opponents continued contested customary relationships with each other, defining their difference by their singular relationships with Victoria. The politics of loyalty were always subject to deeper political currents within Māori society.

The idea that the Empire worked by interlocking European and Indigenous networks of status, as David Cannadine has suggested, is useful in thinking of Māori relationships with Victoria and her empire.[12] The Māori world was clearly hierarchal, based on status that was partly earned and partly inherited. Individuals possessed mana (individual and tribal status) as leaders of tribal collectives.[13] These collectives often overlapped each other. Mana was not determined by extensive interests in the land, but by recognised community leadership. Rangātira acknowledged the mana of others and expected their own mana to be respected in a system of reciprocal relationships. They competed with each other, and competition regularly involved warfare, particularly in the period after initial contact with the European world in the 1820s and 1830s. One of the most difficult features to be incorporated into European ideas of leadership and property ownership was the independence of individual rangātira. Even the most powerful of military leaders relied on the agreement of lesser chiefs, and the whole system required continual negotiation of alliances and relationships, which were often fluid as groups formed and reformed to face new circumstances. Mana was personal and defined by the relationships between individuals, not by their autonomy. Complete submission of one to another was understood as a form of slavery. Negotiated relationships between rangātira were tied to reciprocity, exchange of gifts, intermarriage, and maintaining the relationship between chiefs. In such an environment, loyalty – a question that would become so important after 1840 when New Zealand became a British colony – always carried with it the idea of an alliance between two admittedly unequal leaders, not the subordination of one to the other.

Over the nineteenth century, Pākehā (Europeans), including Queen Victoria, became part of this system of mana. They did so through what Tony Ballantyne has called 'close encounters of Empire' – personal interactions which exchanged knowledge – or networks of intimacy.[14]

Europeans' status was initially determined by their ability to provide access to European goods, ideas, and technology. Before 1840, the most significant European visitors were shore whalers and missionaries. Whalers and other secular visitors cemented their interconnection with tribes through sexual relationships: missionaries with some notable exceptions did not, although many of their children did intermarry.[15] By 1840, some missionaries in particular had escaped being clients of individual rangātira and had been able to form relationships with a wide range of different Māori leaders and their communities.[16]

After the Treaty of Waitangi, networks that were much more hierarchical developed on the European side of these connections, with the Governor at the top, representing the Colonial Secretary and the Queen; his immediate officials, particularly protectors of Aborigines and then native officers; and after 1854 members of the colonial government. These personal networks of association went well beyond Māori relationships with the rich and the powerful, but at a local level involved many others: farmers and traders, land purchasers, and most influentially in the 1840s, missionaries. Missionaries' skills of literacy and ideas of Christianity were avidly adopted by Māori communities as was the role of petitioning and participation in legal proceedings.[17] It was through these networks that knowledge and attitudes were exchanged, and through them Māori developed an understanding of monarchy and incorporated Queen Victoria into their own networks of mana.[18] Although Queen Victoria remained a distant figure, she personified imperial power and could be imagined as the 'great lady who lived in England'.[19] The Queen's mana, like those of rangātira, was rooted in whakapapa (genealogy). Her mana rested in constitutional, political, and symbolic status, but it could only be exercised by a person, uniquely defined by her ancestors, and in her relationships with others similarly defined by their forebears. In 1863, when a group of Māori did meet the Queen at Osborne, they were able to introduce aspects of tīkanga (custom) that underlined the personal relationships of Queen and rangātira (see Clarke Chapter 6 this volume). They performed a tangī (ritual acknowledgement of the dead) for Prince Albert, and in doing so made public acknowledgement of her private grief. To do anything else would have been a major breach of protocol reflecting badly on the mana of the visitors.

Māori understandings of monarchy developed over her reign, but predated Victoria's accession to the throne in 1837. The idea that the British monarchy could be a protector of Māori interests, against those of other European nations, in particular against the risk of European Roman Catholicism, was a key aspect of the Church Missionary Society's representation of Christianity and civilisation in New

Zealand. In 1820, two highly influential rangātira Hongi Hika and Waikato had been taken to England to participate in the writing of a Māori–English dictionary, under the direction of the orientalist, Samuel Lee at the University of Cambridge.[20] Hongi had been treated as a king in his own right when visiting the House of Lords. Like many Māori visitors to London to follow, they were fêted by the great and the powerful, and introduced to King George IV at Carlton House. Hongi famously greeted the King with 'How do you do, Mr King George?' The monarch replied, 'How do you do, Mr King Hongi?'[21] Hongi was far from overawed with the experience and smugly commented that he managed his five wives quite effectively while King George was failing to deal with one, the troublesome and independent Queen Caroline.[22] None of the Māori who later had personal audiences with the Queen appeared intimidated by the experience.

The meeting would have long-lasting influences. Hongi and Waikato appreciated the usefulness of European technology and even of missionaries, and sought to adapt both to their tribal aspirations at home, turning the booty of their trip into muskets, powder, and shot, and beginning a decade and a half of endemic warfare on their return to New Zealand. The meeting with King George would come to be seen as a form of treaty, a promise from the British Crown that while the missionaries would be sent to New Zealand, troops would not. This was for New Zealand a rare example of a promise directly attributed to a monarch, but Victoria was seen as providing such commitments to other Indigenous visitors.[23] This was one of the reasons why the Wellington government prohibited such meetings by the 1880s. Hongi and Waikato's meeting with the King was also recognition of their mana, and after 1840, meeting Queen Victoria would become the aspiration of a succession of Māori visitors. The meeting of such leaders – Victoria and visiting chiefs – recognised the relationship between them, something both sides acknowledged, but also conferred mana on each.

During the 1830s, missionary attempts to convert Māori to Christianity appeared increasingly successful, accompanied by Māori adoption of literacy and introduced crops. Māori occasionally appealed to William IV for protection, beginning in 1831 with a petition from thirteen northern chiefs. From 1833, with the arrival of James Busby as British resident, there was an official British presence in New Zealand. Under his influence, a group of leading chiefs signed a declaration of independence (He Whakaputanga) in 1835, then petitioning William IV 'to be the parent of their infant state … its Protector from all attempts upon its independence'. When the Treaty of Waitangi was signed in 1840, its language clearly focused on the Queen's personal concerns about the impact of Europeans on Māori in the years before 1840 and, even more importantly, once large numbers of expected colonists arrived as a consequence of Wakefield's New Zealand Company experiment in systematic colonisation. The first words of the Treaty are 'KO WIKITORIA te Kuini (HER MAJESTY VICTORIA)', and from these flow a series of concerns and promises. Victoria was 'a kia mau tonu hoki te Rongo ki a ratou me te Atanoho hoki kua wakaaro ia he mea tika kia tukua mai tetahi Rangatira (anxious to protect their just Rights and Property and to secure to them the enjoyment of Peace and Good Order)'. 'Ko te Kuini o Ingarani ka wakarite ka wakaae (Her Majesty the Queen of England confirms and guarantees)' an extensive range of property and legal rights and also granted them 'Her royal protection and imparts to them all the Rights and Privileges of British Subjects'.[24] While Māori were expected to cede their sovereignty, given Māori understanding of mana, signing the treaty carried with it the idea of a new alliance, one that recognised the mana of both rangātira and the Queen.

Such a text would have emphasised the personal nature of monarchy, particularly in a society where mana was fundamentally personal. While considerable attention has been placed on the meaning of the Māori text since the 1970s, reflecting the increasing importance of the treaty in legal proceedings, the prominence given to the Queen was not reflected in the debates by Māori about whether or not to sign. Almost the entire focus of discussion was on whether to accept her representative, Lieutenant Governor William Hobson. Māori had understanding of the outside world, in particular the role of the Governor in the Australian colony of New South Wales, and they debated the practical consequences of New Zealand coming under the Queen's protection. One notable exception was Mananui Te Heuheu of Ngāti Tuwharetoa in the central North Island, who refused to sign the treaty as he saw no reason to put his mana under that of a mere woman.[25]

The idea that the Queen would protect Māori rights through her association with the Treaty of Waitangi emerged in the years immediately after it was signed. Those humanitarian networks that defined the treaty's promises lost political influence with the fall of Lord Melbourne's government in 1841, allowing for the New Zealand Company's star to rise, both within New Zealand and more significantly within the British Parliament. The conflict that had divided humanitarians and the Wakefields in the pamphleteering of the 1830s became imprinted on the land in New Zealand as the New Zealand Company's claims to have purchased 20 million acres of land from Māori were shown to be either fraudulent or illusory. As a result, the New Zealand Company persuaded the Colonial Office that the Company's failure to extinguish title from large areas on which it had settled could be resolved by claiming all uncultivated land as Crown land.

Governor George Grey was also instructed to introduce a new constitution that would give self-government to the company settlers, excluding Māori. Given Māori military power and numeric superiority, Grey was well aware that these instructions were unenforceable. He galvanised humanitarians in New Zealand such as Chief Justice William Martin and Bishop Augustus Selwyn, as well as leading rangātira, against the policy. They coalesced around the promises made by the Queen in the Treaty of Waitangi. Te Wherewhero, the Waikato rangātira who had deliberately declined to sign the Treaty of Waitangi on two occasions, petitioned the Queen, calling on her to uphold the promises of Waitangi:

> May God incline you to hold fast our words, and we hold fast yours forever. Oh Madame, listen! The report has come however, that your Elders (councillors) think of taking the Maoris [sic] land without cause. Behold, the heart is sad, but we will not believe this report, because we heard from the first Governor that with ourselves lay the consideration of our lands, and the second Governor repeated the same, and this Governor also, all their speeches with the same, therefore we write to you to love our people, write your thoughts to us, that peace may abide with the people of these islands.[26]

Te Wherowhero's distinction between the Queen and her ministers would continue to be a significant part of Victoria's appeal. It allowed rangātira to see her as at a distance from her government and as an upholder and potential enforcer of Māori rights.

When Pākehā after 1854 established self-government in a constitution that effectively excluded Māori from participation, the question of whether the Queen stood above the venal world of settler politics became increasingly controversial.[27] The question was not simply whether Māori land and other resources or even chiefly authority could be protected by the Queen, but whether the Queen's laws would keep the peace. A commitment to the Treaty of Waitangi by rangātira was also a commitment to te ture (the new law), although this law was based more on scripture than on common or statutory law. Many Māori adopting Christianity saw the arrival of a British governor as introducing a new era of peace, one that replaced the endemic warfare of the 1820s and 1830s. But by the 1850s, the government was either avoiding any involvement in Māori disputes, or deliberately siding with those Māori prepared to sell land. Māori complained that the law was not being applied equally and maintaining the peace was no more than an instrument of European domination.

With these threats to chiefly authority increasing, the establishment of self-government was the catalyst for an intense Māori debate on the relationship between the Queen, rangātira, and the settler government. Loyalists continued to argue that despite the hostile rhetoric of many settler politicians, the Treaty of Waitangi marked a sacred covenant between Māori and Queen Victoria, centred on the persons of the Queen and the Governor and confirmed by the missionaries, as God's representatives. But other voices were less confident that Māori rights could be protected by a distant Queen. The sceptics paid her the ultimate homage in imitating her by seeking to establish a Māori monarchy. In the debate over the election of a Māori king, Māori nationalists argued that all peoples were entitled to their own self-government and Māori should have a king in the same way that the peoples of Europe had their own monarchs:

> God is good: Israel were his people, they had a king. I see no reason why any nation should not have a king if it likes. The Gospel does not say we are not to have a king. It says, 'Honor the King, love the brotherhood.' Why should the Queen be angry? We shall be in alliance with her, and friendship will be preserved. The Governor does not stop murders and fights among us. A king will be able to do that. Let us have order. So that we may grow as the pākehā [Europeans] grows. Why should we disappear from the country? New Zealand is ours, I love it.[28]

The movement's chief apologist, Wiremu Tamihana, argued that it was no threat to Queen Victoria. The Queen would stand above Māori and Pākehā, providing unity, while each group managed their own lands. Te Wherowhero, who had petitioned the Queen in 1847 and was eventually elected the first Māori king, taking the name Pōtatau, argued, 'The Queen on her piece, the King on his piece, God on both and ever binding them to each other'.[29] Māori had easily adapted the European idea of monarchy from Christian and secular sources: what was much harder was forcing rangātira to accept the curtailment of their own mana by the laws of a Māori king in the leasing and sale of their lands.

Initially, the imperial and colonial governments dismissed the Kīngitanga, the movement to elect a Māori king, as a childlike imitation, doomed to collapse. But, by the early 1860s, as increasing numbers of Māori tribes joined the Kīngitanga or debated doing so, governors saw the movement as a threat to the Queen's sovereignty. Despite many Māori protestations that this was not the case for those joining the Kīngitanga, Victoria was increasingly irrelevant. Prayers were no longer offered for the Queen, and the King would be a king for the Māori as Victoria was a Queen for the Pākehā.[30] Increasingly, as tensions rose, the Kīngitanga rejected the idea that the

Queen could stand apart from European politics because of her special relationship with rangātira.

The loyalist tribes had no doubt in their own minds that the Kīngitanga was a threat to the Queen's sovereignty and rejected it, but by now loyalty to the Queen demanded not just a relationship with her governor, who still had responsibility for native affairs, but with the colonial government. Once war broke out in Taranaki in 1860, loyalists articulated their attachment to Queen Victoria even more firmly. Although Rewi Maniapoto led a group of mainly Ngāti Maniapoto and Raukawa iwi (tribes), from central North Island, to fight against the colonial government in Taranaki, the Kīngitanga itself remained aloof. In an attempt to bolster loyalist opinion and seeking a condemnation of those fighting against it in Taranaki, the Governor called a conference of chiefs at Kohimārama near Auckland in August 1860. There were plenty of expressions of loyalty to the Queen from those tribes who attended, although the event was boycotted by groups loyal to the King. As Manūka of Ngāti Whatūa commented, the speeches sang the same tune, 'love, and the establishment of the Queen's laws'. The Queen was his 'firm friend for ever and ever! "Mercy and truth have met together"'.[31] Tukihaumene, of Ngāti Whakaue, Te Arawa, said 'The Queen shall be our head for ever and ever! This is my word'.[32] From Otakou at the bottom of the South Island, Taiaroa of Ngāi Tahū stated, 'I did not come to support the King: I came to support the Queen'.[33] Matene Te Whiwhi, Ngāti Toa, from Otaki, had with Tamihana Te Rauparahā in 1853 initiated the debate over whether to have a king. But he addressed the conference with:

> I have no other word. I have said all I have to say to you. My words do not run to and fro: [they express] nothing else than the acceptance of the Queen's authority. But with this tribe, and with that tribe, are their own thoughts. We know with the first Governor there was no other word, even up to this time there was but one word; that there should be but one law, and that both races should be united. The authority of the Queen rests upon us. Let us cleave to the good and to the clear customs of the Pakeha.[34]

The assembled rangātira presented a coherent view not just of their relationship with the Queen, but their place in constitutional affairs. They wanted the meeting at Kohimārama to be an ongoing event; one where the Governor would consult with his rangātira, and where unity between the Queen, the Governor, and rangātira would ensure Māori participation in the state and unity between Māori and Pākehā.[35] At least two of those present at Kohimārama would meet Victoria three year later at Osborne House on the Isle of Wight.

When government forces invaded the Waikato in 1863 in an attempt to suppress the Queen's rival and under the pretext of defending Auckland from Māori attack, Māori loyalists were not called upon to take an active part in the war. Anyway, the brunt of the fighting was the responsibility of imperial rather than colonial troops. But even in the Waikato, south of Auckland and the centre of the movement and where Tainui was dominant, not all the tribes had joined the Kīngitanga. Wiremu Te Morehu Maipapa Te Wheoro of the Lower Waikato rejected the King and took office in one of Grey's officially sanctioned rūnanga (Māori committees). Even before the invasion took place, Te Wheoro's attempts to build a courthouse were thwarted by 100 fully armed supporters of King Tāwhiao, who had recently succeeded Pōtatau on his death. They confiscated his timber and then rafted it down the river and handed it back to the government. Once hostilities began, Te Wheoro and his people maintained a supply line for Lieutenant General Duncan Cameron's forces as they proceeded upriver, coming under attack by Ngāti Maniapoto on behalf of the King in September 1863. Cameron promoted Te Wheoro to the rank of captain in the colonial militia.[36] Like many other loyalists, he accepted royal commissions, military rank, and judicial office, along with a Crown pension and other benefits of royal patronage.

Although the war dragged on for over a decade, those who had remained loyal to the Queen had no doubt that they had chosen the winning side. In 1872, as the last few shots were fired, Te Arawa who fought until the end as part of the colonial force in its campaign against Te Kooti Arikirangi Te Turuki, opened their new meeting house, named after their ancestor, Tamatekapua. They had invited their Kīngitanga adversaries, but it was probably in everyone's best interest that they stayed away. Referring to a long list of opponents to the Queen's forces who had been killed, Temuera Te Amohu asked:

> Where was Taekata? Where was Kaingarara? Where was Hakaraia? They were all gone, and most of their followers with them – the last (Kereopa) went the other day. They thought they knew best; they would have their own way. But here we are, the tribes who came on board the Arawa canoe. We have safely reached the shore.[37]

He called on all of those assembled to look around the house, to see the carvings that represented their tūpuna (ancestors). But in looking overhead at the ridge pole, there was the Queen and her laws. 'She is over all, and it is under her shadow all the others abide'.[38] Te Arawa's lands were still intact, but those who had opposed the Queen had lost not only many of their leaders, but many had their lands confiscated. Te Arawa were to find that being on the winning side provided no immunity to losing tribal land. The Native Land Court individualised tribal lands, making them extremely vulnerable to sale. While Te Arawa would remain little affected by the court until the end of the century, other kūpapa (loyalist) iwi were already lamenting their landlessness and political and economic marginalisation and attempting to find ways of resisting or ameliorating the impact of colonisation.

The Kīngitanga was defeated and much its land in the Waikato confiscated, but it was not destroyed. It continued until the early 1880s to control some four and a half million acres in the central North Island. This area became known as the Rohe Pōtae or King Country, and it was not until the mid-1880s that the colonial government was able to assert the Queen's sovereignty over it. In the meantime, King Tāwhiao and the Queen's government engaged in intense large-scale negotiations between the colonial and Kīngitanga administrations. These were attended by Māori leaders from throughout the country who saw any possible agreement between the King and the Queen providing precedents to protect their own aspirations and have their grievances recognised. Such an agreement was never reached, but in the process some major figures changed sides, the most significant being Major Te Wheoro. Te Wheoro was increasingly disaffected; he went from being a mediator between the King and the Queen to being one of Tawhiao's most trusted and useful advisers. In these negotiations, the status of King and Queen were extensively debated.

Tāwhiao and his supporters were substantially isolated in the Rohe Pōtae until 1881, with limited access to European networks, but they continued to share ideas and information with Māori outside the Rohe Pōtae, and there were a few significant mediators between the Kīngitangi and the European world, including a handful of colonial officials and Kīngitanga leaders such as Rewi Maniapoto. Maniaptoto had become a national celebrity based on his heroism during the final battle of the Waikato Campaign at Orākau. In 1881, Tāwhiao began series of highly successful royal progresses through the Waikato towns and in the following year travelled to Auckland where he was treated like a visiting monarch. By this time, the colonial government's refusal to deal with him had undermined his ability to speak on behalf of the tribes within the Rohe Pōtae. In 1883, with his control over the tribes of the King Country all but evaporated, he decided to take Māori grievances to the Queen. He arrived in London in May 1884 and remained until mid-August.[39] The colonial government had spent over a quarter of century undermining the King's authority, and was in no mood to have his regal status recognised in even symbolic terms. The agent general deliberately misled the Colonial Secretary in attempting to downplay Tāwhiao's status in the Māori world and insisted that no meeting of monarchs take place.[40] Tāwhiao was not the first to go to London. Other groups had gone in 1855 and in 1863 and even succeeded in meeting Queen Victoria and members of her family. Hirini Taiwhanga, a Ngāpuhi leader, had unsuccessfully attempted to see the Queen in 1882, although he did get to meet the Prince of Wales.[41]

In leaving the Rohe Pōtae and visiting London, Tāwhiao was taking on a role already well established and far from exclusively Māori: that of an Aboriginal leader taking his grievances to Queen Victoria. His visit had been preceded by that of Cetshwayo kaMpande, the deposed Zulu leader, who had fashioned his mission to appeal to British sympathies and met Queen Victoria.[42] Khama, Sebele, and Bathoen would have similar experiences a decade later.[43] To carry off such a role, Tāwhiao needed to draw on networks of European support for Aboriginal causes that the Kīngitanga had treated with suspicious disdain from the 1850s. Māori visitors to London, particularly those on a political mission, could rely on well-placed humanitarian support, which opened doors to London's elite. This began even before the group left New Zealand, with Sir George Grey providing them with letters of introduction. Taiwhanga had had access to the Aborigines Protection Society to play host to his visit and so did Tāwhiao. Sympathetic supporters rallied to the cause; many of them were women, such as Amelia Saintsbury who provided a house for Māori visitors near Russell Square. Charlotte Weale, who had come to the rescue of the 1863 Māori travelling party, after they were abandoned by the tour's organiser, was still there to offer assistance.

Far from being captured by the Aborigines Protection Society and its secretary, Chesson, the delegation became part of a range of associations, temperance organisations, impresarios (whose royal boxes were offered to them), evangelists, and diplomats. Tāwhiao and his delegation were regularly interviewed, and the visit was widely covered by newspapers and largely sympathetically, though often through a patronising lens. Their residence became an alternative embassy, much better known than the official residence of the High Commissioner. They may not have succeeded in seeing the Queen, but they received a sympathetic hearing from the Colonial Secretary Lord Derby, and were hosted in a series of dinners and garden parties by the Lord Mayor and a number of members of Parliament. All of this occurred in defiance of the government in Wellington, which had to be content with surreptitiously working with the Colonial Secretary's office to undermine Tāwhiao's mission, fearing that any public opposition to Tāwhiao would be counterproductive and reflect badly on New Zealand.

Tāwhiao was changed by the experience. He and his delegation, who were as much kūpapa as Kīngitanga, developed their own constitutional ideas about the role of the Queen. In this view, Victoria was the

Queen of all, Māori and Pākehā, but the colonial government had arbitrarily gained control over Māori, without Māori consent. The Queen's legitimacy was assured; the colonial government's was not. Māori needed their own self-government, their own parliament. This view joined Kīngitanga and kūpapa, and provided a new consensus in Māori thinking. All of these ideas were developed and further articulated in London and with the support of European advisers. With Sir John Gorst, who had been a government agent magistrate in the Waikato before the war, they melded these ideas into an argument more accessible to the European world. Tāwhiao and his delegation did much to fashion themselves for European audiences. To the British supporters, they were reasonable, polite, well dressed, and appeared to combine all the exoticism of Victoria's distant Empire with Britain's manifest destiny to Christianise and civilise savage bodies, heathen souls, and primitive minds. Above all, Tāwhiao, who had successfully remained aloof from the Empire, now was part of it, a critic and disaffected all the same, but his criticism was aimed at an imperial audience and his disaffection at imperial sympathy.

By the end of the 1880s, there was almost universal Māori support for the Queen, support that was personal, constitutional, and political. This support paralleled Pākehā enthusiasm for Queen Victoria in New Zealand in the last decade of her reign, particularly during the celebration of her Diamond Jubilee. Māori took part in the 1887 Golden Jubilee but were much more on the edges compared with the imperial celebration to come in 1897. However, the same patterns of affection and protest were evident in the way that Māori engaged with imperial loyalty to the Queen. They demanded the rights of citizenship, but at the same time claimed a unique relationship with Victoria, explicit in the Treaty of Waitangi and how it was remembered. They reasserted Māori rights to control, retain, and even reclaim Māori land.[44] The colonial government was not completely blind to such criticisms, but almost inevitably fell back on the comforting platitudes of good race relations and privileged natives now living in harmony with their Pākehā neighbours.

Māori were not being ignored: they were being deliberately included in these important ceremonial events. And they did at least partially play the role that was expected of them, in acknowledging Queen Victoria and in participating side by side with Pākehā. Specifically Māori responses to the celebration were acknowledged, accepted, and incorporated, such as a hangi (a feast, with the food cooked in underground pits).[45] But all of this was only possible because Māori airing grievances at these events could be largely ignored by a Pākehā audience who interpreted Māori protest as no more than ritualised performances, with limited political and no military consequences. Pākehā often only saw what they wanted to see: contented natives, grateful for the gifts brought to them from afar.

In 1887, as part of the Golden Jubilee celebrations at Kaiapoi, north of Christchurch, Wiremu Nahiere of Ngāi Tahū was reported in the *Evening Post* as concluding his speech with, 'We rejoice to honour the Queen, for she is a good woman, who cares for the Māori race, as witness the Treaty of Waitangi'.[46] The newspaper failed to report what he said next: 'But to this day Her Majesty's English subjects have neglected to carry out all the provisions of that deed. Let me implore you to do justice, and not allow our reserves at Greymouth to be taken from us'.[47] The complaint was couched in loyalty to the person of Queen Victoria, the 'good woman', a woman whose moral quality could not be questioned. The Treaty of Waitangi, her treaty, achieved the same status. What followed was a general criticism of the failure of the European world to live up to both the Queen's righteousness and the provisions of the treaty. But at the end, there was a specific grievance: the threat to the Greymouth reserves, one of the few pieces of land left to Ngāi Tahū, who in 1840 had customary interests in most of the South Island. This brief appeal intertwined the constitutional and the political with Victoria the person and applied it to specific and present threats.

A Māori military contingent was selected to accompany the Premier Richard Seddon to attend the Diamond Jubilee in London in 1897.[48] The spotlight was on the colonial premiers and their military contingents as Victoria had banned the royal houses of Europe from the event.[49] Once the proposal had been announced, Māori leaders debated how they would present themselves to the Queen. Would it be as a group of warriors, dressed in korowai (cloaks, often decorated with bird feathers) and with moko (tattooed faces)? Such images of Māori were popular, romanticising the Māori past, and many rangātira from an earlier age were having their portraits painted in such dress, wistfully looking backwards. This was the image that had been long cultivated for presenting Māori to the Queen.[50] Even when wearing European dress with aplomb, Tāwhiao and Te Wheoro were photographed in cloaks while they were in London (see Figure 2.1; compare with Figure 2.2). Instead, Māori chose to be examples of modernity, who could compare favourably in education and culture with the European world. It was not a warrior past that would be celebrated, the world of Hone Heke who fought against British imperial forces and his own kin in the 1840s, but rather the world of his grandnephew, Hone Heke Ngapua MA, LLB, and member of the House of Representatives.[51] The Māori contingent of twenty were drilled and mounted and rode almost indistinguishably from the twenty New Zealand-born Europeans. Captain Hoani Paraone Tunuiarangi from

Figure 2.1 Tāwhiao, the Māori king, and Major Wiremu Te Wheoro (Te Morehu Maipapa), in London, 1884.

Rangitane and Ngāti Kahungunu in the Wairarapa participated in the review on 2 July, and was presented to Queen Victoria. She awarded him a Jubilee Medal and presented him with a sword.[52]

At home, Māori were also willing and expected to take a full part in the Jubilee celebration, and the form of these performances was extensively negotiated with the organisers, where these organisers were settler communities and their leaders. Enthusiasm and the extent of negotiation were more muted in the case of Waikato, the central North Island and in Taranaki, where the confiscation of Māori land remained a heartfelt grievance, still exacerbated by government policies affecting what little lands remained. The procession in New Plymouth had no Māori participation at all, but even here, where many of their leaders had been imprisoned without trial in the previous decade, the Parihaka leaders apologised for their non-appearance. Their excuse

Figure 2.2 Te Morehu Maipapa (also known as Major Te Wheoro), Ngai Naho Chief and Member of Parliament for Western Māori, 1879–84.

was a tangi (funeral), which meant they could not attend and neither could the Parihaka brass band.[53] In the South Island, Ngāi Tahū kaika[54] (villages) were formally asked to take part, and were offered free railway passes and refreshments.[55] In Auckland, Kaipara Māori took the initiative, requesting train passes and suggesting a mock battle with Māori using traditional weapons against Pākehā with modern arms.[56] In Tauranga, where land had been confiscated, a conference was held between Ngāi Te Rangi and the mayor, leading to extensive Māori participation in the festivities.[57] Pākehā planning the celebrations were likely to fit Māori into a romantic stereotype, but were happy instead to have Māori brass bands march alongside other bands. In Wanganui, organisers wanted to see 'a large war canoe ... fitted up, and seated with a number of old dusky warriors, in war paint and feathers'.[58] Instead, the Waitotara Māori Band performed and was welcomed by a vigorous haka (war dance), but there was no canoe.[59]

In most areas, Māori participated in the general celebrations, but in Rotorua, Te Arawa hosted an event of their own. Around 700 assembled at Ohinemutu on the lakeshore. A large flag, which had been presented to the tribe by the Duke of Edinburgh in 1870, was given pride of place. A bust of Queen Victoria, also presented by the Duke and which to that time had been kept in the meeting house, Tamatekapua, was brought outside and placed in a carved house dedicated to her (Figure 2.3). It was surrounded with fine mats and pounamu (jade) taonga (treasures). Haka were performed by armed toa (warriors). The music was provided by the community's band, and European visitors were entertained in the wharenui (meeting house).[60] The tribe also presented its own illuminated address to the Queen. By the late nineteenth century, loyalty to the Queen was for these tribes an essential component of tribal identity and pride. It celebrated participation in the modern world and equality with Europeans. It was a major point of difference between Te Arawa, a tribe already extensively engaged in tourism, and their more alienated neighbours who had opposed the British Crown in the 1860s.

Seddon had difficulties with his hand-picked contingent in London. Under Tunuiarangi's leadership, they took the opportunity to petition the Queen, asking that the remaining area of Māori land, now little more than a sixth of the country's area, and generally poor land at that, be made inalienable.[61] The petition was presented to Joseph Chamberlain, secretary of state for colonies, and Tunuiarangi was invited to the House of Commons to explain their concerns. The protest caused surprisingly little embarrassment to Seddon, who was fond of parading New Zealand as the perfect example of enlightened colonisation.[62] While the government was intent on promoting New Zealand

Figure 2.3 The statue of Queen Victoria at Ohinemutu.

as a place of ideal race relations, where contented Māori would provide an exotic experience of geysers and mud pools to free-spending tourists, Māori leaders had other agendas. They used the Queen as a focus of protest, sometimes to make a point shared by all Māori, such as concerns about the impact of the Māori land laws, while for others, a relationship with the Queen was used to bolster tribal identity and chiefly influence with premiers and ministers. Māori success as soldiers or graduates reinforced Seddon's smug belief in British humanitarianism and racial amalgamation, but these were also sources of pride for Māori communities themselves. Loyalist Māori would soon demand the right to fight in South Africa, with Seddon's strong support, but met with imperial resistance to mobilise coloured, colonial troops. Despite this, a number of individual Māori joined the New Zealand South African contingent.[63] Tunuiarangi's protest did not damage his relationship with Seddon. The Premier later appointed him to the board responsible for choosing sites for scenic preservation, and he was promoted to major.[64]

By the end of Victoria's reign, Māori were part of the Empire. Victoria provided much of the cohesion, symbolism, and constitutional focus to allow this to happen. Attempts at constitutional autonomy, such as the development of the Kīngitanga, had not been a reversion into some idealised pre-imperial world. They had been built on ideas about sovereignty, nationhood, and monarchy that emerged in the 1840s as Māori attempted to forge their own relationship with Queen Victoria. The relationship was not simply one-sided. Victoria was incorporated into Māori systems of status: she had mana, and she represented the power and authority of the British Empire. For Māori rangātira who had taken Christianity seriously, she also provided the moral compass for the Empire. This was particularly significant in New Zealand because of the Treaty of Waitangi and the promises that were contained in it. Māori debates over the significance of the Queen did not take place in isolation either. Individual rangātira considered the Queen in the context of their own tribal aspirations and the challenges that they faced, but they did so through their contact with wider networks that involved both Māori and European debates and knowledge. The primary objective for all of these tribal communities was to achieve some control over a dramatically changing world, where Europeans appeared to own the future. Victoria provided a way of participating in empire, because her name mobilised networks of humanitarian and other European groups who could be relied on as allies in representing Indigenous causes to both colonial and imperial governments. Māori began to experience through these networks a sense that they were not unique and were part of an Indigenous world within the Empire.

Following Victoria's death, Māori would become even more committed to performances of loyalty, particularly during the royal tours of 1901, 1926, and 1954. Questions about the legitimacy of the New Zealand Parliament in Wellington would be put aside as a new generation of leaders used participation in political parties and influence with Cabinet to defend Māori aspirations and perspectives. Only from the 1970s would Māori raise new questions about the legitimacy of New Zealand's Pākehā-dominated parliament. By this time, the role given to Queen Victoria in nineteenth-century Māori thinking had been largely forgotten, and loyalty to the Queen by those ancestors who were kūpapa became a source of embarrassment. Māori challenged themselves and Pākehā about loyalty to the nation state, but the place of Queen Victoria and the idea of empire and their contribution to Māori survival had been selectively forgotten.

Notes

1 For the treaty signing, see Claudia Orange, *The Treaty of Waitangi* (Wellington: Allen & Unwin Port Nicholson Press with assistance from the Historical Publications Branch Dept. of Internal Affairs, 1987); Vincent O'Malley, Bruce Stirling, and Wally Penetito (eds), *The Treaty of Waitangi Companion: Māori and Pākehā from Tasman to Today* (Auckland: Auckland University Press, 2010).
2 See, for instance, the recent general histories, James Belich, *Making Peoples: A History of the New Zealanders from Polynesian Settlement to the End of the Nineteenth Century* (Auckland: Penguin, 1996), pp. 270–1; Michael King, *The Penguin History of New Zealand* (Auckland: Penguin Books, 2003), pp. 256–8; Paul Monin, 'Maori Economies and Colonial Capitalism', in Giselle Byrnes (ed.), *The New Oxford History of New Zealand* (South Melbourne: Oxford University Press Australia and New Zealand, 2009), pp. 145–6.
3 Zoë Laidlaw, '"Aunt Anna's Report": The Buxton women and the Aborigines Select Committee, 1835–37', *Journal of Imperial and Commonwealth History*, 32:2 (2003), 1–28; see also, Elizabeth Elbourne, 'The sin of the settler: The 1835–36 Select Committee on Aborigines and debates over virtue and conquest in the early nineteenth-century British white settler empire', *Journal of Colonialism and Colonial History*, 4:3 (2003), http://muse.jhu.edu/journals/journal_of_colonialism_and_colonial_history/v004/4.3elbourne.html, accessed 19 January 2016; Alan Lester, *Imperial Networks: Creating Identities in Nineteenth-Century South Africa and Britain* (London and New York: Routledge, 2001); Mark Murphy, 'The Peaceable Kingdom of Nineteenth Century Humanitarianism: The Aborigines Protection Society and New Zealand' (MA thesis, University of Canterbury, 2002).
4 One of the earliest studies was Keith Sinclair, 'The Aborigines Protection Society and New Zealand – A Study in Nineteenth Century Opinion' (MA thesis, Auckland University College, 1946). See also: Peter Adams, *Fatal Necessity: British Intervention in New Zealand 1830–1847* (Auckland: Auckland University Press, 1977); Claudia Orange, 'The Treaty of Waitangi: A Study of its Making, Interpretation and Role in New Zealand History' (PhD thesis, University of Auckland, 1984); Mark Hickford, *Lords of the Land: Indigenous Property Rights and the Jurisprudence of Empire* (Oxford: Oxford University Press, 2011). A recent report of the Waitangi Tribunal has reviewed in depth the Treaty of Waitangi and the move to intervene in New Zealand. This discussion is helpful, but the findings are of limited value. See Waitangi Tribunal, 'He Whakaputanga me te Tiriti / The Declaration and the Treaty: The Report on Stage 1 of the Te Paparahi o Te Raki Inquiry [volume 2]' (Wellington: Waitangi Tribunal, 2014).
5 Erik Olssen, 'Mr. Wakefield and New Zealand as an experiment in post-Enlightenment experimental practice', *New Zealand Journal of History*, 31:2 (1997), 197–218.
6 Philip Temple, *A Sort of Conscience: The Wakefields* (Auckland: Auckland University Press, 2002).
7 James Heartfield, *The Aborigines' Protection Society: Humanitarian Imperialism in Australia, New Zealand, Fiji, Canada, South Africa, and the Congo, 1836–1909* (London: Hurst, 2011).
8 See, for instance, Appendices to the Journals of the House of Representatives, 1865, A6, pp. 22–3, Te Oha Taotao, Katikati, Te Koou and their tribes to the Aborigines Protection Society, 29 October 1864, thanking the Society for its efforts in trying halt to war in New Zealand.

9 The commonality of such presentations is illustrated by Neil Parsons, *King Khama, Emperor Joe, and the Great White Queen: Victorian Britain through African Eyes* (Chicago, IL: University of Chicago Press, 1998); Vivian Bickford-Smith, 'African nationalist or British loyalist? The complicated case of Tiyo Soga', *History Workshop Journal*, no. 71 (2011); Hilary Sapire, 'Ambiguities of loyalism: The Prince of Wales in India and Africa, 1921–2 and 25', *History Workshop Journal*, no. 73 (2012), 37–65.

10 Andrew Thompson, 'The languages of loyalism in Southern Africa, c. 1870–1939', *English Historical Review*, 118:477 (2003). Michael McDonnell raises similar problems in his 'Facing empires: Indigenous histories in comparative perspective', in Kate Fullagar (ed.), *The Atlantic World in the Antipodes: Effects and Transformations since the Eighteenth Century* (Newcastle upon Tyne: Cambridge Scholars Publishing, 2012), pp. 225–6.

11 Ravi de Costa, 'Identity, authority, and the moral worlds of indigenous petitions', *Comparative Studies in Society and History*, 48:3 (2006), 669–98.

12 David Cannadine, *Ornamentalism: How the British Saw Their Empire* (London: Penguin, 2002).

13 Angela Ballara, *Iwi: The Dynamics of Maori Tribal Organisation from c. 1769 to c. 1945* (Wellington: Victoria University Press, 1998).

14 Tony Ballantyne, 'Strategic intimacies: Knowledge and colonization in southern New Zealand', *Journal of New Zealand Studies*, 14 (2013), 4.

15 Angela Wanhalla, *Matters of the Heart: A History of Interracial Marriage in New Zealand* (Auckland: Auckland University Press, 2013).

16 Judith Binney, *The Legacy of Guilt: A Life of Thomas Kendall* (Auckland: Published for the University of Auckland by the Oxford University Press, 1968); J. M. R. Owens, 'Christianity and the Maoris to 1840', *New Zealand Journal of History*, 2:1 (1968), pp. 18–40; Judith Binney, 'Christianity and the Maoris to 1840: A Comment', *New Zealand Journal of History*, 3:2 (1969), 143–65.

17 Ann Curthoys has drawn attention to such networks in Aboriginal petitioning: Ann Curthoys, 'Taking liberty: Towards a new political historiography of settler self-government and indigenous activism', in Kate Fullagar (ed.), *The Atlantic World in the Antipodes: Effects and Transformations since the Eighteenth Century* (Newcastle upon Tyne: Cambridge Scholars Publishing, 2012), pp. 247–50.

18 The idea of seeing the Empire as a net, a mesh of interconnected networks is usefully developed by C. J. Bayly and Tony Ballantyne. C. A. Bayly, *Empire and Information: Intelligence Gathering and Social Communication in India, 1780–1870* (Cambridge: Cambridge University Press, 1996); Tony Ballantyne, *Orientalism and Race: Aryanism in the British Empire* (Basingstoke: Palgrave, 2002).

19 *Auckland Star*, XXVI:4501 (1 November 1884), p. 2 (newspaper references can be found on PapersPast, http://paperspast.natlib.govt.nz/, accessed 1 February 2016).

20 See Paul Moon, *A Savage Country: The Untold Story of New Zealand in the 1820s* (Auckland: Penguin, 2012); Ormond Wilson, *From Hongi Hika to Hone Heke: A Quarter Century of Upheaval* (Dunedin, NZ: McIndoe, 1985); Binney, *The Legacy of Guilt*.

21 D. U. Urlich Cloher, *Hongi Hika: Warrior Chief* (Auckland: Penguin Books, 2003), p. 141.

22 Arthur S. Thomson, *The Story of New Zealand: Past and Present, Savage and Civilized* (London: J. Murray, 1859), p. 255.

23 Keith Thor Carlson, 'Rethinking dialogue and history: The King's promise and the 1906 Aboriginal delegation to London', *Native Studies Review*, 16:2 (2005), 1–38.

24 The operative text is regarded as the text in te reo Māori text, and the English translations come from the English draft. The two texts are not identical, although the differences between them have been overstated, www.nzhistory.net.nz/politics/treaty/read-the-treaty/english-text, accessed 25 October 2013. See Michael Belgrave, *Historical Frictions: Maori Claims and Reinvented Histories* (Auckland: Auckland University Press, 2005), Ch. 2.

25 Claudia Orange, *An Illustrated History of the Treaty of Waitangi* (Wellington: Bridget Williams Books, 2004), p. 42.

26 Te Wherowhero and other chiefs to the Queen, 8 November 1847, Grey to Earl Grey, 13 November 1847, British Parliamentary Papers (BPP), vol. 6, 1847–50, 1002, p. 899.
27 Curthoys, 'Taking liberty'.
28 Paora, Paetai, 1857, in Thomas Buddle, *The Maori King Movement in New Zealand: with a Full Report of the Native Meetings Held at Waikato, April and May, 1860* (Auckland: Published at the New-Zealander Office, 1860), p. 9.
29 Richard Taylor, *The Past and Present of New Zealand: With its Prospects for the Future* (London: W. Macintosh, 1868), p. 123.
30 Buddle, *The Maori King Movement*, p. 8.
31 Secretary of the Conference, 'Proceedings of the Kohimarama Conference, comprising Nos. 13 to 18 of the Maori Messenger', *Maori Messenger: Te Karere Maori* (6 August 1860), p. 11, http://nzetc.victoria.ac.nz/tm/scholarly/tei-BIM504Kohi-t1-g1-t5-body1-d2.html, accessed 23 February 2015.
32 *Ibid.*, p. 14.
33 *Ibid.*
34 *Ibid.*, p. 16.
35 Claudia Orange, 'The Covenant of Kohimarama: A ratification of the Treaty of Waitangi', *New Zealand Journal of History*, 14:1 (1980), 61–82.
36 Gary Scott, 'Te Wheoro, Wiremu Te Morehu Maipapa', from the *Dictionary of New Zealand Biography. Te Ara – the Encyclopedia of New Zealand*, updated 30 October 2012, www.TeAra.govt.nz/en/biographies/1t87/te-wheoro-wiremu-te-morehu-maipapa, accessed 10 November 2014.
37 HT Clarke to Undersecretary, Native Department, 14 February 1872, Further reports from officers in Native District, in continuation of papers presented on 27 August 1872, Appendices to the Journals of the House of Representatives (AJHR), 1872, F3A, p. 7.
38 *Ibid.*
39 Roger Blackley, 'King Tāwhiao's big O.E.', *Turnbull Library Record*, no. 44 (2012), 36–52.
40 National Archives, Wellington, MA 23/2/4b, Bryce to Grindstone, 27 May 1884.
41 Orange, *An Illustrated History*, pp. 101–2.
42 Catherine E. Anderson, 'A Zulu King in Victorian London: Race, royalty and imperialist aesthetics in late nineteenth-century Britain', *Visual Resources: An International Journal of Documentation*, 24:3 (2008), 299–319.
43 Parsons, *King Khama*.
44 Belgrave, *Historical Frictions*.
45 A Māori feast, where the food is slow cooked in a pit covered with earth. The method is still used to prepare large quantities of food for mass gatherings.
46 *Evening Post*, XXXIII (21 June 1887), p. 2.
47 *Hawera & Normanby Star*, IX:1656 (22 June 1887), p. 2.
48 Richard Seddon and the colonial contingent were captured on film, see: www.filmarchive.org.nz/assets/Media/video/F11225.mov, viewed 30 May 2014, or http://www.ngataonga.org.nz/catalogues/moving-image-catalogue/media/-queen-victoria-s-diamond-jubilee-procession-22-june-1897-f11225 (viewed 18 January 2016).
49 Walter L. Arnstein, 'Queen Victoria's Diamond Jubilee', *The American Scholar*, 66:4 (1997), 591–7.
50 George Angas's portraits of Māori in the 1840s feature Māori deliberately dressed in fine cloaks, as he informed rangātira that the portraits were to be presented to Queen Victoria. George French Angas, *Savage Life and Scenes in Australia and New Zealand: Being an Artist's Impressions of Countries and People at the Antipodes* (London: Smith, 1847). Angas also was responsible for creating popular European images of Zulus, see Anderson, 'A Zulu King in Victorian London', pp. 300–1.
51 *Otago Daily Times*, issue 10737 (27 February 1897), p. 4.
52 Angela Ballara, 'Tunuiarangi, Hoani Paraone', from the *Dictionary of New Zealand Biography. Te Ara – the Encyclopedia of New Zealand*, updated 30 October 2012, www.TeAra.govt.nz/en/biographies/3t44/tunuiarangi-hoani-paraone, accessed 21 October 2013.

53 *Taranaki Herald*, XLVI:10952 (23 June 1897), p. 2.
54 Ngā Tahu dialect for the more common North Island, kainga.
55 *The Press*, LIV:9721 (7 May 1897), p. 3.
56 *Auckland Star*, XXVIII:110 (13 May 1897), p. 7.
57 *Ibid.*, XXVIII:138 (15 June 1897), p. 1.
58 *Wanganui Herald*, XXXI:9152 (19 May 1897), p. 2.
59 *Ibid.*, XXXI:9180 (23 June 1897), p. 2.
60 *Auckland Star*, XXVIII:155 (6 July 1897), p. 8.
61 *New Zealand Herald*, XXXIV:10502 (23 July 1897), p. 5.
62 Tom Brooking, *Richard Seddon: King of God's Own: The Life and Times of New Zealand's Longest-Serving Prime Minister* (Auckland: Penguin, 2014), pp. 217–19.
63 Mike Dwight, *Walter Callaway: Maori Warrior of the Boer War* (Thames: M. Dwight, 2010).
64 Brooking, *Richard Seddon*, pp. 367–8.

CHAPTER THREE

'The faithful children of the Great Mother are starving': Queen Victoria in contact zone dialogues in western Canada

Sarah Carter

During Victoria's reign, Indigenous diplomats, politicians, and speakers drew on an oratorical tradition, one that developed in the maritime and eastern North American colonies and incorporated references to the British monarchy in kinship terms that confirmed themselves as equals of the Europeans. They called on the monarch's representatives to act with honour, justice, integrity, and generosity, to protect them from injustice and oppression, and to guard their rights over and above the arbitrary rule of trading companies or settler governments. They were also accustomed to being lectured about just, benevolent monarchs from generations of British fur traders, and later, missionaries, government officials, and bureaucrats joined in the chorus.[1] Representations of a compassionate and generous Queen Victoria were used by colonisers over the many decades of her reign and beyond to sustain and reinforce the narrative of Canada's humane and fair treatment of its Indigenous people. In contrast to the situation in the United States where violence and chaos prevailed, according to this narrative, Canada had nurtured loyal and docile allies who revered the British monarch. Erased from this narrative is that Canada's First Nations deployed the symbol of Victoria to draw attention to injustice and to call for justice.

While the British drew on 'Great Mother' and 'red children' metaphors to emphasise the inferior position of the colonised people of the Empire, to 'fix, rank and subdue' them, Indigenous people resisted this emphasis on their inferiority and drew on the image and symbol of the female monarch to project their equality, their special relationship based on mutual respect and trust, and to demand fair treatment from settler society.[2] Indigenous people repeatedly reminded the Queen's representatives of treaty promises that had been ignored. They persisted in these appeals even though they were repeatedly and consistently ignored. Faced with shrinking autonomous space, as settler power was consolidated, and without the right to vote, they were at the mercy of those who could.³ They had no other means of redress. Petitions to the Canadian House of Commons were ignored unless signed by voters. As historian Keith Carlson has written (about a 1906 Aboriginal delegation to the King), 'For strategically minded Aboriginal leaders it [an audience with the monarch] demonstrated that it was possible to bypass local provincial and federal officials and speak directly with powerful European authorities who ostensibly commanded the respect, and even obedience, of those prominent Canadian officials who consistently failed to listen to indigenous concerns and grievances'.⁴ Even when appealing to subsequent British monarchs, it was Victoria who was invoked as the source of promises to care and protect.⁵

The oratorical tradition in Canada of the 'Great Mother' and her 'red children' has been noted in studies of treaty-making, royal or vice-regal visits, and the delegations of Indigenous people to England.⁶ In other British colonies, Indigenous people saw the monarch as a source of redress for their treatment at the hands of settlers.⁷ As chapters in this collection demonstrate, Indigenous people appealed to the monarch during vice-regal and other ceremonial occasions, and they sent petitions, letters, and delegations. They asked the Crown to defend them against oppressive local governments, pointed out failures to meet obligations, and articulated their rights to land and resources. Colonial authorities helped to cultivate a familial relationship and the image of a nurturing and benevolent monarch. In New Zealand, missionaries and officials drew on Māori understandings of political relationships in their representations of the monarch and her subjects. Historian Lachy Paterson explains that Victoria was defined as matua (parent) to her Māori tamariki (children). Māori were encouraged to agree to the Treaty of Waitangi (1840) through 'assurances that it was proof of the Queen's love for them, and of her desire for a close relationship with Māori'.⁸ In Australia, colonial authorities also encouraged loyalty to the monarch, and according to historian Ann Curthoys, 'This strategy had an unintended consequence: over time, Indigenous people began to see the Queen as an alternative source of authority, as someone who could help them in their battle with settler governments and peoples, especially in their quest for the return of their land'.⁹ Appeals to Victoria have been interpreted by Elizabeth Burrows as 'strategic political and communicative resistance strategies' in Van Diemen's Land.¹⁰ In Tahiti, Australia, and New Zealand according to Tracey Banivanua Mar, Indigenous people 'attempted to reach beyond local colonial circumstances to an external, higher, or universal authority such as the Crown ... to adjudicate the partisan bias of colonial concerns'.¹¹ Many Africans, writes John Lonsdale, saw Victoria as 'not only a Queen but a Mother', and they appealed to royal justice to defend them against local colonial oppressions.[12]

While there were commonalities in the deployment of images and symbols of Queen Victoria across settler colonies as Indigenous people sought to transcend local colonial authorities, there were also variations and distinct usages because of diverse histories and diverse colonial entanglements and deeply local concerns. Burrows and Banivanua Mar see appeals to Victoria (that often took the form of letters or petitions) as evidence of Indigenous people adopting imperial languages and traditions, and of a growing literacy and knowledge of colonial communication practices. While this is the case in the Canadian context, the British too had to adapt. They learned to adopt Indigenous diplomatic and familial languages and traditions from the time of the Conquest of 1760. The result was a hybrid dialogue that was dynamic, relational, and engaged, involving many voices and perspectives, conforming to Mikhail Bahktin's notion of the dialogic in which there is 'constant interaction between meanings, all of which have the potential of conditioning others'.[13]

This dialogue is fraught with interpretive challenges, and it is impossible to glean a 'true' meaning not only of what was said, but what was understood. The records that survive of these were translations, and often poor translations. There might be a common use of terms such as the 'Queen', but there were very different meanings attached. Records of speeches and dialogues were used by authorities to grandstand loyalty and awe for the monarch, and were exaggerated and hyperbolic. Supposed proclamations of reverence and awe served a host of purposes. Did for example, 'Little Pine', a 'Christian Chippewa Chief' of Ontario, state as claimed in an 1872 publication that 'we Indians know our Great Mother, the Queen of the English nation is strong, and we cannot keep back her power, any more than we can stop the rising sun. She is strong ... but my people are weak'?[14] Oral histories do not provide a 'corrective' to these fraught documentary sources, but they shed light on Indigenous understandings today, and point to the persistence of narrative memories of the Queen's bounty and promises.

References to Queen Victoria in contact zone encounters throughout her reign and beyond were a shared phenomenon across the British colonies of North America, and the territory that became Canada. This is remarkable considering the vast distances and diverse Indigenous people and languages. In 1841 (and for decades after) various Mi'kmaq communities of Nova Scotia petitioned Queen Victoria, expressing their sense of betrayal that treaties had been violated by the British, and that they had lost their land and livelihood.[15] The chief who signed the 1841 petition sent wampum and 'paper talk to tell the Queen I am in trouble. My people are in trouble'.[16] They had no hunting grounds, no clothing, and no timber. They received no answers to these petitions, but were continually assured by the British that the Queen was devoted to their welfare. In 1846 an assembly of chiefs and principal men of Canada West (Ontario) were told that 'your Great Mother, the Queen' was giving directions to the Indian Department for their future, and she wanted them to be 'religious, industrious and happy'.[17] The British were reminded of these assurances when treaty promises were reneged and when settlers invaded without treaties. In 1849 the Chippewa of Lake Huron objected to miners on their land, who were desecrating even their graves. Governor General Lord Elgin was asked: 'Was it for this that we voluntarily became the children of our great mother the Queen?'[18] In 1854 the Six Nations of the Iroquois sent an address to the 'Great Mother' 'as faithful and active allies of your Crown', offering their services in the war in the Crimea, noting that 'the ancestors of your red children never failed to assist in the battles of your illustrious ancestors'.[19] In 1860 the Anishinabe woman Nahnebahnwequay visited Queen Victoria about land rights and reported home that 'the Queen bowed to me and said, "I am happy to promise you my aid and protection"'.[20]

The people of the Northwest Coast were also lectured to and themselves drew on symbols and images of the Queen, despite the fact that there were no treaties made with the vast majority of them. In the later 1870s the Nlaka'pamux attempted to cultivate an alliance with the Queen to resolve the land question and to help them retain self-government.[21] In 1882 a British Columbia chief told the land commissioner that his people no longer had access to fish and timber and that 'we know the Queen does not want us to die, you told us, and others have told us she is good, then we [want] her to help us as her children, and we will be good too like her'.[22]

While these encounters and appeals to the Queen share characteristics they emerged from very different contexts across time and space. A focus on the Saulteaux (Plains Ojibway or Anishinabe) of the Red River settlement provides deep understanding of one context, through a range of 'contact zones' over many decades when both colonisers and colonised drew on and manipulated representations of Queen Victoria.[23] The Saulteaux were at the 'coalface' of the waves of colonisation as they occupied what was to become the 'gateway to the West'. They contended with traders, missionaries, soldiers, government authorities, settlers, treaties, reserves, and railways. They adapted quickly to changing circumstances and were trappers and boatmen during the fur trade as well as fishers and farmers, and by the end of the nineteenth century they were the most prosperous and successful Indigenous farmers of the West at their St. Peter's reserve. But their reserve was coveted by settlers and investors, because it was prime agricultural land but also because initially it was to be on the route of the transcontinental railway (although it was later rerouted). By the end of Victoria's reign, pressure mounted to remove them from their valuable land, leading to the fraudulent 'surrender' of their reserve in 1907.

Through a focus on the imagery deployed by both sides in some of these encounters or dialogues over the many years of Victoria's rule, this study stresses how both First Nations and British/Canadians found it advantageous and pragmatic to stress the monarch's feminine and maternal qualities. An image of Victoria as a nurturing, compassionate, tender, watchful, and devoted mother, 'full of love and generosity', was crafted and frequently pressed into service by both sides.[24] These were images and symbols that were widely promoted to generate the loyalty of all Victoria's far-flung colonies and subjects. The British Empire was configured as a family with the Queen as mother, resident in the 'Mother Country', and the colonies her children. As historian Dorothy Thompson has argued, the Queen served different ruling ideologies during her long reign.[25] Initially she was a youthful, pure, and revitalising force in contrast to her corrupt uncles, and in her later years she was mother of the country and Empire. Victoria was a potent feminine icon to which multiple meanings were assigned.[26]

Chief Peguis was the leader of the Saulteaux of Red River until his death in 1864, and he was a skilled orator. In records of his speeches and addresses, he incorporated and manipulated images of the monarch, initially the 'Great Father'.[27] While Peguis used the term 'Great Father', it is clear that at times he referred not to the British sovereign, but to the Creator, the Great Spirit, or 'our Great Father', to whom the land belonged. In this way he pointed out the presumption of any mortal person, including the King, to claim to own the land, and the presumption of any person to claim to be the 'Father of us all'. In an 1815 speech that Peguis gave to Hudson's Bay Company officials, he laid out a belief system that placed the British King beneath the Great Spirit, contesting and challenging British claims of superiority and land ownership.[28] The land, Peguis said, did not belong to the British, and 'are not my Lands – they belong to our Great Father, for it is he only that gives us the means of existence, for what would become of us if he left us to ourselves – we would wither like the Grass in Plains was the Sun to withdraw its animating beams'.

Peguis and other and later Indigenous speakers did not depict the monarch as an omnipotent and omniscient being, although it was often important to exaggerate her power, knowledge, and compassion as a rhetorical tool. References to the monarch were generally accompanied by references to the Great Spirit or the Creator, and the monarch's abilities and powers, and respect due to her, paled in comparison. In response to the persistent claim by the British that the land was the Queen's even in advance or in the absence of treaties, many Aboriginal orators, like Peguis, insisted that the land belonged not to the British monarch, or to them, but to the Great Spirit.[29] (On the West Coast a chief informed a land commissioner in 1882 that 'the Queen did not put us here – God put us here'.[30]) As historian Neil Parsons has written about South Africa, 'The idea of the Great (White) Queen or Great (White) Mother as invested with "a sort of mysterious reverence" was one that was assiduously propagated by and exploited by British imperialists'.[31] It was the British who insisted that she was 'the Queen who was more than mortal', that 'only transcendent virtue could have wielded such a beneficent influence over alien and savage peoples so remote, so dissimilar, and so numerous'.[32]

References to the British monarch were reserved for occasions when Indigenous people were in dialogue with non-Indigenous people, otherwise the concept or device had no utility or power. For example when the Saulteaux met the Dakota at Fort Garry in 1860 to conclude a treaty between them, there was no mention of the British monarch in the record of the speeches made on that occasion, and there were many celebrated orators present.[33] Several of the visiting Dakota, however, wore George III medals (awarded after the War of 1812), and it was noted in *The Nor'Wester* that 'the Sioux cherish a warm friendship for the English whom they denominate "Saginosh"'.

An image of a just and caring monarch was also introduced in Saulteaux, Cree, and Assiniboine territory through the 1817 treaty made with Thomas Douglas, the fifth Earl of Selkirk, that permitted Scottish settlers to settle and farm. The agreement was with the 'Sovereign, Lord, King George the Third'.[34] Missionaries arrived the year after this treaty, and they too conveyed messages of a benevolent and watchful monarch. The Saulteaux would have been aware that Victoria had replaced her uncle on the throne in 1837 through Hudson's Bay Company (HBC) and missionary contacts. The Anglican Church Missionary Society (CMS), active at Red River and among the Saulteaux, promoted dutiful respect for the Queen, their 'Great Mother', who protected the Church.[35] Missionaries claimed that their converts prayed for 'their "Great Mother," their Sovereign Lady over the Waters'.[36] A significant number of Anishinabe visited the Queen, and knowledge of her would have been circulated and shared.[37] Peter Jacobs, an Ontario-born Anishinabe, was a Methodist catechist, and he worked in Manitoba. He visited England from 1842 to 1851 and on his return to mission work spoke about the 'Great Female Chief' with whom he met at least twice.[38] Jacobs received from Her Majesty a magnificent robe and a framed portrait of herself.[39]

Although Peguis initially had a stormy relationship with the CMS who established themselves in his 'Indian settlement' (later St. Peter's parish) on the Red River in 1833, by the late 1830s, he had reasons to seek an alliance with the CMS and agreed to baptism.[40] He used the occasion of his baptism in 1838, however, to assert his equality with royalty across the sea. He took the name William King, and his wife, who was baptised two years later, took the name 'Victoria'. His sons when baptised took the surname 'Prince'. Thereafter Peguis and family were featured in missionary publications as exemplars of intense loyalty to the Church and the Queen, and as supporters of British civilisation and colonisation. In an 1845 publication about a visit to Red River of the Bishop of Montreal, a letter from Henry Prince, acting for his father, was quoted. It praised the missionaries as 'if they had not pitied us, we should have been still Heathens'.[41] It concluded: 'We pray every day for our great Mother, The Lady Chief, Victoria, and for her relations, and also for our Chief Praying Fathers, and our Praying Fathers'. With these and other records of the words of Indigenous people, it is dangerous to assume that they are their unadulterated, unmediated words. In the case of Peguis and the Saulteaux, however, it is clear that they took advantage of many opportunities to declare their fealty to the Crown, and they had good reasons to do so. By the mid-nineteenth century, Peguis was calling upon the 'Great Mother' to protect his people from injustice and oppression, and his sons in later decades also deployed the image of a maternal figure who would not let her children be mistreated.

Despite his conversion and his celebrated loyalty and devotion to the monarch, Peguis became a sharp critic of the expansion of colonisation at Red River without consultation and permission. Peguis insisted that he had never 'sold' land to the HBC or to Selkirk, and protested that 'the said Company mark out and sell our lands without our permission'.[42] In 1857 Peguis became involved with the Aborigines Protection Society (APS), and a lengthy oration attributed to him was published in *The Colonial Intelligencer or Aborigine's Friend*. It was likely composed with the help and encouragement of Alexander K. Isbister,[43] a critic of the HBC who was involved with the APS. An image of Victoria as a just and compassionate monarch was marshalled: 'We hope our Great Mother will not allow us to be treated so unjustly, as to allow our lands to be taken from us in this way'. The letter continued that Peguis hoped that 'the Great Mother will ... not only protect us from oppression and injustice, but grant us all the privileges of the whites'.[44] His letter concluded by asking the APS to take action: 'Will you, then, use the proper means of bringing before the great Council of the nation [Parliament] and through it to our Great Mother [the Queen], who will shew herself more truly great and good by protecting the helpless from injustice and oppression than by making great conquests'. But Peguis's final words, 'wishing that the Great Spirit may give you every good thing', called on a greater power than the Queen. In a second letter published two years later Peguis concluded by asking that 'the Great Mother ... take us all under her own protection'.[45]

The 1860s was a time of uncertainty and turmoil at Red River: confederation was debated throughout that decade, and then created in 1867, and the plan was to acquire the West from the HBC, but First Nations and the Metis were not consulted about any of these monumental changes. In 1867 a letter or petition written 'in the Indian language' to Edward, the Prince of Wales from the Aboriginal people (likely the Saulteaux) of the Red River settlement was on display at Fort Garry.[46] It was reported to be a unique, remarkable document, written in red, white, and blue ink, on birch bark, and bordered with gilt. It asked the Prince to visit them: the Prince had visited Eastern Canada in 1860 and had been greeted by many Indigenous nations who used the occasions to reaffirm their allegiance to the Crown, and to draw attention to the legal, economic, and political inequalities they faced.[47] The invitation was addressed 'To the first born of our Great Mother, across the great water. Great Chief whom we call Royal Chief'.[48] It stated that should the Prince visit he would be free to hunt buffalo on their land (which likely would have appealed to 'Bertie'), and that he would be guarded and attended to. The old men would show him their medals, 'which they received for being faithful to the father of our great mother'. It was not made clear, however, why the Prince was being invited. The invitation received a reply from the Prince who asked Governor General Buckingham to 'communicate to the chiefs his satisfaction on receiving their address', and to say that he was unable to visit 'but it would have been gratifying to his Royal Highness to comply with the invitation of the chiefs'.[49]

From the time of Chief Peguis, the Red River Saulteaux strategically demonstrated and performed their Britishness and 'loyalty' to the monarch. As mentioned, Peguis was on good terms with the HBC (initially), and had assisted the Scottish Selkirk settlers who arrived in 1812. In 1869–70 Chief Henry Prince did not side with the Métis in the resistance. However, Prince used the occasion of an 1869 meeting with a military official to say that while the 'rebels' were living in plenty on what they had robbed from the Queen, 'the faithful children of the Great Mother are starving and very poor'.[50] He warmly welcomed the troops under the command of Colonel Garnet Wolseley in 1870 and sent St. Peter's men to assist the 'loyal party'. The Princes further demonstrated their loyalty in 1884 when Chief William Prince and a group of thirty St. Peter's voyageurs accompanied Colonel Wolseley up the Nile for the rescue of General Charles Gordon at Khartoum.[51] This was described in an English journal of the late nineteenth century as 'surely the strangest contact between East and West that the world has ever seen'.[52]

Treaty negotiations were occasions when references to Victoria as a fond and caring mother figure flourished. The influence of and pressure from outsiders in crafting an image of a benevolent maternal monarch figure in Saulteaux oratory must be acknowledged, but they also attached their own social and cultural meanings. Among the Anishinabe, all family members were obliged to care for each other, and relatives included not just the nuclear family but those who shared the same clan, or dodem.[53] They were addressed as 'brother' or 'sister' and obligations extended to them. The Anishinabe projected family metaphors onto a multitude of situations, and a parent–child idiom was 'the function of a particular type of diplomatic contact with European governments'.[54] Anthropologist Bruce M. White found a rich tradition of Anishinabe orators asking Europeans for milk, the first food that nurtured and sustained an infant, and that was infused with symbolic meaning. White wrote: 'Milk is the first gift that a child receives when he is born ... It is the quintessence of all gifts that a parent gives to a child, because it flows freely from the mother to the infant and is given with absolutely no thought of a return gift. The obvious exchange for mother's milk is the loyalty of child to parent, perhaps, one of the strongest manifestations of kinship'.[55]

Recent oral histories with Saulteaux and other First Nations of Western Canada indicate how central the image of Victoria as a tender and watchful mother was to the treaty relationship that they forged. Treaties were understood to have created an irrevocable, perpetual familial relationship with the British Crown, based on concepts, principles, and laws defined in Cree as wahkohtowin (good relationships).[56] The Queen is understood to have adopted the First Nations as her children through the treaties. Conduct between a mother and child is characterised by mutual respect and reciprocal duties of nurturing, caring, loyalty, and fidelity. According to one Cree Elder, the 'Queen came to offer a traditional adoption of us as our mother. "You will be my children", she had said'.[57] Another stated that Commissioner David Laird told them that 'the Great Mother, the Queen [would] hold you in the palm of her hand and protect you and look after you just like a child. In other words, the great Mother would become your mother, since you are accepting the treaty'.[58] Yet ultimately the promises made by First

THE FAITHFUL CHILDREN OF THE GREAT MOTHER ARE STARVING

Nations were not to the Queen, but to the Creator, the Great Spirit, that that they would conduct themselves in accordance with the laws, values, and principles give to them by the Creator.[59]

At treaty negotiations of the 1870s there were few examples of complete agreement or common ground, but there was substantial accord and compatibility on the projection of Victoria as a compassionate and caring mother to her Indigenous children. First Nations of the West understood, and were told by treaty commissioners, that their treaties were with the British Crown and specifically with the Queen. Treaty commissioners stated that they were acting under the detailed instructions of the Great Mother, and that they were her 'red children'. At Treaty 1 in 1871 Lieutenant Governor Adams Archibald opened the proceedings with a profusion of references to the Great Mother, the Queen. The message was clear that it was *her* treaty, that *she* was directly involved in the planning and promises to be made and had given direct and explicit instructions to the commissioners. They would be treated with fairness, compassion, benevolence, as a mother cared for her children. Archibald pronounced that 'Your Great Mother wishes the good of all races under her sway. She wishes her Red Children, as well as her White people, to be happy and contented. She wishes them to live in comfort'.[60] Archibald said that when they heard the Queen's representative speak: 'you are listening to your Great Mother the Queen, whom God bless and preserve long to reign over us'.[61]

The symbolic language used by the treaty commissioners would have confirmed and corroborated kinship ties. Treaty commissioners stressed the equality of the treaty partners with expressions such as, 'We are all children of the same Great Spirit, and are subject to the same Queen'. They said that the Queen 'wished to place her red subjects on the same footing as the whites.'[62] As the authors of *Bounty and Benevolence* have argued: 'such metaphors might not have been regarded as Eurocentric paternalism in 1871; rather, with such symbolic language, the Queen's representative assured the Indians that a treaty would create an enduring relationship with the Crown'.[63]

The Saulteaux and other First Nations negotiators of Treaty 1 sought ways to guarantee their sovereignty, a future livelihood, and protection against economic hardship, and they too made extensive references to the Queen, drawing on well-established rhetorical strategies and kinship terms that functioned as diplomatic devices. As 'Sheship' said on the first day: 'I am thankful today that I have heard a message from our Great Mother, the Queen ... I am glad I have heard good tidings from my mother; and if I live till tomorrow, I will send a requisition to her, begging her to grant me wherewith to make my living'.[64] And these were not token or subservient designations. Native American people 'conceptualize kinship in terms of sharing, generosity and nurturance'.⁶⁵ The ideal symbol of the concept of kinship was the relationship of an individual with his or her mother with whom the strongest bond exists. Treaty commissioners were addressed as brothers, emphasising their equality, and in Plains societies, one could not refuse anything to a brother without giving offence. A tactic was used of establishing a common humanity and equivalence with their treaty partners.

At later treaty negotiations, Saulteaux spokesmen made extensive references to the concept of a caring and nurturing mother: Victoria. At Treaty 4 in 1874 the Saulteaux leader Kanooses asked, 'Is it true that you are bringing the Queen's kindness? Is it true you are bringing the Queen's messenger's kindness? Is it true you are going to give my child what he may use? Is it true you are going to give the different bands the Queen's kindness? Is it true that you bring the Queen's hand? Is it true you are bringing the Queen's power? ... Is it true that my child will not be troubled for what you are bringing him?' Commissioner Alexander Morris assured them that the Queen was their mother and cared for them: 'It is good for the Indians to make treaties with the Queen – good for them and their wives and children. Game is getting scarce and the Queen is willing to help her children'.⁶⁶

First Nations were not beguiled or bamboozled by talk of the Great Mother at treaty talks. For both sides, the Queen as mother was a diplomatic device. Treaty commissioners were not prepared for the nature and intensity of First Nations bargaining as they called on the Queen to shelter, protect, and care for them as a mother would. Arriving with the initial offer of small reserves and annuities, the treaty commissioners ultimately had to deliver much more.⁶⁷ First Nations insisted that reserves and annuities were not adequate for future needs; they demanded more land as reserves, larger annuities, agricultural implements and cattle, teachers and schools, housing, buggies, hunting equipment, and freedom from taxes.

Henry Prince or 'Red Eagle' (Mis-koo-kenew) (1819–99), son of Peguis, was a main negotiator of Treaty 1 and principal chief of the region. Prince made numerous references to the Queen, and in his speech on the fifth day 'expressed strong attachment to the British flag'. He bargained for better terms through his references such as 'it is said, the Queen wishes the Indians to cultivate the ground. They cannot scratch it – work it with their fingers. What assistance will they get if they settle down?'⁶⁸ The medals he wore are likely those that commemorated Treaty 1 and the Selkirk Treaty (Figure 3.1).

Some non-Indigenous observers at Treaty 1 were convinced that declarations of fealty or loyalty to the Queen were little more than tongue-in-cheek rhetorical devices. Robert Cunningham, journalist

Figure 3.1 Henry Prince (Mis-koo-kenew/Red Eagle), a son of Chief Peguis, was a negotiator of Treaty 1, Chief of the St. Peter's Band, and a renowned orator.

and politician, stated in the House of Commons in 1873 that 'when one looked at the tear that twinkled in the eyes of these Indians when the great mother question was brought up, he could not help coming to the conclusion that it was all a farce'.[69] Cunningham was concerned however that there was profound dissatisfaction with the 'niggardly spirit' of Canada in complying with the terms of the treaties. Another member of Parliament from Manitoba, Dr John Christian Schultz, stated in the House of Commons in 1873 that there was widespread anger with the non-implementation of treaty promises, and he warned that a keen sense of loyalty to the Queen and Crown was a 'stereotyped opinion' that prevailed in Eastern Canada, and was not as deep and reverential as supposed, and would not prevent or preclude violence.[70] He was not convinced that the George III medals that they displayed were 'proof of their hereditary loyalty to the crown, and an argument against the possibility of difficulties' as so often claimed. Schultz warned his colleagues against placing too much reliance on that which is at best but a very intangible idea of the relations between the crown and themselves, and that whenever they are convinced that they have been unfairly dealt with, or as they themselves would express it, 'the face of "Okemaqua," their great mother, has been hid from them,' that the feeling of injustice will produce the same results north of the 49th parallel, as they have to the south, notwithstanding the sentiment of loyalty to the British Queen which undoubtedly exists.

As Cunningham and Schultz made clear, the Saulteaux were far from contented in the years after their treaties. The Peguis people, now residents of St. Peter's reserve (surveyed as reserve number one in 1873), were particularly vocal and active, led by Henry Prince and his brothers. And while some of this was resolved through the 1875 recognition of the validity of the oral or 'outside' promises made in 1871, discontent remained. Prince wrote letters and petitions, and had meetings with government officials and politicians.[71] References to the Queen in petitions and oratory were reserved for vice-regal visits. These were not, at least in the early post-treaty decades, staged and scripted events. In fact, Department of Indian Affairs (DIA) officials tried to discourage them, and eventually did succeed in containing and controlling them. For First Nations, these visits affirmed and renewed the treaty relationship. They featured Indigenous diplomacy, protocols, and ceremonies as in the treaty negotiations. These visits were also opportunities to remind their treaty partner of obligations and commitments that were not being honoured.

1877 was the first vice-regal visit to the West when Lord and Lady Dufferin travelled to Manitoba. Their visit established a pattern that was to prevail in subsequent tours until about 1900. Governors general were honoured and welcomed with Indigenous ceremonies, presents were exchanged, mutual expressions of loyalty were made, and Indigenous leaders spoke of the promises not kept and their inability to make a living with the land and resources they retained. In August 1877 the Dufferins attended a gathering at St. Peter's Reserve where they were honoured with displays of ceremony, music, dancing, and oratory. Chief Joseph Prince was attended by two standard bearers, one carrying the British flag. In his address to the Dufferins, which they were assured was written by the Indians themselves, Prince said that

> we present to you our homage and loyalty, and the unalterable attachment of our race to the Great Mother ... as we point to the centre of heaven, the seat of the Great Spirit, we offer our united voice of thanksgiving for safely conducting you ... As we present the stem and pipe of peace to your Lordship, we point also to the rising sun – towards the

throne of our Great Mother, as the emblem of our devotedness to the Queen's sacred person.[72]

Yet the main point made by Prince was that there was profound discontent. He said that he hoped the visit would be a 'harbinger of peace and tranquility throughout this land so that the evil spirit of discontent may be ever eradicated from the minds of your red subjects, as mist clears from the atmosphere and we behold a serene sky, and, through your great influence on behalf of our races, we may hereafter enjoy a confidence and security under the care of your rule'. He said that his people had 'confidence in our Great Mother's power and goodness that under your Excellency's administration tranquility and happiness will reign through the land'. Prince stressed that his people had helped to defend the Red River settlement from the Dakota 'before our Great Mother came her with her flag'.

Dufferin's address in reply contained many reassurances of Victoria's personal interest in their welfare, that 'your Great Mother has often written to me to inquire about you, and before I took this journey expressly commanded me to tell you that she loves you'. Despite these warm assurances, Prince spoke once again, and in the same vein. According to a reporter he 'then sought to improve the occasion by ventilating certain grievances. He said that they would have been able to show his Excellency still finer crops had the Indians possessed sufficient agricultural implements to till their land with; ... and brought up several other matters. His Excellency remained listening to an apparently inexhaustible speech with exemplary patience'. When Dufferin replied that he would raise these issues with the government, the St. Peter's people were displeased, stating that they 'wished to obtain categorical replies then and there'. Dufferin insisted however that he could not act without the advice of his councillors. The visit concluded with a tour of the school on the reserve where 'conspicuous at the head of the room were framed portraits of the Queen and of the late Prince Consort'.

It is difficult to know whether press accounts of meetings with and speeches of First Nations are reliable. In seems likely however that the descriptions of the speeches at Dufferin's meeting at St. Peter's are reasonably accurate, despite the reporter's sometimes condescending or mocking tone. The particulars of the meeting between Dufferin and the St. Peter's Saulteaux were excised from the official published account of his visit west, in order to create the impression that all was well, and that 'the extinction of the Indian title upon liberal terms' was carried out with 'tact, discretion and ability'.[73] In the official account it was noted only that 'a very large number of Indians were assembled at St. Peter's and his Excellency made them a speech in which he addressed them as the children of the Queen'.[74] There was no mention of the speeches made by the St. Peter's people, except an oblique and dismissive reference in his closing speech to the 'citizens' of Winnipeg at a banquet where Dufferin said that on the reserves he visited he heard 'a few petty grievances of a local character they thought themselves justified in proffering', but on the whole found them 'contented and satisfied ... implicitly confiding in the good faith and paternal solicitude of the Government'.[75] The 'petty grievances' were dismissed and ignored, bolstering the narrative of the unwavering loyalty of the Queen's 'red children', while erasing their criticism of and challenge to this narrative.

The Princes continued in the tradition of their father and grandfather Peguis to call on the compassion of Victoria, casting her as a watchful, nurturing, and protective mother. In 1882, concerned about the flooding on their reserve, Councillor John Prince spoke to the Inspector of Indian Agencies for his people: 'My fellow being. We call you brothers for we are all children of the Great Mother. We look to you today to use your mouth on our behalf to the Chief Councillor at Ottawa, who attends to our affairs. The Queen gave us a new Chief, [the prime minister?] and we look to her to uphold him in his position while he does what is right'.[76]

In the summer and fall of 1881, Canada's Governor General the Marquis of Lorne embarked on a tour of Western Canada that covered over 8,000 miles and involved many meetings, audiences, or 'pow-wows' with First Nations people. These were not staged and scripted audiences. He arrived at a time of acute desperation, starvation, and disease among the Plains people (although he said nothing of this in his glowing reports on the land and its resources). Lorne did not visit St. Peter's although he was in Winnipeg, and was invited by Chief Henry Prince and his councillors, who sent His Excellency a letter stating that they thought 'a great deal of our Great Mother the Queen, and we were holding her Flag since we were born'.[77] If Lorne hoped to avoid a community where he might be presented evidence of discontent among Victoria's 'children', he was mistaken as he was confronted with this almost everywhere he travelled. He was informed that people were starving, that they could not make a living by the treaties, that the treaty terms were inadequate or unfulfilled, and they were unable to farm with the lack of assistance and implements.[78] First Nations called on their treaty partner, the Crown, in the person of the Governor General (addressed as 'brother'), who was also the son-in-law of the Queen, to live up to their obligations to nurture and cherish them as a mother would. Instead they were being neglected, deprived, and starved.

There were over 4,000 Cree, Saulteaux, and Assiniboine assembled at Fort Qu'Appelle for example, where their main speaker was

Figure 3.2 Chief Crowfoot addressing the Marquis of Lorne at Blackfoot Crossing (Alberta) September 1881. (Drawing by Sydney Hall) Crowfoot said they were hungry, and could not survive on their rations. He held up a teacup to demonstrate the small amount they were given daily.

Saulteaux headman Louis O'Soup. He spoke of their lack of food, clothing, and implements. He concluded: 'Now let us settle things we may not see each other put all our complaints to right for we may not be alive. The Queen will be glad if you do … the Queen will be sorry to hear if she learns we all died'.[79] At this gathering, speaker Pahsung referred to the Queen as the 'Mistress of Everything' (Figure 3.2).

Following the Metis resistance of 1885 that was met with an overwhelming military force intended to subdue all of the Indigenous people of the West, delegations of 'loyal' leaders were sent to Ottawa, in the hope that they could return with descriptions of the technological, military, and political might they encountered. Louis O'Soup was among these but was not silenced and overawed. When asked by a reporter about the loyalty of his people to the Queen, he replied that they 'would never take the warpath against the Great Mother. How many times have I said this? Why am I asked again? I speak the truth'.[80] Yet he also took the same occasion, 'with many forcible gestures', to speak of their want of implements and oxen and state that they were treated unfairly. He complained that the Treaty 7 people were treated better, that 'we are not so well treated. The Blackfeet are the worst children the Queen has, and we are good and loyal'.[81]

In 1901 the St. Peter's people attempted (unsuccessfully) to prevent pressure to rob them of their valuable reserve and throw it open for non-Indigenous settlement by reminding settlers of the solemn promises made to them by the Queen and calling on the King to honour those promises. In a 1901 letter to *The Selkirk Expositor*, acting Chief David Prince wrote that their treaty was made with 'our great mother the Queen', that their reserve was 'to stand forever', that 'we want no person or persons to interfere for our reserve as it was only a piece of land that we have kept for our childrens for the use of the lifetime, and if any body says that the Indians wants to be removed to the other place, tis not true that we will not have a least idea to give up our reserve', that they would 'have to call upon our great Father the King his power in accordance of our bargain', and that 'the public must know that we will not be consent give up our reserve, and if the Government consent to break our reserve that the treaty will have to break, then we will demand our country to come back to us again'.[82] Facing settler pressure and with a federal government that actively promoted reserve land surrender, the St. Peter's people were powerless. Their reserve was erased from the landscape, and the people unwillingly relocated.

Yet the St. Peter's people did not give up, and well into the twentieth century continued to call on the honour of the agreement made with the 'Great Mother'. In 1917 Chief John Prince wrote to the superintendent general of Indian Affairs reminding him of the treaty promise that they could not be conscripted to fight, stating that in 1871 they were told that 'our Great Mother Queen should never fight us in her war because I was told that time she wants to look upon us as a child'.[83] (Fifty St. Peter's/Peguis men volunteered and served in the First World War.)[84] In 1933 the Peguis Chief Alex Greyeyes sought redress for band members arrested for 'squatting' on their former reserve by invoking the 'Great Mother', or 'Grand-mère blanche', and in an audience with the member of Parliament for Selkirk he 'took from his pocket a copy of the treaty agreement of August 3, 1871 ... pointing to the words on which he said his band relied. Queen Victoria promised 160 acres of land, on which no white man might trespass, and promised if white men did so she would punish them herself'.[85] As Maria Nugent has demonstrated in her chapter in this collection, the figure of Queen Victoria has had a long afterlife in the narrative memories of Indigenous Australian people, passed down through generations as a female relative, a mother, provider, and symbol of justice, although the contexts have changed.

Expressions of loyalty to Victoria as the 'Great Mother' were generally accompanied by censure, indictment, and denunciation of broken promises and of the relationship that was supposed to assist them in the face of settler pressure to dispossess them of their land and resources. But these calls for justice were excised from the Canadian memory and narrative, while their declarations of loyalty were warmly remembered, leaving an impression that the Queen was in fact a compassionate, tender, and kind mother to 'her Indians'. Examples abound because Canada was fiercely determined to depict a wise and just regime in comparison to the United States.[86] Odes to the loyalty of the Indians to their Great Mother were found throughout travel, promotional, and missionary literature about and from Canada. In 1881, Conservative English politician Alexander Stavely Hill wrote in the conclusion to his book *From Home to Home: Autumn Wanderings in the North West* that in Western Canada,

> allegiance to their Sovereign Mistress has held full sway, and the Indian has learnt to love the great white Mother as the embodiment of that true justice and respect for right which can be found only under a stable and solid Government. Thus have they helped to bind us all together as England and her Colonies should ever be bound, and to maintain the spirit in which she and her children should ever be united, however great the distance from Home to Home.[87]

Through the authority of 'the "Great Mother," as they term our beloved Queen ... the Canadian Government has been enabled to make fair treaties, and retain the confidence, respect and goodwill of the Indians, a state of affairs in striking contrast with the difficulties experienced by the Americans in their dealings with the red men'.[88] According to a Red River merchant writing in 1884, the Queen was 'amongst the red men of the Canadian prairies ... reverenced in a manner that cannot but bring a throb of pride to every truly loyal British heart. The 'Great Mother' (for that is the name by which our Queen is known to the red man) is to him the personification of goodness, truth and power'.[89]

Nowhere in any of these comforting narratives is it mentioned that declarations of loyalty to Victoria were accompanied by sharp criticism and admonishment. If a recent campaign to have Canada's Victoria Day changed to 'Victoria and First Peoples Day' as a means of recognising and celebrating a venerable relationship is to reflect the traditions of the past, then this national holiday would also have to be a day when First Nations would be invited to call for the humane and fair treatment that still eludes them.[90]

Notes

1. Sarah Carter, '"Your Great Mother across the salt sea": Prairie First Nations, the British monarchy and the vice-regal connection to 1900', *Manitoba History*, 48 (Autumn 2004/Winter 2005), 42–5. On the term 'father' in Indigenous-French relations in Quebec, see Peter Cook, 'Onontio gives birth: How the French in Canada became fathers to their Indigenous allies, 1645–73', *The Canadian Historical Review*, 96:2 (2015), 165–93.
2. Wade Henry, 'Imagining the Great White Mother and the Great King: Aboriginal tradition and royal representation at the "Great Pow-wow" of 1901', *Journal of the Canadian Historical Association*, 11:1 (2000), 90.
3. Cole Harris, *Making Native Space: Colonialism, Resistance, and Reserves in British Columbia* (Vancouver: University of British Columbia Press, 2002), p. 155.
4. Keith Thor Carlson, 'Rethinking dialogue and history: The King's promise and the 1906 Aboriginal delegation to London', *Native Studies Review*, 16:2 (2005), 9.
5. See, for example, 'Pact with Great White Queen provides defense of Indians', *The Globe* (Toronto) (28 March 1925), p. 1; and 'Indians Air Grievances: May Appeal to London', *The Globe and Mail* (Toronto), (17 March 1949), p. 11.
6. Sarah Carter, 'Aboriginal people of Canada and the British Empire', in Phillip Buckner (ed.), *Canada and the British Empire* (Oxford: Oxford University Press, 2008); Henry, 'Imagining the Great White Mother', 87–108; Ruth Phillips, 'Making sense out/of the visual: Aboriginal presentations and representations in nineteenth-century Canada', *Art History*, 27:4 (September 2004), 593–615; Ian Radforth, 'Performance, politics, and representation: Aboriginal people and the 1860 royal tour of Canada', *The Canadian Historical Review*, 84:1 (March 2003), 1–32; Roger Talbot, *Negotiating the Numbered Treaties: An Intellectual and Political Biography of Alexander Morris* (Saskatoon: Purich Publishing Ltd., 2009); J. R. Miller, 'Victoria's "Red Children": The "Great White Mother" and native-newcomer relations in Canada', *Native Studies Review*, 17:1 (2008), 1–23.
7. Ann Curthoys, 'Indigenous subjects', in Deryck M. Schreuder and Stuart Ward (eds), *Australia's Empire* (Oxford: Oxford University Press, 2008), p. 94.
8. Lachy Paterson, *Colonial Discourses: Niupepa Māori 1855–1863* (Dunedin: Otago University Press, 2006), p. 56.
9. Curthoys, 'Indigenous subjects', 94. See also Maria Nugent, '"The Queen gave us the land": Aboriginal people, Queen Victoria and historical remembrance', *History Australia*, 9:2 (2012), 182–200; Jessie Mitchell, '"It will enlarge the ideas of the natives": Indigenous Australians and the tour of Prince Alfred, Duke of Edinburgh', *Aboriginal History*, 34 (2010), 196–216; Ann Curthoys and Jessie Mitchell, '"Bring this paper to the Good Governor": Aboriginal Petitioning in Britain's Australian Colonies', in Saliha Belmessous (ed.), *Native Claims: Indigenous Law Against Empire, 1500–1920* (New York: Oxford University Press, 2012), 182–204.
10. Elizabeth Burrows, 'Resisting oppression: The use of Aboriginal writing to influence public opinion and public policy in Van Diemen's Land from 1836–1847', *Media History*, 20:3 (2014), 221.
11. Tracey Banivanua Mar, 'Imperial literacy and Indigenous rights: Tracing transoceanic circuits of modern discourse', *Aboriginal History*, 37 (2013), 19.
12. John Lonsdale, 'Ornamental constitutionalism in Africa: Kenyatta and the two queens', *The Journal of Imperial and Commonwealth History*, 34:1 (March 2006), 88–90.
13. Mikhail Bakhtin, *The Dialogic Imagination: Four Essays*, ed. Michael Holquist, trans. Caryl Emerson and Michael Holquist (Austin: University of Texas Press, 1999), p. 426.
14. *Little Pine's Journal: The Appeal of a Christian Chippeway Chief on Behalf of His People* (Toronto: Copp Clark, 1872), p. 14.
15. William C. Wicken, *Mi'Kmaq Treaties on Trial* (Toronto: University of Toronto Press, 2002), p. 222.

16 Penny Patrone (ed.), *First People, First Voices* (Toronto: University of Toronto Press, 1983), p. 54.
17 *Minutes of the General Council of Indian Chiefs and Principal Men Held at Orillia, Lake Simcoe Narrows...* (Montreal: Canada Gazette Office, 1846), pp. 5, 9.
18 'The Chippewa Indians and the mining companies of Lake Huron', *The Morning Post* (London, England) (20 August 1849), p. 7.
19 'Canada', *The Royal Cornwall Gazette, Falmouth Packet and General Advertiser* (Truro, England) (21 July 1854), p. 2.
20 Quoted in Celia Haig-Brown, 'Seeking honest justice in a land of strangers: Nahnebahwequa's struggle for land', *Journal of Canadian Studies*, 36:4 (Winter 2002), 147. See also Donald B. Smith, *Mississauga Portraits: Ojibwe Voices from Nineteenth-Century Canada* (Toronto: University of Toronto Press, 2013): 68–97.
21 Harris, *Making Native Space*, pp. 154–5.
22 Quoted in *Ibid.*, p. 185.
23 Mary Louise Pratt, *Imperial Eyes: Studies in Travel Writing and Transculturation* (London: Routledge, 1992). Pratt defines contact zones as 'social spaces where disparate cultures meet, clash and grapple with each other', p. 4.
24 Alexander Morris, *The Treaties of Canada with the Indians of Manitoba and the North-West Territories* (Toronto: Belfords, Clarke and Co., Publishers, 1880), p. 104. These were the words of Treaty Commissioner Alexander Morris at the 1874 Treaty 4, or the Qu'Appelle Treaty, to the Saulteaux chief The Gambler.
25 Dorothy Thompson, *Queen Victoria: Gender and Power* (London: Virago, 1990).
26 Janet Marie Winston, 'Unsettling Images of Empire: How Twentieth Century Narratives Reimagine Queen Victoria' (PhD. dissertation, University of Iowa, 1998).
27 Carter, 'Your Great Mother', 36–7.
28 Hudson's Bay Company Archives (HBCA), 'Peguis' Search File (B235/a/3 fos. 28 – 28d). This speech was made at an assembly led by Peguis and Yellow Legs in June 1815. HBC surveyor Peter Fidler addressed the assembly in an effort to inspire loyalty to the HBC at a time of intense competition with the North West Company.
29 Morris, *The Treaties of Canada*, pp. 104–5. See also Harris, *Making Native Space*, p. 188.
30 Quoted in Harris, *Making Native Space*, p. 188.
31 Neil Parsons, *King Khama, Emperor Joe, and the Great White Queen: Victorian Britain through African Eyes* (Chicago, IL: University of Chicago Press, 2004), p. xvii.
32 C. de Thierry (Jessie Weston), 'Victoria as Empire Builder', *Review of Reviews* (March 1901), p. 259.
33 'An Indian Council: The Sioux at Fort Garry', *The Nor'Wester* (14 March 1860), p. 3.
34 Alexander Morris, *The Treaties of Canada with the Indians* (1880 rpt.: Toronto: Coles Publishing Co., 1979), 15.
35 Church Missionary Society, *An Historical Notice of the Formation of the Church Missionary Society's North-West America Mission and its Progress to August, 1848* (London: Seeleys, 1849), p. 54.
36 David Anderson, *Church of England, Diocese of Rupert's Land* (London: Hatchard and Co., 1864), p. 62.
37 Charles Stuart, *A Short History and Description of the Ojibbeway Indians Now on a Visit to England* (London: 1844); Kate Flint, *Transatlantic Indians: 1776–1930* (Princeton, NJ: Princeton University Press, 2009), pp. 220–5.
38 Flint, *Transatlantic Indians*, p. 222.
39 John Maclean, *Henry B. Steinhauer: His Work Among the Cree Indians of the Western Plains* (Toronto: Methodist Young People's Forward Movement for Missions, 1907), p. 10.
40 Carolyn Podruchny, '"I have embraced the white man's religion": The relations between the Peguis Band and the Church Missionary Society, 1820–1838', in David H. Pentland (ed.), *Papers of the 26th Algonquian Conference* (Winnipeg: Algonquian Conference, 1996), p. 376.

41 George J. Mountain, *The Journal of the Bishop of Montreal, During a Visit to the Church Missionary Society's North-West America Mission* (London: Seeley, Burnside and Seeley, 1845), p. 180.
42 *Nor'Wester* (14 February 1860), p. 3.
43 See Harold C. Knox, 'Alexander Kennedy Isbister', *Manitoba Historical Society Transactions Series* 3 (1955–6), available at www.mhs.mb.ca/docs/transactions/3/isbister_ak.shtml, accessed 20 January 2016. See also Adele Perry, 'Designing dispossession: The Select Committee on The Hudson's Bay Company, fur-trade governance, Indigenous peoples and settler possibility', in Zoe Laidlaw and Alan Lester (eds), *Indigenous Communities and Settler Colonialism: Land Holding, Loss and Survival in an Interconnected World* (Basingstoke: Palgrave Macmillan, 2015), pp. 158–172.
44 Quoted in Donna G. Sutherland, *Peguis: A Noble Friend* (Winnipeg: Derksen Printers, 2003), pp. 140–1.
45 Quoted in *Ibid.*, p. 143.
46 *British Daily Colonist* (Victoria, BC) (22 May 1867), p. 2. Whether the letter was ever sent is not clear.
47 Radforth, 'Performance, politics, and representation'.
48 *British Daily Colonist* (22 May 1867), p. 2.
49 *Ibid.*, 5 October 1867.
50 W. R. Butler, *The Great Lone Land: A Narrative of Travel and Adventure in the North-West of America* (London: S. Low, Marston, Low and Searle, 1872), p. 127.
51 Anthony P. Michel, 'To represent the country in Egypt: Aboriginality, Britishness, Anglophone Canadian identities, and the Nile Voyageur Contingent, 1884–5', *Social History/ Histoire Sociale*, 39:7 (2006), 45–77.
52 'A.W.', 'The problem of the American Indian', *The Speaker: The Liberal Review* (16 July 1898), p. 76.
53 Bruce M. White, '"Give us a little milk": The social and cultural meanings of gift giving in the Lake Superior fur trade', *Minnesota History*, 48:2 (Summer 1982), 61.
54 *Ibid.*, 65.
55 *Ibid.*, 67.
56 Harold Cardinal and Walter Hildebrandt, *Treaty Elders of Saskatchewan: Our Dream is That Our Peoples Will One Day Be Clearly Recognized as Nations* (Calgary: University of Calgary Press, 2000), p. 34.
57 *Ibid.*, p. 33.
58 Pat Weaselhead (Blackfoot), Interview 2, 'Statement on Treaty 7', Hinton, Alberta, 5 March 1976, available at University of Regina oURspace, http://ourspace.uregina.ca:8080/xmlui/handle/10294/640, accessed 20 January 2016.
59 Cardinal and Hildebrandt, *Treaty Elders of Saskatchewan*, p. 7.
60 Morris, *The Treaties of Canada*, p. 28.
61 *Ibid.*, p. 30.
62 'The Chippewa Treaty', from *The Manitoban* (5 and 12 August 1871), appendix to D. J. Hall, '"A serene atmosphere"? Treaty 1 revisited', *The Canadian Journal of Native Studies*, 4:2 (1984), 349.
63 Arthur J. Ray, Jim Miller, and Frank Tough, *Bounty and Benevolence: A History of Saskatchewan Treaties* (Montreal: McGill-Queen's University Press, 2000), p. 66.
64 'The Chippewa Treaty', appendix to Hall, 'A serene atmosphere'?, p. 342.
65 Raymond J. DeMallie, 'Kinship: The foundation for Native American society', in Russell Thornton (ed.), *Studying Native American Problems and Prospects* (Madison: University of Wisconsin Press, 1998), p. 329.
66 Morris, *The Treaties of Canada*, p. 124.
67 Ray *et al.*, *Bounty and Benevolence*, p. 72.
68 'The Chippewa Treaty', appendix to Hall, p. 354.
69 'Speeches on the Indian Difficulties in the North-West', delivered by Robert Cunningham and Donald A. Smith (Ottawa: Free Press, 1873), p. 7.
70 'Indian Affairs in the North West Territories: Delivered by Hon. Dr. Schultz, M.P. in the House of Commons of Canada', 31 March 1873 (n.p.: 1873?), p. 4.

71 Sarah Carter, '"They would not give up one inch of it": The rise and demise of St. Peter's Reserve, Manitoba', in Zoe Laidlaw and Alan Lester (eds), *Indigenous Communities and Settler Colonialism: Land Holding, Loss and Survival in an Interconnected World* (Basingstoke: Palgrave Macmillan, 2015).
72 *Manitoba Free Press* (20 August 1877).
73 George Stewart Jr, *Canada Under the Administration of the Earl of Dufferin* (Toronto: Rose-Belford Publishing Company, 1878), 550.
74 *Ibid.*, 525.
75 *Ibid.*, 549.
76 Dominion of Canada, *Sessional Papers*, Annual Report of the Department of Indian Affairs for the Year Ended 31 December 1882, p. 185.
77 Archives, Argyll Estate, Inveraray Argyll Scotland, Henry Prince and Councillors to His Excellency the Marquis of Lorne, 6 August 1881, Volume of Formal Addresses.
78 Carter, 'Your Great Mother', 40–3.
79 Library Archives Canada (LAC) Record Group 10, Indian Affairs (RG 10), vol. 3768, file 33642, 6.
80 Quoted in Deanna Christiensen, *Ahtahkakoop: The Epic Account of a Plains Cree Head Chief, His People, and Their Struggle for Survival, 1816–1896* (Altona: Friesens, 2002), p. 578.
81 *Ibid.*, p. 579.
82 Quoted in Tyler and Wright Research Consultants Ltd., 'The Alienation of Indian Reserve Lands During The Administration of Sir Wilfrid Laurier, 1896–1911', No. 4 Peter's Reserve (Prepared for the Manitoba Indian Brotherhood, 1978), p. 128–9. Grammatical and spelling errors are in the original.
83 Quoted in James Dempsey, *Warriors of the King: Prairie Indians in World War One* (Regina: Canadian Plains Research Centre, 1999), p. 38.
84 David T. Borutski and Janette K. Murray, 'History of Indian Bands in Southern Manitoba', unpublished study, Manitoba Legislative Library, 1986, p. 135.
85 *The Globe* (Toronto) (11 December 1933), p. 1; *La Liberté* (20 December 1922), p. 5.
86 Edward Ermatinger, *The Hudson's Bay Territories: A Series of Letters on this Important Question* (Toronto: Maclear, Thomas and Co., 1858), p. 12.
87 Alexander Stavely Hill, *From Home to Home: Autumn Wanderings in the North West* (London: Sampson, Low, Marston, Seale and Rivington, 1881), p. 425.
88 'Anglo-Canadian', *Canada* (London: G. Street and Co., 1882), pp. 16–17.
89 Alexander Begg, *Seventeen Years in the Canadian North-West: A Paper Read on April 8, 1884 at the Royal Colonial Institute* (London: Royal Colonial Institute, 1884), p. 15.
90 See http://victoriaandfirstpeoplesday.ca/, accessed 19 January 2016.

CHAPTER FOUR

The politics of memory and the memory of politics: Australian Aboriginal interpretations of Queen Victoria, 1881–2011

Maria Nugent

In late 2011, Euahlayi man Michael Anderson, from Goodooga in New South Wales, addressed the Occupy Movement in London. A seasoned activist, forty years earlier he was one of four young Aboriginal men who had established the Aboriginal Embassy on the lawns of the Australian Parliament House in Canberra to protest against the federal government's refusal to recognise Aboriginal land rights.[1] Still energetically pursuing proper recognition of Aboriginal rights and sovereignty, Anderson explained to his twenty-first-century London audience that 'the old people were told back then, and it came down through the generations, that Queen Victoria gave us our land and recognised us as independent people'.[2] In fact Anderson was in London that year in search of evidence to prove the veracity of what the old people had apparently been told, having become belatedly convinced that their assertions about Queen Victoria's action and acknowledgement had greater substance and significance than he and other activists of his generation had previously countenanced.[3]

When Anderson referred to the old people in his speech, he might well have had someone like William Barak in mind. One hundred and thirty years earlier, Barak, from the Coranderrk settlement outside Melbourne, told a visiting journalist that 'this land was given us by Sir Henry Barkly [the then Governor] in the name of the Queen'.[4] Barak's statement, which has been preserved because it was printed as part of a longer article in a Melbourne newspaper, is among the earliest records of Aboriginal people in the south-east Australian colonies of Victoria and New South Wales articulating the history of Aboriginal reserves created in the second half of the nineteenth century in these terms.[5] His sparse history applied to the Coranderrk settlement specifically, but in time Aboriginal people in other settlements founded during Queen Victoria's reign would come to describe the land on which they were built as personally given grants from Queen Victoria to them.[6] This was an interpretation that circulated widely, and which persisted and persists still. During the decades between William Barak's statement in 1881 and Michael Anderson's comments in 2011, many other Aboriginal people from other settlements and 'nations' explained their rights and claims to reserved land in similar terms. 'Queen Victoria gave us the land', or words to that effect, became a common refrain, during much of the twentieth century especially. This abbreviated version of colonial history with Queen Victoria at its heart is the focus of this chapter.[7] By tracing the contexts and occasions on which this epigrammatic history was told over generations, my aim is to examine how Aboriginal people in Australia's south-east implicated the figure of Queen Victoria in their lives and predicaments, and as each new generation recycled and reworked inherited stories about her according to their own times and situations.[8] In what ways, I ask, was continued reference to Queen Victoria as the ultimate and personal source of reserve land enduringly useful to generations of Aboriginal people? What did (and does) it mean to evoke Queen Victoria's name when asserting claims to certain tracts of land or for authorising particular kinds of political action? What explains the long afterlife of the claim that land was given (back) to Aboriginal people in the name of the Queen?

A number of writers, including some in this volume, have sought to plumb the depths of Queen Victoria's symbolic and cultural weight that made her available for sustained interpretation. From the outset of her reign, as a young female monarch representing a break with tradition and with her immediate predecessors, she became the embodiment of British ideals of justice, charity, and benevolence.[9] On colonial frontiers and within cross-cultural contact zones, an array of government officials, missionaries, and settlers wove references to Queen Victoria into efforts to explain to Aboriginal people ideas of imperial interest in and proposals for the 'protection' of them (see Nettelbeck Chapter 9 this volume).[10] Historian Heather Goodall provides this speculative example of such frontier conversations:

> To convey the meaning of Crown land, the monarch's ownership of all land in the colony had to be stated. Although there is little direct evidence, the later Aboriginal insistence that Queen Victoria promised them land suggests the [land] commissioners did stress the Queen's involvement; she was portrayed as a benefactress who now owned all 'Crown Land' and was offering these small tracts to Aboriginal people.[11]

In line with other scholarship on Indigenous people's storytelling about or involving Queen Victoria, an important aspect of her meanings is the ways in which she personified an idealised imperial moral order, but one which settlers and their governments failed to deliver or live up to. Constant recall of Queen Victoria – and long after her death – can be understood then not so much as the repetitive recounting of actual events as the invocation of an image of the world as it ought to be. In this sense, it is possible to suggest that as device, figure, or symbol Queen Victoria works within Aboriginal people's stories about colonisation as a memory that seeks to make present an absence.[12] Not surprisingly, as will become clear, her name was most often evoked by Aboriginal people in the face of threat or in the wake of loss.

We might usefully reflect on the ways in which Aboriginal claims, centred on the figure of Queen Victoria, work as a *lieu de memoire*, a feature of which, as Pierre Nora explains, is 'to capture a maximum of meaning in the fewest signs'.[13] While as a narrative element the figure of Queen Victoria remained useful, especially as an image of justice, virtue, and provision, the contexts for telling the stories that incorporated her changed. *Lieux de memoire*, Nora continues, 'only exist because of their capacity for metamorphosis, an endless recycling of their meaning and an unpredictable proliferation of their ramifications'.[14] The claim about Queen Victoria granting land and recognising Aboriginal people 'as independent' was passed down across four or so generations, and although there was very little change in its form, it nonetheless possessed a good deal of malleability as it was able to be applied to diverse circumstances. Its longevity provides scope to consider questions of what it was (and is) that makes the figure of Queen Victoria so repeatedly relevant within Aboriginal people's narrative traditions.[15]

This sentence-long history is a not a wholly inaccurate account of the gazettal of Crown land reserves for Aboriginal settlements – as Crown land, all reservations were made under Queen Victoria's imprimatur.[16] However, my argument is that explaining the meaning of the claim only by reference to such events misses the point. This compelling history, simply told, was the product of considerable interpretative labour. Most evidence suggests it was an interpretation that emerged belatedly, finding expression only some time after the event (the granting of reserve lands) to which each local variant of the statement ostensibly referred. As anthropologist Gillian Cowlishaw has observed, Aboriginal people have to work hard to provide an account of themselves under colonial conditions.[17] Indeed the story's very starkness – its deceptive simplicity – is evidence for the depth of thought that went into it. It is no easy matter to represent the complex and contradictory conditions of lives and experiences as colonised people – caught in the bind between being subjects of the British Crown and asserting their own sovereignty – in terms so recognisable and memorable as a story that travelled and was sustained through repeated telling. Another anthropologist, Jeremy Beckett, has reminded us, 'any story worth telling, and certainly any story worth repeating must have some measure of meaning beyond its particularity, even if that meaning falls short of the "generic"'.[18] Teasing out the meaning of this story, beyond its particularity, is my concern here.

In this chapter, I investigate some of the situations and occasions in which Aboriginal people evoked Queen Victoria's name in the stories they told, and repeated the claim that she had been the personal source of reserve lands. I identify three main phases. The first belongs to the closing decades of Queen Victoria's reign. I argue that during this phase the public assertion that land had been given (back) to Aboriginal people under the Queen's name worked like a form of oral petitioning in the sense that, as Ravi de Costa argues, petitioning was a means for describing a 'moral world' in which 'particular claims are legitimate and sensible'.[19] The second phase commences after Queen Victoria's death in 1901, and broadly spans the first half of the twentieth century. Within this context, Queen Victoria was typically recalled as a foundational figure within stories that were told in defence against the loss of reserve land, as a powerful contrast to settler greed, and as a bulwark against bureaucratic amnesia. The third phase spans a period beginning in the 1960s that coincided with the emergence of a national politics of land rights, in which the meanings that the figure of Queen Victoria had held were revised and gradually jettisoned. As many historians have noted, claims to land were articulated less on historical terms and more on the basis of inalienable Indigenous and ancestral rights in land.[20] But this was also a time, I suggest, in which Queen Victoria became even more embedded within regional, local, and family stories as her name was mobilised within new kinds of personal and communal memory work that was engaged with matters of identity, inheritance, tradition, and continuity.

In the name of the queen

When in 1881 William Barak condensed the history of the Coranderrk settlement into a statement about the land having been given to them by the Governor in the Queen's name, almost twenty years had passed since the original gazettal to which his statement ostensibly referred had taken place. From its foundation in 1860 and its gazettal as an Aboriginal reserve a few years later in 1863, the Coranderrk people, in company with a much-liked overseer, had developed a viable farming community. Coranderrk was a settlement critical to the survival of

Aboriginal people displaced from their ancestral lands by the pastoral frontier. By the late 1870s and early 1880s, however, the autonomy that the Coranderrk people had begun to achieve was under threat by government authorities intent on undermining Aboriginal people's independence.[21]

William Barak had good reason, then, in 1881 to remind his interlocutors that the land on which the Coranderrk settlement was built, largely through its residents' own labour, had been given to them by the Governor with the full weight of the Queen's authority which that office possessed. When he made the statement, an inquiry was under way into the conditions of the reserve and its future, with some members of the Board for the Protection of Aborigines advocating the settlement's closure.[22] Such threats provoke and inspire storytelling about people's rightful claims to the place they regard as their home. In this particular context, it made sense to remind the board of inquiry and the readership of the Melbourne press that this piece of land had been returned to the residents of Coranderrk with the full authority of the Queen's imprimatur, and it was not for later, local governments to overturn.

Most historians argue that the belief about Queen Victoria's personal involvement in the Coranderrk land grant, which Barak's statement to some degree implies, was partly a result of the Coranderrk people's own efforts to engage her in their affairs. In 1863, the same year that the gazettal occurred, they had sent a delegation to the Governor's levee held in honour of the Queen's birthday (see Edmonds Chapter 8 and Clarke Chapter 6 this volume). There they presented a decorated address expressing their affection for Queen Victoria and indicating their qualification (almost) for 'becoming imperial citizens', or as Tim Rowse put it, they 'declared their acquired fitness to be subjects of a just Crown'.[23] They also presented a cache of gifts (Figure 4.1). The very next month their reserve was formally gazetted. When a short time later they received a letter from the Queen thanking them for the gifts and assuring them of her interest in them, the conditions it seems were ripe for a belief to emerge that she had some hand in the formal provision of land on which they could establish themselves and carve out their future. Anthropologist Diane Barwick points out that the belief was basically mistaken, based as it was on mere coincidence, but nevertheless suggests that the sequence of events had given the Coranderrk people confidence that direct appeals to colonial governors and the Queen could bear fruit.[24] As literary historian Penny van Toorn glosses it, 'Whether or not the Queen intervened, the people of Coranderrk were correct in their perception that deputations and letters to people in high places were an effective way of asserting their needs and defending their interests'.[25]

THE POLITICS OF MEMORY AND THE MEMORY OF POLITICS

Figure 4.1 A deputation from Coranderrk attended the Governor's levee in May 1863 in Melbourne, Victoria, on the occasion of the Queen's birthday and in celebration of her eldest son's recent marriage. In addition to an address, they presented gifts for the Queen, her two sons and her new daughter-in-law.

This, though, is all speculation – a retrospective account of the possible origins of a belief rendered in a simple statement.[26] The evidence of its existence does not emerge until the early 1880s with William Barak's documented comment to the visiting journalist, which is subsequently affirmed and elaborated by some of the Coranderrk people's allies and supporters. A few months later, for instance, the Reverend Robert Hamilton wrote the Chief Secretary in Victoria, explaining that 'they [the Coranderrk people] believe they are in danger of losing the little piece of country which they say they have received from the Queen'.[27] Not long afterwards, Ann Bon, a champion of the Coranderrk people and friend to William Barak, wrote that 'Coranderrk, they state they received from the Queen at the hands of Sir Henry Barkly as a small substitute for the country they have lost'.[28] This version of history, it seems, was taking shape and solidifying, in part through processes of accretion, cross-referencing, and repetition.

Of course, the absence of earlier evidence does not necessarily mean that the belief about the Queen's involvement in land matters had not been circulating before then among Aboriginal people at Coranderrk and indeed elsewhere. Shared beliefs and stories that circulated among Aboriginal people as spoken words often went unrecorded. Nevertheless, it does seem too narrow to seek to explain this particularly powerful and persistent claim, which gives Queen Victoria centre stage, only – or primarily – by reference to particular past events. What is also required is to consider its possible inspirations, provocations, and implications at the many moments when it was publicly articulated.

William Barak knew how to craft words to good effect. He was a Woiwurrung headman (ngurungaeta), a status that was accorded partly in recognition of a man's way with words. By Barak's own account, he was ngurungaeta (or speaker) because he 'spoke straight and did no wrong'.[29] He was generally known for his oratory style and his command of what historian Jane Lydon has described as the 'Aboriginal tradition of public declamation'.[30] When he said that 'this land was given us by Sir Henry Barkly in the name of the Queen', Barak painted a word picture of the power structure that shaped Aboriginal people's existence. They were now dependent on the Crown for land, which they understood as fundamental for their survival and which had been their long-term aim to secure. By this time all land that was not under freehold title was described as Crown land. This was, as historian Mark McKenna writes, 'the most powerful reminder that those lands had been seized unlawfully, without treaty or negotiation. To this day, the very words "crown land" help to conceal the truth that the lands and waters of Australia belonged to Aboriginal people'.[31] In the absence of treaties or other agreements, Barak articulated another foundational covenant: that the land for their settlement had been given to them in the Queen's name.

At the same time, in this statement Barak named the authorities that the Coranderrk people acknowledged and were prepared to deal with: the Queen and her local representative, the colonial Governor. He repeated this preference in 1886 when he 'made clear [the] wish for "the ... Coranderrk blacks ... to be under the Queen, the Governor, [and] the Chief Secretary"'.[32] The implication was that they would not or did not recognise the authority of local governments over them, such as the Board for the Protection of Aborigines. It was those settler authorities, made up of men who believed they knew more about Aboriginal people than Aboriginal people knew about themselves, that were intent on undermining the Coranderrk people's autonomy. In this context, the monarch and the colonial Governor were seen as preferable authorities and potential sources for justice and recognition. As Ann Curthoys notes, 'over time, Indigenous people began to see the Queen as an alternative source of authority, as someone who could help them in their battle with settler governments and peoples, especially in their quest for the return of land'.[33]

In this sense, it is possible, I think, to regard Barak's statement as a description of the world not just as it is, but also as it ought to be. It is, at its core, a description of a moral world in which the Crown (properly) recognises Aboriginal people as due land and as having a right to hold it. Although Barak's statement was not a petition in the conventional sense of constituting a direct appeal for something, it nevertheless has the quality of a petition, as described by Ravi de Costa in his discussion of Indigenous petitioning in the British world. He describes the ways in which petitions, including those written to the monarch, are not just an 'interaction of the identity of the petitioner and the authority being petitioned'. They are also 'implicit descriptions of the moral worlds in which particular claims are sensible and legitimate', and 'thus petitions act to articulate the identity and status of the petitioner and that of authority in a shared moral order'.[34] Barak's 1881 statement does just this. It works to express the fundamental relationship between Aborigines and the Crown with land at its centre. And in this sense, the statement describes a shared moral order in which Aboriginal people's claims for certain kinds of recognition, provision, and entitlement were rendered legitimate.

Despite the proliferation of this story in the early 1880s, there is little evidence that it continued to be a prominent part of Aboriginal people's political and narrative repertoire for the remainder of Queen Victoria's reign. Again, it is possible that it continued to be an explanation that Aboriginal people shared among themselves, in ways that went unrecorded, but in the remaining two decades of the nineteenth century there are few, if any, instances of it being used as it had been by William Barak in 1881. Nonetheless, Aboriginal people continued to act in concert with all that it implied. They continued to appeal to and articulate their relationship to Queen Victoria and her local representatives in various ways, including by petitioning and sending delegations to governors and parliamentarians.[35] However, it was only after her death that stories about her flourished and spread.

'Our Late Most Gracious Sovereign "Queen Victoria"'

One might expect that Queen Victoria's valency within and usefulness for Aboriginal people's politics would diminish with her death, as new generations either turned to her descendants as a source of appeal or away from the distant monarch as a potential saviour. But the opposite appears true: her rhetorical value and use as a narrative device increased posthumously. References to 'Queen Victoria' proliferated within Aboriginal people's explanations of their situations, and she became a permanent fixture in their dialogue with settler society and governments. Storytelling incorporating the figure of Queen Victoria was, in many respects, a twentieth-century phenomenon, and one that occurs whenever and wherever a politics of memory and a memory of politics meet.

In the immediate aftermath of Queen Victoria's death, Aboriginal people in certain settlements in Victoria and New South Wales had good reason to recall the supposedly royal origins of the reserves they called home as their tenure of them was repeatedly threatened.[36] In a period in which 'dispersal' and 'assimilation' became popular catch-cries for government officials responsible for Aboriginal affairs, there were plenty of occasions on which it seemed a good idea for Aboriginal people to invoke the dead Queen's name, to recall what they regarded as her 'foundational' deeds towards them, and to remind their interlocutors of their 'special' relationship to her. Ironically, the dispersal of some Aboriginal people, young men in particular, contributed to increased movement and communication between disparate Aboriginal settlements that made the spread of this story possible. Through them, politically astute counter-narratives travelled, 'ignit[ing] a new, politically formidable sense of social cohesion among previously atomised groups'. By this and other means, the hitherto 'hidden' interpretations 'of different groups could ... coalesce and consolidate into more fully-developed counter-hegemonic public transcripts that in turn supported open expressions of insubordination' or resistance, as van Toorn argues.[37]

At the start of the twentieth century at the Lake Condah settlement in south-west Victoria, Ernest Mobourne spearheaded a campaign against the government's plans to close it down as part of its policy to disperse most of the Victorian Aboriginal population into the wider community and to concentrate the remainder on just one reserve, Lake Tyers on the opposite side of the state.[38] On occasion, Mobourne included reference to Queen Victoria in the historical explanations he gave as to why the residents should be allowed to remain on the reserve, such as when he wrote in 1907 to the local ratepayers association seeking their support for the Lake Condah residents' cause. After explaining that 'our forefathers, fathers, and ourselves understood that it was ours to own to live on while life lasted', and that they had demonstrated their ownership by 'putting up fences, clearing ground, building houses, &c, besides a nice lovely church and a school where we and our children receive instruction', he ended his appeal by saying 'for we understood at the first that it was granted to us by Our Late Most Gracious Sovereign "Queen Victoria" our mother to let us live and die here'.[39]

Mobourne (born c. 1862),[40] like others of his generation, had participated in various occasions during Queen Victoria's reign in which her imputed largesse towards Aboriginal people was acknowledged and appreciation for it shown. In 1890, for instance, during Governor Hopetoun's visit to the region, Mobourne and another young man, Albert White, were signatories to an address presented that day, which included expression of their 'heartfelt thanks to Her Majesty the Queen under whose just and kind rule and protection it is our happy lot to be placed, for all the care which is bestowed upon us with regard to our spiritual and moral welfare, and for the liberal supplies provided for the daily needs of our selves and our children'.[41] Strangely, though, the next sentence of the address was a prediction of their future demise. 'We feel, however, that it will be only a few more years and we [the Aborigines] will all have passed away, and we pray and hope will have exchanged the home here below for one which is beyond and abiding, while it will be the lot of those who now occupy this country, which was formerly the home of our fathers, to increase'. Like many such texts, the address was probably prepared with help from (or indeed *by*) the resident missionary, even though a newspaper account insisted it was 'all being the work of the aborigines themselves'.[42] Nearly twenty years later, Mobourne and others were certainly not interpreting the Queen's provisions as interim measures until their passing. By then, they were evoking the late Queen's apparent goodness towards quite opposite ends: their survival and endurance into the future and forever. Queen Victoria's largesse had become a central element in arguments against the closure of the settlement and thus in direct opposition to the government's policy aims, which were by that time designed to bring about the end of Aboriginal people's separate existence. No longer youthful mouthpieces for that version of history, instead Mobourne and others were engaged in imagining and realising an alternative future for themselves and Aboriginal people more broadly, in which Queen Victoria's putative past actions were the foundations on which their local futures were to be based.

The situation was more complicated in New South Wales, where there was a much greater number of reserves created through a more diverse set of circumstances and arrangements than was the case in Victoria. But threats to Aboriginal people's continued tenure of some of them were no less real. Here, too, the claim that Queen Victoria had given reserve lands to Aboriginal people as compensation for dispossession and in recognition of their rights had taken root.[43]

One settlement that the NSW Aborigines Protection Board had slated for closure in the early part of the twentieth century was Warangesda on the Murrumbidgee River. It had been established in 1880 as an independent mission, but was incorporated into the network of reserves managed by the government-appointed board. Like Coranderrk and another settlement, Maloga (and later Cumeragunga), Warangesda had been prosperous and independent for a time. By the late 1920s, however, the residents' efforts to forestall the government's intentions to disband it had come to nothing. Decrying their situation, in a letter to the editor of the *Sydney Morning Herald* one of the residents, James Murray, explained that: 'The first piece of land that was given to us, we are told, was a gift from the late Queen Victoria, and that it should never be taken away'. On this occasion, Murray named his sources, including the first missionary in charge of Warangesda; the Inspector General of Police during the 1880s and 1890s, when elements of the government's 'protection' policies were deputised to police; and 'other prominent men'. The letter accused the NSW premier of selling the land from under them: 'That statement [regarding the Queen] has always held good until the Lang government had us evicted and pulled the roofs off our huts'.[44] Yet despite their appeals and their opposition to the government's course of action, the ballot for the land went ahead, and the Aboriginal residents of Warangesda were dispersed.

As these various examples show – and many others could be added – the abbreviated rendition of a complex history of relations and rights, crystallised in the claim that Queen Victoria gave us the land in perpetuity, or something along those lines, was not only a condensed explanation that made sense to Aboriginal people, but was also given as a history lesson that ignorant bureaucrats needed to learn. This was a story told for the sake of others. Remarking on the impressive strength of the historical memory of the Aboriginal people she worked with in Melbourne in the early 1960s and from whom she first learnt about the political history of Coranderrk, Diane Barwick noted that 'their tales of how they were driven from Coranderrk and how this land was lost influenced the ways in which subsequent generations responded to the planning by later officials who *knew nothing of the past*'.[45] A deep memory was (is) a vital resource when dealing with government, particularly when faced with a steady stream of officials for whom having only a slight grasp of history was considered an advantage, even qualification, for the job. Of the Aboriginal people with whom she worked, Barwick noted that by contrast 'their memories had not been obliterated with each change of policy or administrative personnel'.[46]

Sustained memory work in answer to bureaucratic amnesia, wilful or otherwise, could not though prevent the heavy hand of government. By the 1920s, Lake Condah, Coranderrk, and Warangesda and some other Aboriginal settlements had been disbanded and sold off, but even among their dispersed residents storytelling that centred on the figure of Queen Victoria continued. Emphasis though had shifted towards the trickery and fraudulent ways that 'greedy' whites had allegedly assumed ownership of sites that were believed to have been 'grants from the Queen'.[47] As I have argued elsewhere, in regions where old reserves had been lost or revoked, the Queen Victoria claim was woven into broader 'narratives of grievance' about the ways in which land-hungry settler Australians mistreated and exploited Aboriginal people.[48]

At the same time, within Aboriginal people's personal and collective memories these lost settlements became increasingly associated with a remembered period of Aboriginal independence that was characterised by a degree of prosperity and a sense of optimism or hope. The old places, which became physically inaccessible to Aboriginal people as they were farmed by whites or broken up into small allotments for returned soldiers, became sites of memory of a 'golden age' of Aboriginal autonomy and of limited recognition of their rights. Historians Bain Attwood and Andrew Markus have argued that Aboriginal politics during the 1920s and 1930s was partly impelled by past personal experiences and bitter memories of the loss of Aboriginal reserves, including those that had become associated with the Queen's largesse and her apparent recognition of Aboriginal people as both the original owners of the land and as dispossessed people in need of compensation.[49] They argue that politics in this period was motivated less by historical memories of the violent pastoral frontier as by the later losses Aboriginal people suffered when the settlements on which they had been able to begin to rebuild their lives and communities were taken from them by the state.

That the late period of Queen Victoria's reign was associated not only with the gazettal of reserve lands but also with some recognition of rights is evident in a statement that an Aboriginal man, Joe Anderson (also known as King Burraga), made in a letter to a prominent anthropologist, A. P. Elkin, in 1936.[50] Seeking Elkin's support,

Anderson wrote that 'cruel treatments have been playing a big part all over Australia deprived of all our Rights which had been given us in the 90s during the Reign of our Good old Queen Her Majesty Victoria'.[51] Although Anderson does not underline it here, recognition of those rights was understood as having come about in no small measure through Aboriginal people's own efforts, which had included, as already mentioned, directly appealing to Queen Victoria and drawing her into a personal relationship. His statement works, then, to draw together a memory of politics with a politics of memory.

That memory of politics worked in other ways as well, not least in authorising Aboriginal modes of politics in the early decades of the twentieth century. This was a period in which Aboriginal people were faced not only with increasingly authoritarian and interventionist governments, but also with racially motivated opposition from white people among whom they lived. These conditions contributed to various political campaigns, in which some Aboriginal people pushed against the arbitrary and unequal conditions imposed on them. Within such local contexts, the mention of a historical connection to Queen Victoria had its uses. It could, it seems, work as a means to authorise oneself as an active political subject and even to justify one's political methods, such as appealing directly to the reigning monarch. For instance, in the late 1920s, an Aboriginal woman, Jane Duren, at Bateman's Bay on the New South Wales south coast petitioned King George V protesting against the exclusion of Aboriginal children from the local school as well as the loss of reserve lands, and appealing for his intervention. Writing directly to the British monarch in the 1920s about a seemingly minor and local issue appeared almost anachronistic. Within the larger archive that surrounds the petition, however, can be found letters of support for Duren written by non-Aboriginal people, one of which provides a clue to what made her petitioning sensible. It states that Duren and her family 'are all half-caste, but they are all descendants of the Butler family, who had their reserve granted to them by the Late Queen of England'.[52] This snippet is suggestive of the ways in which Jane Duren might have publicly presented her own genealogy and family history, incorporating into her own biography a special relationship with the distant monarch, a practice that might best be described as 'fictive kinship'.[53] This might be thought of as a continuation of an earlier practice, in which the life story of an Aboriginal person, especially women or girls, came to incorporate, and in some cases were predominantly framed by, reference to closeness or correspondence with Queen Victoria.[54]

This mode of authorising one's political actions and standing by reference to historical relations with an earlier monarch has parallels in other settler colonies in the same period. Canadian historian Keith Thor Carlson, for instance, describes the ways in which a Salish man, Isipaymilt, publicly presented himself after he had participated in a delegation in 1906 to London to have an audience with King Edward VII. During his appearance at a Royal Commission held in 1915, Isipaymilt carried a photograph of himself with Edward. Carlson argues that 'in addition to his hereditary prerogatives, Isipaymilt's authority derived in part from his intimate association with Britain's king'.[55] And he pushed the commissioners to make good the promises that had been made.

Something similar, but on a smaller, more intimate scale, is suggested in a letter written by an Aboriginal man, Fred Carmichael, from the Lake Tyers Aboriginal Station in Victoria. Writing to the Australian Governor General in Canberra in 1930, Carmichael prefaced his request for a vice-regal favour by evoking two 'royal' connections. 'I'm a full – blooded Aboriginal by birth decent [sic] from Royal Blood', he wrote, before adding that, 'I used to write letters to Queen Victoria in my young days'.[56] The reference to his descent from 'royal blood' likely refers to a practice widespread in the Australian colonies to anoint certain Aboriginal people as kings and queens.[57] By adding to his own royal pedigree his practice of corresponding with the British Queen suggests a special, or privileged, relationship to the monarch, which works to preface and justify his approach to the Governor General with his concerns. These various evocations of royal connections are used by Carmichael to bolster his prerogative to write directly to the Governor General to request a personal favour. His request concerned the return of his child, who had been taken from him under the state's child removal practices. The outcome of his appeal is unknown.

'Not a great white person, a great white lie'

After the Second World War, Aboriginal people in south-east Australia continued to have reason from time to time to evoke Queen Victoria's name and to remind their interlocutors of her putative past deeds. This was particularly so for those Aboriginal people who had, through a complex of reasons as well as some good fortune, remained resident on reserves that had been created during the later decades of Queen Victoria's reign. When those reserves came under threat as a result of a new round of government intervention motivated by a policy of assimilation in the 1950s and 1960s, some space opened up for the claim to circulate again. Certainly it was expressed publicly and repeatedly at Lake Tyers in Victoria and La Perouse in New South Wales, two long-standing Aboriginal settlements that came under threat of closure in the early 1960s.[58] But this was also a period in which a new generation of activists, both Aboriginal and non-Aboriginal, questioned the continuing political and rhetorical relevance of Queen Victoria as a moral reference point. When an article appeared in the local Communist Party newspaper, *The Guardian*, referring to 'a popular belief among Aboriginal people that Reserves such as Lake Tyers were given to the Aboriginal people by Queen Victoria', the author was inclined to describe it as a 'folk tradition' and to note that 'unfortunately [it] has no legal basis'.[59] At La Perouse, a non-Aboriginal supporter put it more bluntly when he explained to a government inquiry that: 'We had to tell them that [it] was not so'.[60]

Other activists sought to revise the belief about Queen Victoria's goodness not by quietly dismissing it, but rather by publicly arguing that Australian governments had made a lie out of it. On Australia Day in 1972, prominent Aboriginal activist Kevin Gilbert wrote an opinion piece for a national newspaper, penned in response to the federal government's statement that it would not support Aboriginal land rights, in which he evoked the benevolent image of Queen Victoria that had existed for much of the twentieth century and which he acknowledged still had some currency among Aboriginal people. Making reference to a recent struggle over a small reserve, not much larger than six acres, at La Perouse near Sydney, which the New South Wales Aborigines Welfare Board (which replaced the NSW Protection Board in 1939) had been trying to revoke, Gilbert explained to his readership that: 'The greatest, most generous European image in the minds of Aboriginals was Queen Victoria. This great monarch, they claim, deeded the La Perouse mission land back to them'.[61] He continued his editorial by exclaiming: 'Queen Victoria! The Queen may or may not have treated so justly with the Aborigines, but she is in their minds, the most just and vital European to have emerged from the European ranks'. Drawing this tradition into the wider, national sphere of land rights then being pursued by Aboriginal people across the country but stymied and opposed by the current federal government, Gilbert suggests a wholesale reassessment of the comforting figure of the protective Queen Victoria was due. 'Now we are told', he continued, 'that it was all just sheer fantasy – not a great white person, but a great white lie! There is no land for us. We have been truly dispossessed'.[62] Even here though, it is clear, that Queen Victoria still had some uses within explicitly political rhetoric.

The same day that Gilbert's piece was published in the national press, Australians woke to the news that four young Aboriginal men (one of whom was Michael Anderson referred to earlier) had established an Aboriginal Embassy under a beach umbrella on the lawns of Parliament House in Canberra. The Aboriginal Embassy, which later became known as the Tent Embassy, would be a focus for Aboriginal land rights, which were increasingly being argued for and claimed on the basis of 'tribal' or 'ancestral' rights rather than 'historical' factors, such as the ones Queen Victoria encapsulated. This context made the Queen Victoria claim increasingly anomalous, and this is registered in the apparent uneasiness with which some activists and their allies handled the long-standing claim, especially as they worked on campaigns to secure land and rights to it with Aboriginal people who remained convinced that Queen Victoria had been the source of their reserves.[63] Increasingly, the claim would be described by commentators as explicable and understandable in the sense of providing psychological comfort in the face of inexplicable injustice, but ultimately misplaced and useless. In a series of comments, social scientist C. D. Rowley, who was responsible for the first historically informed study of Aboriginal people and race relations in Australia, which was published in a series of volumes in the late 1960s and early 1970s, interpreted the belief as indicative of a wider phenomenon in which the downtrodden hold tenaciously to ideas of justice interrupted: 'Many believed that Queen Victoria had herself given them the poor reserves, that the land within the boundaries really belonged to them; that in some unjust way officialdom had intervened between the source of justice and those who needed it', he wrote.[64] But ultimately he also pronounced it as a tragically misguided and almost completely exhausted belief. Writing in 1978, he observed that: 'Even ten years ago only the old folk could believe in the justice of Queen Victoria'.[65]

Declarations of its end were probably premature. The claim that Queen Victoria granted the land continued to be heard during the 1980s and 1990s, most often given voice in the context of Aboriginal community and oral history work that flourished around that time.[66] By then it had become embedded in regional, local, and family histories. The emphasis within these renditions is typically on the actions and agency of an Aboriginal person, a 'matriarch' usually, who was alive during Queen Victoria's reign and who is remembered by descendants as the person responsible for pushing the monarch to grant to them small pieces of ground that would become the sites where Aboriginal communities 'grew in strength from shared experience of struggle and extraordinary social change'.[67] For instance, historian Margaret Somerville found that at Coonabarabran in central New South Wales the form of the claim about Queen Victoria as the source of the reserve land revolved around an Aboriginal matriarch, Mary Jane Cain, who was believed to have written to Queen Victoria requesting a plot of land.[68] As her descendants assert: 'She wrote to the Queen and got the property', in ways that suggest not only

Cain's agency in the matter, but also imply a measure of equivalence and proximity between the two matriarchs.[69] Emphasis within historical remembrance on individuals appealing to the Queen for grants of land gives further weight to Goodall's argument that the story about Queen Victoria as the source of land was only told in relation to reserves for which Aboriginal people had made direct appeals, such as by petition, letter, delegation, or other modes to settler governments or imperial authorities.[70] This was, she argues, a narrative that privileged Aboriginal people's agency in insisting upon their rights to land, not only to small reserves set apart for their use but more broadly as well, and in having those rights recognised by 'the highest levels of the British state'.[71] That subsequent community-based historical remembrance tended to give prominence to Aboriginal women in this regard – as the appellants for or recipients of land grants – is worth underlining. It suggests traces of other histories embedded within the Queen Victoria claim. Some anthropologists and historians, for instance, have noted that during the later part of Queen Victoria's reign the status of some Aboriginal women, especially those living on 'independent' reserves and settlements, changed as they gained new authority through increased economic independence or as they accepted leadership roles under missionary influence.[72] For some of these women, as Rowse observes, 'Queen Victoria ... was a persuasive exemplar of empowered womanhood'.[73] Stories told in Aboriginal families and communities well into the late twentieth century, which connect some of these matriarchs with Queen Victoria as though they were parties to a foundational exchange or compact, are suggestive of this earlier history of Aboriginal women's empowerment. They acknowledge as well the part that women played during the twentieth century in keeping communities together. At the same time, and more obviously, the stories as narrated in the late twentieth century continued to work, as they always had, as explanations of how Aboriginal people had secured land for themselves and for their survival, and as narratives that enacted, performed, and underwrote their claims and rights to particular portions of land.

When Michael Anderson addressed the Occupy Movement in London in 2011, he was continuing a practice that had been performed at least since the early 1880s: he was implicating the British Crown, expressed by reference to Queen Victoria, in Aboriginal people's dispossession as well as identifying it as the authority to redress the injustice that had been done in its name. His public pronouncements in Britain in the opening decades of the twenty-first century connect in interesting ways with William Barak's statement made in the closing ones of the nineteenth. They represent two instances within an evolving tradition among Aboriginal people in which Queen Victoria's name is used as shorthand for a host of ideas and associations.

But this is not a simple story of historical continuity. While as embodiment of empire and personification of justice and virtue, Queen Victoria has remained enduringly useful to Aboriginal people as a narrative device in the stories they tell and the statements they make as part of their ongoing dialogue with settler society, the situations *in* which and *for* which her name and memory is invoked have been and continue to be diverse and multifaceted. The figure of Queen Victoria is used to remind settler Australians about previous provisions made to Aboriginal people by imperial and colonial authorities as well as to ensure that later generations of settlers were not allowed to forget that 'promises' and 'covenants' had since been broken. At the same time, her name has been a mnemonic device for recalling histories of Aboriginal people's own political activism and their persistent efforts to seek redress for their dispossession by the British. Queen Victoria is a source and carrier for historical memory; and a figure onto which to project desires, idealisations and hopes. Through their own representations of her status and authority, Aboriginal people presented an image of what proper sovereignty should look like. For the historian, then, tracking through the archives the repeated evocation of Queen Victoria's name becomes a means by which to trace the 'subtle shifting conjunctions'[74] of a politics of Indigenous memory and a memory of Indigenous politics.

Acknowledgements

The research for this chapter was supported by an Australian Research Council Discovery Project grant (DP110100230) and an Australian Research Council Future Fellowship (FT100100073). Dr Allison Cadzow did much of the archival research for which I am very grateful. For their comments and suggestions, thanks especially to Ann Curthoys, Paul Gillen, Heather Goodall, Ann McGrath and Glenda Sluga, and to all the participants at the 'Queen Victoria in the Colonies' symposium at The Australian National University in December 2013.

Notes

1 See Gary Foley, Andrew Schaap, and Edwina Howell (eds), *The Aboriginal Tent Embassy: Sovereignty, Black Power, Land Rights and the State* (London: Routledge, 2013), pp. 117–21.
2 Michael Anderson, 'Occupy London Speech', December 2011, http://treatyrepublic.net/content/defining-phase-our-struggle-michael-anderson, accessed 30 November 2014.

3 'Aboriginal leader takes fight to Europe', *Herald Sun* (1 December 2011).
4 'The Coranderrk Inquiry', *Argus* (19 October 1881).
5 Most historians argue that the association drawn between Queen Victoria and land grants for Aborigines had an earlier history, suggesting that it had its origins in the mid-nineteenth century. Heather Goodall, for instance, speculates that it could have developed in the 1850s in New South Wales, when Crown land commissioners sought to explain to Aboriginal people the meaning of reserves for their use and reinforced in the 1880s by the NSW Protector of Aborigines. See Heather Goodall, *Invasion to Embassy: Land in Aboriginal Politics, 1770–1972* (Sydney: Allen and Unwin, 1996), pp. 56, 102. In Victoria, Bain Attwood suggests it might have emerged via explanations given by protectors of Aborigines, such as William Thomas, of Earl Grey's proposal in the mid-1840s to establish reserves for Aborigines and in which the Queen's authority might well have been invoked. See Bain Attwood, *Rights for Aborigines* (Sydney: Allen and Unwin, 2003), p. 15.
6 A number of historians have discussed either particular instances of the claim or the phenomenon more generally. See, especially, Goodall, *Invasion to Embassy*, pp. 101–3, 231, 298, 326, 343, 357; Attwood, *Rights for Aborigines*, pp. 15–16, 27, 29–30, 60–1, 245, 347; Diane Barwick, *Rebellion at Coranderrk* (Canberra: Aboriginal History Monographs, 1998), pp. 66–7; Jane Lydon, *Eye Contact: Photographing Indigenous Australians* (Durham, NC: Duke University Press, 2005), pp. 39–50; Maria Nugent, '"The Queen gave us the land": Aboriginal people, Queen Victoria and historical remembrance', *History Australia*, 9:2 (2012), 182–200; Tim Rowse, *After Mabo: Interpreting Indigenous Traditions* (Melbourne: Melbourne University Press, 1993), pp. 13–16.
7 Nugent, 'The Queen gave us the land', pp. 182–8.
8 The question of what to call the sentence-long story is difficult to resolve. Various terms have been used, including belief, oral tradition, memory, myth, and folk story. All of these descriptions are quite loaded, implying judgements about authenticity and accuracy. While I refer to it interchangeably as a 'story' or 'history', my preference is to describe it as a 'statement' or 'claim', which captures its brevity and declarative quality.
9 See, for instance, Margaret Homans, *Royal Representations: Queen Victoria and British Culture, 1837–1876* (Chicago, IL: Chicago University Press, 1998); Margaret Homans and Adrienne Munich (eds), *Remaking Queen Victoria* (Cambridge: Cambridge University Press, 1997); John Plunkett, *Queen Victoria: First Media Monarch* (Oxford: Oxford University Press, 2003); Dorothy Thompson, *Queen Victoria: Gender and Power* (London: Virago, 2001); David Cannadine, *Ornamentalism: How the British Saw Their Empire* (London: Allen Lane, 2001); Helen Irving, 'Thinking of England: Women, politics and the Queen', in J. Hoorn and D. Goodman (eds), *Vox Republicae: Feminism and the Republic*, special issue of *Journal of Australian Studies*, 47 (1996), 33–41.
10 See Goodall, *Invasion to Embassy*, p. 102; Ann Curthoys, 'Indigenous subjects', in Deryck M. Schreuder and Stuart Ward (eds), *Australia's Empire* (Oxford: Oxford University Press, 2008), pp. 94–6.
11 Goodall, *Invasion to Embassy*, p. 56.
12 Paul Ricoeur, *Memory, History, Forgetting* (Chicago, IL: University of Chicago Press, 2004).
13 Pierre Nora, 'Between memory and history: Les lieux de mémoire', *Representations*, 26 (Spring 1989), 19.
14 See Nora, 'Between memory and history', p. 19.
15 Luise White, *Speaking with Vampires: Rumor and History in Colonial Africa* (Berkeley: University of California Press, 2000), p. 18.
16 As Mark McKenna notes, 'The gradual dispossession of Aboriginal Australia occurred under the imprimatur of the crown'. Mark McKenna, *This Country: A Reconciled Republic?* (Sydney: UNSW Press, 2004), p. 16.
17 Gillian Cowlishaw, *Blackfellas, Whitefellas and the Hidden Injuries of Race* (Melbourne: Blackwell Publishing, 2004), pp. 85–6.

18 Jeremy Beckett, 'Aboriginal histories, Aboriginal myths: An introduction', *Oceania*, 65:2 (December 1994), 100.
19 Ravi de Costa, 'Identity, authority, and the moral worlds of Indigenous petitions', *Comparative Studies in Society and History*, 48:3 (2006), 670. For reference to Queen Victoria as a moral standard, see: Andrzej Olechnowicz, 'Historians and the modern British monarchy', in A. Olechnowicz (ed.), *The Monarchy and the British Nation, 1780 to the Present* (Cambridge: Cambridge University Press, 2007), p. 23.
20 See, for instance, Russell McGregor, *Indifferent Inclusion: Aboriginal People and the Australian Nation* (Canberra: Aboriginal Studies Press, 2011), pp. 169–73.
21 Attwood, *Rights for Aborigines*, Ch. 1; Barwick, *Rebellion at Coranderrk*, Chs 4–8.
22 For detailed discussions of this history, see: Richard Broome, '"There were vegetables every year Mr Green was here": Right behavior and the struggle for autonomy at Coranderrk Aboriginal Reserve', *History Australia*, 3:2 (2006), 43.1–43.16; Giordano Nanni and Andrea James, *Coranderrk: We Will Show the Country* (Canberra: Aboriginal Studies Press, 2013), pp. 20–32.
23 Sukanya Banerjee, *Becoming Imperial Citizens: Indians in the Late-Victorian Empire* (Durham, NC: Duke University Press, 2010); Tim Rowse, 'Aboriginal respectability', in T. Rowse (ed.), *Contesting Assimilation: Histories of Colonial and Indigenous Initiatives* (Perth: API Network, 2005), p. 50.
24 Barwick, *Rebellion at Coranderrk*, p. 66.
25 Penny van Toorn, *Writing Never Arrives Naked: Early Aboriginal Cultures of Writing in Australia* (Canberra: Aboriginal Studies Press, 2006), p. 125.
26 For a discussion of the limitations of such an approach, see White, *Speaking with Vampires*, p. 5.
27 Public Records Office, Victoria (PROVic), 1226/4R, Hamilton to Chief Secretary, 23 March 1882, cited in Attwood, *Rights for Aborigines*, p. 16.
28 PROVic, 1226/4, A. Bon to Under Secretary, 29 May 1882, cited in Attwood, *Rights for Aborigines*, p. 16.
29 Cited in van Toorn, *Writing Never Arrives Naked*, p. 130.
30 Lydon, *Eye Contact*, p. 162.
31 McKenna, *This Country*, p. 71.
32 Attwood, *Rights for Aborigines*, p. 27.
33 Curthoys, 'Indigenous subjects', p. 94.
34 de Costa, 'Identity, authority, and the moral worlds of Indigenous petitions', p. 670.
35 For a discussion of Aboriginal petitioning in this period, see Ann Curthoys and Jessie Mitchell, '"Bring this paper to the Good Governor": Indigenous petitioning in Britain's Australian colonies', in Saliha Belmessous (ed.), *Native Claims: Indigenous Law Against Empire, 1500–1920* (New York: Oxford University Press, 2012), pp. 193–7.
36 The most comprehensive history of Aboriginal people and land in New South Wales is Goodall, *Invasion to Embassy*. See also Peter Read, '"A rape of the soul so profound": Some reflections on the dispersal policy in New South Wales', *Aboriginal History*, 7:1 (1983), 23–33; Peter Read, 'Breaking up these camps entirely: The dispersal policy in Wiradjuri country, 1909–1929,' *Aboriginal History*, 8:1 (1984), 45–55. For Victoria, see: Richard Broome, *Aboriginal Victorians: A History Since 1800* (Sydney: Allen and Unwin, 2005), Ch. 9 and Part 3; Attwood, *Rights for Aborigines*, Ch. 1.
37 Penny van Toorn, 'Hegemony or hidden transcripts?: Aboriginal writings from Lake Condah, 1876–1907', *Journal of Australian Studies*, 29:86 (2005), 22.
38 Jan Critchett, *Untold Stories: Memories and Lives of Victorian Kooris* (Melbourne: Melbourne University Press, 1998).
39 PROVic, B5755, An appeal to the ratepayers from Ernest Mobourne for all the Lake Condah aborigines, 2 July 1907.
40 Jan Critchett, 'Mobourne, Ernest (1862–1918)', *Australian Dictionary of Biography*, http://adb.anu.edu.au/biography/mobourne-ernest-13103, accessed 1 December 2014, originally published in *Australian Dictionary of Biography, Supplementary Volume* (Melbourne: Melbourne University Press, 2005).

41 'Presentation of addresses', *Portland Guardian* (28 March 1890), p. 2.
42 *Argus* (27 March 1890), p. 8.
43 Goodall, *Invasion to Embassy*, p. 343. See also: Heather Goodall, 'Aboriginal history and the politics of information control', *Journal of Oral History Association of Australia*, 9 (1987), 23–7.
44 'Warangesda Aboriginal Reserve, Letter to the Editor', *Sydney Morning Herald* (2 June 1926), p. 17.
45 Barwick, *Rebellion at Coranderrk*, p. 2 (emphasis added).
46 *Ibid.*, p. 3.
47 See Nugent, 'The Queen gave us the land', pp. 189–91. For other references to the Queen Victoria claim around the 1940s, see Beckett, 'Aboriginal Histories, Aboriginal Myths', p. 105; Marie Reay, 'Native thought in rural New South Wales', *Oceania* (December 1949), 98–9.
48 Nugent, 'The Queen gave us the land', pp. 189–91.
49 Bain Attwood and Andrew Markus, *Thinking Black: William Cooper and the Australian Aborigines' League* (Canberra: Aboriginal Studies Press, 2004), p. 15.
50 For a discussion of Joe Anderson/King Burraga, see Heather Goodall, 'King Burraga and local history: Writing Aborigines back into the story', in Royal Australian Historical Society, *Bridging the Gap – Proceedings of the Royal Australian Historical Society's Annual Conference* (Sydney: RAHS, 1988), pp. 40–8.
51 Cited in Bain Attwood and Andrew Markus (eds), *The Struggle for Aboriginal Rights: A Documentary History* (Sydney: Allen and Unwin, 1999), p. 74.
52 State Records, NSW (SRNSW), 5/14819, 'Letter from A. Hamilton to Mr Lang, Premier of NSW', 14 April 1926.
53 This was a term used by Elizabeth Elbourne in a keynote address, 'Family Ties: Kinship and the Imperial Household in the British Empire, 1770s–1840s', at the NZHA Conference, University of Otago, Dunedin, New Zealand, 21 November 2013.
54 See, for instance, Diane Barwick, 'And the lubras are ladies now', in Fay Gale (ed.), *Woman's Role in Aboriginal Society* (Canberra: Institute of Aboriginal Studies, 1974), p. 60; Rowse, 'Aboriginal respectability', p. 56.
55 Keith Thor Carlson, 'The Indians and the Crown: Aboriginal memories of royal promises in Pacific Canada', in Colin M. Coates (ed.), *Majesty in Canada: Essays on the Role of Royalty* (Toronto: Dundurn Press, 2006), p. 71.
56 'Frederick Carmichael, Lake Tyers, to the Governor General, Lord Stonehaven', 14 August 1930, reproduced in www.humanrights.gov.au/publications/track-history-us-taken-away-kids-commemorating-10th-anniversary-bringing-them-home, accessed 13 February 2015.
57 See Jakelin Troy, *King Plates: A History of Aboriginal Gorgets* (Canberra: Aboriginal Studies Press, 1993).
58 Attwood, *Rights for Aborigines*, pp. 237–53. For history of threat to La Perouse reserve, see: Maria Nugent, *Botany Bay: Where Histories Meet* (Sydney: Allen and Unwin, 2005), pp. 136–9, 164–72.
59 'Lake Tyers and the Aborigines of Gippsland', The *Guardian* (2 May 1963), p. 5.
60 John Curwen Horner, Evidence, 22 August 1966, *NSW Joint Committee on Aborigines Welfare* (Sydney: NSW Government Printer, 1966).
61 Kevin Gilbert, *The Australian* (26 January 1972). See: Attwood, *Rights for Aborigines*, p. 347.
62 *Ibid.*
63 See Peter Tobin, *Aboriginal Land Rights in NSW: Demands, Law and Policy*, Endorsed by the Black Caucus, Sydney, the Black Rights Moratorium Committee, Sydney and Abschol (North Melbourne: Abschol, 1972).
64 C. D. Rowley, *A Matter of Justice* (Canberra: Australian National University Press, 1978), p. 109.
65 *Ibid.*
66 See for instance: Peter Read (ed.), *Down There with Me on the Cowra Mission: An Oral History of Erambie Aboriginal Reserve, Cowra, New South Wales* (Sydney: Pergamon Press, 1984); Margaret Somerville, *The Sun Dancin': People and Place*

in Coonabarabran (Canberra: Aboriginal Studies Press, 1994); Individual Heritage Group, *La Perouse: The Place, the People and the Sea* (Canberra: Aboriginal Studies Press, 1988).
67 Marilyn Wood, 'The journey to "Forked Mountain"', *Aboriginal History*, 25 (2001), 202.
68 Somerville, *The Sun Dancin'*, pp. 51–2.
69 Cited in *Ibid.*, p. 51. Similarly, one finds repeated references to Queen Emma Timbery at the La Perouse settlement as the recipient of a land grant from Queen Victoria. See for instance: Janet Hawley, 'Peacemakers for 200 years', *Sydney Morning Herald* (30 December 1987), citing Marjorie Timbery as saying: 'My husband, John Timbery, was born on the La Perouse reserve, which was a grant from Queen Victoria to Queen Emma Timbery'.
70 Goodall, *Invasion to Embassy*, pp. 101–3. In her discussion, Goodall points out that stories about land being granted by Queen Victoria only pertained to reserves to which Aboriginal people had themselves made specific demands, and concludes from this that the stories were not only about rights to land being recognised at the highest level of the British Empire but were also crucially a testament to Aboriginal people's own agency in struggling for and securing rights to land.
71 *Ibid.*, p. 103.
72 Barwick, 'And the lubras are ladies now', p. 60.
73 Rowse, 'Aboriginal respectability', p. 56.
74 Bill Schwarz, *The White Man's World* (Oxford: Oxford University Press, 2011), p. 8.

PART TWO

Royal relations

CHAPTER FIVE

'My vast Empire & all its many peoples': Queen Victoria's imperial family

Barbara Caine

A new year! What will it bring? May God bless all my beloved Children, Grandchildren, relations & friends. May He protect my dear Country my vast Empire & all its many peoples! This is my daily prayer.
Journal of Queen Victoria, 1 January 1894

Interest in Queen Victoria has been considerable in recent years. New biographies seem to emerge almost every year, indicating the continuing fascination with her childhood, accession, and married life.[1] The paradox of having a female monarch within the framework of Victorian constructions of gender – a paradox that was keenly felt and articulated several times by Queen Victoria herself[2] – has been addressed by a number of feminist scholars, while both political and cultural historians have turned their attention not only to the changing nature of the monarchy as an institution in the nineteenth century, but also to the ways in which it was understood and represented in the press and visual culture (see Figure 5.1).[3] Very little of this new work addresses her relationship to what she sometimes referred to as 'my vast Empire & all its many peoples'. This is a curious omission in view of her strong interest in some imperial questions and her importance as an imperial symbol in the final decades of the nineteenth century.

The limited work there is on Queen Victoria and the British Empire points to the difficulties historians have in coming to terms both with her imperial approach and enthusiasms, and with the extent and limits of her power in imperial matters. Many historians suggest that imperial and more particularly colonial questions were not of great interest to her. Yet even while accepting this view, S. H. Pugh points out that from the mid-1850s onwards Queen Victoria began to ask for more and more information about the colonies and to demand that she see colonial dispatches regularly. The Colonial Office in turn sought her approval of various courses of action it was taking. Moreover, Pugh concedes, she maintained a steady and on the whole a beneficent influence on the nominations of colonial governors, insisting that candidates be men of standing and that names might be submitted to her before soundings were taken to ensure that she was satisfied on this point.[4]

As this suggests, one crucial question that needs to be addressed centres on the nature and limits of Queen Victoria's power and influence in imperial and colonial matters, something which, as we will see, was not quite clear either to her or to her governments. She did not visit any part of the Empire and hence never knew it first hand. Nor did she have the extensive sources of independent information that familial links provided when it came to continental Europe. There, as Walter Arnstein points out, she 'was at the centre of a monarchical epistolary network that was often better informed than the British foreign office'.[5] When it came to imperial and colonial matters, however, she was dependent on the Colonial Office or on particular acquaintances or advisers with a range of their own interests and concerns. Her diaries confirm the view held by several historians about the ways in which her interest in imperial matters shifted from one place to another, changing over time, with India as the dominant concern in the early years of her reign and southern Africa becoming increasingly important in her later years.

But the diaries also suggest that Queen Victoria's racial attitudes were considerably more liberal and tolerant than were many of her contemporaries. There was unquestionably an element of orientalism in her fascination with some young Indians and even Africans. But she had a strong sense of the claims of many of them and a deep interest in their personal lives and stories. One of the few values she shared with her oldest son, Arnstein suggests, was that neither of them looked down on a person because of his or her race. She commented on a number of occasions in her journals on her concern that colonial administrators treated Indigenous peoples unjustly and failed to recognise their human claims. But by and large, the main ways in which her ideas were made manifest was in the strong interest that she took in particular individuals with whom she came into contact – and sometimes in the imperial or colonial frameworks or policies that had brought them to her notice. These people in whom she took an interest included Indians, Māori, and Zulus and other Africans, and the singling out of a few individuals perhaps helped to resolve the paradox of her repeated statements of belief in the importance of fair and generous treatment of such people while she believed so firmly in the importance and legitimacy of imperial expansion.

Figure 5.1 *The Secret of England's Greatness* (Queen Victoria presenting a Bible in the Audience Chamber at Windsor), Thomas Jones Baker, c. 1863. According to the National Portrait Gallery: 'The scene depicted is based on a popular but unfounded anecdote current in the 1850s. [W]hen asked by a diplomatic delegation how Britain had become powerful in the world, 'our beloved Queen sent him, not the number of her fleet, not the number of her armies, not the account of her boundless merchandise, not the details of her inexhaustible wealth ... but handing him a beautifully bound copy of the Bible, she said "Tell the Prince that this is the Secret of England's Greatness"'.

Empire and a constitutional monarchy

Almost from the moment that she ascended the throne, Queen Victoria was aware of the difficulties involved in being a constitutional monarch. She had complained to Lord Melbourne, she noted in her journal, 'Of my situation, and of the position of a constitutional monarch being such a hard one; he agreed, but said: "You must bear it, it is the lot which has been cast upon you; you've drawn the ticket," which I said I wouldn't bear and complained I was so much Plagued, *now*.'[6]

But even with Melbourne's tough advice, Victoria had difficulty in accepting some of the constitutional limitations imposed on her and some of the conventions that now surrounded royalty. She was particularly resistant to the notion that these limits applied not only to her role in government, but also to her capacity to staff her household as she chose. Her refusal to accept them led to 'the bedchamber crisis' of 1839, which arose when she refused to bow to the majority party in the House of Commons in choosing her household. She liked the Whig ladies of the bedchamber who had come to her with Lord Melbourne's prime ministership, and refused to dismiss them when Melbourne resigned and the Tory, Sir Robert Peel, was invited to form a government. Peel refused to become prime minister under these circumstances, and Lord Melbourne stayed on for another couple of years. By this time, Queen Victoria had married Prince Albert and so had the benefit both of his understanding of the situation and of his company, which made her ladies in waiting less important as companions. Hence when Melbourne again resigned in 1841 and Peel nominated his supporters as the household staff, the Queen gave way without complaint.

It was not just obstinacy or self-will that created difficulties for Queen Victoria, but a genuine lack of clarity in her situation. Britain lacked a written constitution or any document that defined precisely what her powers were. The Act of Settlement of 1701 gave the British monarch much the same powers as those of the president of the United States: as commander-in-chief of the army and navy, the monarch had the power to declare war, make peace and negotiate treaties with foreign countries, and appoint all major officers of state including judges and diplomats sent abroad.[7] As governor of the Church of England, the monarch chose bishops and the two archbishops who presided over the Church. Within the imperial framework, the monarch also appointed colonial governors. These powers had changed across the eighteenth and early nineteenth centuries, however, and by the time Queen Victoria came to the throne, it was generally expected that decision-making in all these areas would be done by the prime minister and the government of the day. The monarch might appoint the prime minister, but even this had become a formality as she could no longer choose or dismiss governments at will or control elections and put together a government of her choice.

But while convention now decreed that the Queen acted as a nominal figure, carrying out the wishes of the government of the day, even this was not clearly laid down, nor was there any clarity about what additional powers the Queen might have, or the kind of influence that she might exercise by virtue of her social prestige, her personal relationships – or her longevity. Many historians now accept that both outside analysts and those who interpreted constitutional conventions for the monarch and for the parliament tended to assert their own views rather than to base their opinion on any clear traditions or legislation.[8] Walter Bagehot's *English Constitution*, often seen as the most authoritative statement of the mid-Victorian period, is a case in point. Bagehot does not cite any authority and to some extent was simply expressing his own views. His work itself came to be seen as *the* authority, Michael Bentley argues, in large part because it expressed a view that was widely held at the time and meshed with an argument being put forward by constitutional historians, like Stubbs, Seeley, and Dicey, who 'constructed a past as a progression from royal to parliamentary or even democratic government, and whose current constitutional theory placed the taming of the monarchy at its centre'.[9] In Bentley's view, however, Bagehot was simply wrong and the powers of the Queen, although hard to define, were much greater than he thought.[10] Bagehot laid down the three prerogatives of the monarch as to be consulted, to encourage, and to warn. But in Bentley's view, the combination of her social power, her capacity to demand attendance from the prime minister wherever she happened to be, her indefatigable capacity for writing letters, and the sheer strength of her will meant that Queen Victoria often got her way on subjects not deemed to be within her control including the appointment of prime ministers and colonial governors and bishops.[11] And Bagehot entirely omitted the Empire. Writing in the 1860s, when imperial questions were not as important as they later became, it did not occur to him even to include an imperial role, although, as Arnstein argues, by the end of the century 'head of the heterogeneous British empire' was possibly Queen Victoria's most important ceremonial role.[12]

It is interesting to see how this question of the extent and the limits of Queen Victoria's power as a constitutional monarch played out in the imperial realm. It arose as an issue quite early in her reign. In regard to Canada, Ged Martin has argued that Queen Victoria actively exercised the prerogatives that Bagehot laid down, demanding especially that she be consulted when it came to the appointment of governors general.[13] She was guided in her approach, first by Lord Melbourne and then more significantly by Prince Albert, who took a very special interest in both Canada and Australia, seeing them as possible places for his younger sons to make careers. She took an even greater interest in India, where, some historians have argued, she exercised a power far more like that of European absolute monarchs than of their constitutional English counterparts.

Queen Victoria's attention was directed towards India in the early 1840s, partly, Miles Taylor suggests, because of the appointment of the Duke of Wellington as commander-in-chief of the British Army and of Lord Ellenborough as Governor General, both men with whom she was in contact. Ellenborough wrote to her directly, rather than going through the government, and she approved several of his actions, including granting medals to the victors of the Afghan campaign and the annexation of Sind in the northern Punjab in 1843, after a war in Afghanistan. After seeing her letter, the prime minister, Sir Robert Peel, wrote to the Queen, making clear, in a very carefully worded letter of October 1843, that while she might write to the Governor General of India, she should not express her own opinions either about Indian policy or about the conduct of the Governor General in her letters. It was not advisable, Peel wrote, 'to state your Majesty's opinion with regard either to the policy of retaining Scinde, as being of the greatest importance to the security of the Indian Empire'. The regular and constitutional channel for conveying her opinion would be through her servants, the relevant members of his government. In this particular case, as India was still formally governed by the East India Company, it was even more complicated, and 'instructions do not proceed from your Majesty's servants, directly signifying your Majesty's pleasure, but are conveyed in despatches to the Governor-General, signed by the three members of the Secret Committee of the Court of Directors'.[14] The matter was a particularly delicate one, as while some members of his government were sympathetic to Ellenborough's annexation of Sind, the directors of the East India were not. Shortly after this, the directors of the East India Company decided to recall Ellenborough, disliking what they saw as his aggressive policy, his theatrical love of display, and his overbearing demeanour in communicating with them. Peel announced their decision to the Queen – and had again to counsel her against making her opposition to this known to the directors, suggesting as an alternative that she bestow on him 'the rank of an Earl and the Grand Cross of the Bath' at a future date.[15] In all of these careful negotiations, one can see that Peel was clearly aware of how complicated these processes and arrangements were, and to remove any suggestion that he was responsible for them, he stressed that he was merely pointing out the 'constitutional channel'. But Queen Victoria continued to take a very close interest in India, in continued extensions of British territory, and in the fate of some of the Indian princes who were deposed when their territory was annexed.

A personal approach

This concern for particular individuals, and often also a personal attachment to them, was one of the most notable features of Queen Victoria's approach, not only to India, but also to some of the colonies. In some cases, Queen Victoria intervened to assist or support an individual; in others she notionally 'adopted' a particular child, deeming herself its godmother and making provision for educational and other needs. The idea of a godmother was a rather vague one in the nineteenth century, with no legal obligations and no clear religious or moral ones either. There is little discussion of the relationship in histories of the nineteenth century, and the novels in which a godmother features, such as Charlotte Bronte's *Villette*, depict a situation in which a close friend of a deceased mother is named a godmother and takes an occasional interest in a godchild, inviting him, or more often her, to visit for the holidays from time to time, but playing little part in her daily life. Queen Victoria's relationships with her godchildren varied. Some were like the fictional depiction: she provided money for a child's education, or occasionally had him or her to visit, but had little other contact. Others were welcomed as visitors to Windsor and Osborne where she made plans for their adult lives – often ones that did not come to fruition. But in all cases, the relationship was an occasional rather than a regular one as she invited people to visit when something prompted her to do so, or she provided money when it was asked for, rather than having a continuous relationship with a particular godchild. The most prominent of these adoptees were Indians from princely states, but they also included Africans, a Hawaiian prince, and a Māori baby.

The first person Queen Victoria took up seems to have been Princess Gowramma, daughter of Chikka Veerarajendra, the last King of Coorg. In 1852, some years after being deposed and exiled to Benares, Veerarajendra took his favourite young daughter, then aged eleven, to England ostensibly to ensure that she had a Christian education, but also as a way to make representations about a pension for himself. The little girl was presented to the Queen on her arrival and immediately became a favourite. The Queen attended her baptism, which was performed by the Archbishop of Canterbury – and amazed everyone by announcing herself as the godmother of Princess Gowramma. She presented Gowramma with a leather-bound autographed copy of the Holy Bible, embellished with gold-plated trimmings. Gowramma was frequently invited to court and was much liked.[16]

A couple of years later, in 1854, Princess Gowramma was joined by the young Maharaja Duleep Singh. He too had been deposed in 1849 when the Punjab, of which he was crowned Prince at the age of five, was annexed by the East India Company. His property and jewellery were confiscated, and he was put under the care of a British official. He converted to Christianity and was sent to England in 1854 to further his education. He too was presented to Queen Victoria and became for a time her special favourite. 'His youth, amiable character, and striking good looks, as well as his being a Christian, the first of his high rank who has embraced our faith, must incline every one favourably towards him,' she noted, 'and it will be a pleasure to us to do all we can to be of use to him, and to befriend and protect him'.[17] There is no suggestion here that he was wrongfully deposed or that his lands and personal fortune might be returned. But the Queen did come to feel strongly that he and others in a similar situation were entitled to some recompense for their land and titles and some security both for themselves and for their dependants. In a statement that serves to underline her sense of fellow feeling for Duleep Singh and others who, like him, had once been crowned rulers, she suggested to the Marquis of Dalhousie, the Governor General of India, that some form of reparation should be made – and that they should be allowed to live in aristocratic ease. 'It strikes the Queen to be an arrangement difficult to be justified, in a moral point of view', she wrote,

> to give these poor people – who after *all* were once so mighty – *no* security beyond their lives. Whilst we remain permanently in possession of their vast Empire, they receive a pension, which is not *even* continued to their descendants. Would it not be much the best to allow them, instead of a pension, to hold, perhaps under the Government, a property, which would enable them and their descendants to live respectably, maintaining a certain rank and position?[18]

The presence of these two young Indian royals, both of whom were Christian, raised for Queen Victoria and others in court circles the possibility of a marriage. But even though the Queen made her desire for this very clear, it did not eventuate. Neither Princess Gowramma nor Duleep Singh seemed to have followed court protocols or expectations. Princess Gowramma caused a scandal by having a relationship with a stable boy, and Duleep Singh was not prepared to accept her behaviour. He in turn became increasingly truculent and difficult. He apparently expressed his resentment at seeing the Queen wearing his family jewels, including the Koh-I-Noor diamond, by referring to her as Mrs Fagin behind her back, and his gambling and other excesses became increasingly problematic. Although more and more anxious and concerned about Duleep Singh's behaviour, Queen Victoria continued to try to assist him and to allow him to visit her. Both her often-expressed sympathy 'for these poor deposed Indian Princes' and her fascination with their physical appearance and manners help explain her patience with Duleep Singh, which was much greater in his case than it was in regard to her own children. He was, she noted in his adolescence, 'extremely handsome, speaks English perfectly, & has a pretty, graceful & dignified manner'. Even as he aged and lost his youthful looks, this early impression seems to have carried weight. Both Princess Gowramma and Duleep Singh came to rather sad ends, as the Princess contracted an unsatisfactory marriage and then died in her early twenties, while Duleep Singh spent decades living way beyond the means that the

British government was prepared to make available to him, trying vainly to get some restitution of his property.[19]

It was not only Indians who received personal attention and special favours from the Queen, but occasionally also other Indigenous people from Africa, Hawaii, and New Zealand. Here, too, her interest was usually directed to people connected to royal or chiefly households. Thus in the early 1850s, at much the same time as she took up Duleep Singh, Queen Victoria adopted Sarah Forbes Bonetta, a young Yoruba girl from West Africa, who had been orphaned at the age of five in the Okeadan wars and taken to Dahomey, in present-day Benin. Dahomey was a centre of the Atlantic slave trade, but Bonetta's royal birth prevented her from being sold. Instead, she was taken to the palace of the King Ghezo of Dahomey where she was effectively his slave. She was rescued while still a child by a captain of the Royal Navy, Frederick E. Forbes, who convinced the King to give her as a gift to Queen Victoria. Forbes renamed her Sarah, adding his own name and that of his ship, HMS *Bonetta*. The child was apparently exceptionally beautiful and talented both musically and in terms of her language skills. Like Forbes, the Queen was entranced, adopting the girl as a goddaughter, paying for her to be educated so that she could serve as a missionary, and including her in some family occasions. The Queen gave her a lavish gift when in 1861 she married James Davis, a freed slave from Sierra Leone who had become a wealthy businessman. Subsequently, when the couple fell on hard times, Queen Victoria continued her financial support, and when Sarah Davis died of consumption in 1880, leaving a young daughter, Queen Victoria became her godmother too, paying for her education in England (see Figure 5.2).[20]

A decade later, she adopted a young Māori boy who was born in London shortly after his parents had paid her a ceremonial visit. In a journal entry for 1863, Queen Victoria recorded a meeting with thirteen New Zealand chiefs accompanied by three of their women. Her description makes clear her fascination with their exoticism of dress and physical appearance, but also her sense of their seriousness and of her obligations to them:

> They were half in native, half in European dress. The women wore silk petticoats with their strange cloaks of matting, & feathers in their hair. The men also had cloaks, some skins, thrown over them, carrying spears & hatchets, & feathers stuck in their hair. The greater number of the men were much tattooed, and the women, on their mouths. All had fine eyes & beautiful, glossy black hair, but not good features, except 3 of the men who were tall & good-looking. They all kissed my hand & behaved extremely well. Several of the men undid their mantles, spreading them at my feet, & some did the same with their arms, – as a symbol

Figure 5.2 Sarah Forbes Bonetta (Sarah Davies).

of allegiance. I, through the interpreter, expressed my interest in their welfare, sorrow at the war having broken out & my satisfaction at seeing them. I promised they should be governed, & thanked for their beautiful lament. When they were asked if they had anything to say, one stepped forward & expressed the greatest loyalty, declaring they had nothing to do with the war. They deeply regretted they had not come sooner when they would have seen dearest Albert. To see me had been their greatest joy. I bowed and went upstairs.[21]

The chiefs were members of a touring group organised by William Jenkins, a Wesleyan lay preacher of questionable standing, who had been an interpreter for the Nelson provincial government and brought the chiefs to Britain in part to demonstrate to them the might and the technological and military power of Britain. But he intended also to deliver a series of lectures in England, using the Māori party to demonstrate songs and dances. It seems clear that the Māori who signed up for the tour were badly exploited, travelling steerage and inadequately fed on board ship. In London, they were shown many of the sights and introduced at aristocratic and even royal receptions. But Jenkins lacked the funds to pay for the tour, and the chiefs were soon dependent on public subscriptions and charitable aid. The meeting with Queen Victoria was secured early on in their visit, but they had to stay for some time after that as there was no money to pay for their return journey. When the chiefs visited Queen Victoria, she noticed that one of the women, Hariata Pomare, was pregnant and expressed a wish to be the child's godmother. Having done so, she arranged for lodgings for the young couple with the Māori-speaking wife of a missionary, providing a christening gift for the baby, which she presented personally, and paying for the family to return to New Zealand (see Clarke Chapter 6 this volume). Her subsequent interest was intermittent, although apparently she expressed a wish that the boy would serve in the navy, but it is unclear whether or not he did so.[22]

From queen to empress

While Queen Victoria seems to have accepted many of the conventions pointed out to her by Peel, she continued to challenge general ideas and assumptions about her role and powers – and her title. In the course of the early 1870s, she came strongly to feel that she should not only be queen, but also empress. Disraeli, as prime minister, accepted this view and submitted a Royal Titles Bill to Parliament. Initially she had wished to become Empress of Great Britain, Ireland, and India. But in the face of the opposition with which this proposal was met, both in Parliament and in the press, Disraeli suggested that it be limited to Empress of India.[23] Both the Queen and Disraeli were surprised by the extent of the opposition. It came from many quarters and was not united, but one underlying theme was the concern that both historically and in contemporary Europe imperial titles belonged to absolute and autocratic forms of government. By contrast, the designation king – or queen – was the appropriate one for an English constitutional monarch. An imperial title, Gladstone argued, implied rule 'without the constraints of law and constitution'. It was 'wholly repugnant to the tastes, the temper, and the tradition of this country', in the view of the *Westminster Review*, a view shared by dozens of other British newspapers and periodicals. Queen Victoria was deeply distressed that there should have been this opposition, and wondered if it had been made sufficiently clear to people that it was her wish to assume this new title![24]

The controversy that this bill aroused serves as a useful reminder that, while often now thought of as symbolising all things British,

Queen Victoria was seen by many contemporaries and thought of herself very much as a European. Her mother, Princess Victoria of Saxe-Coburg-Saalfield, was a German princess, whose brother, Victoria's devoted Uncle Leopold, became King of Belgium. Victoria, who was fluent in both French and German, often wrote to him in one or other of these languages. Her European ties were expanded by her marriage to her cousin, Prince Albert of Saxe-Coburg-Gotha. Thus through birth, marriage, and then the marriages of her own daughters and granddaughters, Queen Victoria was related to all the royal houses of Europe: German, Russian, Swedish, Norwegian, Bulgarian, Greek. These European connections were often commented on critically during her lifetime, especially after her marriage to Prince Albert. Several historians and biographers insist that the European connection, and the question of her status amongst European royalty, was Queen Victoria's primary concern in becoming an empress. The declaration of the German Empire in 1871 raised particular problems, David Starkey suggests, because this meant that in time Queen Victoria's oldest daughter who had married the German crown prince would become an empress – and might outrank her mother![25]

This is not to suggest that India was unimportant to Queen Victoria. On the contrary it exercised her greatly. But in her own mind, she was already Empress of India. She made this point clear in 1872 when she refused to meet Burmese envoys unless they prostrated themselves in their customary fashion when appearing before sovereigns. 'As Empress of India I must insist on this', she wrote in her journal, noting that her insistence had worked. She went to the Throne Room and 'received the Ambassadors, 4 in number, who knelt down at the door, walked up & knelt again at the foot of the Throne, bowing their heads to the ground. An Address was read, which the 1rst Ambassador laid at my feet, as well as a lacquer box'.[26]

Despite her intense desire to have herself proclaimed empress, Queen Victoria took no part in the public celebrations that greeted this event. Her absence from them provides a useful point from which to raise the question whether and how the new title affected her role in relation to imperial questions. Although some contemporaries feared that becoming an empress would expand her power, few historians would now support the idea that it did so. On the contrary, Miles Taylor has argued, the formal adoption of the title 'Empress of India' marks the point at which 'most of Victoria's imperial powers – both formal and real – had been reduced or removed'.[27] She had long had close relations both with some Indian princes and with a number of viceroys. However, Liberal policy in imperial questions and the reform of the army had reduced the scope for royal patronage. Even in the choice of imperial and colonial governors, the power of the Crown was lessening as that of the government and of the Colonial Office increased. This view, that the authority of the Queen diminished once she became empress, is shared by scholars interested in representations of the Queen in literature and culture, who point to a general sense of the diminution of queens and empresses in popular representation from the mid-1870s onwards.

The proclamation of Queen Victoria as Empress of India did, however, change the way the British Empire was positioned and functioned there. Lord Lytton, the Indian viceroy, organised a vast and elaborate durbar in Delhi to celebrate the proclamation of the Queen as Empress. This occasion, he said, 'was a unique opportunity, not merely for broadening the base of imperial government through a popular symbol but for materially strengthening the government thorough a new understanding with the princes of India'. Held in the old Mughal capital, the durbar depicted Queen Victoria 'as the direct heir of the Mughal dynasty in whose name her Viceroy proceeded to receive the ritual fealty of India's remaining princes and maharajas'. As David Washbrook has recently argued, as Empress of India, Victoria now took her legitimacy from the Indian past 'wherein she became the Great Mughal and committed herself to sustaining, changeless and unchangeable, the hierarchical order of a traditional Indian society'. In doing so, she relinquished the symbolic role she had played earlier as a link to India's modern future. This linking of Queen Victoria to the Mughal tradition and India's past, Washbrook argues, benefited the traditional princes of India – but brought an end to other more liberal developments that had been expanding the role of Indians within the Raj.[28]

Queen Victoria and the scramble for southern Africa

This suggestion about the reduction or removal of Queen Victoria's imperial powers from the mid-1870s is certainly borne out in relation to Africa, which became a subject of increasing interest to Queen Victoria from about this time. The annexation of the Transvaal by Britain in 1877, the Zulu Wars that began in 1879, and then the whole move to partition Africa and extend British control over much of southern Africa were matters of immense public interest in Britain in which the Queen fully shared.

Prior to this point, although receiving letters and dispatches especially about southern Africa, Queen Victoria rarely commented on Africa or on Africans. One of her few journal entries to mention anything about Africa was a report of a family excursion to visit 'a party of Zulu Kaffirs, from Natal' who were being exhibited in London. 'The party', she noted in her diary,

> Consisted of 11 men, a young woman, only 16 years old, the wife of the Chief & a dear little Baby of 15 months old. They were most curious, wild, fine looking people, with the woolly hair, thick lips & flat noses of the Negroes. They are of a rich copper colour, with splendid chests & muscles. ... The woman was very short. ... I stroked & played with the Baby. The men sang some of their war songs & went through some of their war dances, & deliberations on war, mock fights, &c – all very extraordinary, & really frightful, from the state of fury they worked themselves up into with leaps, & bounds & making the most awful sounds. Their singing is very strange, – all in chorus. These people have no idea whatever of religion, but are very intelligent & ready to follow whatever advice, – as to behaviour &c – is given them. They live very happily together. The women are treated as a very inferior being, but not used unkindly.[29]

As the extensive literature on Sarah Baartman demonstrates, exhibiting Zulu and other 'kaffirs' was not uncommon across the nineteenth century, either in the form of a 'spectacle of empire' or as a way of displaying the particular ethnographies and the physical features and characteristics of lesser or primitive races.[30] Queen Victoria's concerns that the group lived happily together and that the merchant, a Mr Caldecott, who had brought the group to Britain and acted as interpreter, 'has promised to take them home',[31] are perhaps as notable here as are her assumptions about the Zulus' savagery, lack of religion, and preparedness to follow any advice given them.

There are few other references to Africa in the journals of Queen Victoria until the 1870s. One of the earliest in that period is a comment on a visit by Bishop Colenso, the Bishop of Natal, who visited England in the mid-1870s to protest against the very harsh measures, including imprisonment and expropriation of land, being taken by British authorities against Zulus who would not obey what they saw as unreasonable demands. She supported him, applauding

> His noble, disinterested conduct in favour of the natives who were so unjustly used, and in general her very strong feeling (and she has few stronger) that the natives and colored races should be treated with every kindness and affection as brother, not – as alas, Englishmen too often do – as totally different to ourselves, fit only to be crushed and shot down! ... (In general all her Colonial Governors should *know* her feelings on this subject of the native races).[32]

But she did not continue to support Colenso or his views when he came into conflict with her other advisers, and, for the most part, those with whom she had closest contact and who helped shape her views were men, such as Lord Chelmsford and Bartle Frere, who were strongly committed to the need to expand British imperial control over southern Africa and to destroy any form of African independence.

It was in the course of 1879, during the first year of the Zulu Wars, that Queen Victoria seems to have become imaginatively engaged with Africa and particularly with the nature and characteristics of African tribes. The context for all of this is made clear in a number of journal entries dealing with that conflict and how it might be resolved. Her views were close to those of the Conservative government as is indicated in a journal entry of August 1879 reporting a conversation with the prime minister, Lord Salisbury, in which he said that the conflict with the Zulus was a very difficult one that would take a long time to resolve. 'The people would have to give up their arms, – Csetshwayo be deposed, & the country divided amongst several Chiefs', she wrote.[33] Queen Victoria, who had received several letters depicting Cetshwayo as cruel and dangerous from the British high commissioner, Sir Bartle Frere, as well as gifts of Zulu spears, shared these views.

The following month, when Cetshwayo was in exile in Cape Town, Queen Victoria reported in her journal a conversation that had occurred with Lord Chelmsford after dinner. Speaking of the Zulus, he said,

> They could easily run 40 miles in a day, & have been known to go 80! They are very fine, powerful men, varying in colour from a yellowish brown, to quite black. They are not exactly Negroes, & are supposed to be half Arab. They have only been in possession of that country, since the beginning of the present century. ... there is no similar race further north, in the interior. The *friendly* Zulus are just the same people. The Kaffirs are different, & not near so formidable. The Swazis, are not near so brave, but very cruel, – the Pondos, not good fighting men. The Zulus are not particularly cruel, but in war will kill every white man, as they consider it lawful & necessary. They disliked the war, & after Ulundi, all, including the women & children, came round to him & his Staff, & shook hands with them, seeming quite happy. They are very merry by nature, even in the streets, jumping & dancing about.[34]

Here as elsewhere, one can see her carefully noting what are seen as the distinguishing features of these different groups – and perhaps also expressing something almost like admiration for the Zulus as 'fine, powerful men'. She also noted comments from Colonel Pemberton on what wonderful soldiers the Zulus were, and how absolutely loyal to their King.

Once deposed, Cetshwayo wrote many letters pleading his cause to the Queen and seeking to come to Britain to do so in person. The government was opposed to him doing so, and the Queen was too. Influenced as she was by Frere, she did not believe that Cetshwayo should be returned to power in Zululand and thought that it should be directly annexed. The election of Gladstone and the Liberal Party in 1880 brought with it both an opposition to the idea of annexation and a sense that Cetshwayo should be allowed to come to Britain to plead his own cause as he wished to do. The Queen accepted this, and when he finally got to England, he had a brief meeting with her. Her description of the meeting, as Bridget Theron has argued, was much less patronising or filled with racial stereotypes and racist overtones than that of Lord Kimberley, head of the Colonial Office.[35] As was so often the case when she was writing about Indigenous men, she noted their physical characteristics and appeal. 'Cettewayo is a very fine man', she wrote in her journal after he had visited,

> In his native costume, or rather no costume. He is tall, immensely broad, & stout, with a good-humoured countenance, & an intelligent face. Unfortunately he appeared in a hideous black frock coat & trousers, but still wearing the ring round his head, denoting that he was a married man. His companions were very black, but quite different to the ordinary Negro. I said, through Mr Shepstone, that I was glad to see him here, & that I recognised in him a great warrior, who had fought against us, but rejoiced we were now friends. He answered much the same, gesticulating a good deal as he spoke, mentioned having seen my picture, & said he was glad to see me in person. I asked about his voyage, & what he had seen, & then named my 3 daughters, at which he said 'ah!'[36]

But there was no discussion of land or restoration of his rule – and no suggestion on her part that she would support such a thing. Cetshwayo, who well understood the ceremonial nature of the visit, did not expect that the Queen would make or announce policy. His significant meetings were with the Colonial Office, and it was there he was told that he could return to Zululand, but would have only a very small territory to rule under British oversight. But what is significant is precisely the way in which the Queen followed the policy and schedule of the Colonial Office, simply providing the ceremonial gloss that was required. There was no suggestion, as there was in regard to India a decade or so earlier, that she might intervene on his behalf.

This entirely ceremonial performance was evident a decade later when the Queen was visited by the three paramount chiefs of Bechuanaland – Khama, Sebele, and Bathoen – in their attempt to prevent their territory being taken over by Cecil Rhodes and his chartered company. They had very much wished to see the Queen and reported themselves greatly pleased to have done so, although, as one of them commented, 'I had no idea she was so short and stout'.[37] But there was no intimation that she had to be persuaded of their cause – or indeed that she was. Public opinion and humanitarian support was rather more important. The concessions they needed had to come from Chamberlain and the Colonial Office and not the Crown.

In the final years of her reign, the role of the Queen in imperial and colonial matters became even smaller. Her personal interest certainly continued – and perhaps even grew. This was so in regard to India, as she surrounded herself with Indian cloth and jewellery and established an extremely close relationship with Abdul Karim, who was first employed as a servant but subsequently became her Hindi teacher and very close friend and adviser. It was evident elsewhere too, such as in her intense interest in the fate of British and imperial soldiers in the South African War, all of whom were sent Christmas chocolates at her request. But the personal interest was removed from any wider political questions.

The diminution of her own power is often evident in the ways in which her image was used and manipulated in imperial celebrations of which she remained a passive spectator. Thus the diamond jubilee of 1897 was celebrated as a 'festival of empire' with military parades and processions of many kinds demonstrating the scope and power of the British Empire. But the great imperial speech to Parliament given in her name on this occasion was not only written and read for her, but was not even submitted for her approval. Her account of the day serves to emphasise her separation from any political activity. It was, she wrote in her journal, 'A never to be forgotten day' involving a drive through cheering crowds, who gave an ovation greater, in her view, than anyone had received before. This was followed by a ceremonial arrival at Buckingham Palace where 'I touched an electric button, by which I started a message which was telegraphed throughout the whole Empire. It was the following: "From my heart I thank my beloved people, may God bless them". At this time the sun burst out'.[38] But her pleasure in the excitement of the day, the warmth of her reception by the crowds, and the electric message to the whole Empire just served to underline the extent to which she had accepted her role as an entirely ceremonial one.

Conclusion

It is clear that Queen Victoria was not in any way inclined to question the imperial expansion that she came to symbolise, nonetheless, as I have argued here, it does seem important to recognise the full extent of her interest in imperial and colonial questions. In a similar way, while no one could argue that she was a consistent advocate of the rights of colonised peoples, it is important to recognise her many statements of concern about them and her relative lack of racial prejudice, a matter that warrants further research. She was forced, from the moment of her accession, to recognise the limits of her power and authority in imperial and colonial matters – although she found a number of ways to challenge and to extend those limits in particular situations. What is most interesting, though, is the deep interest she took in some individuals whose lives had been severely disrupted by colonial expansion and the ways in which she sought to assist and support them. These individual cases are, of course, interesting in themselves as they involve fascinating personalities and situations. But they also seem to provide the only way in which Queen Victoria could resolve the paradox presented by her simultaneous enthusiasm for imperial expansion and her sympathy for some of the victims of that expansion. These relationships of varying degrees of closeness and concern were a way that she could exercise a powerful influence on some aspects of imperial policy and development.

Notes

1 Christopher Hibbert, *Queen Victoria: A Personal History* (London: Harper Collins, 2000); Gillian Gill, *We Two: Victoria and Albert: Rulers, Partners, Rivals* (New York: Ballantine Books, 2010).
2 Dorothy Thompson, *Queen Victoria: Gender and Power* (London: Virago, 2001); Adrienne Munich, *Queen Victoria's Secrets* (New York: Columbia University Press, 1996); Margaret Homans and Adrienne Munich (eds), *Remaking Queen Victoria* (New York: Cambridge University Press, 1997); Margaret Homans, *Royal Representations: Queen Victoria and British Culture, 1837–1876* (Chicago, IL: University of Chicago Press, 1998).
3 David Cannadine, 'From biography to history: Writing the British monarchy', *Historical Research*, 77:197 (2004), 289–312.
4 S. H. Pugh, 'Colonial Office', in John Holland Rose, Arthur Percival Newton, Ernest Alfred Benians, and Henry Dodwell (eds), *The Cambridge History of the British Empire*, vol. I (Cambridge: Cambridge University Press, 1958), pp. 737–9.
5 Walter L. Arnstein, *Queen Victoria* (Basingstoke: Palgrave Macmillan, 2003), p. 180.
6 *Queen Victoria's Journals*, Thursday 5th December 1839, digitised by Chadwyck Healy, http://www.queenvictoriasjournals.org, accessed 30 November 2013.
7 Arnstein, *Queen Victoria*, p. 35.
8 Andrej Olechnowicz, 'Historians and the modern British Monarchy', in A. Olechnowicz (ed.), *The Monarchy and the British Nation, 1780 to the Present* (Cambridge: Cambridge University Press, 2007), p. 37.
9 Michael Bentley, 'Power and authority in the late Victorian and Edwardian court', in Olechnowicz (ed.), *The Monarchy and the British Nation*, p. 164.
10 Olechnowicz (ed.), *The Monarchy and the British Nation*, pp. 13–4.
11 Miles Taylor, 'Queen Victoria and India, 1837–61', *Victorian Studies*, 46:2 (2004), 266.
12 Arnstein, *Queen Victoria*, p. 165.
13 Ged Martin, 'Queen Victoria and Canada', *American Review of Canadian Studies*, 13:3 (1983), 215–34.
14 Sir Robert Peel to Queen Victoria, 30 October 1843, in A. C. Benson and Viscount Esher (eds), *A Selection from Her Majesty's Correspondence Between The Years 1837 and 1861*, published by Authority of His Majesty The King, accessed through http://www.gutenberg.org/files/20023/20023-h/20023-h.html, accessed 30 September 2014.
15 Sir Robert Peel to Queen Victoria, 23rd April 1844, *Ibid*.

16 C. P. Belliappa, *Victoria Gowramma: The Lost Princess of Coorg* (New Delhi: Rupa & Co., 2010).
17 Queen Victoria to the Marquis of Dalhousie, 26 July 1854, in Benson and Esher (eds), accessed through http://www.gutenberg.org/files/20023/20023-h/20023-h.html, accessed 30 September 2014.
18 Queen Victoria to the Marquis of Dalhousie, 2 October 1854, *Ibid.*
19 Evans Bell, *The Annexation of the Punjab, and the Maharajah Duleep Singh* (Boston, MA: Adamant Media Corporation, 2001).
20 The story was told in many daily papers in August 1862 when the marriage of Bonetta to Davis took place. See, for example, *The Caledonian Mercury*, 15 August 1861. See also: Caroline Bressey, 'Of Africa's Brightest Ornaments: A short biography of Sarah Forbes Bonetta', *Social and Cultural Geography*, 6:2 (2005), 253–66.
21 *Queen Victoria's Journals*, 11 August 1863, http://www.queenvictoriasjournals.org, accessed 30 November 2013.
22 Alison Drummond, 'Queen Victoria had a Maori Godson', *TE AO HOU, The New World*, no. 24 (October 1958), http://teaohou.natlib.govt.nz/journals/teaohou/issue/Mao24TeA/c43.html, accessed 10 September 2014. See also: 'Pomare, Hare and Pomare, Hariata', *Encyclopaedia of New Zealand*, http://www.teara.govt.nz/en/biographies/1p21/pomare-hare, accessed 15 July 2014.
23 L. A. Knight, 'The Royal Titles Act and India', *Historical Journal*, 11:3 (1968), 488–507.
24 Richard Williams, *The Contentious Crown: Public Discussion of the Monarchy in the Reign of Queen Victoria* (Aldershot: Ashgate, 1997), pp. 117–20.
25 David Starkey, *Crown and Country: A History of England through the Monarchy* (Harper Collins E-book, 2010), p. 469.
26 *Queen Victoria's Journals*, 21 June 1872, http://www.queenvictoriasjournals.org, accessed 30 November 2013.
27 Taylor, 'Queen Victoria and India, 1837–61'.
28 David Washbrook, 'After the Mutiny: From Queen to Queen-Empress', *History Today*, 47:9 (September 1997), pp. 10–15.
29 *Queen Victoria's Journals*, 14 June 1853, http://www.queenvictoriasjournals.org, accessed 30 November 2013.
30 Saartjie Baartman, also known as Sarah Bartman, was a Khoikoi woman from southern Africa who was exhibited in Europe in the early 19th century in a human zoo setting under the name 'Hottentot Venus'. Particular interest was taken in her large buttocks (steatopygia). See Clifton Crais and Pamela Scully, *Sara Baartman and the Hottentot Venus: A Ghost Story and a Biography* (Princeton, NJ: Princeton University Press, 2009); Rachel Holmes, *The Hottentot Venus* (New York: Random House, 2006); Sadia Qureshi, *Peoples on Parade: Exhibitions, Empire, and Anthropology in Nineteenth-Century Britain* (Chicago, IL: University of Chicago Press, 2011).
31 *Queen Victoria's Journals*, 14 June 1853, http://www.queenvictoriasjournals.org, accessed 30 November 2013.
32 Quoted in Arnstein, *Queen Victoria*, p. 181.
33 *Queen Victoria's Journals*, 5 August 1879, http://www.queenvictoriasjournals.org, accessed 30 November 2013.
34 *Ibid.*, 3 September 1879.
35 Bridget Theron, 'King Cetshwayo in Victorian England: A cameo of imperial interaction', *South African Historical Journal*, 56 (2006), 60–87.
36 *Queen Victoria's Journals*, 14 August 1882, http://www.queenvictoriasjournals.org, accessed 30 November 2013.
37 Neil Parsons, *King Khama, Emperor Joe, and the Great White Queen* (Chicago, IL: University of Chicago Press, 1998), pp. 228–9.
38 *Queen Victoria's Journals*, 21 June 1897, http://www.queenvictoriasjournals.org, accessed 30 November 2013.

CHAPTER SIX

Māori encounters with 'Wikitoria' in 1863 and Albert Victor Pomare, her Māori godchild

Chanel Clarke

On 15 July 1863, Queen Victoria entered the Council Room at Osborne House and was greeted by a party of thirteen Māori accompanied by their interpreter William Jenkins. In this chapter, I discuss why this group had been gathered together to undertake a tour of England, and how they had come to have an audience with the woman they affectionately called 'Our Mother'.[1] Their visit to Britain offers an insight into Māori and European encounters in the nineteenth century. Although the visit itself has been covered by a number of commentators and historians, these accounts have tended to focus on the relationship between the Māori party and their interpreter William Jenkins, including the deterioration of that relationship over the course of the trip.[2] My account instead turns to focus attention on the encounter and ensuing relationship between the Māori group and Queen Victoria.

The Māori party in 1863 was but one of many such Indigenous guests that Queen Victoria herself, or members of her family, received during her reign.[3] Other Māori had visited previously, and others would have audiences afterwards, as Chapter 2 in this volume shows. Queen Victoria was omnipresent in Indigenous people's lives in a symbolic way, either through her representatives on the ground or through material manifestations such as flags, coins, and other objects. In the case of New Zealand, this symbolic relationship was also made manifest in the form of a treaty covenant.[4] Royal audiences provided a different kind of encounter. They were a rare opportunity for her to relate to, and interact on a personal and intimate level with, Indigenous people from Britain's distant colonies. They also offered her the chance to frame the symbolism of 'Great Mother' in a very real and practical way, for instance by becoming godmother to Indigenous children.

For Indigenous people, audiences with Queen Victoria were opportunistically seized upon to affirm and reaffirm allegiances, while also simultaneously providing scope to hold the monarch to account for the often devastating effects of colonisation occurring under her name on their homelands. They were an important means for reasserting their authority and sovereignty, and earnestly pleading their case for support. They also served as a space within which the multiple roles Queen Victoria played, both symbolic and real, were made visible for Indigenous audiences to comprehend and make sense of on their own terms.

While not unique in the broader landscape of Indigenous interactions with Queen Victoria, the visit of this party of Māori is unusual for the rich trove of material that it has left behind. Although visits like this one were often widely reported in the press, or occasionally described in detail by the Queen herself in her journals, in this case the Māori voice and agency is clearly articulated in the surviving record. Some of the party recorded their own impressions, either at the time or afterwards. This chapter will show how this material can be used to reveal Māori ideas and understandings of Queen Victoria. The material, which consists of diaries, letters, photographs, as well as objects of exchange, provides insights into how each party interpreted the other, their attitudes towards one another, and how this was indicative of the broader imperial and colonial contexts within which they were all operating.

Previously overlooked sources of information are also drawn on in the chapter to reveal little-noticed aspects of Māori agency in colonial encounter situations. In particular, the role of dress, a source often neglected in historical studies, offers a different approach to understanding colonial ideologies and Māori responses.[5] Dress is a powerful visual expression of Māori identity and agency within the colonial encounter. However, historians have largely ignored it as a key source as the written word has been given prominence and authority. Dress and the concomitant process of fashion is often seen as frivolous, unimportant, and having little to offer. In recent times, however, material culture studies has advocated for the importance of objects, including clothing and fabrics, in gaining an understanding of past lives, and dress studies has benefited to some extent from this material turn.[6]

Such an object-centred approach is useful here when it is also applied to the other surviving physical remnants of the visit. Objects were exchanged among the parties at the time to acknowledge allegiances and familial relationships, whether real or metaphorical. These objects have continued to have 'lives' and gain significance long after the initial givers and recipients have passed on. One object in particular, a silver gilt christening set presented by Queen Victoria to her Māori godson, Albert Victor Pomare, has become a tangible reminder for descendants, not only of the visit itself, but also the unique personal relationship that was established with the Queen as the result of it.

Gathering the chiefs

The group of Māori that visited Queen Victoria that day in 1863 had been brought together initially by the Wesleyan lay preacher and native interpreter William Jenkins, who had arrived in New Zealand in 1842 with his wife Catherine Jane. The Wesleyan Missionary Society had offered Jenkins a position as a religious teacher and caretaker at the remote Cloudy Bay mission station in the South Island. Jenkins displayed a keen interest in Māori language and customs, and his lay preaching enabled him to further his missionary work amongst Māori. After being posted at various stations, he was dismissed from the Church and moved to Nelson in late 1852, where he established a furnishing and upholstery business and was appointed to the part-time position of provincial native interpreter.[7] In 1856, the decision to dismiss him was revoked, and Jenkins was able to return to his lay work in the Church. Around 1860 he conceived of the idea to take a party of Māori to visit England. He proposed to give a series of illustrated lectures in England, using the group to demonstrate songs and dances. He set up a company to promote the venture and managed to garner both financial and moral support for it from five of his friends and business associates.

Jenkins was keen to get approval for his venture from the Governor, Sir George Grey, which would open the doors to English society, and ultimately it was hoped gain access to the Queen. However, tensions were high in New Zealand with the Māori King Movement having just been established two years earlier in 1858 (see Johnson Chapter 10 and Belgrave Chapter 2 this volume). The idea for the movement was largely derived from the English model of monarchy that Māori were familiar with and had seen in operation. It was to be pan-tribal in membership and would unify Māori under one sovereign but on an equal footing with Queen Victoria. The movement was envisaged as a way to end intertribal conflict, retain Māori land, and provide a separate governing body for Māori. It is fair to say that Grey was lukewarm in his support of the proposed visit owing in part to 'his "peculiar position" as Her Majesty's representative and therefore responsible for the peaceful co-existence of settler and Māori'.[8] With the outbreak of the first Taranaki War in 1860, and with the Māori population declining rapidly as a result of internal wars and disease, if the trip failed it was sure to reflect badly on Grey. Acutely aware of his position, he could not allow the venture to be connected with the New Zealand government in any way.[9]

Although the speculative nature of the trip prevented Grey from committing to it fully, he nevertheless wanted a hand in the selection of those Māori who would travel. Given his present priorities with war in the Waikato imminent, it was clear that loyalist Māori 'would be ideal advocates of that nation's might to their own kinsmen and to rebellious tribes' on their return home.[10] Thus it was probably on his recommendation that Jenkins sought chiefs from amongst the Ngāpuhi who had forged their peace with the Pākehā (Europeans) after the Northern Wars, remained steadfast in their allegiance to Queen Victoria, and refused to rally to the cause of the Māori King.[11]

Jenkins persuaded thirteen Māori to join his tour, nine of whom were from the northern tribes (Figure 6.1). Accordingly, it was felt that those who were chosen to go were to be from good families and chiefs of repute – real Māori nobility.[12] This was to become an important factor later on when Jenkins wished to distinguish his party from that of a troupe of Māori who were performing at the Alhambra Theatre at the same time.[13] This criterion also had implications for the way in which the group understood their own status, not only in relation to Queen Victoria, but also to the English masses, particularly those who had come to call New Zealand their home. The remaining four Māori were from central North Island, Coromandel and Taranaki tribes. Joining them were Jenkins's business partners, both gold prospectors, William Lightband and William Lloyd. On 5 February 1863, they sailed from Auckland on board the *Ida Zeigler* bound for England.

First impressions

One of the first events that the party attended upon its arrival in England was the official unveiling of the Prince Albert Memorial at the Horticultural Gardens in South Kensington. As an obvious visual marker of difference, their dress was a constant source of comment throughout their travels, and the British gaze is clearly represented in newspaper accounts of the time. As the *Spectator* noted on this particular occasion, 'All along the broad walk, most conspicuously, there strolled a party of New Zealand chiefs, tattooed all over, and clothed with what appeared to be coconut matting. ... The matting of the kings might have passed muster, but the painted and engraved faces of the queens contrasted ludicrously with their semi-English costume, including hoops of the latest fashion, to be pleasing to European eyes'.[14]

The image conjured up in the minds of the *Spectator*'s readers, and indeed for those that were present on the day, must have seemed rather bizarre and an apparent novelty as Jenkins noted 'scores of the aristocracy – each vying with the other to get a shake of the hand with one of our New Zealand Princes and Princesses'.[15] However, Māori had been combining both Māori and European dress since early contacts. They adapted their existing garments, and also adopted garments of European manufacture. Mixed styles of dress that incorporated both Māori and European elements persisted throughout the nineteenth century. By the time the well-known painter George French Angas arrived in New Zealand in 1844, Māori, and particularly Māori women and girls, had almost completely adopted European clothing so that there was little distinguishing their dress from that of their European counterparts.[16] The cloak had become one of the few customary articles of clothing that persisted and was employed for its ability to instantly express and maintain Māori cultural identity. Furthermore, depending on the type of cloak employed, the social position of the wearer was communicated. Unfortunately, without the knowledge to translate these inherent meanings, most English observers misinterpreted the Māori party's attire. Either portrayed as a quaint novelty or at worst ridiculed for their clashing styles, the group were denigrated for their apparent parody of 'superior' English fashions.

On the other hand, the occasion provided the Māori party with an opportunity to show English audiences how they had embraced European styles of dressing. The adoption of European dress was regarded as a mark of civilisation and progress,[17] and they were acutely aware of this. How they dressed would have a bearing on how they were perceived and received by English audiences, and in their eyes the less Māori they looked the better. Reihana, probably the most pious Christian of the entire party, confirmed this attitude when he wrote: 'In New Zealand I never liked a mat [cloak]; before I knew Jenkins I disliked all sorts of mats for mostly they are many years old; being not much made now, and the things are nasty, they are often filled with vermin'.[18]

Interestingly it appears that their mixed dress, particularly the wearing of their customary cloaks over their English dress, was largely at the behest of Jenkins. The drive to civilise, so apparent in Jenkins's project, in which the adoption of European dress would have been a key visual indicator of success and the adoption of 'civilisation', was contradicted by his insistence on the wearing of traditional Māori clothing. He deployed Māori dress for its performativity and sensationalist features, but often this ran counter to Māori preferences and sensibilities. Indeed for Reihana it was the heathen nature of Māori dress that caused affront, and the continued hypocrisy in this regard bewildered and aggravated him throughout the trip. Not only were the members of the party expected to wear their customary clothing, but they were also expected to perform traditional dances with which to

Figure 6.1 William Jenkins arranged for the Māori party to visit John Wesley's house while they were resident in London. To commemorate the Jubilee of the Wesleyan Missionary Society, the artist James Smetham was commissioned to depict the occasion. (University of Otago, Hocken Collections, Uare Taoka o Hakena).

illustrate their lectures. As Reihana asserted: 'Jenkins wished us all to practise those wrong things. I never did it in my own country and nor did Paratene since he was baptised'.[19]

Meeting the prince

For the Māori party, dress continued to mark their engagements, but in different ways as it became the material currency for establishing unique relationships between themselves and others. Three days after their outing to the Horticultural Gardens, on 13 June 1863, they had an audience with their Royal Highnesses, the Prince and Princess of Wales, at Marlborough House. After a period of polite conversation and before the couple were about to retire, the old chief Paratene stepped forward and laid his dog skin cloak at the Prince's feet.[20] This was followed by Reihana and Tere each presenting a cloak to the Princess. Jenkins noted in his diary that the cloaks that were exchanged were an Ihupuni and a Kaitaka.[21] It is important to recognise that these types of cloak were typically reserved for those of high rank and standing. The exchange of these particular examples signalled the regard with which the Prince was held. Reihana's earlier comments clearly indicate his awareness of the function of their European-style dress as showcasing their progress towards becoming more civilised, both in appearance and, for the devout Christian, in their adherence to the faith. Despite this, the exchange of traditional cloaks and other significant tribal heirlooms shows that they sought to use familiar tribal customs of exchange to signal their allegiances and in all probability their expectations of reciprocal and mutual support from the Prince and his family.

Further gifts of an ear ornament, a genealogical staff, and, from Hirini, a piece of land, were offered to the Prince.[22] Dispossession from their lands and the desire for self-governance were uppermost in the minds of Indigenous peoples across Queen Victoria's vast empire. Therefore, the offering of land by Hirini in this context is interesting. It is debatable whether the offer was indeed a gift with no expectation of return, or merely the granting of a conditional right to use the land, which is a common practice among Māori that is known as tuku whenua.[23] As was customary, in the tribal context of New Zealand, such exchanges were often undertaken to cement or to reaffirm established allegiances and mutually beneficial partnerships. To what extent Jenkins was able to adequately translate the party's intention in exchanges like these is doubtful. However, the Prince's status as heir to the throne was not lost on the group, and in some ways this visit was an important forerunner and preparation for the main event that was yet to come.

It is useful to compare this occasion with similar ones occurring across the Empire around the same time. Just three weeks previously, on 24 May 1863, several members of the Kulin nation, an alliance of Aboriginal tribes from Central Victoria in Australia, attended Governor Sir Henry Barkly's levee in Melbourne (see Edmonds Chapter 8 this volume). There they presented the Governor with an address to the Queen that was written in both Kulin and English in which they pledged to become her loyal subjects. They also presented the Governor with several gifts for the Queen and her children, including a large possum rug, some baskets, and a number of spears and other weapons and implements.[24] The Kulin had come from Coranderrk, which was located about sixty kilometres north-east of Melbourne, to petition the Governor to set aside Coranderrk for their use as the traditional landowners and to grant them the ability to be self-governing and in charge of their own affairs. Soon after this meeting, the Governor gazetted the reserve at Coranderrk, and the Queen relayed her satisfaction at their allegiance to her, both indications to the Kulin that they had entered into a reciprocal relationship with the Queen.[25] Further to these gifts, the Queen was sent a crocheted collar made by a young Aboriginal girl named Ellen, which she accepted with much pleasure. The adoption of domestic skills such as sewing, knitting, and crochet by Aboriginal girls was encouraged by missionaries and early settlers, and an item like the collar clearly indicated the civilising agenda that Aboriginal people were also experiencing alongside their Māori counterparts at this same time.[26]

A few years earlier in 1860, the Prince of Wales attended similar ceremonies when he represented his mother on the first royal visit to Canada. The tour included multiple opportunities for organised events and public spectacles at which local First Nations had varying involvement. The high point of these ceremonies came towards the end of the Prince's tour of the provinces, when a large group of Aboriginal people gathered at Sarnia.[27] After several addresses and a reply from the Prince, a ritual exchange of gifts occurred where selected chiefs received commemorative medals engraved with the image of Queen Victoria. In exchange, the Prince received a number of weapons, pipes, wampum, and decorative birchbark work.[28]

The ceremonies were carefully planned by colonial administrators to ensure that the right kind of image was presented to the Prince as well as to the local press, and this involved the careful management of Aboriginal dress. Just as Jenkins insisted that the Māori party wear their traditional costumes, Chief Superintendent of the Indian Department Richard Theodore Pennefather also tried to do everything in his power to ensure that Indians appeared in 'Indian costume' during the royal audiences. He even engaged the help of missionaries to ensure that only properly attired Aboriginal people attended the event.[29] This preoccupation with dress and encouraging Aboriginals to wear traditional costume ran counter to departmental policies, which promoted the adoption of European values and practices that included embracing European attire. But European clothes did not convey the same spectacle as the traditional Aboriginal dress of war paint and feathers, so colonial administrators were prone to ignore their own policies when it suited them.

The extent to which Aboriginal dress was indeed 'traditional' and wholly unaltered by European contact is debatable. The surviving images show a somewhat different picture. Images depicted in the *New York Illustrated News* show a mix of semi-tailored fringed coats and trouser-like leggings, styles that were probably developed in the mid-nineteenth century for public performance but that had since gained credence as 'authentic' dress.[30] Some chiefs, particularly those who like Reihana had converted to Christianity, appeared entirely in European dress. The *Christian Guardian*, when commenting on the visit, drew a direct correlation between the Indian Department's insistence on the wearing of traditional dress and the failure of the

Aboriginal attendees to gain redress for their grievances.[31] The deliberate strategy then by some chiefs to don European garb signals that Europeans did not wholly mediate clothing choice, and Indian agency in self-fashioning was still apparent.

Such ceremonies of exchange in a traditional sense signalled the establishment of reciprocal relationships and often access to one another's resources. These royal audiences operated in the same manner, and the objects that were exchanged became symbolic of those allegiances pledged to one another. More importantly, these objects, having been given or received in Queen Victoria's name, were seen by Indigenous peoples as indicative of a direct relationship with her. Although one-off audiences, they were, and still are, constantly recalled by subsequent generations of descendants, gaining in the process an almost legendary quality. The surviving objects also became tangible reminders that Indigenous people could utilise as they continued to petition subsequent governments for recognition and rights to their resources as promised them by the Queen.

Preparing to meet the Queen

For Jenkins, the audience with the Prince and the acknowledgement by their Royal Highnesses ensured that the touring party was 'rising high on the ladder of fame',[32] but not content he was keen that they go higher still. 'I must raise you up to a great height to see the Queen', he wrote.[33] From the outset, he was intent on having an audience with the Queen. To what extent he made this known to the Māori party before they left New Zealand is not clear, but they were probably more than aware of his preparations in the background in pursuit of this goal once they were in England. Jenkins worked to gain support for his venture through the colonial administration and within English aristocratic circles. He engaged the help of Anthony Ashley Cooper, the seventh Earl of Shaftsbury, and upon his request prepared messages from the Māori chiefs to Parliament and royalty. Although Jenkins translated these messages, they nevertheless build a picture of Māori understandings of Queen Victoria particularly as 'Mother' and 'Protector'. In fact, it is clear that the Māori chiefs used these messages as a vehicle to not only assist in seeking an audience with the Queen, but to alert her to some of the pressing issues that they no doubt wanted to raise should they meet her face to face. Paratene, for instance, beseeched the Queen to:

> Listen to what I say about the settler in New Zealand. There are many who say, 'Let the Maories be destroyed and let their land be possessed by the white man.' And it is on this account that many of the natives are

suspicious of the settlers. It is because we have heard these things that we wish to see the face of Our Mother the Queen and to hear from her own lips what the intentions of the English people are towards us the people of New Zealand.[34]

Reihana in his letter reinforced the symbolic status of the Queen as 'Mother' when he wrote: 'Our desire to see this country and the great Chiefs and Our Mother the Queen was great indeed'.[35] Like Paratene, he used the letter as an opportunity to raise the rules of engagement he expected of the Queen's non-Māori subjects, and to seek her moral support in this regard. He hoped that:

> we might converse about the rules of conduct of the Europeans living in New Zealand and also of the rules of conduct of the Maories that you may be informed with whom the fault lies – whether the wrong doing lies with the white man or with the Māori. We rejoice that our friend Jenkins has brought us to this country to England that we may have the opportunity of finding out these things from the fountain head.[36]

In a similar vein, Horomona Te Atua stated, 'When we are permitted to see our Queen then we shall know that we, – the Māori and English, are one. But if the Queen will not see us then what we have to say about New Zealand will remain hidden – it will be lost'.[37]

As all these letters indicate, the Māori concept of kanohi ki te kanohi (face to face) was clearly important and the preferred Māori way of engaging with one another. However, the Colonial Office administrators, like their representative on the ground in New Zealand, maintained a fairly neutral position. As was the case with Grey, the Colonial Office administration had to carefully manage the politics of allowing the Māori party to visit Queen Victoria so close to the outbreak of war back in New Zealand. Additionally, although the visit had decidedly altruistic aims, the underlying sense that the group was ultimately an exhibit was ever present, and Jenkins's motivations were constantly questioned. It was important for the Colonial Office administration to ascertain that Jenkins's intentions were honourable and that he was not taking advantage of his charges by exhibiting them about town 'a la "Barnum"'.[38] Not only was the Queen's honour at stake, but her Māori subjects had to be protected too. After some persuasion by Jenkins, an approach was made on his behalf by the Duke of Newcastle (Secretary of State for the Colonies) for an audience with the Queen, and her consent was given.

Visiting the Queen

The visit to Queen Victoria at Osborne House on the Isle of Wight took place on 15 July 1863. Understandably, the visit was a source of comment by all parties, and remarkably several observations survive to represent the Māori viewpoint. Reihana maintained a journal in Māori, and although parts were probably completed in retrospect, it nevertheless provides an insight into his overall impressions of the country and the people he and the group encountered. In particular, these sources document their preparations for the meeting with Queen Victoria and provide descriptions of the careful self-fashioning of the party. Upon arrival at Osborne, Reihana noted: 'The Duke [of Newcastle] told us to wash ourselves and put on our Māori clothing'.[39] Unlike previous occasions where Reihana bemoaned the pressure to wear their customary cloaks, this time he provides a clear indication of their willingness to abide by the instructions to dress in their native costume. He recorded: 'We did so adorning ourselves with feathers even with albatross feathers. Then we were led into a room where we were to meet the Queen'.[40]

Paratene Te Manu, who described the visit many years later to journalist and historian James Cowan, provided more detail about these preparations, a further indication of the group's careful and deliberate attention to their dress on this occasion:

> We attired ourselves in our Māori garments, which we had carried with us for the ceremony. We put on our waist-mats and our shoulder-capes and our robes and cloaks of the finest woven white flax and some of us had cloaks of pigeon and kākā parrot and kiwi feathers. We set feathers of the huia and the kōtuku (white heron) and the long tailed cuckoo in our hair; and we took in our hands the weapons of the Māori, the spear, the greenstone and whalebone clubs and the hani or taiaha.[41]

The finest feather cloaks were often embellished with kiwi and kākā feathers, and the latter was particularly coveted for its red colour, which was indicative of chiefly status.[42] The further embellishment to the head with huia feathers, again usually reserved for those of high rank, indicated the chiefly make-up of the group and deliberate self-fashioning they employed to indicate this status.

The Queen's own observations provide further elaboration as well as some glimpse of her own perceptions of their dress and physical characteristics. Her diary entry for that day notes:

> they were half in native, half in European dress. The women wore silk petticoats with their strange cloaks of matting, and feathers in their hair. The men also had cloaks, some skins thrown over them, carrying spears and hatchets and feathers stuck in their hair. The greater number of the men were much tattooed, and the women on their mouths. All had fine eyes and beautiful, glossy black hair, but not good features, except three of the men who were tall and good looking.[43]

The adoption of European dress by the Māori party was indicative of their active positioning of themselves as a civilised and cultured people who had given up their former 'pagan' lifestyles and adopted the insignia of elite society. For the chiefs, the royal audience was a chance to use their clothing to mark out their status as equal counterparts with Queen Victoria. Their traditional garments and accessories, which clearly communicated status in a traditional sense, helped them to do this, but whether this was apparent to Queen Victoria is not known. Her description of their dress, very much like the English audiences at the Horticultural Gardens, indicates that she found their mixed styles a novelty and no doubt viewed them as quaint vestiges of past barbaric lives.

Queen Victoria was also adept at manipulating her own image and the audience at Osborne afforded her the opportunity to display her dual private and public roles. Her private life as 'Mother' was on view when three of her children, the Royal Princesses Helena and Beatrice, and Prince Leopold, attended her. This intimate and personal display of motherly duty no doubt helped to reinforce her more public role as 'Mother' to the many Indigenous nations of her empire, Māori included. Several of the chiefs acknowledged her children in their speeches, and her position as a widow was not lost on them either. In accordance with Māori protocol in which the deceased are recognised prior to the living, they also paid tribute to her departed husband Albert, a gesture she found most touching. Jenkins noted that they 'affected her Majesty even to tears'.[44]

The chiefs for their part were intent on using the occasion as an opportunity to alert the Queen to their dissatisfaction about their present situation at home in New Zealand. New Zealand's entree into the British Empire occurred when James Cook sailed into its waters in the latter part of the eighteenth century. However, it was at least another seventy years before Māori became official subjects of Her Majesty when the Treaty of Waitangi, signed by various chiefs in 1840, extended her 'royal protection' and imparted to them 'all the rights and privileges of British subjects'.[45] It was these same rights and liberties that Māori felt were not being upheld. The occasion provided them with the opportunity to present their case directly and unfettered by colonial administrators. As loyalist Māori, they were keen to distance themselves from the present fighting in the Waikato area, which had broken out just three days prior to their visit when British troops had crossed the Mangatawhiri Stream, signalling the beginning of the Waikato campaign. Up until then, this tributary of the Waikato River had formed the frontier between European settlers and Māori Kingites. In his speech, Wharepapa said: 'Perhaps you have heard of the battle that is raging in the Waikato. After we had landed in London we read of it in the newspaper. You might think that it involves all of New Zealand but this fighting is only in Waikato in a small place'.[46] Although he was keen to distance himself from the King Movement and the activities occurring in the Waikato, nevertheless Wharepapa was well aware of the opportunity presented by this occasion and used it judiciously to make the group's case. Loss of land and fear of extermination continued to prey on their minds, and they appealed to the Queen's authority to protect them from her British settler subjects who were intent on making New Zealand the Great Britain of the Southern Hemisphere.[47]

Queen Victoria for her part expressed her interest in their welfare, concern at the war having broken out, and her satisfaction at seeing them.[48] As on previous occasions, to refresh those ties and to ensure that the reciprocal relationship was affirmed, cloaks were presented. Victoria's awareness of her responsibilities are clear from her observations as she describes how 'several of the men undid their mantles spreading them at my feet, and some did the same with their arms, as a symbol of allegiances'.[49] The gifts were, of course, offered as symbols of allegiance but also as reminders of the mantle of protection that the Queen had afforded Māori in her treaty offering. They were a reminder that a partnership pact had been established between the two peoples, and it was her moral duty to ensure that those rights were upheld and that Māori were protected from those British subjects that would seek to cause harm and take away their land.

More than just simple adornments, cloaks also mediated relations between people, both past and present, and it was the spiritual embodiment of past ancestors that Māori also drew on in the exchange as a further reminder of the promises made in the treaty covenant.[50] Cloaks were a commanding visible expression of Māori identity. Although their invisible spiritual potency remained just as powerful to Māori, this was probably not so apparent to Queen Victoria. For her part, she 'promised they should be governed' and thanked them for their 'beautiful lament'.[51] While she made promises to ensure their welfare, the opportunity to signal her reciprocal allegiance to and relationship with the Māori tribes presented itself in a rather unusual way.

Royal godmother

During the visit the Queen noticed that one of the party, Hariata Pomare, was pregnant, and the Queen expressed a wish to be the child's godmother. Furthermore, she requested that if the baby were a boy that he be named

Albert, after her beloved husband, and if a girl, Victoria. At the Queen's expense, Hariata and her husband, Hare Pomare, left Jenkins's party and went to stay with Elizabeth Colenso in Tottenham to prepare for the birth of the baby. Elizabeth was the daughter of a Church Missionary Society (CMS) lay missionary and had grown up in New Zealand, becoming fluent in the Māori language. She married the CMS mission printer William Colenso in 1843 and taught in mission schools around the country. She became estranged from William after his philandering was exposed, and in 1861 she took her children to England to continue their education. In London, she was engaged in philanthropic work with the Church of England, which led to her introduction to Jenkins's party.[52]

On 26 October 1863, Hariata gave birth to a son, and named him Albert Victor. Albert Victor was confirmed at a baptism held at Tottenham, and at the Queen's request, the event was commemorated with a photographic portrait of the couple and their new baby. William Bambridge was engaged to create the portraits, and although never formally recognised, for all intents and purposes he was the Queen's photographer, bearing responsibility for private commissions and the printing and organisation of her vast photographic collection.[53] The following day, the Queen received the couple and the child at Windsor where she requested Bambridge make a further portrait of Hare.[54]

The Queen had wholeheartedly embraced the new medium of photography and was the first British monarch to have her life fully recorded on camera, and, as the medium evolved, so did her image.[55] She grasped that the monarch's role was increasingly symbolic, and the medium of photography allowed her to carefully craft her private and public image to great effect. She had a strong understanding of the monarchy's role as an articulator of moral values, and one way in which she could achieve this was within the framework of family. Through photography especially she was able to create an image of herself as a devoted wife and mother to her immediate family as well as to her extended family across the Empire. With the invention of the *carte de visite*, a format that could be widely reproduced and which allowed the general public for the first time to own a photographic portrait of the Queen,[56] her image indeed became truly global.[57]

John Mayall, who had made a name for being the first to produce visiting-card portraits of the Royal Family, which became enormously popular, made a further portrait of the young Māori couple. In both portraits, the husband and wife are dressed entirely in European fashion with the baby Albert wearing a christening gown and bonnet. The portraits by Mayall were reproduced in the *carte de visite* format, and Hare received four dozen of these to distribute among their relatives on their return home.[58] It is not insignificant that Queen Victoria chose to single out Hare and Hariata as a young family unit to fashion after her own image. The touching photographs depict Hariata, supported from behind by her husband Hare, looking lovingly down at her child, very much in the manner of the Queen's portraits with her own family, especially of her husband before his untimely death (see Figure 6.2). Knowing full well their mobility, especially within the visiting card

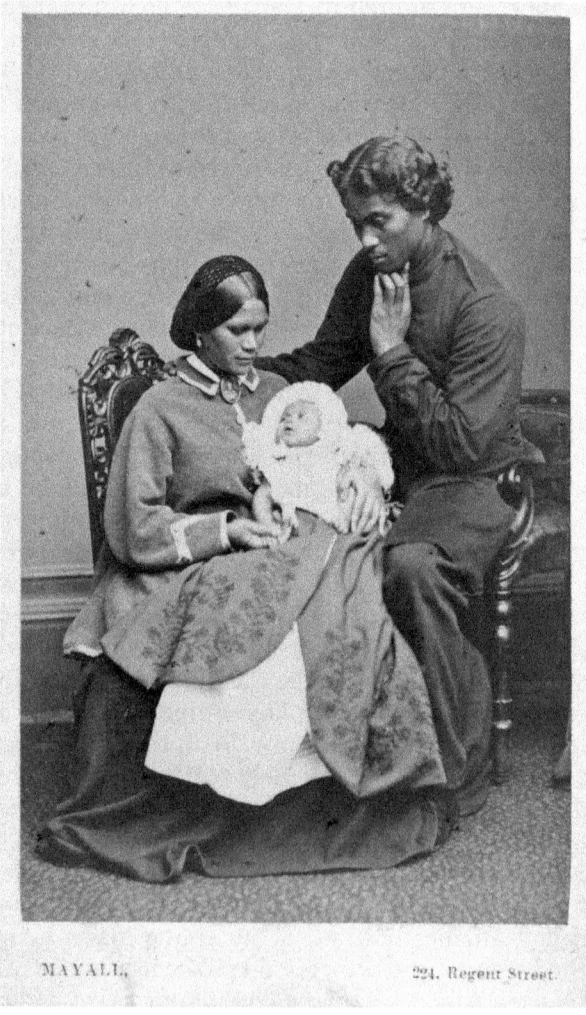

Figure 6.2 Albert Victor Pomare, godson of Queen Victoria, with his parents Hare and Hariata Pomare, photographed by John Mayall at his Regent Street studio in 1863.

MĀORI ENCOUNTERS WITH 'WIKITORIA' IN 1863

format, the Queen in effect could actively promote moral values centred on the family that could be conveyed to her Indigenous subjects.

In recognition of this auspicious event, the name Albert Victor has continued to be bestowed on descendants over the years. My own father, as a descendant of Hariata, was in fact named Albert Victor, and I carry the French version of Victoire for my middle name. This continued naming practice with subsequent generations reinforces the intimate relationship that this small family had with the monarch and links present-day descendants with those past ancestors. In so doing, this practice also acts as a kind of inherited authority by placing present-day descendants in a direct relationship with the Crown in recognition of that forged in the past.

As well as bestowing the gift of her husband's name and her maternal protection as the child's godmother, the birth of the child presented the Queen with an opportunity to exchange material gifts in the form of an engraved gilt christening set comprising a cup, knife, fork, and spoon, all housed in a green morocco leather case (see Figure 6.3).[59]

Figure 6.3 Christening set presented by Queen Victoria to her godson Albert Victor Pomare in 1863. The knife is engraved: To Albert Victor Pomare/from his Godmother Queen Victoria/November 1863.

Interestingly, Albert Victor was one of several of the monarch's godchildren from across the Empire. The year before his birth, Queen Victoria had sent another christening cup to Hawai'i as a gift for the young Prince Albert Kamehameha, the son of King Kamehameha IV and Queen Emma.[60] The relationship between the two families had been established when King Kamehameha wrote asking Queen Victoria to be godmother to their infant son, to which she consented. Unfortunately, due to an illness, suspected to be appendicitis, the young prince died before the Christening gift arrived. A little more than a year later, King Kamehameha followed his son to the grave, leaving Queen Emma grief stricken and bereft much like her British counterpart. For two decades, the queens exchanged letters and were a source of great comfort to each other.[61] Other godchildren included the West African girl Sara Forbes Bonetta and several of the children of the Maharajah Duleep Singh (see Caine Chapter 5 this volume).[62]

The christening sets presented were symbolic on a number of levels. Firstly, they signalled the entry of the native child into the house of God and marked the final step in the process from primitivism towards civilisation and enlightenment. Secondly, they provided tangible material form to the relationship between Queen Victoria and her subjects. Their physical manifestation allowed for her presence while she herself was absent. Although they marked one-off episodic and intimate encounters, at the same time they came to represent enduring and continuous relationships with her subjects at the outer reaches of her Empire. They enabled her to have a personal maternal relationship with these specific children, who in a sense could stand in for all her Indigenous 'children' gaining benefit from her protective mantle.

The legacy of these interactions continues to be emphasised by today's descendants in various public and private contexts. Over the years, the Albert Victor christening set has been withdrawn from the Auckland Museum, where it is currently housed, to be displayed at family reunions and other tribal events. More recently, the set was exhibited within the politically charged space of the Waitangi Tribunal by claimant iwi (tribes).[63] As surviving tangible objects, these gifts play an important role in this space as reminders of cherished relationships and as continued signifiers of loyalty. They are not to be seen as symbols of acquiescence, however, but rather as physical prompts to present-day representatives of the Crown of broken promises and unfulfilled expectations of reciprocity.

Alongside these multiple images of the Queen as mother, godmother, and widow, a further image can be added and that is the Queen as a devout Christian lady. During the audience with the Queen, Hirini

Pakia told her that the 'people of New Zealand are strongly influenced by religion', and Kihirini made touching references to Albert having 'gone to God's right hand'.[64] The extent to which the trip transformed the Māori party as Jenkins had intended is debatable. Several were devout Christians before they left, and their commitment to their faith was evident before they even arrived on English shores. They held daily prayer meetings on board the ship, and Paratene's recollections that 'none of our Englishmen came and had prayers with us; neither did any of our Pakehas read the Bible to us'[65] signal the first instance of their dissatisfaction and increasing disillusionment with their leaders. Although they received mixed messages regarding the religious devotion of the English, the Māori party drew on their understanding of Queen Victoria as a benevolent Christian lady, and therefore sought her assistance in that capacity to advance their cause.

A lasting impact of the trip is the churches that those from the north established at Mangakahia, Ohaeawai, and Kaikohe upon their return home. Although this could be seen as the ultimate success in Jenkins's eyes, it was probably in spite of Jenkins rather than because of him that these edifices were built. Throughout the trip the party became increasingly bitter and frustrated as they were subjected to a roller-coaster of lectures and meetings with little or no payment. The length of time away from their families and the poor English weather began to take their toll. Their predicament came to the attention of Miss Charlotte Julia Dorotea Weale, or Mihi Wira as the party called her, and it was largely thanks to her philanthropy and support that the party made it back home to New Zealand. So it was in honour of Mihi Wira not Jenkins that these churches were built. Interestingly, like Albert Victor, descendants were also named in honour of Mihi Wira and the work she did to ensure the Māori party made it safely home.

Jenkins tried to convince the chiefs before they embarked on their travels that they would rise very high within English society and be great chiefs on their return home. However, despite their meteoric rise within English aristocratic circles, it was apparent to the party that this was because of their novelty and own standing rather than to any help of Jenkins. Indeed, their status allowed Jenkins to participate in circles he would not otherwise have had access to. They were all from families of very high standing in New Zealand and considered themselves equivalent to the English aristocracy, fitting in comfortably with those with whom they mixed. It was Jenkins who would rise above his station with the help of his Māori charges.

Since the signing of the Treaty of Waitangi in 1840, Queen Victoria has loomed large in Māori lives even though she never physically visited New Zealand. Owing to her conspicuous absence, Māori encounters with her were usually through her representatives on the ground or through material forms crafted in her image. The treaty agreement became the basis on which Māori understandings of Queen Victoria were framed, and when the promises made in the treaty failed to be upheld, the visiting Māori party seized the opportunity to meet kanohi ki te kanohi (face to face) with the Queen. They used the meeting to direct the attention of English audiences, and particularly Queen Victoria, towards their grievances back home in New Zealand. Their careful management of dress was critical to enhance their status and prestige on foreign shores and to portray themselves as treaty partners on an equal footing with the Queen. Similarly, Indigenous peoples and Queen Victoria herself had a hand in constructing her own image. Key among these was the image of Queen Victoria as 'Great Mother' in which her protective cloak enveloped all her children including those in her private realm of family, and those within her public realm of empire. This symbolic role was further reinforced with the additional role of godmother, which was realised in a tangible way with the gifting of the christening set to Albert Victor, creating a lasting memory of the visit. The visit to Queen Victoria in 1863 is regularly recalled, and the material legacy of this relationship in the form of the christening set is often re-presented in similar modern-day encounter situations such as Waitangi Tribunal cases where present-day Crown representatives must come face to face with the descendants of those nineteenth-century Māori visitors. These contemporary interactions can tell us a lot about the continued significance of these long-standing relationships. Long after each character has physically gone, that symbolism remains and is probably more potent now than it ever was.

Acknowledgements

My gratitude to Eileen Clarke, Catherine Smith and Angela Wanhalla for their insightful comments on early drafts. Thanks also to the Auckland Museum for assistance to attend the Queen Victoria in the Colonies Symposium at the Australian National University in December 2013, where I presented an earlier version of this chapter, and for its continued support of my research and writing endeavours.

Notes

1 Brian Mackrell, *Hariru Wikitoria! An Illustrated History of the Māori Tour of England, 1863* (Oxford: Oxford University Press, 1985), p. 50.

2 The visit was extensively covered by the English and New Zealand press at the time. Subsequent articles appeared in New Zealand newspapers over the years in relation to the visit and especially the fate of some of the Māori travellers. In more recent times, Brian Mackrell's book-length coverage has been supplemented with smaller articles in academic and local history journals. For instance, see Warren Limbrick, 'A right royal riddle', *Journal of Parnell Heritage Inc.*, 2 (December 2012), 8–12. See also Mandy Treagus, 'Spectacles of empire: Māori tours in England in 1863 and 1911', in Kate Darian Smith et al. (eds), *Exploring the British World: Identity, Cultural Productions, Institutions* (Melbourne: RMIT Press, 2004), and Mandy Treagus, 'Agents or objects? Māori performances in Britain', in Sue Thomas (ed.), *Victorian Traffic: Identity, Exchange, Performance* (Cambridge: Cambridge Scholars Publishing, 2008).
3 Often the Queen's children received Indigenous guests in England or were sent to the colonies to represent the Queen at various official engagements. For instance, the Prince of Wales toured North America in 1860 as the Queen's official representative. The first royal visitor to New Zealand was Prince Alfred, Duke of Edinburgh and second son of Queen Victoria. He arrived at Wellington in 1869 as captain of *HMS Galatea*.
4 The Treaty of Waitangi was first signed on the 6 February 1840 in the Bay of Islands. The treaty is an agreement, in Māori and English, that was made between the British Crown and about 540 Māori rangatira (chiefs).
5 In the context of this chapter, I use the defintion of dress developed by Eicher and Roach Higgins 'as an assemblage of body modifications and/or supplements displayed by a person in communicating with other human beings'. J. B. Eicher and M. E. Roach-Higgins, 'Definition and classification of dress: Implications for analysis of gender roles', in R. Barnes and J. B. Eicher (eds), *Dress and Gender: Making and Meaning* (Oxford and New York: Berg, 1992).
6 In this regard, Appadurai's 1986 work has been particularly influential: Arjun Appadurai (ed.), *The Social Life of Things: Commodities in Cultural Perspective* (Cambridge: Cambridge University Press, 1986). This has been followed by work by Daniel Miller, including his *Material Culture and Mass Consumption* (Oxford: Basil Blackwell, 1987) and Steven Lubar and W. David Kingery (eds), *History from Things: Essays on Material Culture* (Washington, DC: Smithsonian, 1995).
7 Mackrell, *Hariru Wikitoria!*, p. 18. While resident in Motueka, Jenkins became embroiled in a case of theft from local Māori. Refusing to answer the charge, he was dismissed from the Church.
8 *Ibid.*, p. 21.
9 At this time, Māori had moved from a majority population to a minority primarily as a result of internal wars and disease. See M. King, *The Penguin History of New Zealand* (Auckland: Penguin Books, 2003), p. 150.
10 Mackrell, *Hariru Wikitoria!*, p. 21.
11 *Ibid.*
12 *The Wellington Independent* (29 November 1862), p. 2.
13 At the same time the Māori party were in London, another group of Māori were also resident and being employed by a Mr Hegartz for the purposes of theatrical exhibition. Known as the 'Warrior Chiefs', the group had arrived from New Zealand via Australia and were conducting their performances at the Alhambra Theatre.
14 Mackrell, *Hariru Wikitoria!*, p. 38 as quoted in the *Spectator* taken from A. H. Reed, *The Story of Northland* (Auckland: A. H. and A. W. Reed, 1956), pp. 301–2.
15 Diary of William Jenkins, 18 May 1863 to 6 February 1864. Combined transcript taken from two different typescripts held privately, transcribed by Dawn Chambers, www.nzpictures.co.nz/diaryjenkinswilliam1863.pdf. p. 3, 10 June 1863, accessed 30 April 2014.
16 M. Pendergrast, 'The Fibre Arts', in D. C. Starzecka (ed.), *Māori Art and Culture* (Auckland: David Bateman Ltd, 1996), pp. 114–46.
17 S. Buckridge, *The Language of Dress: Resistance and Accommodation in Jamaica 1760–1890* (Kingston: University of the West Indies Press, 2004), p. 35.

18 Mackrell, *Hariru Wikitoria!*, p. 53. Mat was the commonly used term for what is today known as a cloak or covering for the body rather than a floor mat.
19 Ibid., p. 28.
20 Dog skin cloaks (kahu kurī) were made from the skins and fur of the Polynesian dog, which gradually died out in New Zealand. They were descended from the dogs brought to New Zealand from Polynesia on the ancestral canoes of the Māori people in the 13th century. They were small, long-haired dogs about the size of a border collie. Some were black, some white, and others a combination with patches or spots. Considered a prestigious garment, the kahu kurī was usually only worn by those of high status.
21 An Ihupuni is a particular type of dog skin cloak, and a Kaitaka is a highly prized cloak made of flax fibre with a tāniko ornamental border. Both varieties were considered prestigious cloaks and often reserved for those persons of more chiefly status.
22 Mackrell, *Hariru Wikitoria!*, p. 40.
23 See for instance Susan Healy, 'Tuku Whenua as customary land allocation: Contemporary fabrication or historical fact?', *Journal of the Polynesian Society*, 118:2 (2009), 111–34, and I. H. Kawharu (Sir Hugh Kawharu), *Land and Identity in Tāmaki: A Ngāti Whatua Perspective*, Hillary Lecture (2001), Auckland War Memorial Museum, http://tekakano.aucklandmuseum.com/images/common/landandidentitylecturenotes.pdf, accessed 5 November 2014.
24 See Bain Attwood, *Rights for Aborigines* (Crows Nest, NSW, Australia: Allen and Unwin, 2003), p. 16, and Jane Lydon, *Eye Contact: Photographing Indigenous Australians* (Durham, NC and London: Duke University Press, 2005) p. 39.
25 Attwood, *Rights for Aborigines*, p. 16.
26 Lydon, *Eye Contact*, p. 42.
27 Sarnia was chosen for its large Ojibwa reserve and accessibility for visitors coming from the north via Lake Huron and from the east via the Grand Trunk Railway. See Ian Radforth, 'Performance, politics, and representation: Aboriginal people and the 1860 royal tour of Canada', *The Canadian Historical Review*, 84:1 (2003), 11.
28 Ibid., p. 4.
29 Ibid., p. 13.
30 Ruth Phillips, 'Dress and address: First Nations self-fashioning and the 1860 royal tour of Canada', in Susan Kulcher and Graeme Were (eds), *The Art of Clothing: A Pacific Experience* (London: Routledge, 2005), p. 143.
31 Radforth, 'Performance, politics, and representation', p. 18.
32 Diary of William Jenkins, p. 3.
33 Mackrell, *Hariru Wikitoria!*, p. 36.
34 Ibid., p. 50.
35 Ibid.
36 Ibid.
37 Ibid., p. 51.
38 Ibid., p. 45.
39 Auckland War Memorial Museum Library, MS 1069, Reihana Taukawau, Journal, 1863–1883.
40 Ibid., p. 3.
41 Mackrell, *Hariru Wikitoria!*, p. 55.
42 See Patricia Wallace, 'He whatu ariki – he kura, he waero: Chiefly threads – red and white', in *Looking Flash: Clothing In Aotearoa New Zealand* (Auckland: Auckland University Press, 2007), and Hazel Petrie, 'Decoding the colours of rank in Māori Society: What might they tell us about perceptions of war captives?', *The Journal of the Polynesian Society*, 120:3 (2011), 211–39.
43 The Royal Archives, Queen Victoria's Journal, Osborne: 15 July 1863.
44 Mackrell, *Hariru Wikitoria!*, p. 57.
45 www.nzhistory.net.nz/politics/treaty/read-the-treaty/english-text, accessed 30 April 2014.
46 Mackrell, *Hariru Wikitoria!*, p. 57. As Mackrell notes, although the party mentioned the fighting in the Waikato at their audience with the Queen it was in fact the second

Taranaki conflict. The invasion of the Waikato began three days prior to the royal audience, and news of it did not reach England for some time.
47 See James Belich, *Making Peoples: A History of the New Zealanders* (Auckland: Penguin, 2007).
48 Queen Victoria's Journal, Osborne: 15 July 1863.
49 *Ibid.*
50 As well as being employed in a physical sense to protect one from the elements and as a kind of armour, cloaks were also symbolic of the protective nature of interrelationships, and Māori often alluded to this metaphor. For instance, today cloaks are often placed on the coffin of the deceased to connect them to their ancestors and to act as a protective barrier for the person's journey between the worlds of the living and the dead.
51 Queen Victoria's Journal, Osborne: 15 July 1863.
52 www.teara.govt.nz/en/biographies/1c22/colenso-elizabeth, accessed 30 April 2014.
53 A. Lyden, *A Royal Passion: Queen Victoria and Photography* (Los Angeles, CA: The J. Paul Getty Museum, 2014), p. 115.
54 Mackrell, *Hariru Wikitoria!*, p. 81.
55 Lyden, *A Royal Passion*, p. vii.
56 *Ibid.*, p. 180.
57 *Ibid.*, p. vii.
58 Mackrell, *Hariru Wikitoria!*, p. 82.
59 This christening set is currently in the care of the Auckland War Memorial Museum, Auckland, New Zealand (AM 18191).
60 This christening cup is currently in the care of the Queen Emma Summer Palace, Oahu, Hawai'i.
61 See R. Hackler, '"My Dear Friend": Letters of Queen Victoria and Queen Emma', *The Hawaiian Journal of History*, 22 (1988), 101–30, and R. Hackler, 'Albert Edward Kauikeaouli Leiopapa a Kamehameha: Prince of Hawai'i', *The Hawaiian Journal of History*, 26 (1992), 21–44.
62 See P. Bance, *The Duleep Singhs: The Photograph Album of Queen Victoria's Maharajah* (Stroud: Sutton Publishing, 2004), and W. D. Myers, *At Her Majesty's Request: An African Princess in Victorian England* (New York: Scholastic Press, 1999).
63 The Waitangi Tribunal was established in 1975 by the Treaty of Waitangi Act 1975 as a permanent commission of inquiry tasked with making recommendations on claims brought by Māori relating to actions or omissions of the Crown that breach the promises made in the Treaty of Waitangi.
64 Mackrell, *Hariru Wikitoria!*, p. 57.
65 *Ibid.*, p. 27.

CHAPTER SEVEN

Southern African royalty and delegates visit Queen Victoria, 1882–95

Neil Parsons

'Rhodes Must Fall' campaigns by university students in South Africa and Britain have been advocating for the removal of statues of the British South African imperialist Cecil John Rhodes (1853–1902) from campuses. By coincidence, at the same time there has been under production an Anglo-German animated feature film titled *I Am Khama*, which tells of the comeuppance of Cecil Rhodes by three African kings or paramount chiefs who sailed to London to negotiate with Queen Victoria's government in 1895. The film is based on my book *King Khama, Emperor Joe, and the Great White Queen*, published by University of Chicago Press in 1998. Rhodes used to boast that every man had his price. At least in the case of Khama, the price was too high.

The diplomatic mission to Great Britain of Kings Khama, Sebele, and Bathoen in 1895 can be contrasted with the earlier visit of King Cetshwayo of the Zulu in 1882. Between those two dates, royal envoys were also sent by three other Nguni-speaking monarchs: King Lobengula of the Ndebele (Matabele) in 1889, King Ngungunyane of the Gaza (Shangane) in 1891, and Queen Labotsibeni of the Swazi in 1894. My discussion concentrates on the evidence of direct contact between Queen Victoria and the Indigenous rulers from southern Africa who visited her, seen against prior and subsequent knowledge of her as a symbol of British imperial rule. Among southern African rulers, a woman as sovereign was unusual but no fundamental problem – at least for an interregnum between male monarchs. In the words of the Swazi legal maxim, 'If the King is dead, the Queen is King'.[1] By taking kings and royal envoys rather than commoners as the focus, the interaction between 'class' and 'race' in their reception becomes evident. As Catherine E. Anderson notes, in the social hierarchies accepted by Victorians, 'class divisions, whether real or perceived, often trumped racial divisions'.[2] Furthermore, by concentrating on the high politics of diplomacy, it is possible to study the ways in which powerful individuals could use social and political networks to effect and influence change.³

British rule over the Colony of the Cape of Good Hope (1798–1803 and 1806–1910) inherited the problem of Boer settlers penetrating Khoe and Xhosa territories on the eastern frontier. From the 1820s to the 1830s, English settlers in the Eastern Cape pushed Boer settlers northwards on a groot trek (long haul) across the Orange River. In 1852 and 1872, the 'imperial factor' ceded legislative representation and executive responsibility in Cape Colony to a largely white settler franchise. African kingdoms in the interior were confronted by new Boer 'republics' as well as by the British settler-ruled Cape Colony. Sotho and Tswana rulers vainly looked to Britain, the source of their Christian missionaries, for assistance against Boer encroachments. Among Tswana rulers, King Sechele of the Kwena in Botswana, under attack from Transvaal Boers, attempted to travel to Britain in 1853, but ran out of funds when he reached Cape Town.⁴ King Moshoeshoe of the Sotho in Basutoland (Lesotho) sought an alliance with Britain against the Orange Free State Boers. Despite a vicious attack on his capital in 1853 by a British force in support of the Boers, in 1854 he told his people that Queen Victoria was a brooding presence 'sitting on the top of a high mountain, looking down on us, her children. ... Some day, Queen Victoria will come back among us. On that day I shall rejoice as I rejoice at the rising of the sun'.⁵ In 1860, Moshoeshoe rode south to meet Victoria's second son Prince Alfred in the Eastern Cape in a bid to personally cement an alliance. He tried again in 1869, the year before his death, when he sent a diplomatic delegation to England, led by his Christian mission-educated son Tsekelo, but Tsekelo was not granted an audience with Queen Victoria.⁶

The rise to power in the colonial factor – representing British settler interests in cahoots with local British army commanders – can be seen in the careers of two men: Theophilus Shepstone (1817–93) in the British colony of Natal,⁷ and Cecil John Rhodes (1853–1902) in Cape Colony.⁸ Colonial administrator Shepstone was the man behind the British invasion of the Zulu kingdom (KwaZulu) in 1879, conducted 'in spite of Queen Victoria's vigorous protests' and the qualms of the imperial government. Shepstone had previously used a colonial military detachment to seize power in the bankrupt Transvaal Boer republic in 1877. Next, as self-proclaimed supreme chief of all the 'natives' in Natal, he plotted how to conquer and incorporate the Zulu kingdom into Natal. In this he was conspicuously opposed by Bishop Colenso of Natal, his former good friend.⁹

A British army invaded KwaZulu from Natal in 1879. It was defeated in the great Zulu victory of Isandhlwana, but was finally victorious in a battle outside the Zulu capital of Ulundi. On the advice of the Shepstone family, the Zulu kingdom was broken up into competing chiefdoms. After a British force was defeated by Boers on Majuba Hill in 1881, the new Liberal government in London surrendered the Transvaal to its former rulers. Queen Victoria predicted that 'disastrous results would follow the humiliation of a peace made on the morrow of a defeat'.[10]

King Cetshwayo of the Zulu was captured and detained in Cape Town.[11] He expressed his loyalty to Queen Victoria, and began to be treated as a tragic hero. On the advice of Colenso, he wrote to Gladstone, the new Liberal prime minister, and Kimberley, the new colonial minister, in London, appealing to their better natures: 'Talk kindly for me to the Queen'.[12] Cetshwayo – 'although I have a great horror of the sea' – was persuaded by Colenso to travel overseas to further his appeal. Gladstone, who believed that the Anglo-Zulu war had been an unjust 'slaughter of Natives attempting to defend their homes and independence', was agreeable. Queen Victoria was by no means enthusiastic about receiving Cetshwayo, but is said to have been swayed by Colenso's friend Lady Florence Dixie.[13] Cetshwayo arrived on the Royal Mail steamer *Arab* at Plymouth on Thursday, 3 August 1882. His main interpreter was one of the sons of Theophilus Shepstone.[14]

King Lobengula of the Ndebele in Matabeleland sent envoys to petition Queen Victoria in 1889. He had long been wary of the British: Transvaal Boers had warned him that once an Englishman 'has your property in his hand, then he is like a monkey that has its hands full of pumpkin seeds – if you don't beat him to death, he will never let go'. The opening up of the Johannesburg goldfields resulted in a rush of British and Boer concessionaires in the late 1880s.[15] Lobengula comes across as a tragic figure unable to avoid his fate, telling an interlocutor:

> Did you ever see a chameleon catch a fly? The chameleon gets behind the fly and remains motionless for some time, then he advances very slowly and gently, first putting forward one leg and then another. At last, when well within reach, he darts his tongue and the fly disappears. England is the chameleon and I am that fly.[16]

Lobengula preferred to give a mining concession to the London-based Exploration Company that included two of Victoria's sons-in-law (the Dukes of Fife and Abercorn) over Cecil Rhodes's syndicate based in Cape Colony. The Exploration Company organised a delegation to London by Lobengula's two envoys in 1889, in order to stymie Rhodes's syndicate from receiving exclusive approval from the Colonial Office. Of course, from Lobengula's viewpoint, the envoys Mshete and Babayane were as much spies engaged in gathering intelligence, as they were diplomats. A particular remit was to report back if the much-mythologised Queen Victoria was a real person.

Two years later, Rhodes's British South Africa (BSA) Company tried the same ploy as Lobengula by using African diplomatic envoys to try to induce a change in British government policy. The company wished to give its inland territory ('Rhodesia') territorial access to the Indian Ocean, breaching Britain's long-standing recognition of Portuguese sovereignty on the Mozambique coast. Rhodes found an ally in King Ngungunyane of the unconquered kingdom of Gaza (Shangane), another Nguni-speaking military state related historically to the Zulu, Swazi, and Ndebele. For Ngungunyane, an alliance with the British – represented by Rhodes's company – seemed a better alternative than either Portuguese or Transvaal Boer conquest. Two Gaza indunas (councillors), expressive old Mteto and the quieter and younger Nteni, were sent to London in 1891 under the charge of a BSA Company agent. Mteto declared: 'I am the eyes and ears of Gungunyana the King, and I know the heart of Gungunyana as if it were my own heart, and I have come to bring the word of Gungunyana to the great White Queen'. He ended with an exclamation of respect for the majesty of Queen Victoria: Nkos![17]

The Swazi, traditional enemies of the Zulu, were natural allies for the Transvaal Boers. As in Matabeleland, Boer and British concessionaires flooded into Swaziland during the 1880s. The landlocked Transvaal republic wanted control over Swaziland to push its territory to the coast between Portuguese Mozambique and British Natal. Queen Mother Labotsibeni of the Swazi appealed to Britain as a counterbalance against the Transvaal. In October 1894, a delegation of nine Swazi and two white men, led by Prince Longcanga, left for London with James Stuart as their main interpreter. 'Our ancestors', they assured the *Westminster Gazette* when they arrived in London, 'are guiding us'.[18]

In June 1895, the three main chiefs or kings from Bechuanaland Protectorate (Botswana) – Khama, Sebele, and Bathoen – decided to take their cause to London. Cecil Rhodes, as prime minister of the Cape Colony, had announced that the colony would annex the southern part of Bechuanaland in September, while his BSA Company would incorporate the northern part (Bechuanaland Protectorate) into 'Rhodesia'.[19] Khama was already famous as a British ally, a Christian convert, and an enemy of alcohol. He had been invited to attend the centenary celebrations in Britain of the (Congregationalist) London Missionary Society, and he invited Sebele and Bathoen to join him. They hoped to persuade the new colonial minister, Joseph Chamberlain, not to hand over the Bechuanaland Protectorate to Rhodes's company. Either Sebele or Bathoen explained: 'Next to success in the object of our visit, we wish to see the Queen – or, as our people call her, 'the one who listens [Motho-wa-Ditsebe]' or 'the little woman of many days [Mma-Mosadinyana]'.[20] Khama added that many people doubted her existence:

> They think to say she is alive is a lie, and many of my people have mixed notions; they think the Queen is like God, and the Prince of Wales like Jesus Christ. Of course we do not speak of ourselves, but of the very ignorant people. ... If we return and say we have not seen her they will say: 'See, it is as we said, all lies.' We believe it would be of great use from a diplomatic point of view to have audience of her Majesty.[21]

Soberly dressed like respectable bourgeois gentlemen, the three kings criss-crossed England, Scotland, and Wales by train, drumming up support in chapels and churches, chambers of commerce, and provincial newspapers, in small towns and big cities – including Birmingham, Edinburgh, Glasgow, Leeds, Liverpool, Manchester, and the industrial centres of the North of England. At a packed meeting in Leicester, Khama spoke, as interpreted by his secretary:

> We say why should the home [imperial] Government hand us over to the other people without asking us (*Hear, hear*). They hand us over like an ox, but even the owner of the ox looks to where the ox will get grass and water, land, that sort of thing. (*Applause*). I think they ought to have asked us, and found out what we think about it. ... We were progressing very much under the Imperial Government, but now you are teaching us the word of war, and I think these things ought to cease.[22]

The high point for the visits of all foreign royals and envoys was their reception by Queen Victoria at Windsor Castle or at Osborne House on the Isle of Wight. This was usually proffered by the Colonial or Foreign Office as a reward for compliance with government policy. During his visit to England, Cetshwayo was granted a thirteen-minute interview with Queen Victoria. She recorded the audience in her journal:

> I said, through Mr. Shepstone, that I was glad to see him here, & that I recognised in him a great warrior, who had fought against us, but rejoiced that we were now friends. He answered me much the same, gesticulating a good deal as he spoke, mentioned having seen my picture, & said he was glad to see me in person. I asked about his voyage & what he had seen, & [I] then named my three daughters [one daughter, two daughters-in-law standing next to her], at which he said 'ah!' After further commonplace observations, the interview terminated. Both in coming in & going out they gave me the royal salute, saying something all together, & raising their right hands above their heads.

Cetshwayo and his party were given lunch and then walked in the grounds. Victoria watched them from the colonnade of Osborne House: 'As they drove away, Cettewayo caught sight of me, & got up in the carriage, & remained standing till they were out of sight', she recorded in her journal.[23] Cetshwayo was subsequently interviewed by a representative of the Press Association. He said how much he had enjoyed the freedom and attention paid to him on his voyage to England, after his lonely incarceration at Cape Town.

> I asked him if he was gratified with his reception by the public in England since his arrival here. Cetywayo, who up to this point had been sitting with his arms quietly folded across his chest, scarcely moving a muscle, seemed stirred by this question. His face of ebony, before almost emotionless, brightened up with animation, his eyes sparkled, and played, and he gesticulated energetically as he proceeded to explain through the interpreter that the welcome he had received at the hands of the English people was more than he had ever expected.

Cetshwayo referred to Queen Victoria as a 'good, gracious lady', adding: 'She, like myself, was born to rule men. We are alike'. At the end of the interview, he gave the journalist a hearty handshake and wished him goodbye, thereby, or so we are told, nearly exhausting his English vocabulary.[24]

Cetshwayo had arrived at Plymouth comfortably dressed in 'a pilot coat and a peak hat', and on other occasions wore the 'undress' uniform of a British army general, or a dark blue frock coat. He insisted on wearing western dress so that 'government officials would take him more seriously'. A deeper reason is suggested by an observation taken from Namibia: 'If you wear the clothes of your enemy, the spirit of the enemy is weakened. You are wearing the spirit of his brothers'.[25] Victoria was disappointed that 'such a very fine man ... tall, immensely broad, & stout, with a good humoured countenance & an intelligent face' had appeared before her 'unfortunately ... in a hideous black frock coat and trousers'. She arranged for Cetshwayo to sit for the portrait painter Carl Sohn (1835–1908), who portrayed him with a bare shoulder and a necklace of fierce lion's teeth contrasting against his black skin.[26]

When Mshete and Babayane from Matabeleland arrived in England at the end of February 1889, under the patronage of two royal dukes of the Exploration Company, they were soon passed on to the Queen at Windsor. They arrived for their audience 'warmly clad in heavy fur coats'. Queen Victoria's journal on 2 March 1889 records the visit: 'Just before luncheon I received in the Corridor 2 Indunas from Lo Bengula ... Life Guardsmen in full dress with drawn swords were drawn up in the Corridor'. After they had formally presented Lobengula's message, she asked them if they felt the cold. 'How could we feel heat or cold', they are supposed to have said, 'in the presence of the great white Queen'. She then asked them what present they would like for themselves, and they replied that 'they would be delighted to get a pinch of snuff from the Royal hand'. She called for some snuff in an envelope, and 'it was handed by the Queen to the indunas, who took their snuff like gentlemen of the last reign'.[27]

When Ngungunyane's envoys Mteto and Nteni saw Queen Victoria at Windsor on Friday, 10 July 1891, she recorded in her journal the event likewise:

> After luncheon I received in the Corridor, with Life Guardsmen stationed along it, the 2 Indunas of the king of Gazaland, who were presented by the Duke of Abercorn, he being connected with the South African Company ... The Indunas are complete Zulus & the one had that peculiar ring round his head. They held up their arms, giving a sort of cry on seeing me. They protested greatly the measures that had been taken, & asked for my protection. I promised to communicate what they said to [Conservative prime minister] Ld Salisbury.

The Queen gave the envoys a silver cup, inscribed: 'To Gungunyana from Queen Victoria'.[28] When a journalist the next day asked them the stock question about how they reacted to the statue-like soldiers lining the corridors of Windsor Castle, one of the indunas set down his glass of soda water and testily replied: 'I cannot speak in the same breath of your great Queen and of her subjects. We have seen the small stars. Yesterday we saw the moon and the sun'.[29]

The Swazi envoys led by Prince Longcanca were taken to see Queen Victoria at Windsor by colonial minister Lord Ripon in November 1894. Victoria gave them Afghan shawls for the two queens of Swaziland, grandmother and mother of the future King Sobhuza II. Victoria recorded this somewhat matter-of-factly: 'I received 4 Swazi Envoys, sent by the Queen of the Swazis. The Blues were drawn up in the Corridor, & the reception was much the same as on former occasions when African Indunas have been received'.[30]

Joseph Chamberlain accompanied Khama, Sebele, and Bathoen to Windsor in 1895. Unlike the previous envoys received in a castle corridor, they were received in a drawing room: 'After luncheon I went to the White Drawing Room to receive 3 chiefs from Bechuanaland, who are Christians ... The Chiefs are very tall & very black, but their hair is not'. Queen Victoria's journal referred to Khama as 'one of the Chiefs [who] is said to be a very remarkable & intelligent Man ... They brought offerings of skins of leopards & jackals, & I gave them New Testaments

& my photographs handsomely framed, & Indian shawls for their wives'.[31] In Khama's New Testament, she is said to have inscribed, in her own hand, 'The Secret of Khama's greatness'.[32] Sebele was afterwards quoted as saying: 'Her Majesty is a very charming old lady. She has a round beautiful face and a very sweet voice. But I had no idea that she was so small ... When I was in one of Her Majesty's splendid apartments, I was greatly astonished to see an ordinary, tiny housefly! It was a puzzle to me how it got there, as I could hardly believe that even Death could enter such a place'.[33] He later observed that 'the Queen's stables ... were cleaner than any white man's home in Africa'.[34] A few days later, the mission of Khama, Sebele, and Bathoen teetered on the edge of a public relations disaster. During their last triumphal public meeting, a missionary interpreter blunderingly rendered the respectful term Mma-Mosadinyana as 'the old woman' at Windsor.[35]

The Royal Household troops in the corridors who guarded Queen Victoria at Windsor Castle were physically much more impressive than the Queen herself. Mshete and Babayane from Matabeleland were taken through corridors lined by unblinking Life Guards with shining breastplates. As they told a journalist:

> The magnificence of Windsor castle delighted them, but the tall, statuesque guardsmen astonished the indunas. 'These soldiers are only put up for show', said Umshete. 'They are so big and stiff – they cannot be alive.' 'Oh, yes, they are', rejoined Babyjane; 'I saw their eyes move.'[36]

Mteto and Nteni from Gazaland also passed down a line of Life Guards, while the Swazi envoys found the Queen guarded by 'the Blues' (Royal Horse Guards). Among the Tswana kings, Sebele retained a vivid memory of that day when he saw Queen Victoria at Windsor Castle:

> The corridors and the magnificent palace where she lives are all lined with stalwart soldiers, as big as I am, in glittering uniforms. None ever moved ... like the marble statues in the streets of London. While passing along their line I boldly tested one of these giants. I thrust my finger almost into his eye to make certain that he was a living being ... To my great surprise he never flinched, but merely rewarded me with a smile.[37]

The Colonial Office did its best to impress African visitors with military exercises and parades, staged for their intimidation at Aldershot, and with the gun factories and metalworks of the Woolwich arsenal. *The Times*, voice of the British establishment, argued that Cetshwayo should be taught 'the futility of armed resistance to British power' by being shown Britain's 'boundless resources'.[38] After being presented to Queen Victoria in 1880, four envoys from King Mutesa of Uganda in East Africa expressed 'manifestations of extravagant delight' when a 40-ton steam hammer pounded 'a huge mass of red-hot metal' at Woolwich.[39] Cetshwayo and his attendants toured the royal arsenal at Woolwich on Wednesday, 23 August 1882. By contrast, despite 'frequent exclamations of astonishment' among his colleagues, Cetshwayo remained quiet and noncommittal. But, as he left the arsenal, he expressed 'the pleasure I have derived from the visits I have paid to this great workshop of the Queen, my mother', adding:

> I have seen the wonders of the English nation. I have witnessed where England gets her power from, and the might of the works conducted here ... I may say that I have almost ceased to be astonished. I feel I have grown up, so to speak, in a day; that from an intellectual childhood I have suddenly sprung to manhood. I have a great deal to report to my nation when I return which language, I am afraid, will fail to allow me to express ... words, I am afraid, will not describe the wonders of your land.[40]

Before boarding the ship home, Cetshwayo again recalled his visits to Windsor Castle and to the Woolwich arsenal. He added that he now understood what 'civilisation' was, and wished to be civilised himself – but was returning home a pauper. There were loud cheers as the Union packet *Nubian* slipped its Southampton moorings, and yelps from the hunting hounds on board that had been given to the King. This, however, was not Cetshwayo's last taste of England's hospitality. As the ship called in at Plymouth Sound, he was taken on board a Royal Navy gunnery training ship. The captain asked him to press a button. Every gun on one side of the ship fired with an almighty explosion. When the noise died down, Cetshwayo looked round to make sure everyone was safe, and then burst into loud laughter, shaking hands with the captain. It was, he said, the most impressive experience of his whole trip.[41] Bishop Colenso's widow was later to write: 'I believe the personal kindness the Queen showed to their poor captive King when he was in England, shaking hands with him, and giving him valuable presents, won not only his heart, but that of every true Zulu'.[42] (Whites in southern Africa usually declined to shake hands with Africans.)

For Lobengula's envoys Mshete and Babayane, the historian Apollon Davidson points out that every effort was made to convince them 'of both the might and the magnanimity of England'. They were taken to the Alhambra theatre in Leicester Square to see the 'scenery, dresses, glitter and dancing'. At Madame Tussaud's waxworks, some joker told them that 'the figure they saw before them was Cetshwayo in person, punished thus for his unruliness'. They inspected troops in the pouring rain at Aldershot, and witnessed a sham fight with mounted lancers spread out in pursuit. 'Come and teach us how to drill and fight like that', said Babayane, 'and we need fear no nation in Africa'.[43] Mshete and Babayane returned home to Matabeleland reportedly 'hugely delighted' at their reception by the Queen. As *The Times* noted: 'It appears that many of Lobengula's people have been led to believe by the Boers that since the defeat of the English at Majuba-hill, the power of England has been broken, and that the "great white Queen" has passed away. They now say that their eyes have seen her and their ears have heard her voice'.[44] Mshete and Babayane were impressed by the Queen's graciousness, but not by her Colonial Office. In the words of a sympathetic member of Parliament: 'had it not been that the Queen came to the rescue we are very much afraid that they would have gone back to Matabeleland considerably disgusted with the rulers and governors of the Empire'.[45]

The apparent success of Cetshwayo's mission to London carried no weight with the colonial factor back in Africa. He was not restored to his whole kingdom, but found himself king instead of only one of the five parts of KwaZulu. Violence erupted among his former subjects. He died in February 1884, probably poisoned – appalled attendants stopped an autopsy.[46]

Lobengula in Matabeleland is said to have been 'completely won over to Queen Victoria' because 'she sent him ... a great necklace of lion's claws, mounted in gold'.[47] But he was cruelly tricked by the Queen's underlings. The Colonial Office arranged for Rhodes's syndicate to absorb the Exploration Company into its 'British South Africa Company', launched by royal charter in 1889. The next scene in the farce, before it became a tragedy, involved sending Royal Horse Guards officers, sweating under metal breastplates and plumed helmets, to Bulawayo to announce the royal charter to Lobengula. The King attempted to send more messages to Victoria over the next three years, without reply. His last attempt was through two respected indunas who were mysteriously shot dead in 1893, just after they crossed the border of Matabeleland. Lobengula's almost last recorded words were: 'The white men are the fathers of lies.'[48]

For the Gaza of Ngungunyane, the end was equally tragic. While the BSA Company eagerly annexed that part of Gazaland that was on the agreed Rhodesian side of the border, the main part of the kingdom was conquered by a Portuguese army sent, with British compliance, in 1895. Ngungunyane was exiled by the Portuguese.[49] Victoria's gift of a silver cup to Ngungunyane was to remain a source of grievance against the British in Portuguese official circles for many years to come.

The very next day after seeing Queen Victoria in 1894, Queen Labotsibeni's Swazi envoys were abruptly told by the Colonial Office that the British Queen was precluded from accepting their fealty. The 'imperial factor' was bound by a new treaty to be signed in the following month, recognising the Transvaal's Protectorate over Swaziland. The envoys were ordered to return to Swaziland immediately.[50] Faced with effective surrender of their country to the 'unjust and cruel' Transvaal Boers, the Swazi protested:

> We consider that we are the Queen of England's children [wards?]. You have protected us ever since the Zulu war and it is now with sorrow that we learn our Mother the Queen wants to send us from under her wing and hand us over to the hawks that will devour us.[51]

Colonial minister Chamberlain was obliged to listen to British public opinion expressed by newspapers and petitions backing the cause of Khama, Sebele, and Bathoen – not least from his own Birmingham power base. But Chamberlain was compromised by Rhodes's master plan to use the Bechuanaland Protectorate as the 'jumping off ground' for a military incursion to assist a planned coup d'état in the Transvaal. Khama, Sebele, and Bathoen were rushed into a compromise settlement, guaranteeing continued imperial over-rule for their own large reserves – but giving Rhodesia the rest of the country, most importantly a border strip next to the Transvaal ostensibly for a railway.

Only three territories in British Africa persisted through the colonial period as imperial protectorates, ultimately ensuring their eventual independence in the 1960s: two as kingdoms (Lesotho and Swaziland) and one as a republic (Botswana). The annexation of Basutoland (Lesotho) to white settler-biased Cape Colony in 1871 proved disastrous, and led to warfare in 1879–81 – only resolved by the institution of an imperial protectorate in 1884. It guaranteed a large measure of self-rule by the king and council of chiefs, under the Crown rather than under Cape Town.[52] The kingdom of Swaziland managed to slip out of Transvaal control into imperial protectorate status in 1904, as its reward for supporting Britain in the South African War of 1899–1902. More than half of its small territory, however, remained under white settler ownership. The world's longest reigning monarch, King Sobhuza II (1899–1982), survived the colonial period as a defiant neo-traditional autarch.

After initial exultation, Khama, Sebele, and Bathoen returned home painfully aware that they had lost the Kalahari and the Limpopo to Rhodesia. In the following year, however, Chamberlain was obliged to punish Rhodes for the failure of the Jameson Raid to capture the Transvaal. Bechuanaland Protectorate reverted to the 'imperial factor'. Chamberlain thus satisfied the powerful political interests within Great Britain that the three kings had aroused in their support.

The 1895 Chamberlain settlement with the imprimatur of Queen Victoria became the Magna Carta of the Bechuanaland Protectorate.

In 1908, when threatened by incorporation in the upcoming Union of South Africa, Sebele protested: 'I am the inheritance left by the late Queen Victoria the good, under His Majesty the King Edward VII. I do not want any Government except Imperial Government'.[53] By 1922, having lived a decade longer than the other two kings, Khama made the same point in less enthusiastic form:

> I am despised and neglected by the Protectorate Administration. ... The Protectorate is now governed by the laws invented by the Government Officials of which no agreement has been signed between the Late Queen Victoria and myself at the time I invited her to protect me.[54]

The three southern African protectorates or 'High Commission Territories' survived until independence in the 1960s, despite periodic attempts to absorb them by the Union of Southern Africa or, in the case of Bechuanaland, Southern Rhodesia. Political supporters within the imperial parliament stopped them from being given to the colonial factor.

Postscript

As racial segregation was tightened (and renamed *apartheid*) under the Union and Republic of South Africa, longing for the good old days of Queen Victoria flickered on. In 1934, King George V's fourth son, Prince George, was greeted at King Williams Town in the Ciskei by a group of chiefs, of whom many no doubt were 'loyal Fingo' (Mfengu). Everywhere, the Prince was recognised as 'the Queen's great-grandson, not the King's son':

> The mention of Queen Victoria's name brought excited expressions of approval from the natives. Queen Victoria (or 'Vittoree-a,' as the natives pronounce it) is still a fairy godmother to the natives, who pass down from father to son glowing accounts of the guardianship she afforded the native peoples. Modern legislation is measured by the natives in terms of Queen Victoria's actions, and an extremely suspicious eye is cast on any suggestions which seem to infringe the principles of freedom and protection.

When Prince George went on to Mafeking in 1934, he was presented with a magnificent jackal-skin blanket (kaross), because Victoria had appreciated jackal fur so much in 1895.[55]

King Khama's grandson Seretse Khama, later first president of the Republic of Botswana, married an Englishwoman in 1948. A myth persists that the marriage was fulfilling a promise made by the Queen Victoria in 1895 to find a wife from among her people for Seretse's widowed grandfather.[56] The accession of Queen Elizabeth II to the British throne in February 1952 was announced as the return of a benevolent imperial monarch and matriarch. At Kanye in Botswana, Bathoen's grandson expressed 'the hope that having sought the aid of the Crown in the reign of Queen Victoria, the Territory could look forward to many years of peace and prosperity under another Queen'.[57]

In Lesotho, as John Gunther noted in the 1950s, 'The Basuto make much of such facts that they were never a conquered nation, [that they] asked to be taken in by the British in the last century of their own free will, and [that they] had close treaty relations with Queen Victoria, and have always been loyal to the British crown'. Gunther travelled on through Northern Rhodesia (Zambia) and Nyasaland (Malawi), noting again how African chiefs still put their trust in real or supposed treaties with Queen Victoria. They had good reason at the time to fear the federation of their territories with white-settler-ruled Southern Rhodesia.[58] It was hardly surprising if chiefs, hanging on to their 'traditional' political and territorial claims, should hark back to some charter from Queen Victoria as their 'fairy godmother'.

By contrast, attitudes to Queen Victoria have been more ambiguous in Nguni-speaking kingdoms and chiefdoms defeated by the British, or abandoned by the British as allies. In the Transkei of the Eastern Cape, the two large kingdoms of the Thembu and Mpondo had generally seen the British as allies – until the British sold them out in 1909–10 by not declaring the Transkei a British Protectorate outside the Union like Basutoland. The memory of Victoria turned bitter. The young Nelson Mandela among the Thembu was told that 'the white queen brought nothing but misery and perfidy to the black people: if she was a chief, she was an evil chief'.[59]

The older generation of well-educated African nationalists had reason to retain their 'cringe' towards Victoria as the evocation of a golden age of civil rights progressively lost to white minority rule. In the words of historian Silas Modiri Molema, 'Queen Victoria's government [was] regarded ... as a guarantee of justice and honour'.[60] But such elite attitudes did not necessarily reflect mass opinions – or those of younger African nationalists.

At independence in 1966, a special issue of the Botswana government magazine *Kutlwano* featured five pictures of 'Our Nation's Founders': Khama, Sebele, Bathoen, and Queens Victoria and Elizabeth II. In South Africa, a statue of Queen Victoria remains prominently sited near the parliament building at Cape Town. But statues of her have been removed in Zimbabwe and defaced in the Eastern Cape – areas that were conquered more than a century ago in her name. In Zimbabwe, statues of Queen Victoria and other colonial relics have been parked since the 1980s in the gardens of the National Museum at

Bulawayo. In the Eastern Cape, the statue of Queen Victoria that sits outside the main library at Port Elizabeth was daubed with black paint across the face during the night on 9–10 March 2010 (see Figure 7.1). The words Goduka Europe – 'Away with Europe' – were written on the base of the statue. The incident was reported as popular reaction to the rough reception that President Zuma, during a state visit, was receiving from the British press, which characterised him as a serial polygamist and an alleged rapist. Zuma had struck back against the British as imperialists who bore no respect for other cultures.[61] Though the defacement was caught on CCTV, no perpetrators were arrested.

Figure 7.1 Statue of Queen Victoria in front of the Port Elizabeth public library, which was vandalised in 2010, allegedly in 'defence' of President Zuma who was then being criticised in the British press.

Acknowledgements

This chapter is dedicated to the memory of Jeff Guy, Africanist historian and biographer of Bishop Colenso, who died on 15 December 2014. My thanks go to Sarah Carter, Maria Nugent, and Gwil Colenso for comments on earlier drafts.

Notes

1 Hilda Kuper, *Sobhuza II: Ngwenyama and King of Swaziland* (London: Gerald Duckworth, 1978), p. 29.
2 Catherine E. Anderson, 'A Zulu King in Victorian London: Race, royalty and imperialist aesthetics in late nineteenth-century Britain', *Visual Resources*, 14:3 (2008), 299.
3 Jaap Van Velsen, 'Social research and social relevance: Suggestions for research policy and some research priorities for the Institute for African Studies', *African Social Research* (Lusaka), no. 17 (1970), 517–53.
4 Anthony Sillery, *Sechele: The Story of an African Chief* (Oxford: G. Ronald, 1954); Silas Modiri Molema, *Montshiwa 1815–1896: Barolong Chief and Patriot* (Cape Town: C. Struik, 1966).
5 Peter Sanders, *Moshoeshoe: Chief of the Sotho* (London: Heinemann, 1975), pp. 101, 241, 249, 254–5, and 309.
6 Peter Sanders, *The Last of the Queen's Men: A Lesotho Experience* (Johannesburg: Wits University Press and Morija, Lesotho: Morija Museum and Archives, 2000), pp. 128–9. Moshoeshoe's ca. 1866 plea of 'My country is your blanket, O Queen, and my people the lice on it' is not authenticated. Its earliest mention in print may be Eric A. T. Dutton, *The Basuto of Basutoland* (Cape Town: Juta, 1923), p. 44. See also Lord Hailey, *Native Administration in the British African Territories. Part V: The High Commission Territories: Basutoland, The Bechuanaland Protectorate and Swaziland* (London: Her Majesty's Stationary Office, 1953), p. 42.
7 Jeff Guy, *Theophilus Shepstone and the Forging of Natal: African Autonomy and Settler Colonialism in the Making of Traditional Authority* (Scottsville, KwaZulu-Natal: University of KwaZulu-Natal Press, 2013).
8 Robert I. Rotberg, with the collaboration of Miles F. Shore, *The Founder: Cecil Rhodes and the Pursuit of Power* (New York: Oxford University Press, 1988).
9 Norman Herd, *The Bent Pine: The Trial of Chief Langalibalele* (Braamfontrein, Johannesburg: Ravan Press, 1976), pp. 69, 75, 100 and 104–7.
10 Cecil Headlam, 'The failure of confederation, 1871–1881', in Eric A. Walker (ed.), *The Cambridge History of the British Empire, Volume VII: South Africa, Rhodesia and the High Commission Territories* (Cambridge: Cambridge University Press, 1963), pp. 489 and 494–6.
11 See Jeff Guy, *The Destruction of the Zulu Kingdom: The Civil War in Zululand, 1879–1884* (London: Longman, 1979); John Laband, *Kingdom in Crisis: The Zulu Response to the British Invasion of 1879* (Manchester: Manchester University Press, 1992); Ian Knight, *"By the Orders of the Great White Queen": Campaigning in Zululand through the Eyes of a British Soldier, 1879* (London: Greenhill Books and Novato, CA: Presidio Press, 1992); Andrew Duminy and Bill Guest (eds), *Natal and Zululand from Earliest Times to 1910: A New History* (Pietermaritzburg: University of Natal Press and Shuter and Shooter, 1958).
12 P. H. Butterfield, 'From monarch to monarch: Cetewayo's letters to Queen Victoria', *Africana Notes and News*, 28:5 (March 1989), 199.
13 Headlam, 'The failure of confederation', 493; Jeff Guy, *The Heretic: A Study of the Life of John William Colenso* (Johannesburg: Ravan Press 1983), p. 310.
14 Bridget Theron, 'King Cetshwayo in Victorian England: A cameo of imperial interaction', *South African Historical Journal*, 56:1 (2006), 60–87.

15 Daphne Trevor, 'Public Opinion and the Acquisition of Bechuanaland and Rhodesia (1868–1896)' (PhD dissertation, University of London, London School of Economics, 1936), p. 216.
16 Philip Mason, *The Birth of a Dilemma: The Conquest and Settlement of Rhodesia* (London: Oxford University Press/Institute of Race Relations, 1958), p. 105, citing Sidney Shippard (Deputy Commissioner Vryburg) to Hercules Robinson (High Commissioner Cape Town), March 1889. The chameleon quotation has been traced further back by Timothy Glen McLaughlin, 'Appeal to the Empire: African Appeals to Great Britain, 1881–1914' (PhD dissertation, State University of New York, 1984), p. 210, to a High Commissioner's dispatch from Cape Town to the Colonial Office, 20 November 1888.
17 *Pall Mall Gazette* (28 May 1891), p. 1, col. 3; p. 2, col. 1.
18 *Westminster Gazette* (29 October 1894), p. 2.
19 For a fuller account, see Neil Parsons, *King Khama, Emperor Joe, and the Great White Queen: Victorian Britain through African Eyes* (Chicago, IL: University of Chicago Press, 1998).
20 Mosadi-wa-Ditsebe, literally 'woman-of-ears'. The alternative translation of ditsebe as 'sheets-of-paper' instead of 'ears' would also have been appropriate for a bureaucracy.
21 The London *Daily News* (9 September 1895), quoted in Parsons, *King Khama, Emperor Joe, and the Great White Queen*, p. 80.
22 *Leicester Post* (26 September 1895).
23 *Queen Victoria's Journals*, vol. 77, pp. 86–7, 14 August 1882, www.queenvictoriasjournals.org, accessed 2 September 2014.
24 *The Times* (15 August 1882), p. 5, col. 6; 21 August, p. 4, col. 6; Guy *The Heretic*, p. 328. See also Butterfield, 'From monarch to monarch', p. 197–204.
25 Wyn Rees (ed.), *Colenso Letters from Natal* (Pietermaritzburg: Shuter and Shooter, 1958), p. 398; Hildi Hendrickson (ed.), *Clothing and Difference: Embodied Identities in Colonial and Post-Colonial Africa* (Durham, NC: Duke University Press, 1996), p. 1. Theron ('King Cetshwayo in Victorian England', pp. 66–7) suggests that 'Cetshwayo's abject misery at his incarceration and dismay at being regarded as a curiosity ... led to his insistence at dressing in European clothes.'
26 Anderson, 'A Zulu King in Victorian London', p. 300; *Horowhenua Chronicle* (9 May 1910), p. 4, retrieved from papers.natlib.govt.nz, accessed 3 October 2014.
27 *The Times* (2 March 1889), p. 12, col. 6, and 4 March, p. 7, col. 2; *Pall Mall Gazette* (7 March 1889), p. 2, col. 6, and p. 6, col. 5; *Queen Victoria's Journals*, 2 March 1889.
28 *Queen Victoria's Journals*, 10 July 1891.
29 *Pall Mall Gazette* (11 July 1891), p. 4, col. 3.
30 *Queen Victoria's Journals*, 15 November 1894.
31 *Queen Victoria's Journals*, 19 November 1895.
32 Arthur Eustace Southon, *Khama, the Conqueror* (London and Cape Coast: Atlantis Press, 1930), p. 270. This copy of the New Testament was destroyed in a fire at Serowe, ca. 1952.
33 Julian Mockford, *Khama: King of the Bamangwato* (London: Jonathan Cape, 1931), p. 179. I have not found the original location of this quotation.
34 Quoted in the London weekly magazine *South Africa* (10 February 1900), p. 394, col. 3.
35 Molema, *Montshiwa 1815–1896*, pp. 186–7.
36 *The Times* (2 March 1889), p. 12, col. 6; 4 March, p. 7, col. 2; *Pall Mall Gazette* (7 March 1889), p. 2, col. 3 and p. 6, col. 3.
37 Mockford, *Khama*, p. 179.
38 *The Times* (4 July 1882), p. 10, col. 2; 6 July 1882, p. 10, col. 4.
39 *The Times* (14 May 1880), p. 6, col. 5. See also James Walvin, *Black and White: The Negro and English Society, 1555–1945* (London: Allen Lane/The Penguin Press, 1973), p. 198.
40 *The Times* (24 August 1882), p. 7, col. 6.

ROYAL RELATIONS

41 *Pall Mall Gazette* (25 August 1882), p. 10, col. 1; 30 August, p. 10, col. 1; 2 September, p. 8, col. 2; 4 September, p. 7, col. 6; *The Times* (18 August 1882), p. 6, col. 1; 25 August, p. 6, col. 4; 26 August, p. 9, col. 6; 30 August, p. 9, col. 6; 2 September, col. 2 and col. 5; 14 September, p. 7, col. 6.
42 Rees, *Colenso Letters from Natal*, p. 399.
43 Apollon Davidson, *Cecil Rhodes and His Time* (Moscow: Progress Publishers, 1988), p. 151; *Pall Mall Gazette* (21 March 1889), p. 6, col. 2; 26 March, p. 5, col. 3; *The Times* (27 March 1889), p. 9, col. 5.
44 *The Times* (6 March 1889), p. 9, col. 6.
45 *Pall Mall Gazette* (16 March 1889), p. 2, col. 2.
46 Bishop Colenso's daughter Harriette Emily carried on the campaign for the restitution of Zulu monarchy and extended it into opposing the policies of Cecil Rhodes. See Shula Marks, 'Harriette Colenso and the Zulus, 1874–1915', *Journal of African History*, 4:3 (1963), 403–11; Charles Theodore Binns, *The Last Zulu King: The Life and Death of Cetshwayo* (London: Longman, 1963); Guy, *The Destruction of the Zulu Kingdom*; Jeff Guy, *The View Across the River: Harriette Colenso and the Zulu Struggle Against Imperialism* (Cape Town: David Philip, 2001).
47 A. A. Frew, *Prince George's African Tour* (London and Glasgow: Blackie and Son, 1934), p. 172.
48 Stanlake Samkange, *On Trial for My Country* [semi-fictionalised biography of Lobengula] (London: Heinemann, 1966); Stanlake Samkange, *The Origins of Rhodesia* (London: Heinemann, 1969).
49 See also Philip Robert Warhurst, *Anglo-Portuguese Relations in South-Central Africa 1890–1900* (London: Longman, for Royal Commonwealth Society, 1962), pp. 85, 97–9, 103–7; Malyn Newitt, *A History of Mozambique* (London: Hurst and Company, 1995), pp. 348–55; 374–8; Douglas Wheeler, 'Gungunyane the Negotiator: A Study in African Diplomacy', *Journal of African History*, 9:4 (1968), 585–602; McLaughlin, 'Appeal to the Empire', pp. 126–9; Neil Parsons, '"No longer rare birds in London": Zulu, Ndebele, Gaza and Swazi envoys to England, 1882–1894', in Gretchen Gerzina (ed.), *Black Victorians/Black Victoriana* (New Brunswick, NJ: Rutgers University Press, 2003), pp. 124–7; Davidson, *Cecil Rhodes and His Time*, pp. 155–61.
50 James Shadrack Mkhulunyelwa Matsebula, *A History of Swaziland* (Cape Town: Longman Southern Africa, 1972), pp. 73–7; Philip L. Bonner, *Kings, Commoners and Concessionaires: The Evolution and Dissolution of the Nineteenth-Century Swazi State* (Cambridge: Cambridge University Press and Johannesburg: Ravan, 1983), pp. 204–5; Balam Nyeko, 'Prenationalist resistance to colonial rule: Swaziland on the eve of the imposition of British administration, 1890–1902', *Transafrican Journal of History*, 5 (1976), 66–83; Parsons, 'No longer rare birds in London', pp. 127–31.
51 Kuper, *Sobhuza II*, p. 27.
52 Sandra B. Burman, *Chiefdom and Politics under Alien Law: Basutoland under Cape Rule, 1871–1884* (Basingstoke: Macmillan, 1981), p. 174.
53 Frederick Jeffress Ramsay, 'The Rise and Fall of the Bakwena Dynasty in South-Central Africa, 1820–1940' (PhD dissertation, Boston University, 1991), p. 299.
54 Botswana National Archives, ex-Mafeking Registry File J.199, Khama (private letter via Rev. Tom Brown) to High Commissioner Pretoria, 21 August 1922.
55 Frew, *Prince George's African Tour*, pp. 57–8, 145, 156.
56 Thomas Tlou, Neil Parsons, and Willie Henderson, *Seretse Khama 1921–1980* (Braamfontein, Johannesburg and Gaborone: Botswana Society, 1995), p. 9.
57 Botswana National Archives, Secretariat Files, Bechuanaland Protectorate 'Monthly News Letter', February 1952.
58 John Gunther, *Inside Africa* (London: Hamish Hamilton, 1955), pp. 556, 565, 602, 613, 626.
59 Nelson Rolihlala Mandela, with Richard Stengel, *Long Walk to Freedom: The Autobiography of Nelson Mandela* (London: Little, Brown, 1994, Abacus ed., 1995), p. 27.

60 Molema, *Montshiwa 1815–1896*, p. 212.
61 'The day polygamist president Jacob Zuma dined with the "old fashioned imperialists"', *Daily Mail* (London), www.dailymail.co.uk (4 March 2010); 'Queen Victoria statue attacked during Jacob Zuma's UK trip', *The Telegraph* (London), www.telegraph.co.uk (9 March 2010), both accessed 2 September 2014.

PART THREE

Sovereign subjects?

CHAPTER EIGHT

Sovereignty performances, sovereignty testings: The Queen's currency and imperial pedagogies on Australia's south-eastern settler frontiers

Penelope Edmonds

In 1843 near the town of Geelong, in the Port Phillip Bay area of south-eastern Australia, William Adeney, a young man in his twenties and a recent emigrant from England, met a group of Aboriginal people near a squatter's run. Later that day, he recorded the encounter in his diary:

> Met some natives today and had a short yarn with them. Seeing that I looked inquisitively at them they asked me for a sixpence ... the woman said 'give me sixpence' so I took one from my pocket and asked whose head was on it when one of the men replied 'white [woman]'.[1] I told them it was the queen's'.[2]

For the Aboriginal people that Adeney met that day, probably Wathawurrung peoples of the Geelong area, the visage on the coin was merely that of a white woman. The encounter continued:

> '[W]here you quamby [sleep]?' One of the Aboriginal men asked Adeney.
> 'Geelong,' answered Adeney.
> An Aboriginal woman queried, 'name you [?]'
> Adeney replied, 'I said William' and then she imitated it ... After a little more palaver we parted.[3]

In the midst of Wathawurrung country, on cross-cultural borderlands, Adeney sought to assay the currency of Queen Victoria, the British sovereign, among Kulin Aboriginal peoples.[4] In this frontier encounter, seemingly quotidian yet compelling enough for Adeney to record in his diary, is revealed an intriguing sovereignty performance. In a scene rendered as a theatrical vignette, Adeney showed the coin and tested the small Aboriginal group when he asked if they recognised 'the Queen', their now nominal sovereign. This curious colonial moment, based around a single coin, provides a snapshot of unacknowledged and unreciprocated sovereignty. Adeney's frontier vignette compels us to consider Queen Victoria's 'currency' on colonial frontiers, and Kulin peoples' early and then ongoing engagements with the image and idea of the sovereign queen. In particular, this moment, which I argue both was a sovereignty performance and a testing as well as a form of imperial pedagogy, invites questions regarding the uncertain and always partial currency of an imposed sovereignty on new colonial frontiers, and the limits, ambiguities, and fantasies of colonial rule.

Sovereignty is a signal feature of modern politics. It is typically defined as rule, power, authority, and dominion, and its core meaning has traditionally denoted supreme authority within a territory.[5] In the early modern period, sovereignty could denote supreme authority within a territory, but the sovereign also came to hold supreme authority according to a body of law. Territoriality and jurisdiction therefore became a feature of political authority in modernity.[6] Sovereignty, then, has never been wholly abstract, nor is it essential or transcendent. It does not dwell merely in the realms of law or text, and scholars have debated whether a stable, essential notion of sovereignty exists.[7] Just as sovereignty is given meaning through law and territory, it may be material and embodied, as well as symbolically represented, though never absolute. No site could reveal the precarity of European sovereignty better than when empire encroached on and invaded Indigenous lands. New colonial frontiers were 'anomalous legal zones', where the ambiguous and incomplete sovereignty of Europeans had to coexist and was entangled with the laws and customs of peoples over whom they sought to wield supremacy, writes Lauren Benton.[8] In emerging settler colonies, where the 'legal trinity of state nationhood' became 'sovereignty, jurisdiction and territory', writes Lisa Ford, sovereignty in anglophone imperial settings was critically concerned with the 'ordering of indigenous peoples in space'.[9] Ford argues that in the new settler colonies of New South Wales and Australia, as well as in Georgia in the new American republic, a period of plurality – that is, Indigenous sovereignty entangled with an encroaching European sovereignty – endured. This was gradually replaced by a move to a more absolute claim of European sovereignty, or in Ford's words 'perfect settler sovereignty'. Settler sovereignty was consolidated and given meaning by both territory and jurisdiction, she argues.[10] But on new settler frontiers, characterised by such pluralities and anomalous legal codes, and where European authority was insecure, beyond the realms of law and territory, I suggest that sovereignty needed to be made real and brought into being, performed, rehearsed, materially inscribed and reiterated, and even tested and taught to Aboriginal peoples. The curious contestation of sovereignty between Aboriginal people and Europeans on Australian settler frontiers may therefore be observed through paying close attention to cross-cultural moments and to contact history, with its shifting contingencies of ceremony and bodily performance, where people, objects, and rituals and systems of signification came together in a complex, performed interplay of sovereignty claims.[11]

Drawing together themes of political, embodied, and cross-cultural performance and material culture on settler frontiers, I consider the ways in which mobile frontier objects – in this case, coinage bearing the image of Queen Victoria – became points of arbitration and were performatively implicated in protean frontier encounters in Port Phillip, south-eastern Australia. Here recognition, or indeed misrecognition, of sovereignty passed between Indigenous peoples and settlers in surprisingly reciprocal and contradictory ways. In her perceptive exploration of the encounter between history, performance, and colonialism, Diana Taylor argues that embodied performance 'transmits memories, makes political claims, and manifests a group's sense of identity'.[12] Drawing attention to the asymmetries of political and public culture in colonised societies and her quest to examine the relationships between 'embodied performance and the production of knowledge', she argues that 'if performance does not transmit knowledge only the literate and powerful could claim social memory and identity'.[13] In such ways, Indigenous/settler performances on new frontiers could add to, or depart from and indeed subvert, scripted, textual, and legal assumptions and fantastic projections of a complete European sovereignty.[14] Accordingly, Adeney's testing and the Kulin response, one of misrecognition or an unreciprocated sovereignty, could be read as a performance or ritual of critical import. Moreover, it shows an interplay of potent embodied and semiotic claim making that continues to this day.

From the coin scene in 1843, I cast backwards to two years before the commencement of Queen Victoria's reign to explore the possible material (mis)negotiations of the Batman Treaty of 1835 in Port Phillip apparently brokered between settlers and Kulin leaders, in which settlers greatly tested the presumption of the blanket sovereignty of the Crown. With Queen Victoria's ascension to the throne in 1837, just two years after this treaty-making episode, Kulin people entered a new relationship with the female monarch. By 1850, the entire Port Phillip region was inscribed with the monarch's name as the Colony of Victoria. In 1863, two decades after the Adeney vignette, south-eastern Kulin leaders sent a 'Letter to the Queen', an address of loyalty, in which they elicited the Queen's protection. In their minds, this act assisted in securing land for them in the form of a virtuous and filial covenant. Bringing a postcolonial attention to the ambiguous and shifting 'currency' of the sovereign in encounters between settlers and Aboriginal peoples reveals the ways in which they could both shore up European sovereignty and also interrupt it, exposing an always incomplete sovereignty. Lastly, I consider the 'Gold Woman' series (2008) by Aboriginal artist Darren Siwes as an example of contemporary sovereignty assertions by Aboriginal people in the midst of ongoing debates over sovereignty and nation in Australia. Siwes's testing of viewers in his 'Gold Woman' series is a potent reminder that even as the Australian settler state's imposed sovereignty apparently becomes more certain or perfect over time, it is always unstable and open for negotiation in the sphere of creative and cultural politics, where the 'palaverments' and interplay of sovereignty claims endure.

The Queen's two bodies: Frontier 'palavers' and testing sovereignties

Adeney's use of the term 'palaver' to describe his frontier encounter with Kulin people may well have meant that he found the encounter to be idle or flippant. Yet the etymology of the term runs deeper. In the eighteenth century, 'palaver' often referred to a conference between European explorers or colonists and African officials, usually requiring the use of a pidgin language. 'Palaver' denoted a quarrel, or misunderstanding, and of interest here is that it could refer to a matter for arbitration between colonist and Indigenous peoples – a negotiation. The term, deriving from the Portuguese word palavra, was also used to describe a dispute or lawsuit. Colonial officials dubbed 'palaver-men' were responsible for trade and negotiation with local people in West Africa. In Britain, references were made to the 'palaverments' of law (1816).[15] With this in mind, we may read Adeney's encounter with the Aboriginal group as a palaver or a negotiation. As Adeney solicited the correct response to the coin – recognition of the new sovereign – the moment did indeed pertain to the law. It referenced the law of nations and a crucial issue of great import for the lives for Indigenous peoples then and today: sovereignty, its limits and its contestations. Moreover, the palaver related to the relationship between the British sovereign and sovereignty, and in particular, the ways in which power and authority were embodied in Victoria as monarch.

While understandings of sovereignty are complicated by the scope of empire, and the various settings and contexts in which it is enacted, the image of the monarch has remained a central feature. In his classic work *The King's Two Bodies* (1957), Ernst H. Kantorowicz considered the ways that early-modern western monarchies began to develop a political theology, and traced the historical problem posed by the long-held belief in the 'King's two bodies': the 'body-natural' and 'body-politic'.[16] In Kantorowicz's schema, the natural body recognises the corporal element of the monarch, who like all humans is subject to nature and human frailty, and so will age and die. However, the body-politic transcends the body-natural; it is both divine and majestic. This includes all the mechanisms of government (law, order, protection of state, and borders), but also has a mystic element. In the Middle Ages and indeed after the Reformation, the monarch's position was seen to possess divine origins. The theory of the divine right of kings justified the existence of royal power and also confirmed the individual monarch's legitimacy.

In the early days of the colony of New South Wales, many types of foreign currency were in common use. For example, 'British coins circulated with Dutch guilders and ducats, Indian mohurs and rupees and Portuguese johannas', and a great deal of this coin joined the colony as a result of trade with visiting merchant ships. Sterling coinage began to replace foreign coinage from 1822.[17] By 1843 in Melbourne and Geelong, coinage with the head of Queen Victoria was commonly in use. Such coinage circulated in many British colonies as in Britain itself. It literally and repeatedly reified the Queen as sovereign in the currency of the everyday. It is likely that the small group of Wathawurrung people that day were shown an 1843 coin similar to Figure 8.1, which circulated in the Port Phillip region.[18] On one side of the coin is the 'body natural' or profile countenance of the young Queen Victoria.

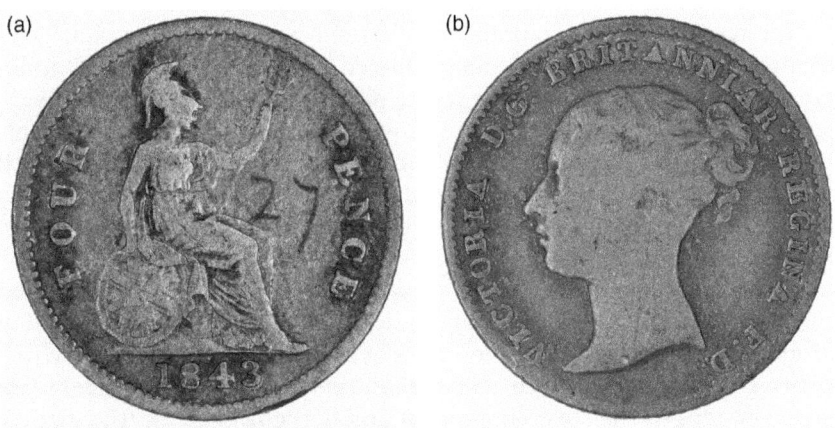

Figure 8.1 A coin dated 1843 with the profile of Queen Victoria on one side. Coins like this were in use in colonial Victoria when William Adeney met a group of Aboriginal people near Geelong.

She faces left, and her hair is bound in a double fillet gathered behind in a knot in a neoclassical style. The inscription reads: 'VICTORIA D: G: BRITANNIAR: REGINA F: D'. On the reverse side of the coin is the 'body politic', the divine and majestic Britannia, the female personification of Great Britain and the British Empire. Seated facing right on a rock, she wears a Corinthian helmet, is armed with a trident and rests her right hand on an oval shield, which bears the three crosses of the Union Flag, conveying themes of maritime and territorial power. The inscription reads: 'FOUR PENCE 1843'.

'From the very beginning', writes Mark McKenna of the British arrival in Australia in 1788, 'monarchy in Australia was performed into being'.[19] Adeney's performance, I suggest, was both a testing and a form of imperial pedagogy, which would become increasingly crucial to the shaping of both Indigenous and British colonial identities in the Australian colonies. On remote frontiers especially, where British settlers experienced feelings of separation and exile, and their Britishness was rendered fragile, the monarchy was seen to be 'at the heart of Australian colonial narratives of belonging', writes McKenna. Yet, as he reminds us, so often monarchy in the colonial setting was an 'act of imaginative recreation'.[20] Further, such imaginative projection should not be understood as mere imperial propaganda, for as David M. Craig has argued, such a view would 'efface' its complexity as well as that of its subjects.[21] As Adeney displayed the coin marked with his sovereign to Kulin people, he thus asserted both his Britishness and his belonging to Port Phillip; the sovereign display grafted a new double identity, British colonial. For the Kulin this performance was an object lesson in imperial citizenship. As Lauren Berlant has argued on the constitution of 'competent citizens' within nations, activities of 'national pedagogy' must been enacted. Berlant speaks of 'technologies of citizenship that seek to create proper national subjects and subjectivities'.[22] Likewise, in the creation of competent imperial citizens, recognising as well as understanding one's appropriate affiliation with the Queen had to be both taught and learned. The increasing 'currency' of the Queen could thus reconfigure European and Indigenous subjectivities in various ways.

In these lessons of empire, coins were the medium of exchange, and the young Queen's physical image, her visage, constituted a key point of arbitration or palaver. Such moments of assay reveal the ways in which coins were entangled with the continuous and uneven engagements with the idea of the sovereign queen and her 'currency' or 'the quality or state of being used or accepted by many people'.[23] In this recursive interplay of claims, 'monarchy' and 'sovereignty' worked as enactment and projection through the 1843 coin. As Louis Marin writes in his *The*

Portrait of the King, 'In the arts of representation are found the real origins and organs of social control ... What then is a king? He is a king's portrait, and that alone makes him king'.[24] In the Kulin act of misrecognition – to their eyes she was a mere white woman – Victoria's portrait, the representation of her power and queenship, and thus her sovereignty, had reached the limits of its currency. In Wathawurrung country, the boundaries of recognition were uncertain and transient. The political cross-currents of recognition (or misrecognition) hovered ambiguously between the body natural, the visual image of a young female human Queen Victoria, and the body politic, that is, Queen Victoria as monarch with the territory, law, and jurisdiction that her sovereignty subtended. In being recognised (or not, in this case), the Queen was thus the *object* of the action, which lends this moment of non-recognition great significance. On one hand, of course, the Kulin saw Victoria's literal embodiment, the body natural: she was a young European female, dressed similarly to well-to-do women on the streets of Melbourne with hair in a neoclassical style. On the other, perhaps this was a wilful misrecognition of strategic import. To recall Marin, just as the recognition of the Victoria portrait made her Queen, the wilful misrecognition of her portrait unmade her as Queen.

The Batman Treaty: Recognising Kulin sovereignty?

The sovereignty of the confederacy of cultural-linguistic groups now referred to as the Kulin Nation was not recognised by the British Crown. Although the 'Batman Treaty' had been brokered in June 1835 (during the reign of King William IV), it was quickly declared null and void by Governor Richard Bourke of the colony of New South Wales, the Crown representative. The only treaty ever to be made in Australia, this dubious agreement made by John Batman on behalf of the entrepreneurial Port Phillip Association claimed that representative 'chiefs' or ngurrengaeta (headmen) of the Kulin Nation had exchanged two tracts of land amounting to 600,000 acres in return for goods such as blankets, axes, flour, mirrors, scissors, 250 handkerchiefs, and the promise of an annual rent or tribute.[25] There has been much debate on the authenticity of the treaty documents and the 'signatures' or sacred inscriptions of eight Aboriginal 'chiefs' or ngurrengaeta of the Wurundjeri-willam clan of the Port Phillip District: it has been suggested Batman might have forged the marks of these headmen on the treaty document thereby performing himself their ceding of territory. The first page of Batman's diary contains the marks or signatures that also appear on the treaty, suggesting that he might have rehearsed the marks apparently belonging to the headmen.[26]

The Batman Treaty, made by a group of private 'Overstraiters' from Van Diemen's Land with Aboriginal peoples of Port Phillip, greatly threatened and undermined the British Crown's blanket claim to its sovereign ownership and jurisdiction over all the land. Further, by treating, however dishonestly, with peoples of the Kulin Nation, Batman had implicitly acknowledged Aboriginal sovereign rights in land, which the Crown had sought to disavow. Port Phillip was also outside the official 'Limits of Location' and so was an anomalous legal zone.[27] Officials in Hobart, Sydney, and London were 'determined that the basic sovereignty of the Crown should not vanish by default'.[28] The Port Phillip Association's claim that the Batman Treaty had gained rights to vast tracts of land, and the subsequent settlement in the area which the treaty presaged, tested not only the Crown's sovereignty claim but also enlivened the possibility of a plurality of sovereignties; it was therefore a renegade manoeuvre.

Fast on the heels of Batman's claim to have signed a treaty with Kulin peoples of the Port Phillip region and the illegal occupation on land around Melbourne and present-day Geelong, Francis Forbes, chief justice of the colony of New South Wales, wrote to Governor Bourke. He advised that the Governor must prevent settlers purchasing land from Aborigines in the erroneous belief that they would have legal title to the land. Forbes concluded his advice by declaring the great importance and urgency of the matter, as Batman and his party would 'surely [be] followed by other persons'. Forbes warned 'much trouble may be occasioned if the Crown seems tacitly to assent to the right of the Savage to sell, and of His Majesty's subjects to buy the land of the Colony'.[29] Tripartite tensions between the Crown's absolute claims to the land and the counterclaims of non-compliant settlers who had in effect recognised the 'right' of Aboriginal landholders 'to sell' are amply apparent.

The significance of a small entrepreneurial group treating with Aboriginal peoples without the Crown's imprimatur was considered by London and the colonial governments to be dangerous, for it signified an acknowledgement of Aboriginal sovereignty and rights in land. Authorities were troubled by the spread of costly settlements beyond their control, and the treaty was quickly voided on the grounds that the Crown alone had an exclusive right of pre-emption. Described as 'pretence', the treaty was declared null and void on 26 August 1835 in a formal proclamation issued by Bourke. The proclamation stated that 'every such treaty, bargain, and contract with the Aboriginal natives ... for the possession of title, or claim to any lands lying and being within the limits of the Governments of the Colony of New South Wales ... is void and shall be of no effect against the rights of the Crown'. Any persons 'in possession of any such land' were to be deemed 'trespassers' and were 'liable to be dealt with in like manner as other intruders upon the vacant lands of the Crown'.[30] In September the proclamation was also published in the Van Diemen's Land press, no doubt to deter other eager Overstraiters from attempting such a journey.[31] In these early years, such palavering with native peoples of Port Phillip was not idle banter, but could alarm colonial officials and have profound legal import across colony and in Britain alike.

The constant invocation of 'the Crown' in this official and legal palaver over the treaty is also marked. Themes of monarchy, sovereignty, and territory dominate the flurry of letters, despatches, and proclamation making. The 'lands of the Crown' and the 'right of the Crown' are cited to assert British imperial sovereignty and jurisdiction extending well beyond the territory of Port Phillip. Bourke's proclamation cited the Crown's vast jurisdiction from the northern 'extremity of Cape York ... to Wilson's Promontory in the South', and 'embracing all the country westward' including 'all the islands adjacent in the Pacific Ocean within the latitude aforesaid ... including Norfolk Island'.[32] In these exchanges, the Crown was not simply the personification of His Majesty King William IV. It was also both metonym and transcendent symbol of an imperial sovereignty stretching over immense expanses of land and sea. Testing the blanket sovereignty of the Crown, and indeed enlivening Aboriginal sovereignty through direct treaty with Aboriginal people, was thus a perilous exercise, for at this time it was a Crown sovereignty whose reach, jurisdiction, and completeness was imagined, and such acts showed it to be perpetually imperfect.

On 20 June 1837, two years after the Batman Treaty and the counter-claims around issues of sovereignty that it produced, the young Queen Victoria assumed the throne. The commencement of her reign symbolically ushered in a new 'sovereign' order, in which Kulin peoples were cast as British subjects.[33] Specifically, they were Queen Victoria's subjects, and governed by her proxy, Governor Sir Richard Bourke, her representative in the colony of New South Wales. One month after Victoria's ascension to the throne, Secretary of State for the Colonies Lord Glenelg wrote to Governor Bourke on 26 July 1837 respecting conduct towards Aboriginal peoples in the Australian settlements:

> Your commission as Governor of New South Wales asserts her Majesty's sovereignty over every part of the continent of New Holland, which is not embraced by the colonies of western or southern Australia. Hence I conceive it follows that all the natives inhabiting those territories must be considered as subject of the Queen, and as within her Majesty's all allegiance. To regard them as aliens, with whom a war can exist, and

against whom her majesty's troops may exercise belligerent rights, is to deny that protection to which they derive the highest possible claim from the sovereignty which has been assumed over the whole of their ancient possessions.[34]

Glenelg articulated an exchange that would often be repeated throughout the Australian colonies: since the British assumed sovereignty over the Kulin's most 'ancient possessions', they were therefore deserving of the 'highest possible claim' – the allegiance and protection of Queen Victoria. Glenelg's pronouncement occurred at the same time as violent frontier warfare was waged between settlers and Aboriginal people in the western districts of Port Phillip.[35] Throughout south-eastern Australia, from the Western District to Gippsland in the east, Aboriginal groups pushed off their lands made surprise attacks on shepherds' huts and squatters' homes, sometimes burning them and taking goods. They often killed hut keepers, especially those who were known to have abused Aboriginal women.[36] They disrupted stock routes and drove off flocks of sheep; in some cases, they, like Europeans, fenced the sheep to use them for food. European reprisals were often swift and vicious. After a visit to outlying stations, Charles Sievwright, assistant Aboriginal Protector for the Western District, related the sense of ominous violence to Aboriginal Protector William Thomas: 'The state of society in the interior towards the poor Aborigines is awful, out of sixteen stations ... but one (Mr. Airy) [was] humanely disposed to the Aborigines, 2 out of 16 ... visited had skulls of Aborigines placed over the door of their huts.[37] Yet officials routinely tried to obscure the high rate of Aboriginal deaths. As one police magistrate remarked in 1839: 'A murder committed by the black is paraded in the papers, and everybody is shocked; but there have been hundreds of cold-blooded murders perpetrated by the whites on the outskirts of the Colony, which we have never heard of'.[38]

The rise of British humanitarianism in the 1830s coincided with the rapid expansion of settlement and its associated frontier violence in the Australian colonies. Following the 1837 *Report of the Select Committee on Aboriginal Tribes (British Settlements)*, which sought to draw attention to the negative and violent effects of Britain's expansionist endeavours on Indigenous peoples, officials were prompted to create a humanitarian system that would 'protect' Aboriginal peoples of south-eastern Australia in the Port Phillip District.[39] The Aboriginal Protectorate system of Port Phillip was instituted by Great Britain's House of Lords and implemented by Lord Glenelg. Established in 1839, the Protectorate experimented with the 1837 Select Committee's recommendations. By 1838, the Chief Protector, George Augustus

Robinson, with the dubious reputation of having 'conciliated' the Aborigines in Van Diemen's Land, was selected along with four assistants. Glenelg stipulated that the protectors were to 'promote the well-being of Aborigines and to represent their interests to the colonial executive or the British government'. They were to physically protect the Aborigines, 'civilise' them, educate them, convert them to Christianity, and instruct them in agriculture and the building of houses.[40] Yet the Port Phillip protectorate system was beset by controversy and mistrusted by squatters and colonial authorities alike, which made it ineffective in its mandate to 'protect' its Aboriginal peoples. It was dismantled in 1849. As would be the case elsewhere, these protection strategies were eventually harnessed to colonial efforts that disenfranchised and dispossessed Indigenous people.[41] Nevertheless, it did change the lives of Kulin people like in no other colony in Australia, and their experience was distinctive.

By 1843, when Adeney met the small Aboriginal group near Geelong, many Kulin people had some knowledge of the Queen, in part through their conversations with missionaries and the assistant protectors. Chief Protector Robinson, for example, was a loyal supporter of Queen Victoria and frequently given over to flourishes of imperial and monarchist gesturing. In 1840, while touring north-eastern Port Phillip, Robinson, accompanied by the Reverend Joseph Docker and Assistant Protector James Dredge, camped at the confluence of the Murray and Ovens Rivers. Here the group carved an inscription into a gum tree announcing their allegiance to the young Queen: 'Robinson and Dredge for Victoria'. As Robinson recorded in his diary, afterwards they wrote a note in the time-honoured mode of explorers in a new land, placed it in a bottle, and buried it at the base of the tree. They next 'drank her Majesty's health with a little brandy mixed in water'. The note read:

> Reverend Joseph Docker and GA Robinson Esp. C.P of Aborigines, James Dredge, Esq. A P. of ditto, Amici, humani generis. Murray river, 2 miles below the junction of the Ovens with the Murray on this occasion the health of Her Most Gracious Majesty Queen Victoria was drunk and the Royal initials inscribed on a gum tree, April 30th, 1840 Vivat Regina Tries (in) Uno'.[42]

The group claimed their allegiance for Victoria, inscribed it in the landscape, and announced their standing as 'Amici, humani generis', friends of the human race, or philanthropists. As Jessie Mitchell observes of the same incident, in his diary James Dredge recorded that at the end of the inscription was the word 'WO-RA-JE-RE', presumably Wuradjeri, a large Aboriginal nation whose country lay to the north.[43] As Mitchell remarks, the inscription is 'alive with multiple meanings'.

The act of inscription itself, plus the burying of a bottle, is typical of the repertoire of adventurers in new and uninhabited lands. But the group, as it well knew, was in the midst of Aboriginal lands, and the 'purpose of the protectors' journey [was] not to claim empty land but rather to monitor the culture and dispossession of the people still living there'.[44] The loyalty pledged to Queen Victoria, 'Vivat Regina' or 'long live the Queen', the occurrence of this sovereignty performance within the Australian landscape, and the inclusion of 'Wo-ra-je-re', as Mitchell argues, 'marked both the land and the protectorate with a significant combination of the imperial and the Indigenous'.[45] But more than this, I suggest they proclaimed Victoria as sovereign *because* this was Aboriginal land, and a dual acknowledgement occurs. Indeed, like Adeney's coin palaver three years later, Robinson instated a double identity – both his Britishness with its associated race pride and his belonging to Port Phillip – through the medium of the monarch, Queen Victoria.

After the Port Phillip Protectorate was deemed a failure and closed in 1849, Kulin people were effectively abandoned by the state and left to find their own way in the colonial economy, where many ended up working for local settlers.[46] The onset of a gold rush spelled further dispossession of Aboriginal land as colonists purchased leases from the Crown and asserted ownership rights, allowing Aboriginal people to remain on the land insofar as they became useful as 'a pool of inexpensive labour'.[47] In 1850 Port Phillip become the Colony of Victoria, taking the eponymous title to signal the Queen's territorial sovereignty.[48] The British Parliament passed 'An Act for the Better Government of Her Majesty's Australian Colonies', which received Royal Assent on 5 August 1850. The Colony of Victoria came into being on 1 July 1851 once legislation was passed by the New South Wales Legislative Council, and was celebrated with a five-day public holiday and festivities throughout the streets of Melbourne.

To become the Colony of Victoria, the Port Phillip District had fought for and achieved separation from the colony of New South Wales in 1850. It then gained responsible government five years later in 1855. As Ann Curthoys has observed, the imperial government handed 'responsible government' to the colonies as a 'way to keep potentially restive settler colonies within the realm', but also to transfer most of the costs of government 'from the metropole to settlers themselves'. This shift gave the settler colonies jurisdiction over Indigenous peoples.[49] Further, as Henry Reynolds has argued, the colonial office surrendered 'responsibility for the Aborigines to the very colonists whom they had frequently accused of trying to exterminate the tribes they encountered'.[50] Curthoys registers the 'double character' of this shift when she notes that settler jurisdiction and responsibility expanded as colonies gained political autonomy from Britain while simultaneously it 'restricted or denied those capacities' to Indigenous peoples. In other words, a 'diminution of indigenous rights and sovereignty was entwined with the expansion of those to settlers'.[51] In other settler colonies such as North America and New Zealand, treaties at the very least acknowledged a relationship or covenant between Indigenous peoples and newcomers and did acknowledge some form of sovereignty, however delimited. Yet, in the Australian colonies, Aboriginal people would be 'British subjects who *appealed* to the Crown rather than subjects who *negotiated* with the Crown', writes McKenna, and their 'protection under British law rested almost entirely in the hands of their dispossessors'.[52] As Curthoys relates, those seeking political change, 'indigenous and settler alike', would therefore encounter a range of bodies and personalities at differing levels of power – 'governors, colonial secretaries, ministers of the Crown, local authorities and police', and therefore, for 'indigenous people knowing where power might lie could be especially difficult'.[53]

From 1835 the Indigenous population in the Port Phillip District plummeted by around 80 per cent within a generation. Thousands of sheep destroyed Kulin food sources and fouled water supplies.[54] The influx of gold seekers in the 1850s further transformed Victoria, pushing more Kulin people off their lands. As trespassers in their own country, Aboriginal people survived on station work, seasonal harvesting, and occasional rations. They developed strategies of accommodation by incorporating new languages, methods of gathering food and resources, and developing new forms of protest. In 1840 the Wathawurrung people from near Geelong asked the missionary Francis Tuckfield for land of their own, and from 1843 the Woiwurrung clan near Melbourne repeatedly called on Assistant Protector William Thomas for 'land in our own country'.[55] By 1847 they also sought new alliances with the previously hostile Kurnai of Gippsland.[56] These early political networks and demands for land as both refuge and compensation would develop into cultures of protest and a 'powerful narrative of entitlement'; and as Curthoys and Mitchell have shown, it would also bring Kulin people and their supporters into political engagement with colonial governments.[57]

By the 1860s, and with the establishment of the Central Board Appointed to Watch Over the Interests of the Aborigines in 1860, Kulin peoples were sequestered on mission stations and deemed wards of the state. Yet, as Curthoys and Mitchell have shown, they could make their political voice known through petitions. This was a 'way of making claims', and often such political action was supported with missionary encouragement and involvement. Nevertheless, it also proffers a unique window into Indigenous experience and worldview.[58]

'The Queen's Letter'

In the Colony of Victoria, peoples of the Kulin Nation were well aware of the identity and power of the white woman on the coin. 'Wherever possible', writes Curthoys, and as demonstrated by other scholars, Aboriginal people 'sought to approach the Queen or her representatives directly'.[59] By the early 1860s, they would articulate affective and affectionate bodily ties of family and kinship and use the discourse of the protective, beneficent Victoria as 'Queen Mother' to appeal for land.

With their land increasingly occupied by colonists, Kulin clans encountered great difficulties finding and settling on land unoccupied by squatters. In 1860, the Woiwurrung and Taungerong clans of the Kulin Nation set up camp at Coranderrk (near the town of Healesville) because squatters already inhabited their chosen site on the Yarra River nearby. According to Diane Barwick, for years 'the Kulin ... [had] been told that the Queen had explicitly commissioned the Governor to protect Aborigines and were apparently aware that this formal consent was required for the reservation of land. The leaders of the camp at Coranderrk Creek originated the idea of attending the Governor's public levee, open to all gentlemen, on 24 May 1863'. This levee was a public reception held in honour of Queen Victoria's birthday, as well as the recently formalised nuptials of the Prince of Wales. The Kulin arranged to walk to Melbourne with gifts to mark the occasion, which included 'weapons for the Prince, and rugs and baskets for the Queen'.[60] Upon learning of this plan shortly before the levee was to take place, the secretary of the Board for the Protection of Aborigines, Robert Brough Smyth, resolved, with the help of former Protector and government adviser on Aboriginal welfare William Thomas, to 'draft and translate a loyal address in the express hope that this would win sympathy for the Aborigines from the "Home Government"'.[61]

Barwick has written that Aboriginal leader Simon Wonga 'gracefully presented the written address with a speech in Woiwurrung' to the 'Great Mother Queen Victoria'.[62] A delegation of 'eight men and five boys' from four Kulin tribes spoke to the Queen's official local representative, the Governor of Victoria at the time, Sir Henry Barkly, of their need for land – in 'good English'.[63] The next month they were granted land. Coranderrk was officially established through a notice in Victoria's *Government Gazette*, and facsimiles of 'a letter from the Queen's Secretary were sent to the Kulin later that year, conveying the Queen's thanks for Wonga's address and her promise of protection'.

Although Barwick argues that the gazettal of a 'reservation of 2,300 acres [931 ha] for their use on 30 June 1863' was probably only coincidentally related to the address of loyalty at the levee,[64] it was nonetheless interpreted by the Kulin people as a covenant with the Queen.[65] 'The coincidence of the Levee, the granting of Coranderrk and the written acknowledgments of the Queen were considered significant and linked events in the hearts and minds of the Kulin', Barry Judd observes. The Kulin treated the Queen's promise of reserve land as both a gift and an acknowledgement of their rightful claims to compensation. They understood that the Queen's gift 'had been granted in perpetuity and [that] the land at Coranderrk would provide a home for them and their heirs and successors'.[66] Maria Nugent (Chapter 4 this volume), however, notes that as Crown land, all reservations were in fact 'made under Queen Victoria's imprimatur'. Nugent argues that the claim that the Queen was the source of land has become a *lieu de memoire* or site of memory for Aboriginal people, and works powerfully as 'an invocation of an image of the world as it ought to be'. This is because the 'narrative element of Queen Victoria remained useful especially as an image of justice, virtue, and provision', she argues.[67] Penny van Toorn has suggested that whether or not the Queen had intervened, the Kulin had 'used the medium of writing not to preserve words over time, but rather to carry their voices over the heads of local officials so that they could be heard by higher authorities to whom the locals were accountable'.[68] In this strategic manoeuvre, the Kulin had effectively bypassed the Central Board for the Protection of Aborigines and directly influenced the government.[69] And they would repeatedly use this strategy. Indeed, as Curthoys argues, 'Indigenous peoples did learn gradually the intricacies of how power was dispersed and adapted their behaviours accordingly'.[70] For the Kulin, the Queen's letter formed part of a very real, and embodied, process of negotiation. The letter served to materially represent the sovereign, not as an abstract power, but as the benevolent, if geographically distant, participant in an exchange. Moreover, the image of the sovereign as the 'Great Mother' reinforced the notion of Queen Victoria as a matriarch, but also highlighted what Kantorowicz identifies as the 'body-natural' of the monarch, acknowledging that the sovereign, like the rest of humanity, was subject to the processes of life, including those associated with mothering. Throughout the nineteenth century, Native peoples of Canada also referred to Queen Victoria as 'Great Mother' and themselves as 'red children', and thus stressed their familial, if subordinate, relationship with her in the same way.[71] The appeal by the Kulin to this motherly side of the sovereign, as opposed to the 'body politic' or law and governance side, perhaps suggests a different way of viewing their relationship to the Queen. It was one that circumvented government machinery, instead focusing on an emotional and personal relationship, yet which nevertheless had its reciprocal obligations. The subsequent return of the 'Queen's letter', in which she apparently recognised Kulin sovereignty over Coranderrk though a personal, filial, and virtuous covenant, further reinforced this perception of the affective workings of sovereignty. Such effects of memory and emotion around the image and idea of the Queen as sovereign are amply resonant in the present in complex, contradictory, and fraught ways.

Relocating sovereignty in 'Gold Woman'

Finally, I turn to the recent artworks by Aboriginal artist Darren Siwes titled 'Gold Girl' and 'Gold Female' (2008) (see Figures 8.2 and 8.3) as a present-day example of both a challenge and a reminder of the plural and unstable nature of sovereignty on postcolonial frontiers.

Figure 8.2 'Gold Girl', artist: Darren Siwes, from the series *Oz Omnium Rex et Regina*, 2008. (© Darren Siwes/Licensed by Viscopy, 2015/ Courtesy GAGPROJECTS, Adelaide, South Australia.)

Figure 8.3 'Gold Female', artist: Darren Siwes, from the series *Oz Omnium Rex et Regina*, 2008. (© Darren Siwes/Licensed by Viscopy, 2015/ Courtesy GAGPROJECTS, Adelaide, South Australia.)

These artworks form part of a series of twelve coin images titled *Oz Omnium Rex et Regina* (King and Queen of all Oz). In this photographic series, Siwes reproduces the visual conventions of Australian state coinage, but uses profiles of Aboriginal people to represent the constructed regal personages of 'Mary I' and 'George I' in a reimagined future, from 2010 to 2042. The series may also pay tribute to the work of photographer Frederick Kruger, a German immigrant to Australia, who, in the late nineteenth century, compiled a portfolio of photographs titled *Souvenir album of Victorian Aboriginals, kings, queens etc.* This collection, designed to be commercially appealing, appeared in the miniature booklet format popular in its day and featured notable Indigenous figures assigned European royal titles.[72] Included in its pages was a photograph of an Aboriginal woman titled 'Queen Mary – Ballarat'.[73] The many late nineteenth-century photographers who marketed similar sets of photographs of 'Native' kings and queens in 'foreign' lands did so not only for the purpose of spectacle or derisive, wry amusement, but also for the purpose of preservation. These images served as elegiac records of people who were thought to be the 'last of' their tribes, a swansong to their race, and a herald to modernity.

Newton has remarked that through the nationally recognisable image of an Australian gold coin, 'Siwes seems to suggest that should a future ruler of Australia be Aboriginal, they will not become whitefellas but keep faith with their own culture'.[74] Another commentator, Ric Spencer, argues that Siwes's 'work is timely, [given that] post Sorry Day we must now give ourselves, as a nation, the opportunity of looking forward, pondering, if you like, new possibilities'.[75] However, rather, than simply keeping 'faith with their own culture' or a post-Sorry Day looking forward, I interpret these works as both a political reappropriation of the classic queen's head on the coin, as well as a powerful assertion and enactment of Indigenous sovereignty in the midst of enduring postcolonial debates over sovereignty and nation in Australia. Such debates are all the more salient in a present political campaign called 'Recognise', which is lobbying for the recognition of Aboriginal and Torres Strait Islander people as first peoples in the Australian Constitution. Siwes's 'Mary I' is a challenge that in its multivalency and visual and textual play both surprises and schools us (the non-Indigenous viewer) in the currency of an Aboriginal head of state.

Siwes's images are multifaceted in their spatial-temporal depictions of monarchy. The title of the series itself, *Oz Omnium Rex et Regina*, denotes these individuals to be the rulers of Oz. 'Oz', of course, may readily be interpreted as a colloquial term for Australia. While connections can be made between Australia and 'Oz', it is also the fantastical setting of Dorothy's adventures in L. Frank Baum's story *The Wonderful Wizard of Oz* (1900). Baum's Oz is a place of fantasy and enchantment, especially in American popular culture, but it is also a utopian realm, which offers the promise of transformation and visions of a better world. In this way Siwes's Oz can be read as belonging to the dream realm, and thus free of the burden of ownership and history attached to the designation 'Australia'. In the context of Australian Aboriginal–settler relations, Oz may also signal a return, a homecoming to a complete Aboriginal sovereignty before European contact, an enactment of political desire that is deeply compelling.

Time is a central feature of this series. 'George' and 'Mary' appear in both their young and old guises. In the Mary sequence, the first coin is marked 'MARY I' / 'AUSTRALIA 2013', evoking the 'Queen Mary' of Kruger's portraits. The second coin, 'MARY I' / 'AUSTRALIA 2041', suggests that twenty-eight years have elapsed. The images present a chronology that is linear and sequential in its projection of time, but one that goes beyond the present and into future time. Significantly, this movement into future time is anchored and made real through the ageing body of the Queen. While the Queen herself wears the mark of human frailty, the markers of her majesty (the body-politic) remain unchanged; she still wears the crown and her presence on the coin shows her sovereignty to remain current.

Above all, the coin is radical in its visual overthrow of the current British sovereign (Queen Elizabeth II), and suggestive of a genuine future reconciliation that recognises some form of Aboriginal sovereignty – indicated by the image of 'Mary I' as the head of state. The imagery is thus radically speculative and challenging, taking us into the realm of the great 'reconciled republic', thus resolving, in McKenna's words, the 'two great symbolic issues of Australian politics' in the 1990s. Siwes thus imagines this republic anew, as does McKenna, who argues that 'the republic and reconciliation are linked intimately to one another', and that the 'only way forward is a reconciled republic, a republic founded on the full recognition of Australia's history'.[76]

Conclusion

The striking Adeney coin vignette invites reflection on the use of the Queen (and King) in the recursive and perpetually incomplete performances of sovereignty marking and sovereignty testing. Sovereignty did not (and does not) reside, nor was it brought into being, only within the realms of law, territory, and jurisdiction. Rather, it could be asserted, enacted, or refuted in complex, fleeting, interpersonal, and embodied exchanges, on the ground in spaces of contestation and emergent settler frontiers, where plural sovereignties competed, and where people, objects, and rituals came together in often ambiguous and contradictory ways. Such imperial pedagogies shaped settler and Indigenous subjectivities in particular, various, and highly relational and affective ways. Imperial fantasies of the sovereign's reach and currency, such as that enacted by Adeney, could be ruptured on the ground by Indigenous people's lack of reciprocation and refusal to recognise the body of the sovereign. The European sovereign's limits are also starkly apparent, precariously dependent on Indigenous recognition in these transient interpersonal and intercultural spaces. As Kulin people became schooled in the sovereign Queen and the lexicon of loyal address through which affiliations might be formed with her, they articulated ties of family and kinship and used the discourse of the protective, beneficent Victoria as 'Queen Mother', recognising her on their own cultural and political terms to achieve their goals of obtaining land and liberties.

Siwes's 'Mary I' points to the future but also to the past, and the past's present. He reverses the specular commerce as he reappropriates the image on the coin, the nation's currency, by replacing it with an Aboriginal woman, Queen Mary. As Lisa Ford has argued, in settler societies 'indigenous recovery ... has taken place in the gaps and fissures of settler sovereignties – spaces that are historically emergent, fluid and contested'.[77] She suggests that 'even at their most racist and self-serving, settler states in Australia were complex institutions; their claims to jurisdiction, their effort at dispossession, even their establishment of formal bureaucratic tyrannies over indigenous peoples were both presumptuous and unconsummated'.[78] Perhaps as non-Indigenous observers, our taken-for-granted notions of sovereignty – established and visually reinforced in such thoroughgoing ways by our quotidian and yet ubiquitous coinage – are being tested and reschooled by Siwes. Like Adeney, Siwes compels us to ask 'who is this woman?', evoking past and future Indigenous sovereignty, the permanent presence of which perpetually worries the settler state, whose sovereignty is always in a state of incompletion.

Acknowledgements

I wish to thank the anonymous reviewers, and Maria Nugent, Camille Nurka, and Alicia Marchant for most helpful comments on this chapter.

Notes

1 The original term used by the Aboriginal men, according to Adeney, was 'Lubra', a now highly contested term. In 1843 it was new in the colonial argot. It referred to an Aboriginal woman, but it quickly took on derogatory, highly racialised meaning. As Liz Conor notes, '"Lubra" first appeared in 1829 in the journals of G. A. Robinson, the self-styled missionary of Tasmania (then Van Diemen's Land). The term appears to derive from "Leuberer" which Robinson took to mean wife. Over time it has become "deeply offensive to Indigenous women"'. Liz Conor, 'The "Lubra" type in Australian imaginings of the Aboriginal woman from 1836–1973', *Gender & History*, 25:2 (August 2013), 230–51.
2 State Library of Victoria, MS 8520A, William Adeney diary, 6th Feb 1843, Mr. Roadknight's run near Geelong, 327.
3 *Ibid.*
4 The 'Kulin' peoples or 'Kulin Nation' refers to the five related cultural-linguistic groups of south-eastern Australian Aboriginal people who are the traditional owners of the Port Phillip region, now greater Victoria. These are the Wurundjeri (speaking Woiwurrung), Wathawurrong, Boonwurrung, Daungwurrung, and Djadjawarrung peoples. See also Richard Broome, *Aboriginal Victorians: A History Since 1800* (Crows Nest, NSW: Allen and Unwin, 2005), p. xxi.
5 'Sovereignty', Stanford Encyclopedia of Philosophy, http://plato.stanford.edu/entries/sovereignty/, accessed 15 November 2014.
6 *Ibid.*

7 *Ibid.*
8 Lauren Benton, *A Search for Sovereignty: Law and Geography in European Empires, 1400–1900* (Cambridge: Cambridge University Press, 2009), p. 30.
9 Lisa Ford, *Settler Sovereignty: Jurisdiction and Indigenous People in America and Australia, 1788–1836* (Cambridge, MA and London: Harvard University Press, 2010), p. 1.
10 *Ibid.* See also: Julie Evans, Ann Genovese, Alex Reilly, and Patrick Wolfe (eds), *Sovereignty: Frontiers of Possibility* (Honolulu: University of Hawaii Press, 2013).
11 See for example Patricia Seed, *Ceremonies of Possession in Europe's Conquest of the New World, 1492–1640* (Cambridge: Cambridge University Press, 1995).
12 Diana Taylor, *The Archive and the Repertoire: Performing Cultural Memory in the Americas* (Durham, NC and London: Duke University Press, 2003), p. xix.
13 *Ibid.*, p. xvii.
14 See also Maria Nugent, '"An echo of that other cry": Re-enacting Captain Cook's first landing as conciliation event', in Kate Darian-Smith and Penelope Edmonds (eds), *Conciliation on Colonial Frontiers: Conflict, Performance and Commemoration in Australia and the Pacific Rim* (London: Routledge, 2015), pp. 193–209.
15 'Palaver', Oxford English Dictionary online, http://dictionary.oed.com, accessed 6 June 2014; *Online Etymology Dictionary*, http://dictionary.reference.com/browse/palaver, accessed 6 June 2014.
16 E. H. Kantorowicz, *The King's Two Bodies: A Study in Medieval Political Theory* (Princeton, NJ: Princeton University Press, 1957), pp. 7–23.
17 www.nma.gov.au/collections/highlights/holey_dollar, accessed 12 June 2014.
18 Reg. No: NU 1103. 'This groat, like most groats of Queen Victoria in the Museum Victoria collection, was collected by George McArthur. All his coins show considerable wear and it is believed that they were collected by him from circulation in Victoria'. Museum Victoria collection webpage, http://museumvictoria.com.au/collections/items/75699/coin-groat-queen-victoria-great-britain-1854, accessed 5 November 2014.
19 Mark McKenna, 'Monarchy: From reverence to indifference', in D. M. Schreuder and S. Ward (eds), *Australia's Empire* (Oxford: Oxford University Press, 2008), p. 261.
20 *Ibid.*, p. 262.
21 David M. Craig, cited in *Ibid.*, p. 276. David M. Craig, 'The crowned republic? Monarchy and anti-monarchy in Britain, 1760–1901', *The Historical Journal*, 46:1 (2003), p. 172.
22 Lauren Berlant, *The Queen of America Goes to Washington City: Essays on Sex and Citizenship* (Durham, NC: Duke University Press, 1997), pp. 30, 31.
23 Merriam Webster dictionary on the term 'currency', www.merriam-webster.com/dictionary/currency, accessed 18 January 2015.
24 Kantorowicz, *The King's Two Bodies*. See also: Louis Marin, *The Portrait of the King* (Minneapolis: University of Minnesota Press, 1998).
25 A. G. L. Shaw, 'Batman Treaty', in *Encyclopaedia of Melbourne* (Melbourne, Cambridge University Press, 2005); Michael Christie, *Aborigines in Colonial Victoria* (Sydney: Sydney University Press, 1979), p. 25; Bain Attwood, *Possession: Batman's Treaty and the Matter of History* (Melbourne: Miegunyah Press, 2009); Penelope Edmonds, *Urbanizing Frontiers: Indigenous Peoples and Settlers in 19th-Century Pacific Rim Cities* (Vancouver: University of British Columbia Press, 2010), pp. 37–40.
26 Attwood, *Possession*, pp. 50, 51. See also State Library of Victoria, http://ergo.slv.vic.gov.au/image/batmans-journal, accessed 14 June 2014.
27 Governor Darling's 1827 'Limits of Location' statute stipulated that settlement could not occur outside a certain coastal penumbra stretching from the northern New South Wales coast to the southern coastal town of Moruya.
28 *Historical Records of Victoria*, henceforth *HRV*, vol. 1, p. 3.
29 National Library of Australia, MS 1293, Francis Forbes, Letter to Governor Sir Richard Bourke, 26 July 1835.
30 *HRV*, vol. 1, p. 14, Governor Bourke's proclamation, dated 26 August 1835.
31 For example, 'Proclamation by His Excellency General Sir Richard Bourke', *Cornwall Chronicle*, Launceston (26 September 1835).

32 *Ibid.*
33 Ann Curthoys, 'Indigenous subjects', in Schreuder and Ward (eds), *Australia's Empire*.
34 *British Parliamentary Papers: Correspondence and Papers Relating to the Government and Affairs of the Australian Colonies 1837–40* (1970), vol. 5, p. 373.
35 See, for example, Lyndall Ryan, 'Settler massacres on the Port Phillip Frontier 1835–1851', *Journal of Australian Studies*, 34:3 (2010): 257–73.
36 Christie, *Aborigines in Colonial Victoria*, p. 64.
37 NSW State Library, MS MLMSS214, microfilm CY2604, frame 44–6, William Thomas journal, April 1839.
38 'Report of the Committee on Police and Gaols', *Votes and Proceedings*, 2, F2815 (1839), p. 75, quoted in R. H. W. Reece, *Aborigines and Colonists: Aborigines and Colonial Society in New South Wales in the 1830s and 1840s* (Sydney: Sydney University Press, 1974), p. 24.
39 *Report of the Select Committee on Aboriginal Tribes (British Settlements)*, reprinted, with comments by the Aborigines Protection Society (London: William Ball, Aldine Chambers, Paternoster Row, and Hatchard and Son, Piccadilly, 1837).
40 Christie, *Aborigines in Colonial Victoria*, pp. 87, 89; M. Lakic and R. Wrench (eds), *Through Their Eyes: An Historical Record of the Aboriginal People of Victoria as Documented by the Officials of the Port Phillip Protectorate, 1839–1841* (Melbourne, Museum Victoria, 1994), p. 13.
41 See Tracey Banivanua Mar and Penelope Edmonds, 'Indigenous and settler relations', in Alison Bashford and Stuart Mcintyre (eds), *New Cambridge History of Australia*, vol. 1 (Cambridge: Cambridge University Press, 2013), pp. 342–66.
42 Ian D. Clark (ed.), *The Journals of George Augustus Robinson 1839–1852* (CreateSpace Independent Publishing Platform, 2014), p. 161.
43 State Library of Victoria (SLV), MS11625, MSM534, James Dredge, Diaries, Notebook and Letterbooks, 1817–1845, James Dredge, 30 April 1840; Clark, *The Journals of George Augustus Robinson*, vol. 1, pp. 248–56.
44 Jessie Mitchell, *In Good Faith? Governing Indigenous Australia Through God, Charity and Empire, 1825–1855* (Canberra: ANU E-Press, 2011), p. 2.
45 *Ibid.*, p. 2.
46 Jessie Mitchell, '"Country belonging to me": Land and labour on Aboriginal missions and protectorate stations, 1830–1850', *Eras Journal*, www.arts.monash.edu.au/publications/eras/edition-6/mitchellarticle.php, accessed 14 June 2014.
47 Larissa Behrendt, *Achieving Social Justice: Indigenous Rights and Australia's Future* (Sydney: Federation Press, 2003), p. 36.
48 See 'An Act for the Better Government of Her Majesty's Australian Colonies', p. 662, on separation and the new colony 'to be known and designated as Victoria'. www.foundingdocs.gov.au/scan-sid-943.html, accessed 15 November 2014. Charles La Trobe, who had been the superintendent of the Port Phillip District, became the new colony's first Lieutenant Governor. See also A. G. L. Shaw, *A History of the Port Phillip District: Victoria Before Separation* (Carlton: Melbourne University Press, 1996), p. 278.
49 Ann Curthoys, 'Taking liberty: Towards a new political historiography of settler self-government and Indigenous activism', in Kate Fullagar (ed.), *The Atlantic World in the Antipodes* (Cambridge: Cambridge Scholars Publishing, 2012), p. 237.
50 *Ibid.*, p. 238.
51 *Ibid.*
52 Mark McKenna, 'Transplanted to savage shores: Indigenous Australians and British birthright in the mid-nineteenth-century Australian colonies', *Journal of Colonialism and Colonial History*, 13:1 (Spring 2012), http://muse.jhu.edu/journals/journal_of_colonialism_and_colonial_history/v013/13.1.mckenna.html#f15, accessed 18 January 2015. McKenna cites Alan Atkinson, "Conquest," in Schreuder and Ward (eds), *Australia's Empire*, pp. 33–53, especially 33–6 and 52.
53 Curthoys, 'Taking liberty', p. 238.
54 See Banivanua Mar and Edmonds, 'Indigenous and Settler Relations', p. 354. George Augustus Robinson (1845), quoted in Richard Broome, 'Changing Aboriginal

Landscapes of Pastoral Victoria, 1830–1850', *Studies in the History of Gardens and Designed Landscapes*, 31:2 (2011), p. 91.
55 Ann Curthoys and Jessie Mitchell, '"Bring this paper to the Good Governor": Aboriginal petitioning in Britain's Australian colonies', in Saliha Belmessous (ed.), *Native Claims: Indigenous Law Against Empire, 1500–1920* (New York: Oxford University Press, 2012), p. 188.
56 See Banivanua Mar and Edmonds, 'Indigenous and Settler Relations', p. 354. R. E. Barwick and Diane E. Barwick, 'A memorial for Thomas Bungaleen, 1847–1865', *Aboriginal History*, 8:1 (1984), p. 9.
57 Curthoys and Mitchell, 'Bring this paper', p. 190.
58 Curthoys, 'Taking liberty', pp. 247, 248.
59 *Ibid.*, p. 248.
60 Diane Barwick, *Rebellion at Coranderrk* (Canberra: Aboriginal History Monographs, 1998), p. 66. This was found at www.nfsa.gov.au/digitallearning/mabo/info/theQueensLetter.htm, accessed 14 June 2014.
61 *Ibid.*
62 *Ibid.*
63 *Ibid.*
64 *Ibid.*
65 See, for example, Sukanya Banerjee, *Becoming Imperial Citizens* (Durham, NC: Duke University Press, 2010).
66 Barry Judd, '"It's not cricket": Victorian Aboriginal cricket at Coranderrk', *La Trobe Journal*, 85 (May 2010), p. 43.
67 Maria Nugent, Chapter 4, this volume: 'The politics of memory and the memory of politics: Australian Aboriginal interpretations of Queen Victoria.
68 Penny van Toorn, *Writing Never Arrives Naked: Early Aboriginal Cultures of Writing in Australia* (Canberra: Aboriginal Studies Press, 2006), p. 125.
69 Rachel Perkins and Marcia Langton (eds), *First Australians Unillustrated* (Melbourne: The Meigunyah Press, 2010), p. 92.
70 Curthoys, 'Taking liberty', p. 250.
71 See for example Sarah Carter, '"Your Great Mother across the salt sea": Prairie First Nations, the British monarchy, and the vice-regal connection to 1900', *Manitoba History* 48 (Autumn 2004/Winter 2005), 35.
72 See Jane Lydon, *Eye Contact: Photographing Indigenous Australians* (Durham, NC and London: Duke University Press, 2005), p. 157.
73 *Ibid.*, p. 157.
74 Gael Newton – Text © National Gallery of Australia, Canberra 2010, in Francesca Cubillo and Wally Caruana (eds), *Aboriginal and Torres Strait Islander Art: Collection Highlights* (Canberra: National Gallery of Australia, 2010).
75 Ric Spencer, 'A profile of symbolic exchange', 2008, http://www.greenaway.com.au/Artists/Darren-Siwes.html#Essay04, accessed 14 June 2014. Spencer's note of 'Sorry Day' refers to the national apology to Australian Aboriginal people by Prime Minister Kevin Rudd on behalf of the Australian Parliament on 13 February 2008.
76 Mark McKenna, *This Country: A Reconciled Republic?* (Sydney: University of New South Wales Press, 2004).
77 Lisa Ford, 'Locating Indigenous self-determination at the margins of settler sovereignty: An introduction', in Lisa Ford and Tim Rowse (eds), *Between Indigenous and Settler Governance* (London, Routledge, 2012), p. 1.
78 *Ibid.*, p. 2.

CHAPTER NINE

Bracelets, blankets and badges of distinction: Aboriginal subjects and Queen Victoria's gifts in Canada and Australia

Amanda Nettelbeck

In colonial encounters over centuries, gifts formed a critical part of how Europeans initiated contact with Aboriginal peoples and established the terms for trade, military allegiance, or peace. At least in this process, if not in others, colonial newcomers attempted to attune themselves to traditional cultural expectations, since gift-giving protocols were embedded in many traditional societies as a means of producing understood relations in the spheres of ceremonial, social, and economic life.[1] By enlisting gifts to enter into those networks of reciprocity and obligation, European explorers, entrepreneurs, and government representatives sought to pursue a range of colonial projects.[2] By the time Queen Victoria came to the throne in 1837, the British practice of distributing gifts to Aboriginal peoples as affirmation of the Crown's goodwill was well established. Most importantly, the beginning of her reign coincided with the rise of the 'humanitarian era' in British colonial policy, in which the achievement of British subjecthood through Christianisation and civilisation was seen as the greatest possible gift to extend to Aboriginal peoples.[3] In reality the humanitarian policy agenda was vexed and short-lived, and by the dawn of the twentieth century when Victoria died, it had long since become reshaped into locally administered programmes of governance that controlled almost all aspects of Aboriginal life. The long period of Victoria's reign, then, witnessed a complex set of transitions in the politics and policies of Aboriginal governance within Britain's empire, which in turn were met with different kinds of Aboriginal resistance and adaptation.[4]

This chapter compares some of the different contexts in nineteenth-century Canada and Australia in which Aboriginal people figured as recipients of the Queen's gifts, particularly on occasions that celebrated or reinforced her sovereignty over Britain's empire. In considering how these gifts were received and how they circulated, it seeks to explore some of the different meanings they generated and the potentially unsettled relationships they implied between Aboriginal people and the Crown. Attempting to understand the positions and motivations of Aboriginal peoples as historical actors is an inevitably problematic project, limited by the very nature of colonial records and complicated by the interpretative dispositions of later readers;[5] but notwithstanding these constraints, the historical records of both countries offer some comparative glimpse into how Aboriginal people regarded the symbolic status of Queen Victoria and made their own use of the gifts given in her name. Canada and Australia share many parallels as sites of British settlement where Aboriginal people were brought within the state's authority through similar legal, administrative, and 'moral' measures designed to transform them fully into their nominal status as the Crown's subjects, but what makes their comparison most interesting is that their histories of Aboriginal relationships to Queen Victoria had quite different points of origin and quite different trajectories.

The historical attachment of Canada's Aboriginal peoples to the British Crown, and to Queen Victoria in particular, has been well noted. Numerous scholars, most notably Wade Henry, J. R. Miller, Sarah Carter, and Ian Radforth, have examined how Aboriginal people's expressed loyalty to the Great Mother served to establish their own special relationship to the Crown, at the same time as it was exploited by local officials to further government agendas.[6] So enduring was this attachment to Queen Victoria that even decades after her death, when later royal visitors toured Canada, Aboriginal delegations came with pictures bearing her image.[7] The origins of this attachment lay in a long history of diplomatic exchanges between Aboriginal people and the British Crown dating back to the fur trade and the military alliances of the eighteenth and early nineteenth centuries, and that during Victoria's reign helped pave the way for the negotiation of treaties.[8] This history of formal diplomacy shaped a more tangible relationship between Aboriginal people and Queen Victoria than was ever apparent in Australia, where there was no history of alliance between the Crown and Aboriginal groups, and no formal acknowledgement of pre-existing Aboriginal sovereignty through treaty negotiations. Nonetheless, despite the absence of a parallel diplomatic history, Aboriginal peoples across Australia's colonies encountered Queen Victoria's representatives in many different kinds of exchange over the long course of her reign. As scholars have argued in relation to specific aspects of this history, such encounters demonstrated the scope as well as the limits of Australian Aboriginal people's capacity to negotiate with the Crown, or with its representatives at the level of the colonial state, in the face of an official culture that refused to recognise the existence of independent Aboriginal polities.[9]

In the histories of both countries, commemorative moments that called forth Aboriginal people's formal status as Queen Victoria's subjects are revealing not only of how they were positioned, or positioned themselves, in relation to the Crown, but also of how they engaged, ignored, or otherwise negotiated their relation to local government authorities. Gifts given to them on behalf of the Crown indicate something of the complexities and contradictions between expressions of imperial unity on the one hand and local cross-cultural struggles on the other, for while these gifts appeared to confirm Aboriginal people's assimilation as Her Majesty's subjects, as objects they also had parallel lives of their own, becoming invested with other meanings and uses that open a partial window onto Aboriginal cultural integrity and independence. In this sense, even as the Queen's gifts apparently fulfilled their role to signal her supreme place as the sovereign of a benevolent empire, they point towards the fractures in the colonial state's assumed jurisdiction over Aboriginal people.

The politics of intimacy and allegiance to the Crown

In Canada, one of the consistent ways in which Aboriginal people expressed a strong sense of their own traditions as cultural polities was through a politics of intimacy with Queen Victoria that drew on the history of their diplomatic relationship with the British Crown. Other historians have explored how Aboriginal bands frequently reminded Crown representatives of this shared bond by framing it in appellations of kinship.[10] In this sense, as Sarah Carter has put it, Aboriginal people's self-reference as the Great Mother's children can be seen not as a gesture of subservience but as a diplomatic device in which the familial relationship symbolised 'mutual respect and reciprocal duties of nurturing, caring, loyalty and fidelity'.[11]

The way in which intimacy with Queen Victoria endorsed rather than undermined Aboriginal people's own sense of cultural relevance and tradition was visible in how they regarded the gifts given on her behalf. While Crown representatives clearly regarded gifts as a necessary protocol for securing Aboriginal loyalty, Aboriginal people received them as a mark of respect due them as the Crown's diplomatic partners. Moreover, they absorbed these gifts into their own cultural traditions and identities. In 1896, Huron chiefs of the Lorette Indian Agency asked the Governor General to forward an address to Queen Victoria requesting that the recognition historically granted them in gifts from the English sovereign, now lapsed but dating from 1825 when King George IV received a delegation of their chiefs and bestowed bracelets and medals stamped with his image, would be continued. These bracelets and medals were worn by Huron chiefs on all their occasions of cultural significance, the petitioners argued; they were a vital part of maintaining 'our old customs' and were material symbols of their authority as chiefs. 'We rely upon you', they urged the Governor General, to 'persuade the Great Queen to give us these bracelets and medals which we shall be glad to wear at the great feasts of the nation'.[12]

The Governor General declined to pursue this request on grounds that the gifts, which he associated with rewards given for Aboriginal allegiance to the Crown in the years following the War of 1812, were not intended to be given 'in perpetuity'. Yet the chiefs persisted in their petition, arguing that the gifts were not given in recognition of loyalty in a time of war but in recognition of their political rank as chiefs within their own national body. For a second time, they argued that a failure to provide 'the bracelets and medals which the then chiefs had and which we the present chiefs have not would prove that our tradition has been abandoned and that our national custom will not be carried out'.[13] Their renewed petition fell on deaf ears, but their claim to the bracelets and medals as an important sign of 'preserv[ing] intact all our old customs' indicates that for them the Queen's gifts marked not just their historical relationship to the Crown, but also the Crown's recognition of their own social and political customs.

If the politics of intimacy with Queen Victoria had continuing valency for Aboriginal people in endorsing their recognisable status as polities, it had decreasing meaning for the Crown's representatives as the nineteenth century progressed. Canadian government authorities were aware of the significance Aboriginal people placed on the Crown's gifts as signs of respect, and when the protocols of diplomatic tradition demanded it, such as during royal or vice-regal tours, they made medals and other gifts ready for distribution to Aboriginal chiefs as commemorative 'souvenirs'. There can be little doubt, however, that beyond a role in securing Aboriginal people's continuing cooperation, they considered such gifts to be little more than a formal gesture to be kept at minimal expense.

When Queen Victoria's son-in-law and Canada's Governor General the Marquis of Lorne toured the North-West Territories in 1881, the Deputy Superintendent General of Indian Affairs Lawrence Vankoughnet considered what arrangements should be made for presents to Aboriginal chiefs. Since no funding had been provisioned for this purpose, he suggested that leftover presents from an earlier tour by Lorne's predecessor Lord Dufferin would suffice to fill the gap; these he suggested would prove 'quite sufficient to give the Chiefs' who came to represent their bands at any points on Lorne's itinerary. He advised the Governor General's secretary that Indian superintendents would be posted at strategic points along the route to present any chiefs to His Excellency, but also 'to prevent any imposture being practiced by Indians not Chiefs': thus 'there will be a considerable saving in the way of presents, if I am correct in the conclusion that His Excellency will not consider it necessary to do more than present the Chiefs or Headmen with some slight memento'.[14]

An earlier memo on arrangements for the police escort that would accompany Lorne's entourage had advised that 'Clothing & Blankets' would make suitable presents for general distribution during the tour, given the state of Aboriginal destitution affecting the prairies; all Aboriginal people of the North-West Territories would 'be looking to the Government for assistance', and the question was how to 'tide over' their state of near starvation without trouble flaring. Gifts from the government would have strategic value in offsetting the risk of unrest, and would be appreciated as a diplomatic gesture.[15] Since there was no dedicated provision set aside for the general distribution of presents it appears that this advice was not followed, although Lorne did carry medals and supplies to be given as rewards to those who showed 'the best disposition to carry out the treaties' and were prepared to

Figure 9.1 'Treaty medal presented to chiefs and councillors of treaties no. 1–7'. Although the distribution of commemorative medals had been an important diplomatic protocol at the signing of treaties, the Canadian government increasingly neglected such protocols as the years passed.

'persevere in getting a living out of the land' (see Figure 9.1).[16] Despite their parsimony, however, Canadian government officials at least remained aware of the diplomatic significance of gift-giving protocols, indicating some continuing acknowledgement of Aboriginal political sentiment. Two years after Lorne's 1881 tour of the North-West Territories, the government's insufficient attention to this sentiment emerged as an embarrassment when a newspaper reported on the 'disappointment of Indian chiefs at not having received the presents' they expected.[17] This was a matter of 'gross neglect', the superintendent general of Indian Affairs noted retrospectively, since '[t]o such things as these the Indians are peculiarly sensitive'.[18]

In Australia's colonies, of course, there was no formal history of diplomatic relationships to support even as compromised an acknowledgement of Aboriginal political feeling as this.[19] Nonetheless, the Canadian practice of presenting medals to chiefs to commemorate their ongoing relationship to the Crown or its representatives can be compared with the practice across Australia's colonies of presenting Aboriginal individuals with engraved breastplates as a means of acknowledging or inducing their loyalty to the colonial state. The first known of these 'badges of distinction' was given by Governor Lachlan Macquarie of New South Wales to the famed Aboriginal mediator Bungaree in 1815, and breastplates also were distributed at one of his earliest annual 'conferences' with local Aboriginal people as a sign of the government's goodwill.[20] In comparison to commemorative medals in Canada, which usually bore the engraved image of a member of the royal family, Australian breastplates were both more individually specific and more distinctively cross-cultural in design, often engraved in the European heraldic tradition of coat of arms, but depicting images of native flora and fauna.[21] As was the tradition in Canada, they were initially given to the men presumed to be Aboriginal leaders in the expectation that their good influence would support colonial endeavours more widely.

As an early gesture of diplomacy, Macquarie's distribution of breastplates to 'chiefs' indicated an implicit acknowledgement that Aboriginal groups comprised distinctive polities, but this acknowledgement waned over time as breastplates became widely given not only by government officials but also by settler entrepreneurs and employers as rewards for acts of fidelity, cooperation, or service. Kingplates comprised a particular class of breastplate: in modified continuity of Macquarie's intent to privilege the position of Aboriginal leaders as agents of influence, they bore the appellation of 'King' (or sometimes 'Queen') alongside the European nickname of the person who wore them. As the nineteenth century progressed, however, this designation became an increasing subject of mirth within a circulating settler sentiment that Aboriginal people survived only as the destitute remnants of an abject and now disappearing race.[22]

Yet breastplates denoted a more complex set of meanings than those assigned by colonists as symbols either of Aboriginal fidelity or of a people in decline. Like commemorative medals in Canada, they could be taken up by Aboriginal people as a symbol of political agency in a cross-cultural space. At the same time as the Huron chiefs of the Lorette Indian Agency were petitioning Canada's Governor General for the Queen's bracelets and medals, Mickey Johnson, an Aboriginal man from Lake Illawarra in New South Wales, suggested to the local member of Parliament that he should receive a kingplate, and arrangements were made to present him with one inscribed with the words 'Mickey Johnson, King'. The press made much comic play on the 'lofty dignity' and 'courtly air' of 'His royal highness' during the presentation, as well as of the homely fact that the local mayor's mother stood in for Queen Victoria by presenting it to him at the 1896 Wollongong Agricultural Show.[23] It also satirised the speech made by King Mickey following his 'coronation', in which he 'dropped into politics' by offering his endorsement to the local member of Parliament and pledging that if Queen Victoria should 'ever need his assistance it would be readily given her'.[24] No doubt, jested Sydney's *Evening News*, when Britain's foes learned of King Mickey's pledge they would abandon all thoughts of war 'as being entirely futile'.

Despite the press's derision, Mickey Johnson's speech can be seen as asserting an affiliation with Queen Victoria that brought his own place in the local scene of Illawarra into play with the very seat of empire. In a wider sense, he claimed and received a certain authority that crossed the political and cultural domains of Aboriginal and white worlds. As a well-known local figure, he was photographed extensively during his lifetime, wearing the kingplate with equal ease over a bare torso or a European suit. In 1899, he was instrumental in establishing a church for the new Lake Illawarra Aboriginal mission; and although apparently a sign of his acceptance of colonial projections, this public status gave him considerable access to the white community that enabled him to argue for his people's interests in the district over the coming years.[25] His influence as a local political figure took on a national scale after his death, his image featuring on a 1938 sesquicentenary commemorative stamp.

In all these respects, in Australia as in Canada, gifts from the Crown or its representatives might be taken by Aboriginal people as reinforcing their cultural and political status in ways that were quite different from colonial expectations of acquiescence to the colonial project.

In so far as Aboriginal people sought to be recipients of such gifts, as the Huron chiefs and Mickey Johnson did from opposite sides of the world in 1896, their wishes cannot simply be configured in terms of self-identification as the Queen's subjects; as Alan Lester and Fae Dussart have argued, they can be seen as acts of mobilisation in which Aboriginal people sought to achieve cultural and political recognition within a global field of empire.[26]

By the same token, Aboriginal people used their formal status as subjects of the Queen's Empire to petition for resources at the local level. That this was a practised pattern in Canada during vice-regal tours was evident in the memo on police escort arrangements for Lord Lorne's tour of the North-West Territories in 1881:

> the demands made by the Indians will be very great and His Excellency will be told that it is impossible for them to live on what Land and money is given them by Treaty. They will ask for more of both, as well as for more oxen, cows, and implements. His Excellency will have to listen to the same story that is told to every one who they think has the power to give them more, and they will on this memorable occasion make a great effort to obtain better terms. This is always the case with Indians.[27]

A similar pattern was evident in Australia when governors toured regional districts. When South Australia's Governor Dominic Daly visited the southern districts in 1864, Aboriginal people turned out to greet him, reportedly in demonstration of their 'loyalty' to the Queen and her representative, but the fact that they had other motivations in mind was made clear by their petition for better provisions on the grounds that settlement had destroyed their access to native game.[28] Their address to the Governor, some parts of the press noted, 'shows that the blacks understand the knack of getting up a memorial quite as well as the whites. They praise his Excellency, they compare themselves advantageously with the blacks who kill whitefellows in the North; they then state their grievances and end by asking not only for "tomahawks and shirts" but also for "tobacco and big one tuck-out"'.[29] As colonial officials were aware, then, Aboriginal people were adept in enlisting the rhetoric of loyalty to the Crown as a means of engaging its representatives at the level of local colonial policy.

Celebrating the Queen's birthday

Perhaps the occasion which most tellingly traced the complex intercultural politics of Aboriginal people's relationship to the Crown over the course of decades was the annual celebration of Queen Victoria's birthday on 24 May, an event that routinely included an allowance of 'presents' or provisions as a reminder of the Queen's solicitous care of her Aboriginal subjects. The nature of Aboriginal people's engagement with the Queen's birthday diverged in Canada and Australia, shaped by the historic differences in their affiliation to the Crown as well as by the different degrees to which their everyday lives were subjected to governmental oversight. Yet in both countries, the material provisions made to them on the Queen's birthday opened up the potential for an independent social and cultural existence that extended well beyond the intended message of the Queen's unifying sovereignty.

The role of Aboriginal people as participants in the 'Queen's Day' celebrations was more overt in Canada than was ever the case in Australia's colonies, a symptom not just of Canadian Aboriginal people's historic links to the British Crown but also of the political attention that treaties enabled them – even if with limited effect – to demand from local government authorities. Keith Thor Carlson and Robin Fisher have considered the political dimensions of Aboriginal attendance at Queen's birthday celebrations in New Westminster, British Columbia, during the 1860s.[30] When Frederick Seymour was appointed Governor in 1864, he invited local Aboriginal constituencies to a Queen's birthday assembly at Government House as an opportunity to show that he would be as solicitous of Aboriginal welfare as his predecessor James Douglas, and they accordingly responded positively with expectations that their land base achieved under Douglas' liberal regime would be protected.[31] Under Seymour's governorship, however, the land policy implemented by Douglas was steadily undermined by Chief Commissioner of Lands and Works Joseph Trutch, who worked to ensure that Aboriginal claims would not stand in the way of colonial settlement.[32] By the end of the 1860s, Carlson notes, the Queen's birthday celebrations at Government House had come for Aboriginal people 'to epitomise government indifference and dismissive paternalism'.[33] In 1875, with Trutch now Lieutenant Governor, Salish chiefs of the Fraser River declined to have any role in Queen's birthday celebrations, writing to the Indian commissioner that '[s]he has not been a good Mother and Queen to us. She has not watched over us that we should have enough land', nor 'compel[led] the British Columbia Government to extend our present reserves'.[34]

In British Columbia, then, the declining trajectory of governmental attention to Aboriginal land interests can be traced in Aboriginal people's declining participation in the Queen's birthday celebrations as an act of political diplomacy. By the end of the 1870s, as Aboriginal populations across the prairies became increasingly confined to reserves, references to Aboriginal participation were notably absent from press reports on the Queen's birthday celebrations that annually attracted large numbers of people into towns.[35] Nonetheless, some Aboriginal reserve populations continued to mark Queen Victoria's birthday each year. The Six Nations Agency's annual receipts for the Queen's birthday events over the 1870s and 1880s, reimbursed by the Department of Indian Affairs, describe a range of activities similar to those held by Anglo-Canadian town populations: additional supplies of food were ordered; bands were organised; races and games were planned. Indian Superintendent Jasper Gilkison reported each year on the fine weather and the success of the festivities, as well as on his efforts to maintain economy. Only once, in 1878, did he report that events were marred 'by several cases of drunkenness' due to whisky brought onto the reserve by outsiders; for this violation he fined the perpetrators fifty dollars and emptied the liquor onto the ground.[36] On the whole, however, he was pleased to report each year that the participants behaved in a manner that 'would have been creditable to any part of the Country'.[37] In 1887, the year of the Queen's Jubilee, he reported that the 'assemblage of Indians appeared larger than on any previous occasion; that the arrangements were well carried out in a manner to the enjoyment of all, and reflected credit upon their general good conduct'.[38]

For Department of Indian Affairs' officials, it seems, celebrating the Queen's Day on the reserve provided a reassuring opportunity for reinforcing Aboriginal attachment to the Crown and demonstrating the residents' advancement in desirable behaviour. It was also seen as a safe avenue of enjoyment through which the dangerous influences of the world outside could be avoided: as John McIver, the Indian Agent on the Cape Croker Agency wrote, 'the Indians ... should be encouraged to [celebrate the Queen's birthday here rather] than going out amongst the whites and be exposed to numerous temptations'.[39] But at the same time, reserve-based Queen's Day celebrations also gave Aboriginal people opportunities for community cohesion beyond the prying eyes of Indian Agents. As agents sometimes acknowledged outright, on reserves with sizable populations it was impossible to keep detailed track of people's movements and activities.[40] Although agents had managerial oversight, Aboriginal people held considerable autonomy in planning Queen's Day events, to which friends and relatives could be invited. The fact that they participated in Queen's Day festivities in large numbers indicates the potential of these occasions for reinforcing social and community ties. Indeed, just as the sovereign's gifts of bracelets and medals became regarded by the Hurons as part of their 'national custom', so too the Queen's birthday annual festivities were considered to be central to the Hurons' 'old customs' on the Lorette Indian Agency.[41]

In Australia's colonies, a government-administered reserve system was, with the exception of Victoria, much slower to evolve than in Canada, and there were no treaties to support the efforts of colonial officials to secure a programme of Aboriginal management. Instead, from early in Queen Victoria's reign, the distribution of 'presents' on the Queen's birthday formed part of administrative efforts to conciliate Aboriginal people to colonial authority and win them over to 'Christianity and civilisation'. In 1839, South Australia's new Governor, George Gawler, initiated a Queen's birthday 'dinner for the natives' in the grounds of Government House, anticipating the way that future colonial officials like British Columbia's Governor Seymour used the Queen's birthday as a diplomatic opportunity. Balanced with its message of the Crown's goodwill, Gawler's Queen's birthday dinner held an explicitly civilising intent. In its first year, this took material form in gifts distributed to each person who came: clothing and a blanket, and a pewter plate engraved with Queen Victoria's image and the letters of the English alphabet.[42]

The Queen's birthday 'dinner for the natives' continued through the 1840s, but as time passed and dispossession drove Aboriginal people further into deprivation, it transformed from an occasion for cross-cultural diplomacy to one when Aboriginal people merely received a 'dole of provisions'.[43] By 1849, the Queen's birthday dinner had become a distribution of rations consisting of a piece of beef, a two-pound loaf, and a blanket, and the Governor did not even attend as the Crown's representative, as he had in former years.[44] By the early 1850s, this annual 'dole' was further reduced, the meat substituted for 'an extra allowance of bread'.[45] The earlier presents presented to Aboriginal people as a sign of the Crown's goodwill had become replaced with the distribution of rations as a sign of the Crown's 'charity'.

The enduring form of this perceived charity was the annual distribution of blankets to Aboriginal people that took place across Australia's colonies on the Queen's birthday.[46] Each year the colonial press reported on the blanket distributions alongside descriptions of the Queen's birthday balls, the picnics, and the Governor's levees from which Aboriginal people were excluded. Amongst some commentators, the annual blanket distribution produced expressions of contempt for the recipients themselves as 'decrepit', 'grotesque', 'mendicant', or even 'defiant'.[47] Amongst others, it was cause for criticism of the government's parsimonious response to widespread Aboriginal deprivation. Settlers sometimes wrote letters to the press pointing out that Aboriginal people were entitled to better recompense for having been 'despoiled of their lands'.[48] But although such commentary acknowledged partial responsibility for the forcible appropriation of Aboriginal land and resources, it was usually assuaged by appeal to a colonial humanitarian rhetoric in which compensation in the form of a blanket was proof of Christian sympathy. By the late nineteenth century, the Queen's blanket had come to hold a fixed meaning within settler culture as a charitable concession to a destitute people fast approaching a state of extinction 'beyond hope of redemption' (see Figure 9.2).[49]

But if the blanket distributions triggered debate about the future of Aboriginal people within the colonial state, they also triggered the question of Aboriginal people's nominal status as subjects of the Queen, in whose name the blankets were annually bestowed. In 1874, *The Moreton Bay Courier* argued that although the connection between 'her Majesty's blankets, blacks, and birthday' was not initially obvious, it became so 'when it is remembered that the gift of a blanket to a black on Her birthday is likely to … impress the recipient, black though he be, with an exalted idea of that lady's power and excellence'.[50] Indeed in some regions, the blanket distribution would close with 'three cheers for the Queen' as an explicit reminder of her connection.[51] Other commentators were more dismissively pragmatic: there was 'no particular reason' why the Queen's birthday should be 'a red-letter day' amongst Aboriginal people, observed a writer in *The Queenslander*. 'At any rate, the loyalty evoked by the

Figure 9.2 'The Queen's Birthday at Brisbane: distribution of blankets to the aboriginals [sic], 1873'.

present once a year of a half-crown blanket on the 24th of May can scarcely be of a very fervent type'.[52] In fact, as distributions of rations spread out to take place at distant depots, the press noted declining numbers of Aboriginal people coming into town to receive the traditional Queen's birthday blanket, rendering its intended message of her benevolent sovereignty even more marginal.[53]

But what meanings and uses might the Queen's blanket have held for Aboriginal recipients? To the chagrin of local authorities, it was clear that blankets circulated amongst Aboriginal people in ways that defied their given intention either as an earlier sign of the Crown's conciliating goodwill or as a later sign of its charity. For a start, blankets held use for Aboriginal people as a form of currency that could be exchanged for coin, rations, or other goods. In 1896, one correspondent to the press noted that the government-issue blankets meant only for Aboriginal use could be found for sale in every store and were used in every public house.[54] Their circulation as objects of trade raised regular concerns that, even before the sun had set on the Queen's birthday, the blankets could be bartered away for liquor.[55] Authorities were also concerned that Aboriginal people's tendency to redistribute the blankets amongst themselves as a shared resource undermined attempts to instil 'civilised' habits and the value of individual possessions. In 1856, New South Wales' Legislative Assembly debated whether 'the money expended in supplying blankets was entirely thrown away, because in many cases they were torn up and divided among the wilder blacks ... while in other cases they were bartered away almost immediately after they were received'.[56] The suggestion was that rather than giving blankets 'in the way of gratuity', they should only be given as reward 'for industrial occupations'.[57]

In reality, blankets were distributed in myriad other contexts than as the Queen's birthday annual 'present', given as payment by settlers and colonial officials as rewards for Aboriginal assistance.[58] That this was so over the course of decades reinforced the reality that they had value and uses for Aboriginal people that had little to do with the idea of the Crown's compassion. They formed a hard currency in Aboriginal people's economic exchanges, and as an internally shared resource they became part of the material repertoire of Aboriginal society.[59] In this sense, Michael Smithson has argued, blankets held an important place within the context of the traditional exchange relationships that regulated and supported Aboriginal cultural identity.[60]

Afterlife of the Queen's gifts

The different trajectories of Aboriginal people's relationship to the Crown in Canada and Australia were visibly manifest at the time of

Queen Victoria's death in January 1901. In Canada, the significance of Aboriginal people's intimate connection to the Great Mother was expressed in the addresses of condolence many bands scripted to their 'brother' and new monarch, King Edward VII. The address of the Chippewas of the Ojibway nation exemplified the idea that Aboriginal people held a privileged relationship to Queen Victoria, stating that while sorrow at 'the death of Our Beloved Mother' was 'shared by all loyal subjects throughout the Empire, we being the subjects of Her more peculiar care, feel the bereavement more keenly'.[61] The Six Nations address carried this special relationship forward to her son through the framework of a bereavement ritual in which the grieving Edward would be nurtured by his brother chiefs and 'allies'. In an inversion of the familiar representations of Queen Victoria herself as the source of loving care for the Empire's peoples, the Six Nations chiefs assured the new King of their own solicitousness. When his tears caused blindness, they wrote, 'your brother Chiefs' will 'wipe off the tears ... so that you may clearly see'; when his head was bowed with sorrow, 'your brother Chiefs' will 'support your head and ... raise you up'. The chiefs closed with a scene of cultural affirmation and equivalence in which they imaginatively accompanied the new British sovereign 'to the grave of Her late majesty our Mother the Queen' where they 'decorate[d] the grave with wreaths, made of sweet grasses and forest flowers'.[62]

Such feeling can hardly be more different from the general dearth of reported Aboriginal responses to the Queen's death in Australia. Certainly, there seemed little incentive for Aboriginal people to associate this event with anything other than the potential disappearance of the blankets, as was noted by one Queensland correspondent to the press. When his Aboriginal employee learned that Queen Victoria had just died, he wrote, the 'elderly blackfellow ... asked me about the blankets which it was usual for the Government to supply', and stated that with the game scarce on the land his people would experience 'great difficulty' if the blanket distributions ended. The correspondent's glib response was an assurance 'that although Kings and Queens might come and go, the annual distribution of blankets to his people would go on for ever'.[63]

Yet while it was evident that Aboriginal people in Canada nurtured their relationship to the Queen more than was the case in Australia, where there was no history of allegiance to lend that relationship political substance, this distinction would be too simple in describing Aboriginal people's more complex relationships to the Crown in both countries, and of their shared scope to elude expectations of acquiescence to British sovereignty. The presentation of gifts or provisions to Aboriginal people by Queen Victoria's representatives carried a set of messages designed to demonstrate their place as Her Majesty's subjects within an overarching framework of benevolent colonial governance that was perceived to define her reign. Over time, the intended meaning of these gifts varied, shaped by the different needs of colonial authorities to civilise, placate, or otherwise incur the cooperation of Aboriginal peoples. In this sense, these material objects or goods often said more about the vexed relationship between Aboriginal people and the local colonial state than they did about Queen Victoria's authority as sovereign of an empire. But above all, the meaning and value of the objects given to Aboriginal people in the name of the Queen always appeared to overreach those they were intended to impart. They were enlisted by Aboriginal people to emphasise their own cultural and political status in a cross-cultural sphere, and they circulated internally within Aboriginal society in ways that expressed continuing social and community cohesion. While for Crown representatives the presents distributed on Queen Victoria's behalf may have articulated the British settler state's jurisdiction over Aboriginal people, the ways in which they were received and used suggest that the Queen's sovereignty over her Aboriginal subjects, and thereby the sovereignty of the settler state, was always incomplete.

Acknowledgement

This chapter was supported by an Australian Research Council Discovery Project grant, DP1095363 'The rule of law in history and memory: Australian and Canadian settler frontiers'.

Notes

1 Anthony Redmond and Fiona Skyring, 'Exchange and Appropriation: the Wurnan Economy and Aboriginal Land and Labour at Karunjie Station, north-western Australia', in Ian Keen (ed.), *Indigenous Participation in Australian Economies* (Canberra: ANU E Press, 2010), pp. 73–90.
2 For instance, Lorraine Aragon, 'Twisting the gift: Translating precolonial into colonial exchanges in central Sulawesi, Indonesia', *American Anthropologist*, 23:1 (1995), 443–60; Patricia Seed, *Ceremonies of Possession in Europe's Conquest of the New World, 1492–1640* (Cambridge: Cambridge University Press, 1995); Herbert Applebaum, *Colonial Americans at Work* (London: University Press of America, 1996); Nicholas Thomas, *Entangled Objects: Exchange, Material Culture, and Colonialism in the Pacific* (Cambridge, MA: Harvard University Press, 1991); Arthur Ray, Jim Miller, and Frank Tough, *Bounty and Benevolence: A History of Saskatchewan Treaties* (Montreal: McGill-Queen's University Press, 2000).
3 British Parliamentary House of Commons, Report from the Select Committee on Aborigines (British Settlements), 7 (1837), no. 425.
4 Alan Lester and Fae Dussart, *Colonisation and the Origins of Humanitarian Governance: Protecting Aborigines across the Nineteenth-Century British Empire* (Cambridge: Cambridge University Press, 2014).

5   Maria Nugent, '"The Queen gave us the land": Aboriginal people, Queen Victoria and historical remembrance', *History Australia*, 9:2 (2012), 192.
6   Wade Henry, 'Imagining the Great White Mother and the Great King: Aboriginal tradition and royal representation at the "Great Pow-wow" of 1901', *Journal of the Canadian Historical Association*, 11:1 (2000), 87–108; Sarah Carter, '"Your Great Mother across the salt sea": Prairie First Nations, the British Monarchy and the vice regal connection to 1900', *Manitoba History* 48 (Autumn/Winter 2004–2005), 34–48; Ian Radforth, 'Performance, politics, and representation: Aboriginal people and the 1860 royal tour of Canada', *The Canadian Historical Review*, 84 (2003), 1–32; J. R. Miller, 'Victoria's "Red Children": The "Great White Queen Mother" and native-newcomer relations in Canada', *Native Studies Review*, 17:1 (2008), 1–23.
7   Library and Archives Canada (LAC), PA-131185, 'Their Majesties greet chieftains of the Stoney Indian Tribe, who have brought a photo of Queen Victoria', 26 May 1939.
8   For instance J. R. Miller, '"I will accept the Queen's hand": First Nations leaders and the image of the Crown in the Prairie Treaties', in *Reflections on Native–Newcomer Relations: Selected Essays* (Toronto: University of Toronto Press, 2004), pp. 217–41.
9   For instance, Michael Parsons, 'The Tourist Corroboree in South Australia to 1911', *Aboriginal History*, 21 (1997), 46–69; Jane Lydon, 'The experimental 1860s: Charles Walter's images of Coranderrk Aboriginal Station, Victoria', *Aboriginal History*, 26 (2002), 78–130; Maria Nugent, *Captain Cook Was Here* (Cambridge: Cambridge University Press, 2009); Jessie Mitchell, '"It will enlarge the ideas of the natives": Indigenous Australians and the tour of Prince Alfred, Duke of Edinburgh', *Aboriginal History*, 34 (2010), 198; Ann Curthoys and Jessie Mitchell, '"Bring this paper to the Good Governor": Indigenous petitioning in Britain's Australian colonies', in Saliha Belmessous (ed.), *Native Claims: Indigenous Law Against Empire, 1500–1920* (New York: Oxford University Press, 2011), pp. 182–203; Maryrose Casey, 'Colonisation, notions of authenticity and Aboriginal Australian performance', *Critical Race and Whiteness Studies*, 8 (2012), 1–18.
10 For instance, Radforth, 'Performance, politics, and representation'; Miller, 'Victoria's "Red Children"'.
11 Carter, 'Your Great Mother across the salt sea'.
12 LAC, RG 10, vol. 2841, file 172,535, Huron chiefs to Governor General, 26 March 1896.
13 *Ibid.*, Huron chiefs to Governor General, July 1896.
14 LAC, RG 7, G23, vol. 2, Deputy Superintendent General of Indian Affairs to Governor General's Secretary, 15 July 1881.
15 *Ibid.*, 'Route Transport Escort' Memorandum 24 March 1881 (no author identified).
16 LAC, G 10, vol. 3768, file 33642, 'His Excellency's Councils with Indians of the North West', forwarded Minister of the Interior, 4 November 1881.
17 *The British Columbian* (21 November 1883).
18 LAC, RG 10, vol. 3666, file 10147, Superintendent of Indian Affairs to Deputy Superintendent of Indian Affairs, 8 December 1883.
19 Mark McKenna observes that until the late twentieth century each royal visit to Australia marked 'a forgetting of the Aboriginal occupation of the continent, in which Aboriginal people were reduced to decorative adornment or viewed as curiosities destined for the museum'. Mark McKenna, 'Monarchy: From reverence to indifference', in Deryck Schreuder and Stuart Ward (eds), *Australia's Empire* (Oxford: Oxford University Press, 2008), pp. 266–7.
20 Keith Vincent Smith, *King Bungaree: A Sydney Aborigine Meets the Great South Pacific Explorers, 1799–1830* (Kenthurst NSW: Kangaroo Press, 1992); *Sydney Gazette* (4 January 1817).
21 David Kaus, 'Aboriginal Breastplates', National Museum of Australia, www.nma.gov.au/exhibitions/captivating_and_curious/the_stories_behind_the_objects/aboriginal_breastplates, accessed 28 January 2016.
22 For instance, 'King Billy of Buninyong: A Biography', *South Bourke and Mornington Journal* (24 August 1887).
23 *The Evening News* (4 February 1896), p. 3.

24 *Ibid.*
25 Michael Organ, *Illawarra and South Coast Aborigines 1770–1900* (Academic Services Division Papers, University of Wollongong, 1993).
26 Lester and Dussart, *Colonisation and the Origins of Humanitarian Governance*, pp. 116–7.
27 LAC, RG 7, G23, vol. 2, 'Route Transport Escort', Memorandum 24 March 1881 (no author identified).
28 *The Maitland Mercury and Hunter River General Advertiser* (16 January 1864).
29 *The Sydney Morning Herald* (6 January 1864), p. 5; *Brisbane Courier* (12 January 1864), p. 2.
30 Keith Thor Carlson, *The Power of Place, the Problem of Time: Aboriginal Identity and Historical Consciousness in the Cauldron of Colonialism* (Toronto: University of Toronto Press, 2010), pp. 211–31; Robin Fisher, *Contact and Conflict: Indian–European Relations in British Columbia, 1774–1890* (Vancouver: UBC Press, 1992), pp. 158–9.
31 Fisher, *Contact and Conflict*, pp. 146–58.
32 *Ibid.*, pp. 162–3.
33 Carlson, *The Power of Place*, p. 212.
34 Cited in Miller, 'Victoria's "Red Children"', p. 13.
35 *The Brandon Mail* (28 May 1891); also for instance *The Prince Albert Times* (30 May 1884); *The Edmonton Bulletin* (26 May 1892). An exception was the year following the North-West Rebellion, when Lieutenant Governor Edgar Dewdney spoke at a Queen's birthday parade in Qu'Appelle to assure onlookers that the government's effort to 'check' Aboriginal disloyalty at that time had 'aided very materially in suppressing the rebellion' (*Qu'Appelle Progress*, 28 May 1886).
36 LAC, RG 10, vol. 2060, file 9851, J. T. Gilkison to Superintendent General of Indian Affairs, 1 June 1878.
37 LAC, RG 10, vol. 222, file 43,496, J. T. Gilkison to Superintendent General of Indian Affairs, 26 May 1886.
38 *Ibid.*, J. T. Gilkison to Superintendent General of Indian Affairs, 27 May 1887.
39 LAC, RG 10, vol. 2973, file 209,525, Indian Agent John McIver to Deputy Superintendent General of Indian Affairs, 5 May 1899.
40 LAC, RG 18, vol. 1139, file 173/1889, Agent Pocklington to Indian Commissioner, 11 December 1889; LAC, RG 18, vol 1077, file 321/1887, Agent Begg to police reported by Inspector Superintendent W.M. Herchmer, 9 June 1887.
41 LAC, RG 10, vol. 2807, file 162,869, Indian Agent Antoine Bastien to Deputy Superintendent General of Indian Affairs, 8 June 1895.
42 *The SA Register* (25 May 1839).
43 *The SA Register* (26 May 1849), p. 2.
44 *Ibid.*
45 *The SA Register* (26 May 1851), p. 2.
46 Michael Smithson notes that although ultimately framed as charity, blanket distributions originated in early administrative efforts to quell frontier violence. Michael Smithson, 'A misunderstood gift: The annual issue of blankets to Aborigines in New South Wales, 1826–48', *Push*, 30 (1991), 75.
47 For instance, *The Clarence and Richmond Examiner* (27 August 1876), p. 2.
48 *Border Watch* (22 January 1870); *The Inquirer and Commercial News* (5 August 1863).
49 *Kalgoorlie Miner* (22 July 1896).
50 *The Moreton Bay Courier* (2 June 1860), pp. 4–5.
51 *The Western Star and Roma Advertiser* (16 May 1896), p. 2.
52 *The Queenslander* (13 June 1874), p. 4.
53 For instance, *The Brisbane Courier* (25 May 1865), p. 2.
54 *The Clarence and Richmond Examiner* (9 June 1896), p. 3.
55 *Bathurst Free Press and Mining Journal* (11 August 1890), p. 2.
56 *Empire* (11 December 1856), pp. 2–3.
57 *Ibid.* This argument framed debates about the distributions of rations more widely in both Australia and Canada. See Amanda Nettelbeck and Robert Foster, 'Food

and governance in colonial Australia and western Canada', *Aboriginal History*, 36 (2012), 29–34.
58 For instance, Quarterly report of the Protector of Aborigines, *The SA Register* (6 November 1854).
59 Christopher Anderson, 'Aboriginal economy and contact relations at Bloomfield River, north Queensland', *Newsletter of the Australian Institute of Aboriginal Studies*, 12 (1979), 34; William Simeone, *Rifles, Blankets, and Beads: Identity, History, and the Northern Athapaskan Potlatch* (Norman: University of Oklahoma Press, 1995), pp. 21–4; John Lutz, 'After the fur trade: The Aboriginal labouring class of British Columbia 1849–1890', *Journal of the Canadian Historical Association*, 3:1 (1992), 69–93.
60 Smithson, 'A misunderstood gift', p. 87.
61 LAC, RG 10, vol. 3027, file 230,470, Resolution of the Special Council Meeting, Chippewa Hill, 26 January 1901.
62 *Ibid.*, Address of Condolence from the Six Nations, 5 March 1901.
63 *The Western Star and Roma Advertiser* (26 January 1901), p. 3.

CHAPTER 10

Chiefly women: Queen Victoria, Meri Mangakahia, and the Māori parliament

Miranda Johnson

In this chapter, I examine two sets of intersecting tensions that emerged in the context of political debate in a Māori parliament known as 'Kotahitanga' or the unity movement. The parliament was established in 1892 and lasted until 1902 and included members and representatives mainly from northern and eastern tribes of New Zealand's North Island. It sought constitutional recognition of its autonomy and the right to represent Māori interests in its own institutional setting, outside of the context of the majority settler parliament. Many members of Kotahitanga expressed abiding loyalty to Queen Victoria as they laid out their demands for autonomy. The parliament is an example of what Andrew Thompson has called the 'broad church' of imperial faith. As Thompson writes, the diversity of imperial faiths, however, often coexisted 'uncomfortably', and in this chapter I consider how the expressions of autonomy and loyalty in the Kotahitanga parliaments existed in significant and productive tension with one another, in the broader context of empire.[1]

In Kotahitanga sittings, another set of tensions between equality and status emerged when some Māori women leaders, represented by Meri Te Tai Mangakahia (see the portrait of her in Figure 10.1), demanded voting and representational rights alongside the men. Such demands echoed those of white settler women in New Zealand at the time who were pushing for their enfranchisement – which occurred nationally (and included Māori women) in 1893 as a new form of liberalism began to be established in the country. However, the argument of Mangakahia for enfranchisement was distinct from arguments propounded by white feminists because she highlighted the roles of high-ranking women in Māori society as customary property-owners, with the entitlements and responsibilities that such tenure implied. It was this customary and hierarchical status and achievement that made *some* women eligible to vote, she implied. Additionally, she suggested that women representatives of Kotahitanga would make a stronger case to Queen Victoria for Māori autonomy, since women leaders in the two customary systems – Māori and British – were more likely to understand each other.

In this story, the two sets of tensions I have identified between loyalty and autonomy, equality and status, are expressed *in relation to* the figure of Queen Victoria. I argue that by centring the figure of Queen Victoria in their various demands, the Māori protagonists of this story laid claim to their own space *beside* the settler state, and *in* the British Empire. This is a story that fits neatly into neither progressive accounts of democratisation in which the enfranchisement of women is a signal event, nor into critical histories of the colonial state in which Indigenous resistance leads to the overthrow of colonial power, or fails to do so. In this chapter, I want to open a space in the historical literature for the consideration of Indigenous agency and thought in terms that do not foreclose the strategies for achieving their political goals that Indigenous peoples have pursued in the face of an encroaching settler state. This chapter – part of a larger project about the intersections between tribalism, liberalism, and gender in empire – is written to that end.

Such forms of agency are undoubtedly complex, and may even seem paradoxical – put bluntly, what agency do the oppressed really have? The problem of their political agency was one that members of Kotahitanga debated among themselves. How could loyal Māori subjects of the Queen request from her the right to be self-sovereign? 'Who will sign for the Maoris when the authority of the Queen has ceased?', asked one member.[2] One of the answers to this question, as we shall see, was that Māori should be self-authorising, yet such an answer was not entirely satisfactory. In order to become self-authorising, as leaders recognised, they needed to be granted the *right* to their own constitutional authority, a grant that had to be made by an authority outside of themselves. Their 'self' needed an authorising 'other' in order to come into being. Did this mean that Māori were always bound to be servants of imperial rule or, worse, wards of the settler state? In this chapter, I argue that Māori made sense of their place within empire, and the possibilities for self-government alongside the settler state, in genealogical terms that respected the importance of ancestral hierarchies for the purpose of maintaining social order. For Māori leaders, including Meri Mangakahia, politics was an interrelated system of reciprocal exchange in which status must be closely and carefully observed. The agency that Māori leaders invoked and enacted was a deeply relational one, and one that observed interdependencies in the achievement of *balance* rather than *equality*.

Respect for ancestral hierarchies did not foreclose the possibility of novelty and the creation of new political forms. An idea that ancestral hierarchies in particular could bring something new into being made sense to many Māori leaders. In a central creation story, it is the children who push the earth-mother and sky-father apart in order to let light into the world. In so doing, however, they do not supplant their parents. And as we shall see, Māori leaders in Kotahitanga who followed the Bible put their faith in an active and protective God who had 'led them safely across the seas'. In these cosmologies, the notion of 'separatism' was quite foreign yet the possibilities of creation and newness – of a world of light; and of emigration – were key narrative events.

Considering Queen Victoria's own ambiguous and ambivalent power and status as titular monarch, self-appointed empress, and constitutional anachronism, her figuration by Māori members of Kotahitanga as *their* Queen is perhaps not to be unexpected. Moreover, it is not only thinking about the Indigenous colonised that raises profound and paradoxical questions of political agency. Margaret Homans has suggested that Victoria's agency was a passive one: for her, 'being is a form of doing'. Victoria held less political power than any monarch before her; nonetheless she presided over the greatest empire Britain had yet controlled. She 'signed' the laws that then came into being; and yet she was 'compelled' to do so. The Queen, explains Homans, 'is always performing her containment, her subjection to the law she commands, for the public gaze'.[3]

Loyalty and separatism in Kotahitanga

The Kotahitanga parliaments, or Pāremata Māori,[4] that met formally for a decade between 1892 and 1902, emerged out of discussions in the 1880s about how tribes in New Zealand might secure the benefits promised them in the Treaty of Waitangi. Leaders in the north, east, and Whanganui district in the south-west of the North Island in particular believed that they needed to form some kind of confederation in order to regain control of their remaining territories and to slow land sales. Their idea of a confederation was a strong one, as the name 'kotahitanga' suggested: it would entail the *unification* of tribes in pursuit of their autonomy. The idea of a confederation was not a new one, and drew on historical precedents including the northern confederation of chiefs who had issued a Declaration of Independence in 1835, prior to the signing of the treaty. Descendants of those chiefs were involved in the establishment of Kotahitanga in the 1890s, with an even greater goal in mind: the unification of *all* the tribes across New Zealand.

The core support for the parliament, however, came from those tribes often called 'kupapa'. The term literally means neutrality in war although it was often mistranslated by Pākeha as 'loyalist' or even used to designate so-called 'friendly tribes' who fought alongside colonial and imperial troops in the wars of the 1860s.[5] Kupapa tribes were also – perhaps more accurately – called 'Queenites', referring to those who supported Queen Victoria rather than the Māori king, whose own tribal supporters formed the main opposition to the colonial state in the wars. Despite the loss of land and life that supporters of the Māori king – 'Kingites' – suffered during and after the wars, the movement still roused considerable political support. Around 1890, the Kingites formed their own parliament, called Kauhanganui or the large convention. Whereas support for the Kotahitanga parliament had petered out by the early twentieth century, the King Movement's Kauhanganui operates today. Some historians have argued that the failure of Kotahitanga leaders to forge a coalition with Kauhanganui is what spelled its demise.[6]

At its height in the mid-1890s, over a thousand people attended the Kotahitanga sittings and the leaders of the movement claimed over 20,000 signatories to a declaration of allegiance.[7] Discussions in the parliament covered a range of issues including electoral representation, the payment of dues to the organisation, and the buying back of land for tribal purposes. Perhaps most notably in early parliamentary sessions, leaders sought the establishment of some kind of 'home rule' for Māori, as Keith Sinclair put it.[8] Sinclair was referring to the bill that the Member of the House of Representatives (MHR) for Northern Māori, Hone Heke Ngapua – descendant of the famous northern chief Hone Heke, and participant in Kotahitanga – brought before the New Zealand parliament in 1894. The 'Native Rights Bill' sought the grant of a constitution from the New Zealand parliament that would enable a Māori parliament to enact laws dealing with the 'personal rights and with the lands and all other property of the aboriginal native inhabitants of New Zealand'.[9]

The bill was, unsurprisingly, defeated in parliament, following a debate that reaffirmed the story of amalgamation that underwrote much 'Native policy' at the time.[10] While some Pākeha members were sympathetic to the injustices suffered by Māori people, no one supported the idea of a separate constitution for Māori. Many regarded the idea as absurd. 'It would be an act of folly to pass the second reading of this Bill, because if they did so it would go forth to the world that these Natives wanted a Constitution of their own as they were not treated in a fair and just manner', opined the member for New Plymouth, E. M. Smith.[11] Others argued that Māori were simply not ready for self-rule. Sir Robert Stout spoke favourably of Heke's presentation, and he thought 'the Maoris should be met, however, he did not think they could compete with Europeans in the race of life.' They had not had the same 'race education that our race had. It had taken us thousands of years to develop our civilisation, and it was perfectly impossible for the Maoris to compete with us on equal terms'. Stout argued for a continuation of special representation for Māori, that is, until they were properly amalgamated into European civilisation.[12]

The Kotahitanga parliament's demand for autonomy, which would enable them to make internal territorial decisions and exercise tribal jurisdiction, countered the idea of amalgamation espoused by these politicians. But the bill they proposed did not advocate a violent secession from the colonial state. This was no doubt due in part to the fact that those who attended Kotahitanga meetings could provide neither the economic nor human resources necessary to mount a military campaign against the state. Despite the assistance the kupapa tribes had given the colonial troops in the 1860s and 1870s, by the 1890s they found themselves in a situation not so different from those who had fought against the colonists: they were, as scholar J. A. Williams pointed out, 'victims not of the Pakehas' war but of the Pakehas' peace'.[13] Some kupapa tribes suffered land loss under the confiscation legislation that was passed during the wars – particularly if their lands were in fertile areas – or were threatened with confiscation. Kupapa tribes, like others, were losing even more land through the native land court process in which individuals or small groups of Māori could secure title deeds and then sell lands to whomever they wanted, without securing the consent of the tribe as a whole to alienation.[14]

Kotahitanga leaders pursued political and diplomatic rather than militaristic solutions to the problems that tribes faced. Indeed, leaders asserted their commitment to principles of peace and to ideals of civil discourse in order to achieve their goals. One of the stated principles in an early meeting was that 'kia kaua e tupu ake he raruraru i waenganui onga iwi o Niu Tireni' ('no trouble should arise among the peoples of New Zealand').[15] Many debates in the parliamentary meetings lasted for several days. According to some members, in fact, the talk went on far too long. 'E pouri ana ahau ki enei korero he moumou taima noaiho e whakaporourarutia ana tatou', chastised N. Haari in an 1893 sitting. ('I am disappointed with this discussion, it's just a waste of time and we are all becoming distracted'.)[16]

The commitment to peaceful political discourse was framed by members' frequently expressed loyalty to the Queen and their charge, as the descendants of those who had forged a covenant with her in the Treaty of Waitangi and other political agreements, to see those promises fulfilled. 'Ko tatou kia kotahi i raro ite Tiriti o Waitangi, me te 71 tona ritenga he pononga nate Kuini', pointed out one member of the 1893 parliamentary sitting. ('We are all one under the Treaty of Waitangi and Section 71, which means that we are servants of the Queen'.)[17] By referring to 'Section 71', the speaker meant the section of the 1852 Constitution Act that permitted local rights of self-government to Māori tribes and that had been given the royal assent. Many Māori interpreted section 71 as a further assurance of what they had been promised in the Treaty of Waitangi: that their lands and possessions would remain their own.

This member's interpretation of the treaty is even more interesting. Did this speaker mean that Māori and Pākeha would become 'all one' – an idea that would become ubiquitous at celebrations of the signing of the treaty in the twentieth century? Or, rather, did he mean that all the tribes were made one – that is, that by agreeing to the treaty's terms, different tribes had become one race or nation of 'Māori', as 'servants' of the Queen and tied together in a genealogical or extended kinship network?

It was as British subjects, loyal to *their* Queen, that many members of Kotahitanga demanded the right to self-government, just as settler subjects had claimed such a right to self-government in previous decades. Indeed, some members clearly imagined that should the tribes be granted what they were owed, as obedient subjects, they would receive a proper hearing and protection from Queen Victoria. As E. Wano explained at Te Kotahitanga in 1893,

> E marama aua tona korero e korero nei ite mea kei raro tatou ite ma a ote Kuini. I kiia ite tuatahi ko te weti iti te hoatu ite tuatahi mo muri te mea rahi, kua inoi ta ou i runga ite mea kua kite tatou e mate ana tatou ite mahi Ture ate kawanatanga. He tika kia ahu ano tatou kite kawana, ka kore katahi ka kau, kia ahei ai kite ki atu kite kuini, e tautoko ana ahau kia uru tona kupu ki roto ite Pire e Heke.
>
> (We come under the authority of the Queen. It is said that the small wedge should be put in first and afterwards the large one. We have asked these things because we have seen that we suffer because of the laws the Government creates. It is right that we should approach the Governor. If nothing comes of that then we cross the ocean in order to tell the queen that he would not sign for us.)[18]

Others argued for a separation – the Māori word is 'motuhake', a word that conveys an idea of severance and the cut that achieves it quite strongly – although to some at the meetings the idea was a new one. Nonetheless, Paraone, from the Whanganui district, argued, 'E tautoko ana aha i ma tatou aka e haina a tatou korero', or that it should be Māori themselves who should sign their proposals.[19] Hamiora Mangakahia, husband of Meri

Te Tai Mangakahia and the premier of Kotahitanga, cautioned against striving for separate authority, which would be tantamount to trampling on the Queen.[20] More complexly, H. K. Taiaroa, a Ngai Tahu leader from the South Island and elected member of the House of Representatives, as well as a former member of the selective Legislative Council, wondered how a unified Māori parliament could become self-authorising when their very political identity had been constituted through their expressed loyalty to the Queen, in the Treaty of Waitangi:

> E tono ana tatou i tenei mana kia wai, Kuini, ko waitt e mangai ote Kuini i naianei, kawana, kote Pire a Heke kaore e tu, heoi ano te mea mana e patu kote Patai nei, ma wai e haina nga maori, kua mutu te mana ote Kuini.
>
> (We request this authority from whom? – the Queen. Who is now the mouthpiece for the Queen? – the Governor. Heke's Bill will not stand. And the thing which they will strike out will be this question – Who will sign for the Maoris when the authority of the Queen has ceased?)[21]

Taiaroa raised a profound question of constitutionalism: who indeed authorises the 'people' in the moment of their sovereign creation? The people do not exist as such until they are brought into being, or constituted, as a people; and in order for this to happen they must be authorised by some outside force.[22] For Taiaroa and many other leaders, as we have seen, the authorising force was both the Queen and the Māori chiefs who had covenanted together in the making of the Treaty of Waitangi. Taiaroa himself was obliged by his own father – the Ngai Tahu chief Te Matenga Taiaora – to ensure 'that the promises made by Wakefield, Kemp and Mantell were fulfilled' for the southern tribe of Ngai Tahu, that is, in regard to lands and food gathering rights. Taiaroa pursued the tribal claim of Ngai Tahu until his own death in 1905.[23]

Like the obedient political subject in Thomas Hobbes' theory of the social contract, Kotahitanga members recognised that they could not simply cast off their obligations to the sovereign power, to whom they had given the right of representation of some of their interests. At the same time, the idea of covenant or treaty was so important to Māori because it framed their demands in terms of nation-to-nation negotiations. In other words, the idea of a covenant allowed Māori to retain a sense of being part of a larger and plural world of nations. Moreover, the notion of a covenant was clearly adopted and adapted from their understandings of the Bible and God's protection of them. The 1892 parliament was opened with this declamation:

> Kia whakapaingia a Ihowa te Atua o Aperahama, te Atua o Ihaka, te Atua o Iharaira Koia nei te Atua o tatou tupuna nana nei ratou i arahai ora mai ite moana nei i whiti mai ai ki enei motu e noho nei tatou. Me hoatu te kororia kia ia ake, ake, ake.

(Praise the Lord God of Abraham, the God of Isaac, the God of Israel, for he is the God of our forefathers who led them forth safely across the ocean to these islands which we now inhabit. Glory be unto him for ever after.)[24]

Furthermore, just as Māori owed the sovereign their loyalty, the sovereign promised to protect them. Again, as Hobbes wrote, 'the end of obedience is protection'.[25]

The loyalty of many of the Māori who met at the Kotahitanga sittings might be interpreted in a variety of ways. Andrew Thompson, for instance, agues that the loyalty of some southern Africans and Māori was 'born of a psychological need for hope: faced with settler rapacity, the imperial state seemed the lesser of two evils'.[26] Or perhaps such loyalty was entirely strategic, a way of earning support for their cause by demonstrating their civility and obedience to the Queen, while highlighting the savage excesses of the colonial state. In other words, perhaps they essentialised the figure of the Queen as all that was good, and themselves as good subjects, in order to bring into even starker relief the badness of the colonial regime.[27] Finally, we might interpret the loyalty of Kotahitanga members as a kind of colonial mimicry, in which leaders adopted signs, institutions, and attitudes of civility in order to demonstrate their own capacity for civilisation.[28]

I offer a fourth interpretation: that expressions of loyalty to Queen Victoria was a narrative device that allowed Kotahitanga members to express their political will in terms that made sense to them, according to their own cultural and political logics. By stating their abiding loyalty to the Queen, and grounding that loyalty in the treaty and other key agreements covenanted with their ancestors, Māori leaders were able to 'wedge' open a space for the articulation of another history, as one of the speakers I quoted above put it. This history criticised the actions of the colonial state and, in particular, refused the *justification* frequently given to those actions: that Māori needed to be amalgamated into European society for their own good. By countering that narrative, Māori who expressed loyalty to the Queen could therefore assert their *own* history, in positive terms, of filial piety and imperial loyalty. This was one that was not dependent on social or racial amalgamation into the world of the majority, but rather appreciated the importance of hierarchy, status, and the responsibilities of leader and led to each other. Thus, Māori at Kotahitanga could retain the pride and dignity for which they sought recognition, at the same time rewriting the script laid out for them in the story of amalgamation.

By discussing the interventions of Meri Mangakahia in a sitting of Kotahitanga, and some of her later speeches, I shall suggest that this narrative device enabled further differentiations and assertions of power and authority. In the case of Mangakahia, a story of loyalty to the Queen enabled her to reassert the figure of 'mana wahine' or female authority. I will suggest, in a more speculative mode, that the identification with the authority Queen by one of her female Māori subjects signalled the way in which Mangakahia had incorporated the British queen into a Māori world that this wahine rangatira, or chiefly woman, was trying to hold onto or perhaps recreate: one in which the landed power of Māori women was recognised as power in its own right.

Equality and status

In the afternoon of 18 May 1893, Meri Te Tai Mangakahia rose to speak to a motion that she had brought before Kotahitanga. Her motion proposed that women, who could speak in the parliament, be given the right to vote, and to stand as representatives in the assembly. Her appeal was no doubt influenced by the women's suffragist movement at the time, and just a few months after Mangakahia proposed an expansion of women's rights in Kotahitanga, the vote was awarded to women in New Zealand – which thus became the first self-governing country to do so (though women could not stand for national office until 1919). Mangakahia's reasons for why Māori women in Kotahitanga (which means one-ness or unity) should get the vote and be eligible to stand in the Māori parliament were, however, distinct from those generally made by the suffragists.

Raewyn Dalziel has discussed two important strains in white women's arguments for suffrage in New Zealand (and which can be found in other settler societies, too). The first was the adoption by settler women of virtues associated with colonial manhood in order to emphasise their contribution to nation building. Thus, in some suffrage writing, white women were described as being brave, strong, and self-reliant, qualities closely associated with colonial masculinity and which marked settler countries like New Zealand as free from the status anxieties associated with Britain. The second argument, one that Marilyn Lake has likewise drawn attention to in the Australian context, depicted women as being equal members of a post-Enlightenment world: civilised and educated. This idealisation relied on a contrast with women of the 'dark ages' and specifically women of the tribe who were 'bought and sold like so much goods', as one suffragist in New Zealand wrote.[29] According to Lake, this argument in which the 'advancement of women – white Western women – was predicated on the backwardness of other women' brings into relief the 'double difference' of white feminists in settler colonies, that is, their peculiar roles as colonised-colonisers.[30]

Figure 10.1 Meri Te Tai Mangakahia.

Neither of these arguments for women's suffrage – ambivalently premised as they were in colonial egalitarianism and colonising racism – were much use to Māori women arguing for the right to vote in their own political domain. Mangakahia's argument emphasised status, responsibility, and intelligent leadership, rather than civilisation, progressivism, or racial hierarchy. She argued that:

1. He nui nga wahine o Nui Tireni kua mate a ratou taane, a he whenua karati, papatupu o ratou.
2. He nui nga wahine o Nui Tireni kua mate o ratou matua, kaore o ratou tungane, he karati, he papatupu o ratou.
3. He nui nga wahine mohio o Niu Tireni ke te moe tane, kaore nga tane e mohio ki te whakahaere i o raua whenua.
4. He nui nga wahine kua koroheketia o ratou matua, he wahine mohio, he kurati, he papatupu o ratou.

(1. There are many women in New Zealand whose husbands have died and who own land under grant or papatupu land [that is, land still held under the authority of the tribe and that had not gone through the Native Land Court process].)
(2. There are many women in New Zealand whose parents have died and who have no brothers, and who own grants or papatupu land.)
(3. There are many intelligent women in New Zealand who marry men who do not know how to run their land.)
(4. There are many women whose parents have grown old and who are intelligent women with grants and papatupu land of their own.)[31]

Mangakahia thus drew attention to the special and distinct roles of Māori women in dealing with their lands on their own behalf and on behalf of their families. She highlighted the achievements of women of status who owned customary land, as marked by her reiterative reference to 'intelligent' women (he wāhine mohio). Such was certainly not an argument that appealed to egalitarian nationalism; and nor was it dependent on marking out barbarous others from civilised selves. It was thoroughly embedded in the values of a hierarchical world in which status meant not only power but the observation of certain responsibilities. The logic of Mangakahia's argument was supported by the elder statesman H. K. Taiaroa: 'i te mea kanui nga wahine whiwhi whenua a ka mahi noa atu ko tatou ki te mahi ture atu mo o ratou whenua. I oti hoki i tera tau kia kohi nga wahine i te £1.0s.0d., na reira me whai mana nga wahine ki te pooti.' ('There are many women who own land'), he concurred, ('and we have all the control to create laws for their lands. Also last year the women managed to collect £1.0s.0d. They should therefore have the right to vote'.)[32]

Mangakahia was herself a high-ranking woman, possibly with land interests of her own. Born in 1868, Meri Te Tai was the daughter of an important Te Rarawa chief, Re Te Tai, from the northern Hokianga in the north of the North Island, and Hana Tera. This was Tera's second marriage, and Meri Te Tai was the eldest of that union thus she may well have inherited land, since the inheritance of land and resource rights in Māori communities is not patrilineal but rather bilineal – a practice that was recognised by the early Native Land Court. Therefore, certain Māori women could hold use-rights over land and resources as individuals. But like all rights-holders, their 'ownership' was contained; rights to land were subject to 'the overriding right of the tribal community and the mana (authority) of the chief over the land and people'. However, the Native Land Court process, as has been well documented, was having a destructive effect on the relationship of leaders and communities and their access to and responsibility for land holdings. The land court process circumvented the tribe by finding a few title-holders whose names would then be placed on certificates that allowed those named to sell land to whomever they liked.[33] The Kotahitanga parliament criticised this very practice: 'the work of [the Native Land Court] was bad from the beginning because it gave the land of tribes or sub-tribes to ten people ... those ten people managed to destroy the land and the people. They posed as the important people who owned the land themselves and the tribe were as slaves', the parliament complained in a petition.[34] Furthermore, during the 1870s, the authority of women as rights-holders in particular began to be undermined by amendments to the colonial land laws. The changes provided that husbands 'should be party to all deeds'.[35] This meant in practice that husbands could exercise a power of veto over land sales, and even negotiate sales without their wives' full consent.

As their husbands (Māori and Pākeha) were given increased authority in regard to the sale of their lands, Māori women were at the same time losing ground politically within the colonial state. They were unable to represent themselves in the national parliament, where decisions about their land rights were being made. This was despite the fact that, for instance, at least thirteen women of rank signed the Treaty of Waitangi documents. In 1840, therefore, a number of women leaders *represented* their communities' agreement to the terms of the treaty through their signatures.[36] Yet in 1867, when separate seats were established for Māori electorates by legislation, voting rights in the 'Māori seats' were limited to Māori men (including 'half-castes'), over twenty-one years of age. The act, which was intended as a temporary provision 'to provide for the better Representation of the Native Aboriginal Inhabitants of the Colony of New Zealand', thus defined 'representation' in terms of gender, as well as race. This did not accord with the roles and functions of chiefly and powerful Māori women. Rather, the act imposed European gender hierarchies on Māori society. Nonetheless, women continued to protest their situation: historian Tania Rei has argued that between 1886–96, Māori women sent at least forty petitions to parliament complaining about the effect of the land laws.[37]

Sometime around 1890, Meri Te Tai married Hamiora Mangakahia, premier of Kotahitanga, becoming his third wife and adding the name Mangakahia to her own. Hamiora, of the Ngati Whanaunga tribe, was thirty years Meri's senior, and Meri moved to live with him at his home on the Coromandel Peninsula – a considerable distance from her own homeland. From an entrepreneurial family with significant political interests, Hamiora's rise to leadership in Kotahitanga was not unexpected. Whether Meri had political interests prior to meeting Hamiora is hard to ascertain; the marriage certainly helped her to bring her voice to prominence in the Kotahitanga debates.

There is no extensive historiography in New Zealand that discusses the political lives of nineteenth-century Māori women. Those historians who have given some attention to Māori women's politics have tended to frame their concerns in tribal or national terms. An essay by Angela Ballara, published in 1993 to mark a century since women's enfranchisement in New Zealand, focuses on Māori women's political activity in the 1890s, a crucial and tumultuous time in Māori life as the new Liberal government pursued an aggressive 'bust up' of large land-holdings and the remaining tribal lands.[38] Ballara interprets the actions of Mangakahia and other wāhine rangatira as a 'structured ... contribution to what they saw as the men's work of creating a kotahitanga or union of the tribes' in order to face the problems of land loss. 'Their efforts', writes Ballara, 'were a response to what they saw as the men's continuing failure'.[39] Other historians who have written about Mangakahia similarly have emphasised her contribution to the discussion about land-holding and political rights within Kotahitanga in the context of colonial threat. Less attention has been given to the latter part of Mangakahia's speech before the Kotahitanga assembly. Mangakahia provided a fifth reason as to why women should be allowed to vote and stand in the parliament:

5. He nui nga tane Rangatira o te motu nei kua inoi ki te kuini, mo nga mate e pa ara kia tatou, a kaore tonu tatou i pa ki te ora i runga i ta ratou inoitanga. Na reira ka inoi ahau ki tenei whare kia tu he mema wahine.

(5. There are many male chiefs in this island who have appealed to the Queen over the problems affecting then, and we have never received any advantage from their appeals. For this reason I ask this House that women members be appointed.)

She continued, 'Ma tenei pea e tika ai, a tera ka tika ki te tuku inoi nga mema wahine ki te kuini, mo nga mate kua pa nei kia tatou me o tatou whenua, a tera pea a whakaae mai a te kuini ki te inoi a ona hoa Wahine Maori i te mea he wahine ano hoki a te kuini.' ('In this way perhaps things will be put right, and it might be suitable for the female members to make appeal to the Queen over the problems which affect us and our lands. For perhaps the Queen will assent [whakaae] to the appeals for her Māori women advisers since she is also a woman'.)[40]

Mangakahia's appeal to and even identification with the femininity of Queen Victoria may seem insignificant or even naïve – especially considering Queen Victoria's distaste for the women's suffragist movement. Unless, that is, we situate this appeal too within the ancestral, genealogical world of politics I have described. Indeed, it appears from this statement that according to Mangakahia, Queen Victoria was a wahine rangatira like her. In Mangakahia's rendering of the sympathy between chiefly *women*, race does not cleave civilisational difference (as it did in the ways that white suffragists differentiated their own enlightened being from that of purportedly victimised tribal women). Mangakahia herself was likely quite familiar with white female authority, since it is thought that she attended a convent school in Auckland in the 1880s, when she would have been in a minority of Māori girls to have done so.[41]

Mangakahia maintained her faith in the Queen's particular concern for the Māori people into later life. On 28 July 1914 – the day the Austro-Hungarian Empire declared war on Serbia – Meri Mangakahia delivered a speech to prime minister William Massey, leader of the conservative Reform Party, in Wellington, as a member of tribal delegation from the Eastern Māori District. She congratulated him on 'giving effect to paragraph III of the Treaty of Waitangi, in consideration whereof her Majesty the Queen of England extends to the Natives of New Zealand her Royal protection and imparts to them all the rights and privileges of British subjects'. And she warned against giving support to another group of Māori leaders, including Sir James Carroll and Āpirana Ngata, because they believed that the 'Treaty of Waitangi is decomposed and buried, and that there is no good in looking backward but look ahead'.[42] Of course, it was in fact Queen Victoria who was by this time dead and buried, but I want to draw attention here to the metaphors of death and decay that Mangakahia used, and her undying faith in the Queen's protection, since I think they may suggest something quite particular about the way in which Mangakahia redeployed her story of chiefly women that could again criticise what she perceived to be the amalgamationist rhetoric of those involved in the settler state.

According to Mangakahia, the vitality of the Māori people hinged on continuing to practise and believe in what the Treaty of Waitangi had promised: that Māori were to become British subjects of the Queen. Like other Kotahitanga leaders, Mangakahia believed that this was not an oppressive kind of subjecthood but one that was premised on recognition of and respect for the integrity of tribal protocol, politics, and landholding, as well as tribal accounts of their own histories. As British subjects, Māori people could ally themselves with and even express loyalty to the sovereign. But they did not, as Thomas Hobbes also cautioned against, have to accede to the now encompassing state's view of the past and present. As Hobbes wrote, 'Therefore I put down for one of the most effectual seeds of the death of any state, that the conquerors require not only a submission of men's actions to them for the future, but also an approbation of all their actions past; when there is scarce a commonwealth in the world, whose beginnings can in conscience be justified'.[43] Perhaps Mangakahia was worried not only about the turning away from the political tradition of the treaty, and the ancestral covenant it represented, but also from the role of chiefly women such as herself as transmitters of traditional knowledge.[44]

Mangakahia was distinguishing, I suggest, between being a British subject, and becoming a New Zealand citizen. The former allowed Māori to retain what was important to them, as distinct tribes. Becoming a New Zealand citizen, however, might require Māori to accede to a version of the past in which the treaty was dead and buried, and a future in which Māori would have to hold the same values as the settlers around them. They would have to become ever more assimilated into the majority population, she feared.

This was the position of James Carroll, whose mother was a prominent Ngati Kahungunu woman, and was the first man of Māori descent to win a general electorate seat. In 1894, when Hone Heke brought the Native Rights Bill authorised by Kotahitanga before the New Zealand parliament, Carroll strongly opposed it. Explaining that he had listened to the speeches of those gathered at the 'Native parliaments', he commented that Māori were 'very prone to dispute amongst themselves' and were perhaps not the best people to represent their own interests. Māori were not yet fully 'British subjects', he went on, for they needed to be 'taken by the hand' and made to 'advance step by step'. The sooner they 'advance[d] into line with [their] European brethren the better it would be for all'. A Māori might, he conceded, feel that he were being 'violently severed from the old associations to which he had been accustomed, and which he revered and desired to conserve; but, notwithstanding all this, it was better that he should feel the momentary pain in order to feel the lasting benefit.'[45]

Mangakahia's ambivalence about what being a citizen might entail, and her stated opposition to the ideas of Carroll and Ngata, were well founded considering her own desire to make present again the authority of chiefly women. In order to do so, she conducted herself confidently as a leader and representative, despite a patronising description of her in *The Press* in 1914 as a 'chieftainess'. Further, Mangakahia did so by incorporating the figure of the British queen into a genealogy of female authority that she sought to reaffirm.

Figure 10.2 *Queen with Moko*, Barry Ross Smith, 2008. (Courtesy: Barry Ross Smith) The incorporation of British monarchs into Māori genealogy and history continues today, as this image of Queen Elizabeth II with moko references.

Acknowledgement

This research was supported under the Australian Research Council's Laureate Fellowship funding scheme (project number FL110100243).

Notes

1 Andrew Thompson, 'The languages of loyalism in southern Africa, c. 1870–1939', *The English Historical Review*, 118:477 (2003), 619–20.
2 H. K. Taiaroa. See the section 'Loyalty and separatism in Kotahitanga' for full quotation.
3 Margaret Homans, *Royal Representations: Queen Victoria and British Culture, 1837–1876* (Chicago, IL: University of Chicago Press, 1998), pp. xix, xxv.
4 'Pāremata' is a transliteration of 'parliament'.

5 See James Belich, *Making Peoples: A History of the New Zealanders from Polynesian Settlement to the end of the Nineteenth Century* (Auckland: Penguin Press, 1996), pp. 243–4.
6 Ranginui Walker, *Ka Whawhai Tonu Matou: Struggle Without End* (Auckland: Penguin, 1990), p. 170; and Lindsay Cox, *Kotahitanga: The Search for Māori Political Unity* (Auckland: Oxford University Press, 1993), p. 70.
7 J. A. Williams is sceptical of the claim and argues that many signed out of deference to the chiefs and a general sense of grievance rather than because they positively supported the parliament. Williams, *Politics of the New Zealand Maori: Protest and Cooperation, 1891–1909* (Seattle: University of Washington, 1969), p. 61.
8 Keith Sinclair, *A History of New Zealand*, rev. ed. (Auckland: Penguin Books, 2000), pp. 201–2. Other accounts of the parliament appear in: Cox, *Kotahitanga*, pp. 61–70; Michael King, *The Penguin History of New Zealand* (Auckland: Penguin Books, 2003), pp. 329–30; Paul Moon, *Ngapua: The Political Life of Hone Heke Ngapua, MHR* (Auckland: David Ling Publishing, 2006), pp. 45–59; Walker, *Ka Whawhai Tonu Matou*, pp. 165–73.
9 Reproduced in W. David McIntyre and W. J. Gardiner (eds), *Speeches and Documents on New Zealand History* (Oxford: Clarendon Press, 1971), pp. 164–5.
10 See Alan Ward, *A Show of Justice: Racial 'Amalgamation' in Nineteenth-Century New Zealand* (Canberra: Australian National University Press, 1974); and Damon Ieremia Salesa, *Racial Crossings: Race, Intermarriage, and the Victorian British Empire* (Oxford: Oxford University Press, 2011).
11 Smith in *New Zealand Parliamentary Debates - Hansard* (NZPD), vol. 85, 10 September 1894, p. 559.
12 Stout, NZPD, vol. 85, p. 557.
13 Williams, *Politics of the New Zealand Maori*, p. 48.
14 Bryan Gilling, 'The Punitive Confiscation of Māori Land in the 1860s', in Richard Boast and Richard S. Hill (eds), *Raupatu: The Confiscation of Māori Land* (Wellington: Victoria University of Wellington Press, 2009), pp. 13–30.
15 Alexander Turnbull Library, Wellington (ATL), Te Kotahitanga Papers, MS-Papers-6373-26, *Nga Korero o Te Hui o Te Whakakotahitanga i tu ki te Tiriti o Waitangi*, Aperira 14, 1892 – The Proceedings of the Meeting for Unity Held at "The Treaty of Waitangi", 14 April 1892, printed by William McLeod, High Street, Akarana, trans. by Jane McRae.
16 ATL, MS-Papers-6373-26, *Paremata i Te Waipatu*, 8 May 1893, p. 39, trans. by Jane McRae.
17 ATL, MS-Papers-6373-26, A. Kume in *Paremata i Te Waipatu*, 8 May 1893, p. 40, trans. by Jane McRae.
18 ATL, MS-Papers-6373-26, E. Wano in *Paremata i Te Waipatu*, 8 May 1893, p. 40, trans. by Jane McRae.
19 ATL, MS-Papers-6373-26, in *Paremata i Te Waipatu*, 8 May 1893, p. 39, trans. by Jane McRae.
20 ATL, MS-Papers-6373-26, Mangakahia, in *Paremata i Te Waipatu*, 8 May 1893, p. 38, trans. by Jane McRae.
21 ATL, MS-Papers-6373-26, H. K. Taiaroa, *Paremata i Te Waipatu*, 8 May 1893, p. 39, trans. by Jane McRae.
22 See Jacques Derrida, 'Declarations of Independence', in Jacques Derrida *Negotiations: Interventions and Interviews, 1971–2001*, trans. Elizabeth Rottenberg (Stanford, CA: Stanford University Press, 2002), p. 47; and Bonnie Honig, 'Declarations of Independence: Arendt and Derrida on the problem of founding a republic', *The American Political Science Review*, 85:1 (1991), 98.
23 Harry C. Evison, 'Taiaroa, Hori Kerei', in the *Dictionary of New Zealand Biography Te Ara – the Encyclopedia of New Zealand*, updated 30 October 2012, http://www.teara.govt.nz, accessed 29 January 2016.
24 ATL, MS-Papers-6373-26, *Nga Korero o Te Hui o Te Whakakotahitanga/ Proceedings of the Meeting for Unity*, 14 April 1892.

25 Thomas Hobbes, *Leviathan, or The Matter, Forme, & Power of a Common-wealth Eccelsiastical and Civill*, ed. Michael Oakeshott (London: Collier Macmillan Publishers, 1962), p. 167.
26 Thompson, 'The languages of loyalism', p. 649.
27 See Diana Fuss, *Essentially Speaking: Feminism, Nature, and Difference* (New York: Routledge, 1989).
28 Homi Bhabha, 'Of mimicry and man: The ambivalence of colonial discourse', in *The Location of Culture* (London and New York: Routledge, 1994), pp. 85–94.
29 Raewyn Dalziel, 'An experiment in the social laboratory? Suffrage, national identity, and mythologies of race in New Zealand in the 1890s', in Ian Christopher Fletcher, Laura E. Nym Mayhall, and Philippa Levine (eds), *Women's Suffrage in the British Empire: Citizenship, Nation and Race* (London: Routledge, 2000), pp. 87–102.
30 Marilyn Lake, 'Between old world "barbarism" and stone age "primitivism": The double difference of the white Australian feminist', in Norma Grieve and Ailsa Burns (eds), *Australian Women: Contemporary Feminist Thought* (Oxford: Oxford University Press, 1994), p. 84.
31 Meri Mangakahia, *Paremata i Te Waipatu*, 18 May 1893, p. 63, trans. by Jane McRae, MS-Papers-6373-26, (ATL).
32 ATL, MS-Papers-6373-26, *Paremata i Te Waipatu*, 18 May 1893, p. 62, trans. by Jane McRae.
33 Angela Ballara, 'Wāhine Rangatira: Māori women of rank and their role in the women's Kotahitanga movement of the 1890s', *New Zealand Journal of History*, 27:2 (1993), 133–4.
34 *Paremata i Te Waipatu*, 18 May 1893, p. 150, trans. by Jane McRae. See also David Williams, *'Te Kooti Tango Whenua': The Native Land Court 1864–1909* (Wellington: Huia Publishers, 1999).
35 Ballara, 'Wāhine Rangatira', pp. 133–4.
36 See Tania Rei, *Māori Women and the Vote* (Wellington: Huia Publishers, 1993), pp. 8–9.
37 *Ibid.*, p. 13.
38 Tom Brooking, '"Busting up" the greatest estate of all: Liberal Māori land policy, 1891–1911', *New Zealand Journal of History*, 26:1 (1992), pp. 78–99.
39 Ballara, 'Wāhine Rangatira', p. 127. See also, Rei, *Māori Women*, and Charlotte Macdonald, 'Meri Mangakahia', in Charlotte Macdonald, Merimeri Penfold, and Bridget Williams (eds), *The Book of New Zealand Women* (Wellington: Bridget Williams Books, 1991), pp. 413–15.
40 ATL, MS-Papers-6373-26, *Paremata i Te Waipatu*, 18 May 1893, p. 63, trans. by Jane McRae.
41 I have not yet been able to verify which convent school she attended.
42 'Government and natives: Maori Appreciation', *The Press* (29 July 1914), p. 10. See also 'Lobby Gossip', *Dominion* (28 July 1914), p. 6.
43 Hobbes, *Leviathan*, p. 506.
44 See, for example, Judith Binney and Gillian Chaplin, *Ngā Mōrehu: The Survivors: The Life Histories of Eight Māori Women* (Wellington: Bridget Williams Books, 2011), p. 4.
45 Carroll, NZPD, vol. 85, pp. 554–5.

SELECT BIBLIOGRAPHY

Ballantyne, Tony (ed.). 'From orientalism to ornamentalism: Empire and difference in history', special issue of *Journal of Colonialism and Colonial History*, 3:1 (2002).

Banerjee, Sukanya. *Becoming Imperial Citizens: Indians in the Late-Victorian Empire*. Durham, NC: Duke University Press, 2010.

Cannadine, David. *Ornamentalism: How the British saw their Empire*. London: Penguin, 2002.

de Costa, Ravi. 'Identity, authority, and the moral worlds of Indigenous petitions', *Comparative Studies in Society and History*, 48:3 (2006), 669–98.

Elbourne, Elizabeth. 'Indigenous peoples and imperial networks in the early nineteenth century: The politics of knowledge', in Phillip Buckner and R. Douglas Francis (eds), *Rediscovering the British World*. Calgary: University of Calgary Press, 2005.

Evans, Julie, Patricia Grimshaw, David Philips, and Shurlee Swain. *Equal Subjects, Unequal Rights: Indigenous Peoples in British Settler Colonies, 1830–1910*. Manchester: Manchester University Press, 2003.

Gorman, Daniel. *Imperial Citizenship: Empire and the Question of Belonging*. Manchester: Manchester University Press, 2006.

Homans, Margaret. *Royal Representations: Queen Victoria and British Culture, 1837–1876*. Chicago, IL: University of Chicago Press, 1998.

Homans, Margaret and Adrienne Munich (eds). *Remaking Queen Victoria*. Cambridge: Cambridge University Press, 1997.

Plunkett, John. *Queen Victoria: First Media Monarch*. Oxford: Oxford University Press, 2003.

Thompson, Dorothy. *Queen Victoria: Gender and Power*. London: Virago, 2008.

Africa

Anderson, Catherine E. 'A Zulu king in Victorian London: Race, royalty and imperialist aesthetics in late nineteenth-century Britain', *Visual Resources: An International Journal of Documentation*, 24:3 (2008), 299–319.

Levine, Roger S. 'Prince Alfred in King William's Town, South Africa: 13 August, 1860', *Rethinking History*, 14:1 (2010), 137–44.

Lonsdale, John. 'Ornamental constitutionalism in Africa: Kenyatta and the two queens', *The Journal of Imperial and Commonwealth History*, 34:1 (March 2006), 87–103.

Parsons, Neil. *King Khama, Emperor Joe, and the Great White Queen: Victorian Britain through African eyes*. Chicago, IL: University of Chicago Press, 1998.

Price, Richard. *Making Empire: Colonial Encounters and the Creation of Imperial Rule in Nineteenth-Century Africa*. Cambridge: Cambridge University Press, 2008.

SELECT BIBLIOGRAPHY

Reed, Charles V. *Royal Tourists, Colonial Subjects and the Making of a British World, 1860–1911*. Manchester: Manchester University Press, 2016.
Sapire, Hilary. 'Ambiguities of loyalism: The Prince of Wales in India and Africa, 1921–2 and 1925', *History Workshop Journal*, 73 (2012), 37–65.
Theron, Bridget. 'King Cetshwayo in Victorian England: A cameo of imperial interaction', *South African Historical Journal*, 56:1 (2006), 60–87.
Thompson, Andrew. 'The languages of loyalism in Southern Africa, c. 1870–1939', *The English Historical Review*, 118:477 (June 2003), 617–50.

Australia

Curthoys, Ann. 'Indigenous subjects', in Deryck M. Schreuder and Stuart Ward (eds), *Australia's Empire*. Oxford: Oxford University Press, 2008.
Curthoys, Ann and Jessie Mitchell. '"Bring this paper to the Good Governor": Aboriginal petitioning in Britain's Australian colonies', in Saliha Belmessous (ed.), *Native Claims: Indigenous Law against Empire, 1500–1920*. New York: Oxford University Press, 2012.
McKenna, Mark. 'Monarchy: From reverence to indifference', in Deryck M. Schreuder and Stuart Ward (eds), *Australia's Empire*. Oxford: Oxford University Press, 2008.
Mitchell, Jessie. '"It will enlarge the ideas of the natives": Indigenous Australians and the tour of Prince Alfred, Duke of Edinburgh', *Aboriginal History*, 34 (2010), 196–216.
Nugent, Maria. '"The queen gave us the land": Aboriginal people, Queen Victoria and historical remembrance', *History Australia*, 9:2 (2012), 182–200.

Canada

Carlson, Keith Thor. 'Aboriginal diplomacy: The Queen comes to Canada and Coyote goes to London', in J. Marshall Beier (ed.), *Indigenous Diplomacies*. London: Palgrave Macmillan, 2009.
——— 'The Indians and the Crown: Aboriginal memories of royal promises in Pacific Canada', in Colin M. Coates (ed.), *Majesty in Canada: Essays on the Role of Royalty*. Toronto: Dundurn Press, 2006.
Carter, Sarah. 'Aboriginal people of Canada and the British Empire', in Phillip Buckner (ed.), *Canada and the British Empire*. Oxford: Oxford University Press, 2008.
——— '"Your Great Mother across the salt sea": Prairie First Nations, the British monarchy and the vice-regal connection to 1900', *Manitoba History* 48 (Autumn 2004/Winter 2005), 34–48.
Henry, Wade. 'Imagining the great white mother and the great king: Aboriginal tradition and royal representation at the "Great Pow-wow" of 1901', *Journal of the Canadian Historical Association*, 11:1 (2000), 87–108.
Martin, Ged. 'Queen Victoria and Canada', *American Review of Canadian Studies*, 13:3 (1983), 215–34.

SELECT BIBLIOGRAPHY

Miller, J. R. '"I will accept the Queen's hand": First Nations leaders and the image of the Crown in the Prairie Treaties', in *Reflections on Native-Newcomer Relations: Selected Essays*. Toronto: University of Toronto Press, 2004.

────── 'Victoria's "red children": The "Great White Queen Mother" and native-newcomer relations in Canada', *Native Studies Review*, 17:1 (2008), 1–23.

Phillips, Ruth. 'Dress and address: First Nations self-fashioning and the 1860 royal tour of Canada', in Susan Kulcher and Graeme Were (eds), *The Art of Clothing: A Pacific Experience*. London: Routledge, 2005.

Radforth, Ian. 'Performance, politics, and representation: Aboriginal people and the 1860 royal tour of Canada', *The Canadian Historical Review*, 84:1 (March 2003), 1–32.

New Zealand

Belgrave, Michael. *Historical Frictions: Māori Claims and Reinvented Histories*. Auckland: Auckland University Press, 2005.

Belich, James. *Making Peoples: A History of the New Zealanders from Polynesian Settlement to the end of the Nineteenth Century*, Auckland: Penguin Press, 1996.

Treagus, Mandy. 'Agents or objects? Māori performances in Britain', in Sue Thomas (ed.), *Victorian Traffic: Identity, Exchange, Performance*. Cambridge: Cambridge Scholars Publishing, 2008.

────── 'Spectacles of empire: Māori tours in England in 1863 and 1911', in Kate Darian Smith *et al*. (eds), *Exploring the British World: Identity, Cultural Productions, Institutions*. Melbourne: RMIT Press, 2004.

Williams, J.A. *Politics of the New Zealand Maori: Protest and Cooperation, 1891–1909*, Seattle: University of Washington, 1969.

INDEX

Underlined page numbers refer to illustrations.

Aborigines Protection Society 56, 66, 84
addresses (formal) 25–6, 28, 33, 37, 44, 63, 71, 81–2, 84–5, 90–2, <u>93</u>, 100, 104, <u>105</u>, 109, 116, 136, 150–1, 189, 200–1, 205, 212, 217, 223
Adeney, William 187–92, 197–8, 205–6
agency *see* Indigenous peoples: agency
Albert Prince of Wales *see* Edward VII
Alfred, Duke of Edinburgh (son of Queen Victoria) 12–13, 25–49, 167
Alhambra Theatre (London) 147, 174
amaGcaleka 29, 35
amaMfengu 29, 37, 48–9
amaNgqika 29, 32–5, 37
amaThembu 27, 178
  see also Tamboekies
amaXhosa 27, 29, 31–3, 35–7, 48–9, 54, 167
amaZulu 29, 32, 43, 46, 56, 66, 126, 137–40, 166, 169, 172, 174–6
Anderson, Joe (King Burraga) 111–12
Anderson, Michael 100–1, 114, 116
Angas, George French 148
Anishinabe (Ojibway, Chippewa) 17, 81, 83, 86
Archibald, Adams 87
archives 8, 11, 112, 117
Assiniboine 83, 92
Auckland 63–5, 71, 147, 160, 241
Australia 1–3, 6, 8–9, 12, 14, 16–7, 30, 79, 100–1, 106, 111–15, 117, 129, 150, 187–90, 192–3, 195–9, 203–5, 210–11, 215–18, 220, 222–3, 236

autonomy *see* Indigenous peoples: autonomy

Babayane (Tswana King) 168, 171, 173–5
Bagehot, Walter 128–9
Barak, William 100–7 *passim*, 116
Barkly, Sir Henry (Governor of Victoria) 100, 105–6, 150, 200
Barolong 29, 40–2
Barwick, Diane 104, 110–11, 200–1
BaSotho 29, 38–41, 167
Basuto 40, 178
Bathoen (Tswana King) 66, 140, 166, 169–70, 172–3, 176, 178
Batman Treaty 189, 193–5
benevolence 4–6, 26–7, 42, 49, 78–9, 86–7, 101, 114, 161, 178, 201, 222, 224
Blackfoot <u>93</u>
blankets 177, 193, 210, 214, 220–3
Bloemfontein 38, 41–2
Boers 31–2, 38–9, 41–2, 167–9, 175–6
Bonetta, Sarah Forbes 133, <u>134</u>, 160
Botswana (Bechuanaland) 25, 140, 166–7, 169–70, 172, 176–8, 180–2
Bourke, Richard (Governor of NSW) 193–5
bracelets 212, 216, 219
breastplates 173, 175, 215–16
British colonial identity 192, 198
British Columbia 81, 218, 220
British South Africa Company (BSA Company) 175
Burraga *see* Anderson, Joe
Buxton, Thomas Fowell 55–6

[249]

INDEX

Cain, Mary Jane 115
Cameron, Duncan (Lieutenant General) 64
Canada 1–4, 8, 12–14, 16, 30, 56, 78–81, 85–6, 89, 92, 95, 129, 151, 201, 210–13, 215–18, 220, 222–3
Cape Colony (Colony of the Cape of Good Hope) 167, 169, 178–9
Cape Croker Agency 219
Cape Town 25, 28, 30, 33–6, 41, 139, 167–8, 171, 176, 178
Carmichael, Fred 113
Carroll, Sir James 241–2
carte de visite 157
  see also photographic portrait
Cattle Killing episode 31–3, 36
ceremonial, ceremony 25, 27–31, 35, 43–8 *passim*, 47, 67, 79, 90, 129, 133, 140–1, 151–2, 154, 189, 210
  see also Jubilees, Queen's day
Cetshwayo kaMpande (Zulu King) 25, 29, 43, 66, 139–40, 166, 168, 170–1, 173–5
Chamberlain, Joseph 71, 141, 169, 172, 176
Chesson, Frederick 56, 66
Chikka Veerarajendra (King of Coorg) 131
Chippewa (Anishinabe, Ojibway) 80–1, 223
christening gown 157
christening sets 15, 145, 159, 160, 162
Christian Guardian 151
Christianity 9, 26–7, 29–30, 33, 36–7, 48, 56, 58–9, 61–2, 67, 73, 80, 131–2, 148, 150–1, 160–1, 167, 169, 172, 197, 210, 220–1
Church Missionary Society (CMS) 55–6, 58, 83–4, 157
Church of England 128, 157
Ciskei 25, 177
cloaks 68, 133, 148–50, 154, 156, 162
  see also dress, dog skin cloaks
clothing 81, 93, 145, 147–8, 151–2, 154–5, 171, 214, 220
  see also dress
coins 15, 17, 144, 187–92, 196, 198, 200, 203–6, 222
  see also currency
Colenso, Elizabeth 157
Colenso, John (Bishop of Natal) 138, 167–8, 174
Colenso, William 157
colonial factor 167, 175, 177
  see also settler politics
Colonial Office 5, 15, 30, 60, 125, 137, 140–1, 153, 168, 173, 175, 198
commemorations, commemorative practice 9, 16, 88, 149, 151, 157, 212–17 *passim*, 214
commemorative medals 70, 83, 85, 88, 89, 129, 151, 212–13, 214, 215–16, 219
constitutionalism 14, 63, 67–8, 73, 127–30, 135, 228, 234
Coranderrk 100, 103–7, 110–1, 150, 200–2
Coromandel 147, 239
costume 39, 140, 147, 151, 154
  see also clothing, dress
Cowan, James 154
Cree 28, 83, 86, 92
Crowfoot (Blackfoot Chief) 93
Cunningham, Robert 88–90
currency 4, 144, 187–93 *passim*, 204–6, 222
  see also coins

Dakota (Sioux) 83, 91
de Costa, Ravi 56, 103, 107
Department of Indian Affairs (Canada) 81, 90, 94, 151, 213, 215, 219
Diamond Jubilee (1897) *see* Jubilees
diplomacy, diplomatic practice 9, 11, 15, 38, 66, 78, 80, 86–7, 90, 127–8, 166–70 *passim*, 211–18 *passim*, 220, 232
Disraeli, Benjamin 135
Dixie, Lady Florence 168
dog skin cloaks 149
  see also cloaks

[250]

INDEX

Douglas, James 218, 220
Douglas, Thomas (Earl of Selkirk) 83–4
Dredge, James (Assistant Protector) 196–8
dress 15, 44, <u>47</u>, 67–8, 81, 133, 145, 147–52, 154–7, 162, 170–1, 174, 193
  see also clothing
Duleep Singh, Maharajah 131–3, 160
Duren, Jane 112

Earl Of Shaftsbury (Anthony Ashley Cooper) 152
Edward VII (formerly Albert Prince of Wales) 30, 55, 66, 85, 113, 151, 170, 177, 200, 223
elections 62, 79, 128, 140
  see also suffrage, voting
Elizabeth II (Princess Elizabeth) 25, <u>243</u>
Emma (Queen of Hawaii) 160
Evening News (Sydney) 216
Evening Post (Christchurch) 68

fashion 145, 147–8
feathers 44, 68, 133, 151, 154
feminists 125, 228, 237
'fictive kinship' 112
First Nations (Canada) 13, 78, 82, 85–8, 90–2, 95, 151
Ford, Lisa 3, 188, 206
Fort Qu'Appelle 2, 92

Gawler, George (Governor of South Australia) 220
Gaza *see* Shangane
Gcaleka *see* amaGcaleka
Geelong 187, 191, 194, 197, 199
gender 26, 125, 229, 239
genealogy 58, 112, 150, 233, 241–2
George III 83
George IV 59, 212
George V 27, 112
George VI 25–6
gift-giving, gifts 9, 15–17, 28, 35–6, 40, 46, 50, 57, 68, 86, 104, <u>105</u>, 110, 133, 135, 139, 150–1, 156, 159–60, 162, 175, 200–1, 210–24 *passim*
  see also presents
Gladstone, William E. 135, 140, 168
Golden Jubilee (1887) *see* Jubilees
Gorst, Sir John 67
governance 3, 14, 31, 201, 210
  see also Indigenous peoples: self-governance
Gowramma, Princess of Coorg 131–2
Grahamstown 37, 41
Grey, Sir George 30–1, 33–4, 36–7, 39–42, 47, 61, 64, 66, 146–7, 153
Greyeyes, Alex 94
Griqua 32, 40, 42
Gungunyane *see* Ngungunyane
Guy, Jeff 180

He Whakaputunga 59
Heke, Hone 68, 231, 242
hierarchy 31, 57, 137, 166, 228–30, 235–9 *passim*
  see also rank, status
Hika, Hongi 59
Hobbes, Thomas 234, 241
Hobson, Captain William (Lieutenant Governor of New Zealand) 54, 60
Horticultural Gardens (London) 147, 149, 155
House of Commons Select Committee on Aborigines 55, 196
Hudson's Bay Company (HBC) 82–5
humanitarian, humanitarianism 4, 55–6, 60–1, 66, 72–3, 141, 196, 210, 221
hunting 33, 41–2, 81, 85, 88, 174
Huron 212–13, 216–17, 219

identity 28, 57, 71–2, 103, 107, 145, 148, 156, 189, 192, 198, 222, 234
  see also colonial identity

INDEX

imperial citizenship 7, 192
imperial factor 167, 175
imperial pedagogy 192, 205
India 2, 30–1, 35, 126, 129–30, 135–7, 140–1, 173, 191, 218–19
Indian Department *see* Department of Indian Affairs (Canada)
Indigenous peoples 1–18 *passim*, 28–9, 31–3, 37, 48, 56–7, 59, 73, 78–94 *passim*, 101, 103, 107, 117, 126, 133, 140, 144–5, 150, 152, 155, 159, 160, 162, 166, 188–90, 192, 196–206 *passim*, 229–30
   agency 115–16, 145, 152, 216, 229–30
   autonomy 4–5, 15–16, 29, 39, 55, 57, 73, 104, 107, 111, 228–30, 232
   interpretations of Victoria 1–3, 6, 8–10, 12, 100–2, 233, 235
   politics 9, 111, 117
   protection of 3, 5, 26–7, 29, 32, 39–41, 45, 56, 59–60, 81, 85, 87, 101, 106, 109–10, 155–6, 172, 177, 189, 196, 199, 200–1, 233–5, 241
   protest by 13, 54, 57, 67, 71–3, 100, 112, 138, 172, 199, 239
   resistance 35, 79, 85, 93, 108, 173, 210, 229
   self-governance 17, 150
   self-rule 176, 232
   visits to Queen Victoria: 55–6, 59, 66, 81, 83, 113, 132–5, 140, 144–50, 153–6, 162, 166–79 *passim*
Isandhlwana (battle) 167
Isle of Wight 63, 153, 170
iwi 63, 65, 160

Jacobs, Peter 83–4
Jameson Raid 176
Jenkins, William 134–5, 144, 146–8, 149, 150–3, 155, 157, 161
Johnson, Mickey ('King') 216–17

Jubilees 27, 49, 67–8, 70, 141, 210, 219

Kaffraria 32, 46
Kamehameha IV 160
Kamehameha, Prince Albert 160
Kanooses (Saulteaux leader) 88
Kawâhkatos (Cree Chief) 8
Khama, Seretse 177
Khama (Tswana King) 66, 140, 166, 169–70, 172–3, 176–8
Kimberley, Earl of (John Wodehouse) 140, 168
King Country *see* Rohe Pōtae
Kingites *see* Kīngitanga
King Williams Town 49, 177
kingplates 215–16
Kīngitanga 13, 57, 62–7, 73, 146, 155, 231
kinship (Indigenous North American) 78, 86–8, 200, 205, 212, 233
   see also fictive kinship
Kohimārama 63
Kok, Adam lll 42
Kotahitanga *see* Māori: Parliament
Kulin 150, 187–90, 192, 200–2, 205
kūpapa 65–7, 74, 231–2
Kurnai 199
KwaZulu 25, 29, 32, 43–6, 140, 167–9, 175

La Perouse (place) 113–14
Labotsibeni (Swazi Queen) 166, 169, 175
Lake Condah 108–9, 111
Lake Tyers 108, 113–14
land 5, 7–9, 14–16, 32, 39, 42–3, 45, 48, 54, 56–8, 60–2, 64–5, 67–8, 71–2, 79–85, 88, 90–2, 94–5, 100–4, 106–7, 110–12, 114–16, 131–2, 138, 140, 146, 150, 152, 156, 170, 188–9, 193–6, 198–201, 203, 205, 215, 217–18, 220, 223, 230–4, 236, 238–41
   compensation (recompense, redress) 5, 94, 110, 117, 199, 220, 221, 132

[252]

INDEX

Crown land 7–8, 61, 101–2, 106, 201
dispossession 3, 6, 17, 29, 54, 117, 150, 198, 206, 220
Māori 61, 67, 70, 146
rights 15–16, 79, 81, 100, 103, 114–16, 194, 238–9
tenure 108, 110, 228
settler hunger for 42, 103
see also Native Land Court (New Zealand)
Lehulere, Samuel 42
Leopold, Duke of Albany (son of Queen Victoria) 155
Leopold, King of Belgium (uncle of Queen Victoria) 136
Lesotho (Basutoland) 40, 42, 167, 176, 178
Lesseyton (Eastern Cape) 37
letters 28, 40, 42, 66, 79–80, 84–5, 90, 92, 94, 104, 110–13, 116, 129–30, 137, 139, 140, 153, 160, 189, 195, 200–2, 220
Lobengula (Ndebele King) 166, 168–9, 172, 174–5
London Missionary Society 169
Longcanga (Swazi Prince) 169, 172
Lord Derby (Edward Henry Stanley) 66
Lord Dufferin (Frederick Hamilton-Temple-Blackwood, Canadian Governor General) 90–2, 213
Lord Melbourne (William Lamb) 60, 127–9
Lorette Indian Agency 212, 216, 219
Lorne, Marquis of (Canadian Governor-General) 2, 92, 93, 213–15, 217
Lovedale 35, 37, 41
loyalty 5–7, 13–14, 16, 26, 28–30, 35–8, 40, 42–4, 48–9, 54–7, 62–4, 67–8, 71, 73–4, 78–9, 82, 84–6, 88, 90, 92–5, 134, 139, 147, 150, 155, 160, 168, 177–8, 189, 197–8, 200–1, 205, 211–12, 215, 217, 221, 223, 228–30, 232–6, 241

Mafeking (Maheking) 177
Majuba Hill (battle) 168, 175
Malawi (Nyasaland) 178
Maloga 110
mana 57–60, 62, 238
Mandela, Nelson 27, 178
Mangakahia, Meri Te Tai 228–9, 234, 236, 237, 238–42
Maniapoto, Rewi 63, 65
Manūka 63
Māori 13, 59, 61, 146, 152–3, 229, 232, 234
land *see* land: Māori
Parliament 16, 67, 228–36, 239–42
King Movement *see* Kīngitanga
Martin, William (Chief Justice of New Zealand) 61
Matabeleland 168–9, 171, 173, 175
material culture 11, 27, 145, 189
Mayall, John 157–8
medals *see* commemorative medals
Melbourne 100, 103–7, 110–11, 127, 150, 191, 193–4, 198–200
memorials 30, 37, 48, 57, 147, 217
memory 1, 8, 17, 26, 80, 94, 95, 110, 162, 178, 189, 202
lieux de memoire 102, 201
memory studies 8
memory work 103, 111
politics of 8, 14, 17, 102, 103, 108, 111–12, 117
Métis 85, 93
Mfengu *see* amaMfengu
Mi'kmaq 80
missionaries 4, 27, 33–4, 38, 41, 54–5, 58–9, 62, 79, 81, 83–4, 95, 101, 109–10, 116, 133, 135, 146, 151, 157, 167, 169, 173, 197, 199–200
Mobourne, Ernest 108–9
monarchism, monarchy 10–11, 26–8, 30, 31, 36, 57–8, 62, 73, 78, 125, 129, 157, 192, 195, 204

[253]

INDEX

Moroka 29, 38, 40–2, 48
Moshoeshoe (BaSotho King) 29, 38–42, 48, 167
Mozambique 169
Mpande, ka Senzangakhona 29, 44–5
Mpondo 139, 178
Mshete 168, 171, 173–5
Mteto 169, 172–3
Murray, James 110
Mzilikazi (Ndebele King) 41

Nahnebahnwequay 81
Namibia 171
narrative 1–2, 5, 11, 16, 30, 78, 80, 92, 94–5, 102, 107–8, 111, 116, 192, 199, 201, 230, 235–6
Natal 12, 29–33, 43, 138, 167, 169
Native Land Court (New Zealand) 65, 232, 238–9
Ndebele 41, 166, 168–9
Nelson (place) 134, 146
New Plymouth 70, 231
New South Wales 60, 100, 108, 110, 112–15, 188, 191, 193–5, 198, 215–16, 222
New York Illustrated News 151
New Zealand 1–3, 8, 12, 16–18, 30, 54–7, 59–62, 66–8, 71, 73, 79, 133, 135, 144, 146–8, 150, 152–3, 155–7, 161–2
newspapers 1, 4, 17, 66, 68, 100, 109, 114, 135, 147, 156, 170, 176, 215
Ngapua, Hone Heke 68, 231
Ngāpuhi 66, 147
Ngata, Āpirana 241–2
Ngoza ka Ludaba (Chief Goza) 44, 45, 46, 47
Ngqika *see* amaNqgika
Ngungunyane (King of the Gaza) 166, 169, 172, 175
Nguni 166, 169, 178
Nlaka'pamux 81
North-West Territories (Canada) 213–15, 217
Northern Wars (New Zealand) 147

Nteni 169, 172–3

O'Soup, Louis 93
Ojibway (Anishinabe, Chippewa) 81, 223
Ontario 80–1, 83
Orange Free State 32–3, 38–9, 41–2, 167
Orange River Sovereignty 39, 41
orations, oratory 9, 12, 11, 37, 78–9, 82–4, 86, 89, 90, 106
Osborne House 58, 63, 131, 162, 153–5, 170–1

Pahsung 2, 93
Pākehā 57, 62–3, 67, 70–4, 147, 161, 231, 232–3, 239
Pakia, Hirini 160–1
palaver 187, 190, 192, 195, 198
Pāremata Māori *see* Māori: Parliament
Parihaka 70–1
Parliaments 9, 107
    British 60, 66, 84, 128–9, 135, 141, 152, 175, 177, 198
    Maori *see* Maori: Parliament
    settler
        Australia 100, 114
        Canada 89, 94
        Cape Colony 178
        New South Wales 216
        New Zealand 55, 67, 73, 228, 234, 239, 246
Peel, Sir Robert 128, 130, 135
Peguis (William King) 82–5, 88–90, 92, 94
performance 9, 11, 16–17, 27–9, 35, 45, 57, 68, 70, 73, 140, 151, 187, 189, 192, 198
    see also war dances
petitions 28, 37, 56–9, 61–2, 71, 79–81, 85, 90, 103, 107, 112, 116, 150, 152, 168, 176, 199, 213, 216–17, 239
Pietermaritzburg 44, 47
photographic portraits 40, 157, 158
photographs 4, 15, 17, 40, 46, 68, 113, 145, 157, 158, 173, 203, 216

[254]

INDEX

politics *see* Indigenous peoples: politics, settler politics
Pomare, Albert Victor 144–5, <u>158</u>, 159–60
Pomare, Hare 157, <u>158</u>
Pomare, Hariata 135–6, 156–7, <u>158</u>
Pondos *see* Mpondo
Port Elizabeth 17, 29, 334, 37, 179
Port Phillip 187, 189, 191–2, 194–6, 198–9
Port Phillip Association 193–4
Port Phillip Protectorate 196–8
portraits 13, 15, 33, 40, 68, 84, 91, <u>127</u>, 157–8, 171, 193, 204, <u>237</u>
presents 54, 70, 71, 104, <u>105</u>, <u>127</u>, 145, 149–51, 156, 159, 172, 177, 213–20, 222
 see also gifts
Prince, David 94
Prince, Henry (Chief Red Eagle) (Mis-koo-kenew) 84–5, 88, <u>89</u>, 90, 110
Prince, John 92, 94
Prince, Joseph 90
Prince, William (Saulteaux Chief) 96
Prince Albert Memorial 147
Prince George, Duke of Kent (son of King George V) 177
Prince William (Duke of Kent) 1
Princess of Wales (Alexandra, wife of Albert, Prince of Wales) 149
protest *see* Indigenous peoples: protest

Queen's Day (Queen Victoria's Birthday) 95, 217–21
Queenites *see* kūpapa
Queenstown (Eastern Cape) 34, 37

race, race relations, racism 5, 26–7, 29, 32, 36, 54, 63, 67–8, 72, 87, 90–1, 112, 115, 126, 131, 138–41, 166, 177, 198, 204, 206, 216, 232–3, 235, 237, 239, 241
rangātira (Māori chiefs) 54, 57–63, 68, 73

 see also wahine Rangātira
rank (social) 78, 131–2, 136, 147, 154, 213, 228, 238–9
 see also hierarchy, status
Red River Settlement (Winnipeg) 81–5, 91, 95
Reihana Taukawau 148–51, 153–4
resistance *see* Indigenous peoples: resistance
Rhodes, Cecil 140, 167–70, 175–6
Robinson, George Augustus (Chief Protector) 197
Rohe Pōtae 65–6
royal tours 9, 12, 17, 25–49 *passim*, 73, 79, 85, 90–2, 144–6, 150–1, 162, 211, 213–17 *passim*

Saintsbury, Amelia 66
Salish 113, 218
Sandile, Mgolombane 29, 32–7, 48
Sarhili (amaXhosa King) 29, 35, 48
Saulteaux (Ojibway, Anishinabe) 81–8, 88, 90–3
Schultz, John Christian 89–90
Sebele (Tswana King) 66, 140, 166, 169–70, 172–3, 176–8
Seddon, Richard (New Zealand Premier) 68, 71–3
self-fashioning 66–7, 152, 154
self-governance *see* Indigenous peoples: self-governance
self-rule *see* Indigenous peoples: self-rule
Selkirk Treaty 88, 94
Selwyn, Augustus (Bishop of New Zealand) 61
settler politics 13
 see also colonial factor
Shaka ka Senzangakhona 31, 43
Shangane 166, 169, 172–3, 175
Shepstone, Sir Theophilus 31, 43–6, 167–8, 140, 167–8, 170
Sheship 87
sites of memory *see* memory
Siwes, Darren 190, <u>202–3</u>, 204–6
Six Nations Agency 219
Six Nations of the Iroquois 81, 223

[255]

INDEX

Smith, Sir Harry 31, 39–40
Sobhuza II (Swazi King) 27, 172, 176
Soga, Tiyo 33–7
Sohn, Carl 171
Sotho see Basotho
South Africa 1, 6, 9, 12, 17, 26–8, 30–1, 35, 49, 73, 83, 166, 177–8
South African (Anglo-Boer) War 141, 176
South Australia 217, 220
sovereignty 5, 10, 15–16, 29, 38, 41, 60, 62–3, 65, 73, 87, 100, 103, 145, 169, 187–206 passim, 210–11, 218, 222–4
  performances 187–206 passim
  testing 188–93, 195, 205
Spectator 147
speeches 9, 17, 33, 35, 37, 44, 61, 63, 68, 80–3, 88, 91–2, 100, 141, 155, 200, 216, 236, 240–2
St. Peter's Reserve 90–1
statues 72, 178, 179
status (social) 5, 12–13, 16, 31, 57–8, 65, 73, 106–7, 116–17, 136, 147, 153–5, 161, 213, 216–17, 224, 228–30, 235–8 passim
  see also hierarchy, rank, mana
Stutterheim 33–5
suffrage 236–7
  see also elections, voting
Swazi 139, 166, 169, 172–3, 175
Swaziland 27, 169, 172, 176
Sydney Morning Herald 110

Taiaroa, H. K. 63, 234, 238
Taiwhanga, Hirini 66
Tamatekapua 64, 71
Tamboekies 37
  see also amaThembu
Tamihana, Wiremu Tarapipi 62
Taranaki War 63, 70, 146–7
tattoos 68, 133, 147, 154
Tāwhiao (Second Māori King) 64–7, 69
Te Amohu, Temuera 64
Te Arawa 63–5, 71
Te Atua, Horomona 153

Te Hautakiri Wharepapa 155–6
Te Heuheu, Mananui 60
Te Kooti, Arikirangi Te Turuki 64
Te Manu, Paratene 149, 152–4, 161
Te Morehu, Maipapa (Major Wiremu Te Wheoro) 64–5, 68, 69, 70
Te Rauparahā, Tamihana 63
Te Tuahu, Kihirini 161
Te Wherowhero, Pōtatau (First Māori King) 61–2, 64
Te Whiwhi, Matene 63
Thaba Bosiu 38
Thaba Nchu 41–2
The Colonial Intelligence or Aborigines Friend 84
The Exploration Company 168, 171, 175
The Guardian (Australia) 114
The Moreton Bay Courier 221
The Queenslander 221
The Selkirk Expositor 94
The Times 173, 175
Thembu see amaThembu
Thomas, William (Assistant Protector) 196, 199–200
tours see royal tours, Indigenous peoples: visits to Queen Victoria
Transkei 26, 178
Transorangia 29
Transvaal 32, 137, 167–9, 176
treaties 1, 8, 80–1, 82, 86–90, 92–5, 106, 128, 144, 156, 175–6, 178, 199, 211, 214, 217–18, 220
  see also names of individual treaties
'Treaty 1' 87–9
'Treaty 4' 8, 88
'Treaty 7' 93
tribal 45, 57, 59, 65, 71–3, 115, 146, 150, 160, 229, 231–2, 234, 238, 240–1
  see also Indigenous people
Trollope, Anthony 48
Tshipinare (Barolong Chief) 41–2
Tswana 29, 38–9, 40–1, 167
Tukihaumene 63

INDEX

Tunuiarnagi, Captain Hoani Paraone 68, 71, 73

Van Diemen's Land (Tasmania) 79, 194–5, 197
vice-regal tours *see* royal tours
visiting card *see carte de visite*
Victoria (colony, state) 108, 113, 198–200
Victoria, Queen
  constitutional monarch 14, 127, 129, 135
  death 3, 6, 13, 30, 54, 73, 102–3, 107, 108, 211, 223
  discursive production of 9, 17
  Empress 30, 135–7, 230
  exemplar of empowered womanhood 116
  fairy godmother 177–8
  female monarch 5, 16, 27, 78, 83, 94, 101, 125, 189, 192–3, 202, 203, 236, 240–2
  godmother 15, 130–1, 133, 135, 144, 156, 159–60, 162
  Great Mother 5, 78–95 *passim*, 144, 162, 200–1, 211–12, 223
  Great White Queen 13, 25, 27–9, 37, 166, 169, 172, 175
  journals 12, 14–15, 125–7, 133, 136–41, 145, 170–3
  Mistress of Everything 2, 93
  Mma-Mosadinyana 170, 173
  Motho-wa-Ditsebe 170
Victoria Day *see* Queen's Day
voting 79, 228, 236–40
  see also elections, suffrage

Wāhine Rangātira (chiefly woman) 236, 240–1
Wahkohtowin 86
Waikato (place) 61, 64, 65, 67, 70, 147, 155–6

Waikato Campaign 64, 67, 134, 147, 153, 156
Waikato River 155
Waitangi, Treaty of (Te Tiriti o Waitangi, 1840) 155, 161–2, 230, 232–5, 239, 241–2
Waitangi Tribunal 17, 160, 162
Wakefield, Edward Gibbon 55
wampum 80, 151
'war dances' 43–4, 45, 46, 71, 138, 151
Warangesda 110–1
Wathawurrung 187, 191, 193, 199
Weale, Charlotte Julia Dorotea (Mihi Wira) 66, 161
Wellington (New Zealand) 59, 66, 73, 241
Wesleyan Missionary Society 55, 146, 149, 243
Western Canadian Treaties 86–90, 92, 95
  see also Treaty 1, Treaty 4, Treaty 7
Westminster Gazette 169
Westminster Review 135
William IV 59, 193, 195
Windsor Castle 127, 131, 157, 170–3
Woiwurrung 106, 199–200
women's suffrage 236–42
Woolwich arsenal 173–4
World War I 94, 241
World War II 26, 113
Wuradjeri 197

Xhosa *see* AmaXhosa

Zambia (Northern Rhodesia) 178
Zimbabwe (Southern Rhodesia) 166, 169, 175–8
Zulu *see* AmaZulu
Zulu Wars 137, 139, 167–8, 176
Zululand *see* KwaZulu
Zuma, President Jacob 179